"Roger Williams is well known for [...]
This careful, intelligent anthology highlights and [...]
long life as writer, activist, and citizen in New England, his understanding of local Native Americans, and his relationship to the policies—endorsed (or criticized)—of his fellow colonists towards those people.
Filled with unexpected evidence at every turn!"

—DAVID D. HALL, professor emeritus of New England church history, Harvard Divinity School

"Diplomacy, conflict, beliefs, betrayal, sovereignty, alliances, and politics...this book has them all. The "divide & conquer" strategy that you see
play out throughout the writings included in *Reading Roger Williams*
gives an inside view into Roger's thoughts, perspectives, and personal
& professional goals. Although eye opening, it is painful and affirming
to our oral history that he was not our FRIEND. He had many personal,
professional, economic, political and ideological ambitions that were self-
serving and certainly not in the best interest of the Indigenous people as
he espoused in his rhetoric."

—LORÉN SPEARS, Narragansett Tribal Citizen and Executive Director, Tomaquag Museum

"Who was Roger Williams? You will learn to know him in this carefully
curated collection both as a radical puritan who worked for the liberty
of conscience as he understood it, and as a self-proclaimed 'friend of the
Indians' who joined in the settler colonial conquest of Narragansetts,
Pequots, and other Native peoples. This is an essential guide to Williams
and to the contradictions and cruelties of the seventeenth-century
English colonial world."

—TISA WENGER, professor of American religious history, Yale Divinity School

"*Reading Roger Williams* is no mere compilation of an icon's works.
Drawing on the best recent scholarship and placing carefully selected
excerpts of Williams's public and private writings alongside the words of
his contemporaries, the authors embed a very human Williams in rich
historical contexts. Readers hoping to understand the religious, political,
and personal underpinnings of English attempts to colonize Indigenous
America can find no better guide on their journey."

—DANIEL K. RICHTER, professor emeritus of American history, University of Pennsylvania

"Roger Williams is among the most controversial figures in colonial America. Some historians dismiss him as almost irrelevant; others consider him enormously significant. For example, W. K. Jordan, author of the classic *Development of Religious Toleration in England*, said Williams provided 'the most important contribution' to the development of toleration in the seventeenth century—a century which included Locke. *Reading Roger Williams* allows readers to make their own decision."

—JOHN M. BARRY, author of *Roger Williams and the Creation of the American Soul: Church, State, and the Birth of Liberty*

"Notoriously cranky, complex, and diverse, Roger Williams shines as a religious liberator and repels as an exploiter of Natives. Prolific, provocative, brilliant, and often dense, his writings both need and reward the insights so richly applied by three deft scholars with deep expertise in colonial New England and its Native context. This collection reveals Williams as the most compelling, maddening, and revealing colonist of his century."

—ALAN TAYLOR, author of *American Colonies: The Settlement of North America*

"Revealing Roger Williams to be a highly capable, complicated, and irascible man who betrayed his own principles without fully realizing what he had done, this excellent documentary history is exceptionally well-conceived. The editors situate carefully chosen documents in historical context to reveal both the idealism and the tragedy of New England's founding."

—AMANDA PORTERFIELD, author of *Conceived in Doubt: Religion and Politics in the New American Nation*

Reading Roger Williams

Reading Roger Williams

*Rogue Puritans, Indigenous Nations, and the
Founding of America—A Documentary History*

LINFORD D. FISHER
SHEILA M. McINTYRE
JULIE A. FISHER

PICKWICK *Publications* · Eugene, Oregon

READING ROGER WILLIAMS
Rogue Puritans, Indigenous Nations, and the Founding of America—A
Documentary History

Pickwick Publications
An Imprint of Wipf and Stock Publishers
199 W. 8th Ave., Suite 3
Eugene, OR 97401

www.wipfandstock.com

PAPERBACK ISBN: 978-1-5326-3943-2
HARDCOVER ISBN: 978-1-5326-3944-9
EBOOK ISBN: 978-1-5326-3945-6

Cataloguing-in-Publication data:

Names: Fisher, Linford D., author. | McIntyre, Sheila M., author. | Fisher, Julie
A., author.

Title: Reading Roger Williams : Rogue Puritans, indigenous nations, and the
founding of America—a documentary history / Linford D. Fisher, Sheila M.
McIntyre, and Julie A. Fisher.

Description: Eugene, OR: Pickwick Publications, 2024. | Includes
bibliographical references and index.

Identifiers: ISBN 978-1-5326-3943-2 (paperback). | ISBN 978-1-5326-3944-9
(hardcover). | ISBN 978-1-5326-3945-6 (ebook).

Subjects: LCSH: Williams, Roger, 1604?–1683. | Christianity and culture—
New England—History. | Indians in North America—New England—Religion.
| New England—Religious life and customs.

Classification: BV741 F57 2024 (print). | BV741 (epub)

07/10/24

The Correspondence of John Cotton Junior, edited by Sheila McIntyre and Len Travers. Boston, Mass:
The Colonial Society of Massachusetts, copyright © 2009. Used by permission. All rights reserved.

The Correspondence of Roger Williams, edited by Glenn W. LaFantasie, Robert S. Cocroft,
Glenn H. Horton, Pamela A. Kennedy, Christian A. King, and Deborah van Dam. Hanover
and London: Brown University Press/University Press of New England, copyright © 1998.
Used by permission. All rights reserved.

The Journal of John Winthrop, 1630–1649, edited by Richard Dunn, James Savage, and Laetitia
Yeandle. Cambridge, Mass.: The Belknap Press of Harvard University Press, copyright © 1996
by the President and Fellows of Harvard College. Used by permission. All rights reserved.

Contents

Illustrations and Maps

Illustrations

Maps

Acknowledgments

WE ARE INDEBTED TO all of the scholars who have wrestled with Williams's texts before us, but Glenn LaFantasie and his team (Robert S. Cocroft, Glenn H. Horton, Pamela A. Kennedy, Christian A. King, and Deborah van Dam) deserve special gratitude. The two-volume *Correspondence of Roger Williams* published by the Rhode Island Historical Society in 1988 made our work so much easier and sets an aspirational standard for documentary editors in general. We thank Dr. LaFantasie for permission to use his work as extensively as we have. Readers may want to skip all the biographies listed in our bibliography and spend some time in the two-volume collection of letters that Glenn and his team created—the introduction, essays, editorial notes, and footnotes would be a perfect place to start to understand Williams more deeply. Their work is approachable, learned, and detailed, and we encourage readers to dig into those letters next.

Ted Lewis at Wipf and Stock reached out several years ago with an idea for a one-volume Williams reader and he has been very supportive of our work. We thank Ted, along with the editorial team at Wipf and Stock, especially Chris Spinks and Matthew Wimer, for their guidance as we worked on this collection. With thanks, too, to Lynn Carlson and Compass Cartographic for the wonderful maps produced so efficiently and responsively.

We are also thankful for the time and input of a number of friends and tribal members who provided perspectives and insights that helped make this volume stronger and more nuanced. This includes Edward Andrews, Chrystal Mars Baker (Narragansett and Niantic), Dawn Dove (Narragansett), Charlotte Carrington-Farmer, Mack Scott (Narragansett), Owen Stanwood, and Adrian Weimer. Jo Fisher saved us from many poor word choices, usage problems, grammar flaws, and typos. Any remaining errors are ours alone.

Sheila: While I was delighted that Kenneth Minkema suggested my name to Wipf and Stock for this project, I knew that Williams was simply too tricky a subject to handle alone. I thank Linford Fisher and Julie Fisher for their willingness to work on this collection with me; it has been a joy to learn from such talented historians over the past six years. Austin Raetz, Liam Kingsley, and Mahala Nyberg—Presidential Scholars and students at SUNY Potsdam—took an independent study seminar in documentary editing, where we edited two of Williams's published works: *Experiments in Spiritual Health* and *Fox Digg'd Out*. Funding from the Dorf foundation, through SUNY Potsdam's Lougheed Center for Applied Learning, supported their transcription and annotation work. A sabbatical granted in 2022–2023 allowed me time to help complete this collection.

Julie: While Roger Williams may have been and even remains a divisive figure, the people that I have met while studying him have been a generous, kind, supportive, curious, and engaging community that I treasure. They are scholars, educators, artists, park rangers and, more often than not, assume many roles. Over the years, I am richer and humbled by the conversations I have had with Charlotte Carrington-Farmer, John McNiff, Ramona Peters, Nancy Brown, Charlotte Taylor, Sara Damiano, and Elizabeth Perry. A number of librarians and archivists make this work possible, but I will be forever indebted to the Rhode Island Historical Society and Dana Signe K. Munroe for their assistance. And while conversations about Roger Williams may not be everyone's idea of dinner conversation, I have enjoyed many wonderful evenings discussing this uncommon character with David J. Silverman and I look forward to many more. The thoughtful debates with my co-editors and their tenacious work renders me grateful yet again. My sincerest gratitude to both Lin and Sheila for the collection that we did not intend to write and is better for it.

Linford: Living and working in Rhode Island for the past fourteen years has provided ample opportunity to have conversations about Roger Williams with many people, including tribal members, undergraduate students, PhD students, colleagues, members of the general public, and local historians. Each one—from the biggest Williams boosters to the staunchest critics at public talks—deserves some credit for shaping the various perspectives and interpretations contained in some sections in this volume. This project received an early boost from Claire Fishman in 2016, at that time an undergraduate history concentrator at Brown, who helped pull together and transcribe many of the documents that focus on Williams's life in Indian Country. With thanks, too, for the support I received from the Brown

Department of History for various aspects of this project. Finally, thanks to Sheila for spearheading this project, and for the invitation to co-edit, along with Julie. Such collaboration and conversations are one of the many joys of academic projects.

Abbreviations

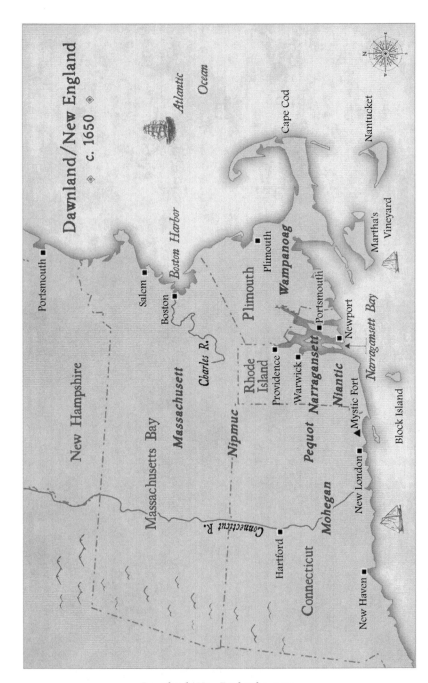

Dawnland / New England c. 1650.
Map by Lynn Carlson, Compass Cartographic ©2023.

Introduction

Roger Williams Statue, Providence, Rhode Island.
Photo by Linford D. Fisher, 2023.

HIGH ABOVE THE CITY of Providence, Rhode Island, looms a solitary figure. Carved from granite and standing fifteen feet tall, an imposing likeness of Roger Williams is perched on the bow of a granite rowboat, head up, with one hand outstretched over the city. Situated under a large granite arch at the edge of Prospect Terrace, this statue commands the best view of downtown Providence and even overlooks the Roger Williams National Memorial, established in 1965. The statue—and the coffin beneath it that contains Williams's remains—was part of a commemorative effort in 1936 surrounding the three hundredth anniversary of the founding of Providence and was completed in 1939. This is Roger Williams in his most iconic form: solitary, in command, and presiding over the city he founded.

The real Roger Williams was different in almost every way. Williams was rarely alone, he was not exactly in command of anything he was involved in, and he spent his entire life trying to hold onto and enact a vision for Rhode Island that came crashing down around him late in his life. Most importantly, perhaps, the city and colony Williams helped to found was deep in Native country—a "Lyons den," he called it at one point—situated between the powerful Narragansett and Wampanoag nations, with the Nipmuc, Niantic, Pequot, Mohegan, and Massachusett nations also in close proximity. The Williams that emerges from the documents in this collection is immersed in a dynamic world of Native politics, engaged in regional and trans-Atlantic debates and conversations about religious freedom and the separation of church and state, and situated at the crossroads of colonial outposts and powerful Native nations.

Williams, if he is known at all by modern readers, is perhaps best known for his ideas. And indeed, the texts in this volume chart his uncompromising vision of full religious liberty and the separation of church and state. He believed no one should be "molested, punished, disquieted, or called in question," as the 1663 royal charter for Rhode Island put it, "for any differences in opinione in matters of religion," so long as those opinions do not disturb the public peace. Williams defended the rights of Jews, Catholics, Muslims, and atheists to live free from governmental coercion. As Williams noted in a letter to the town of Warwick in 1665, such full liberty made Rhode Island the freest place in the English empire, and perhaps the world. Williams was not singular in his defense of religious liberty; he drew on a rich history of English nonconformity, and the nearby Dutch colony of New Netherland permitted some religious toleration. And Rhode Island's "lively experiment" in full religious liberty could not have lasted long without the support of King Charles II.[1] Still, these were radical ideas in their time, and, as implemented in Rhode Island, they allowed for a kind of religious liberty unknown in the colonial world.

And yet, Williams was no modern religious and cultural pluralist. Even as he defended religious protections for both personal belief and public worship, he took every opportunity to challenge and even attack people with whom he disagreed. This included his Boston ministerial nemesis, John Cotton, with whom he vehemently disagreed in several lengthy publications, as well as the Quakers, with whom he debated in person in Newport and against whom he published a 503 page screed in 1676.

1. As Evan Haefeli argues, "England kept Rhode Island free. Rather than a beacon anticipating the United States, it was an extension of English authority, one of a growing number of colonial enterprises for which England's new king in 1660 permitted religious toleration." Haefeli, "How Special Was Rhode Island?" 22.

At times, Williams is also portrayed by modern interpreters as a "friend" to Natives (something he believed himself to be), as symbolized by the Narragansett who allegedly greeted him in 1636 with the phrase, "What cheer, Netop!" But in the pages below, we show that Williams was also hopelessly part of the settler colonial project. Yes, he learned Native languages and stayed with them in their wetus (wigwams); and yes, he published a fascinating Narragansett Indian language phrasebook and cultural commentary in 1643 (*A Key Into the Language of America*). But he also acted in obviously self-serving ways, used derogatory language for Natives throughout his writings, and when things counted most, he almost always sided with the English colonial project of which he was a part, especially during the two major Native wars in his lifetime.

The end result is a raw and honest view of Williams in which many of these realities—no matter how contradictory—are true. He was a pioneer of religious liberty, and yet he was a Native enslaver and part of a process that dispossessed regional Indigenous populations. He provided a refuge for religious and political dissidents, and yet found ways to publicly provoke those around him. We have organized the texts in this book to allow these complexities and contradictions to take center stage by opting for a largely chronological approach rather than a strictly thematic one. Not only does this approach better mirror the events of his time and how he experienced them, it emphasizes how the different aspects of his life—theology, politics, religion, languages, Indigenous relationships—were always happening simultaneously for him. Only later did writers divide these aspects of his life into neat categories and chapters. A chronological approach allows this edition to follow the rather chaotic and contradictory course of Williams's life rather than attempt to dictate it.

Roger Williams and His Times

Williams was born in London in approximately 1603 to parents that we might now describe as middle class. He came of age during a time of relative peace and prosperity for England, although in his religious circles, things were less than settled. Starting with King Henry VIII, England officially broke away from the Roman Catholic Church in 1534 as part of the Protestant Reformation (starting with the Augustinian German monk Martin Luther, who first protested Catholic excesses in 1517). Henry VIII's motivations were more complicated, since he was also seeking a divorce from Catherine of Aragon and wanted instead to marry the younger Anne Boleyn. But the break with Rome was real, and completely reshaped English history. It led to a series of monarchs who either favored the Protestant reforms (like Edward VI and Lady Jane Grey) or entirely embraced the Catholic Church, as with Mary Tudor, whose reign from 1553–1558 plunged England back into a firmly Catholic (and Protestant-persecuting) country. The reign of Queen Elizabeth from 1558–1603 brought more stability as the queen sought to unify a country under the Church of England that was doctrinally Protestant but still favored some Catholic ritualism.

Elizabeth's compromise did not please the "hotter sort of Protestants," however, and led to a large and long-lasting movement to purify the Church of England.[2] "Puritans," as they were called, desired what they saw as a simpler, more biblically based mode of church organization and worship, one rooted in preaching and simplicity. Most puritans desired to stay within the Church of England (even as they did not fully conform to its liturgy), although some groups believed it was too corrupt to remain within it, and therefore separated entirely. Williams was indelibly shaped by the ethos of both forms of puritanism, although as he grew into adulthood he proved adept at moving in a number of circles, both politically and religiously. Thanks to the sponsorship of the famed English jurist Sir Edward Coke, he was able to attend the Charterhouse School starting in 1621 and have an inside track on internships at the highest levels of English governance. Bolstered by his Charterhouse education, Williams attended Pembroke College at Cambridge University in 1624, which was known for its puritan sympathies.[3] Upon graduation, he was ordained as a minister in the Church of England and took up a private chaplaincy for Sir William Masham in Essex. After a failed attempt to marry the wealthier Jane Whalley, he married Mary Bernard, daughter of the prolific English minister Richard Bernard, who had deep puritan tendencies but ultimately conformed to the Church of England.

As the political environment shifted around him, and as Williams's own thinking tilted more towards separatism, he decided in 1630 that perhaps the new colony of Massachusetts Bay in New England would be a better place to follow his conscience. Upon arrival, it took just under five years for English leaders to banish Williams. After turning down a high profile teaching pastor post at the First Church in Boston, Williams moved his family first to Salem, and then to the separating puritan colony of Plimouth, and then back to Salem again. Along the way, he increasingly drew criticism and concern for his views regarding the propriety of the king's grant of Native lands for colonial settlement, as well as the impropriety of civil

2. Collinson, *Elizabethan Puritan Movement*, 27.
3. Winslow, *Master Roger Williams*, 51–58.

governments punishing people for not outwardly conforming to religious requirements. These and other positions put him at odds with the Massachusetts Bay Colony's civil and religious authorities, and eventually even his own church in Salem. In October 1635, Massachusetts Bay banished him, although due to illness, officials permitted him to delay his departure until he had recuperated. Not content to lie still, however, Williams continued to write and teach, prompting immediate banishment. In the winter of 1636, he narrowly escaped capture by leaving the colony before he could be deported back to London.

Williams's solitary wintertime escape is iconic, and the memory of being banished colored his writings for the rest of his life. Thirty-four years later, Williams told Governor Thomas Prence and Major John Mason that he could still feel the cold: "I tooke his prudent Motion as a Hint and voice from God, and . . . steerd my Course from Salem (though in Winter snow wch I feele yet) unto these parts."[4] While Williams remembers striking out alone, his destination had already been planned by a small cadre of sympathizers in Salem, who had agreed to start a new settlement at the head of the Narragansett Bay. Williams made his way south to the east side of the Seekonk River, in present-day Rumford, Rhode Island, and gathered his family and supporters there for a few months before being forced to move west a few miles, outside of the jurisdiction of the Plimouth Colony. Williams and his followers received permission from the Narragansett sachems to settle at the site of the present-day city of Providence, at the confluence of the Moshashuck and Woonasquatucket Rivers, at the head of the Narragansett Bay. Within a few years, Williams helped facilitate the founding of Portsmouth and Newport, both on Aquidneck Island (then called Rhode Island) in the Narragansett Bay, also populated by religious and political dissenters of various stripes. As with so many aspects of Williams's life, his banishment reveals contradictions: He clung to the idea of exile and yet he was central to the English colonial project.

For the rest of his life, Williams struggled to enact and defend a colony based on full religious liberty and the separation of church and state. Rather than an orderly progression from founding a few towns to a full-fledged colony, Williams found himself loosely at the helm of a chaotic collection of colonists, residents, dissenters, dissidents, and scoundrels who all had different ideas about what Rhode Island should be. Most vexingly, Samuel Gorton drove an early wedge in Williams's vision by securing a separate and large purchase in 1643 from the Shawomet Indians just south of Providence. Gorton then placed himself and his acquired land under the authority of the

---

4. *Correspondence of Roger Williams*, 2:610.

Massachusetts Bay Colony, which was eagerly eyeing up a way to break up the detested Rhode Island settlements and gain access to Narragansett Bay. The debacle caused great consternation to Williams, who sailed to London in 1643 to get a patent for the three towns of Providence, Portsmouth, and Newport as a protection against the Massachusetts Bay leaders and other enterprising colonists. Although this particular incident mostly resolved in the creation of the town of Warwick and later incorporation into the colony of Rhode Island, Williams also faced other internal strife, such as bickering over Providence land plots and a forged, later addition to the original deed for the city of Providence given by the Narragansett sachems. His quarrelsome nature also drew him into extended and public debates with the Quakers, a radical English Protestant movement whose members had been persecuted in Massachusetts Bay. Williams believed they should be protected in their beliefs and public worship, but he vigorously tried to prove in person and in print that their views were wrong. Williams scholars have suggested that by the time the 1663 charter was granted by the crown, the colony had already been "home to a fractious democratic community of ill-used Quakers, Diaspora Jews, and a bevy of other beleaguered groups, mostly Protestant and frequently unconventional. There were few places like it."[5]

More importantly, Williams found himself completely over his head in terms of local Native politics and affairs. The powerful Narragansett nation, which had invited Roger Williams to settle, expected reciprocal obligations for their hospitality, which required constant diplomacy by Williams and others. Governor John Winthrop and Massachusetts Bay leaders continually looked to Williams for help in navigating Native politics, leading to a complicated relationship among Williams, Narragansett sachems, smaller tributary tribes of the Narragansett, and individuals and groups within Rhode Island and Massachusetts Bay who wanted to leverage Native lands and connections for their own benefit. Williams framed himself as a friend of the Narragansett and regional Natives, but his actions repeatedly demonstrated that, in the end, he protected his own interests and sided with the larger English colonial project—even with the Massachusetts Bay Colony that had exiled him. Williams's involvement in two major wars with Natives in New England, as described in the documents below, irrevocably altered the world for specific Native nations and ultimately ensured the permanent presence of English (and, later, American) towns and colonies. The Pequot War (1636–1637) demonstrated the genocidal potential of English colonization, and King Philip's War (1675–1678) ruptured all of southern New England and marked the end of a particular phase of Native American

5. Beneke and Grenda, *Lively Experiment,* 3.

political and military sovereignty in the region. Williams was at the center of both of these conflicts, writing letters, making deals, hunting down "enemy" Indians, and buying and selling Native captives for profit.

When Williams died in 1683, Rhode Island had survived, yes. But at what cost? After 1676, colonists eagerly snatched up Wampanoag and Narragansett land on both sides of the Narragansett Bay. Thousands of colonists poured into Rhode Island who, over time, did not share Williams's exact vision for religious freedom or even attempt to peacefully coexist with their Native neighbors. And still, Williams remained a contrarian to the end. His last essay, written sometime after 1679 but not published until 2014, is an extended treatise against the famous missionary to Native Americans, John Eliot, largely regarding infant versus believer's baptism, but also partially analyzing Eliot's methods of evangelizing Natives. For the Narragansett, the colonial nightmare that Roger Williams inaugurated continued with a steady erosion of their land base, state detribalization in the 1880s, and federal recognition in 1983 that has been all but nullified by the state of Rhode Island.

Interpreting Roger Williams

Starting with James David Knowles's *Memoir of Roger Williams: The Founder of the State of Rhode-Island* in 1834, Williams has been the subject of hundreds of articles and books. Books about Williams can tend towards admiration, with a recent writer giving him credit for "the creation of the American soul."[6] It is very tempting to praise Williams. As scholar Teresa Bejan writes, modern readers see in Williams "an inclusive, proto-multicultural vision of a tolerating society ahead of its time and far beyond that of other early modern thinkers."[7] As a result, Williams is sometimes enlisted in causes that would surely surprise him: In 2020, *Roger Williams' Little Book of Virtues* hit the shelves, promising that modern day readers will find "hope in the rise of the nones who, like Williams, follow their own spiritual path and create spaces that embrace women, POC, LGBT folks, and others marginalized by the institutional church."[8] In many studies, Williams is described as an exception to the puritan New England rule—more modern and more acceptable to twenty-first-century readers than his counterparts are. So while there was much about Williams that strikes modern readers as remarkable—and we agree—we do not aim for praise or criticism. Instead, we want readers to see Williams as more complicated than earlier studies often describe.

6. Barry, *Roger Williams and the Creation of the American Soul.*
7. Bejan, "When the Word of the Lord Runs Freely," 66.
8. Garrison, *Roger Williams's Little Book of Virtues.*

On the one hand, we know a lot about his ideas, since Williams published more than 1,800 pages of pamphlets and books and wrote probably hundreds of letters, of which 175 survive. But there is so much we do not know, especially about his earlier years, the everydayness of his life, or the inner workings of his own household and marriage. For example, Williams spent many months of the year at his trading post at Cocumscussoc, twenty miles from home, leaving his wife, Mary, alone with their six children in Providence.[9] Roger and Mary exchanged letters during these long absences, but all of those letters are now gone.[10] Williams and Governor John Winthrop maintained regular correspondence from 1636 to 1645, but that exchange is now one-sided, since Winthrop's letters to Williams no longer exist. There are many such gaps: only a single letter survives from his most turbulent period in Massachusetts Bay, a handful from his earliest days in England, and none from early Spring 1641 to Summer 1645, which included his first return trip to England to secure a patent for the Providence Plantations colony.

That said, unlike many texts from the seventeenth century, accessing Williams's published books and correspondence is now relatively easy, requiring no trips to archives or special libraries. His published writings were collected and reprinted in six volumes from 1866 to 1874 by the Narragansett Club entitled *The Complete Writings of Roger Williams*, which were later reprinted by Russell & Russell in 1963, adding a seventh volume. In 1988, Glenn LaFantasie and his team published an incomparable two-volume edition of his correspondence, including lengthy and learned annotations and introductions. Rhode Island's Tomaquag Museum published the most recent edition of *A Key Into the Language of America* in 2019; it is the first edition of the *Key* edited by Narragansett language experts and includes annotation and commentary by Indigenous scholars, elders, and knowledge-keepers, Lorén Spears and Dawn Dove. All of these volumes are available from any online bookstore, and many are free on public domain internet archive sites like hathitrust.org. Even looking at a sample of the original manuscripts has become easier as the Rhode Island Historical Society has made their entire holdings of his letters available on-line.[11] But, if accessing Williams's texts is relatively easy, reading Williams is another matter entirely.

9. We are grateful to Charlotte Carrington-Farmer for sharing her unpublished work on Mary Bernard Williams; "More than Roger's Wife: Mary Williams and the Founding of Providence." *New England Quarterly*, forthcoming 2024.

10. In chapter 4, we included the sole surviving few words in Mary's own handwriting, which was simply an address sheet that was meant to cover a letter she addressed to Roger—a letter she never sent.

11. See Rhode Island Historical Society's "Roger Williams Online Gallery," https://

Put simply, Williams can be rambling, cranky, and hard to understand, especially for readers new to seventeenth-century style. Even compared to other early New England ministers, Williams's writing is dense and disorganized, something Williams admitted in a 1638 letter to Governor John Winthrop: "I sometimes feare that my lines are as thick and over busie as the Muskeetoes."[12] Many scholars who study Williams comment on his writing choices. Perry Miller warned readers that Williams's "eccentric spelling, wild use of italics, and barbarous paragraphing" are "formidable terrors."[13] Even the masterful Glenn LaFantasie described Williams's letter-writing style as "gnarled and convoluted."[14] But historian Alan Simpson put it best: "Students have been known to open one of Roger Williams's pamphlets, under the impression that they were going to meet a familiar figure, only to shut it hastily again with the feeling that there must have been some mistake."[15]

Perhaps because his writings are so thick and hard for modern readers to wade through, many scholars have selected out the parts that suit their needs, leaving Williams's intellectual complexity in separate pieces. An important goal for our work was to reflect the breadth of Williams's work (and life) in a single volume. Other scholars have compiled one-volume collections of Williams's work, but ours is the first that includes selections from all of his published works, as well as some of his correspondence. We have tried to avoid crafting a "greatest hits" collection of Williams quotations. That said, readers familiar with Williams's publications may notice that we included a lengthy portion of *The Bloudy Tenent* (1644), but much less from *Bloody Tenent Yet More Bloody* (1652). And we devoted more space to *George Fox Digg'd Out* (his 1672 account of several days of debate with Quakers) than most scholars have. Pragmatic considerations (and a concern for the reader) forced us to select from the thousands of pages that Williams authored, and we are well aware of the impact of those choices. Equally important are the dozens of letters in this volume that truly give the full range of topics, places, and people that Williams's life engaged. This book is not a definitive collection, but rather an attempt to immerse the reader in Williams's world. Our hope is that while this might be the first Williams collection for some readers, it won't be the last.

---

www.rihs.org/roger-williams-online-gallery/.

12. Roger Williams to John Winthrop, c. early June 1638 in *Correspondence of Roger Williams*, 1:159.

13. Miller, *Roger Williams*, v.

14. LaFantasie, "Introduction," *Correspondence of Roger Williams*, 1:xxvi.

15. Simpson, "How Democratic was Roger Williams?" 53.

We wanted to allow Williams to come alive in this collection as the complicated and unpredictable human he was—and that goal informed our choices throughout. So, perhaps surprisingly, *Reading Roger Williams* includes documents that were not written by Williams—Governor John Winthrop's and Governor William Bradford's diary entries about Williams, the Massachusetts Bay Colony's banishment order, the "submission" of the Narragansett in 1644, and an order for the sale of Indigenous people into slavery following King Philip's War that Williams signed. We chose to include these texts because we want readers to see Williams in context. Pulling Williams forward into our own time is an unavoidable hazard of being an historian, and he is intriguing in part because he seems so much more modern than his contemporaries. But this collection tries to invite the reader back into his time by surrounding him with some of his own period's documents, especially when they help fill in gaps or complicate the (sometimes overly fawning) traditional depiction of Williams.

Most of the materials produced by Williams are from an English colonial perspective and therefore do not contain Native voices and perspectives. Read closely, Williams does include some Native voices in some writings, but they are still filtered through his own agendas and ideas. It therefore felt important to try to understand Williams through the lens of present-day Narragansett tribal members. Throughout this collection, you will see some of their perspectives interspersed with the introductory materials. These inclusions do not reflect the fullness of Native perspectives on Williams, nor do the Narragansett individuals who so graciously commented on this book speak for all Narragansett or all Indigenous peoples. Still, these present-day voices are an important corrective to the one-sided archive that usually informs and frames histories of Rhode Island and Williams. As Narragansett and Niantic tribal educator Chrystal Mars Baker has noted, "So much of Narragansett history is lost or unknown because of colonization and its changes to the landscape of what is Rhode Island; buried beneath the structures and systems established by such men as Roger Williams and all others. It is written on the landscape and environment which existed pre-contact and are no longer the same."[16]

A Note on Transcription and Annotation

An introduction prefaces each document in this volume to help situate the reader and offer some guidance with seventeenth-century names, language, and terms, but our hope is that we have not directed the reader's

16. Chrystal Mars Baker, correspondence with the authors, January 24, 2023.

interpretation of the text itself. The longer pieces—those representing books Williams published—have introductory notes as well as additional guidepost notes in *italics* throughout the transcription to guide the reader through the longer texts. We have kept the spelling and punctuation of the original editors, but their editorial principles already span more than a hundred years of documentary editing best practices, and we understand that this leads to variation among texts. Italics appear throughout Williams's printed volumes with no pattern or predictability, and scholars suggest that these italics may reflect the printer's intention, rather than the author's; so, we have not kept them.[17] In this collection, we refer to Indigenous people using several different terms: Indian, Native American, Indigenous, and whenever possible, by their own tribal or First Nation name. Williams often used tribal names in his publications and correspondence, and this is the preference for scholars writing today. When it is not possible to identify a specific nation, we use those broader terms interchangeably. In the original texts, the words Williams used remain unchanged by us. We have deliberately not modernized any words. While it may be tempting to make Williams easier to read by changing his language to help him sound more like us—a decision many scholars have made—we did not want to interfere that much in the reader's experience with Williams.

Roger Williams National Memorial, Providence, Rhode Island.
Photo by Linford D. Fisher, 2023.

17. For a discussion of author/printer text decisions, see: Simpson, *Proof-reading in the Sixteenth, Seventeenth, and Eighteenth Centuries;* Moore, *Primary Materials Relating to Copy and Print in English Books.*

Chronology[1]

c. 1603	Born in Smithfield, England
c. 1618–1621	Worked as apprentice scribe/assistant for Sir Edward Coke, jurist
1621 June	Student at Charterhouse School
1623 June	Admitted to Pembroke College, Cambridge, matriculated June 1624[2]
1627 July	Received AB degree
1628 Dec–1629 Feb	Left Cambridge, accepted position as chaplain to nonconformist Sir William Masham, Essex
1629	Courted Jane Whalley, unsuccessfully proposed in April
1629 Dec 15	Married Mary Bernard
1630 Dec 1	Departed for Massachusetts Bay Colony on the *Lyon*, with Mary
1631 Feb 9	Arrived in Boston, offered a Boston ministerial position, which he refused
1631	Moved to Salem briefly, then to Plymouth
1633	Left Plymouth in late Spring, returned to Salem by Sept
1633 early Aug	Daughter, Mary Williams, born in Plymouth
1633 Sept 3	John Cotton arrived in Boston with letter of safe passage from Parliament

1. *Correspondence of Roger Williams*, 1:xciii–xciv; Winslow, *Master Roger Williams*; Field, *Errands into the Metropolis*, 26–47; Gilpin, *Millenarian Piety of Roger Williams*, 141; Camp, *Roger Williams*.

2. Winslow discusses the unusually long delay between admission and matriculation in *Master Roger Williams*, 58.

1635 April 12	Accepted position of teacher at Salem Church
1635 Oct 9	Banished by order of the General Court of Massachusetts Bay
1635 late Oct	Daughter, Freeborn Williams, born in Salem
1636 Jan	Fled Salem alone, arrived in Narragansett Bay fourteen weeks later
1636 Spring	Started settlement at Providence, Mary Williams and children arrive
1638 Mar 24	Narragansett sachems (Miantonomo and Canonicus) deed him land of Providence
1638 late Sept	Son, Providence Williams, born
1639 May 1	Roger and Mary Williams excommunicated from Salem church
1639	Gathered a Baptist church in Providence
1639 July	Left Providence Baptist congregation, and never joined another church
c. 1639	Opened a trading house at Cocumscussoc, about twenty miles south of Providence on the water (near present-day Wickford, Rhode Island)
1640 c. July 15	Daughter, Mercy Williams, born
1640 July 27	Williams and other Providence settlers signed civil compact
1642 Feb 15	Son, Daniel Williams, born
1643 June–July	Sailed for England from New Amsterdam port
1643 Sept 7	*A Key into the Language of America*—his first book—published in London
1643 Dec	Son, Joseph Williams, born
1644 Feb 5	*Mister Cotton's Letter Examined* published in London
1644 Feb 9	*Queries of Highest Consideration* published in London
1644 Mar 14	Parliament granted patent for Providence Plantations
1644 July 15	*The Bloudy Tenent of Persecution* published after his departure from London
1644 Aug 9	*The Bloudy Tenent of Persecution* ordered burned by Parliament

1644 Sept 17	Williams landed at Boston with letters of safe passage to Rhode Island
1644–1647	Served as chief officer of Providence Plantations
1645	*Christenings Make not Christians* published in London
1649 Mar	Chosen deputy president of Providence Plantations
1651	Sold his trading post at Cocumscussoc to business partner, Richard Smith
1651 Nov	Sailed for second trip to London
1652 Mar 30	*Fourth Paper, Presented by Major Butler* published in London
1652 April	*Hireling Ministry None of Christs* published in London *Experiments of Spiritual Life and Health* published in London
1652 April	*Bloody Tenent Yet More Bloody* published in London
1652 Sept	*Examiner Defended* published in London
1654 c. June	Returned from London
1654 Sept 12	Elected president of Providence Plantations
1657 May	Stepped down from presidency
1663 July 8	King Charles II granted royal charter to Rhode Island and Providence Plantations
1672 Aug	Debated Quakers in Newport and Providence
1675 Dec 19	Aided by Rhode Island, the United Colonies (Massachusetts Bay, Plimouth, and Connecticut) attack the Narragansett fort in what was later called the Great Swamp Massacre
1676 Mar 29	Indigenous bands attacked and burned Providence & Williams's house
after 1676	Mary Bernard Williams died at Providence
1676	*George Fox Digg'd out of his Burrowes* published in Boston
c. 1679–1683	Wrote "A Brief Reply to a Small Book Written by John Eliot" in margins of *An Essay Towards the Reconciling of Differences Among Christians*
1683 Jan–Mar	Died at Providence

Chapter 1

"My Native Country," 1603–1630

WILLIAMS GREW UP MIDDLE-CLASS *in a merchant family in London, attended the Charterhouse School thanks to his patron, Sir Edward Coke, and then graduated from Pembroke College at Cambridge with his bachelor's degree in the summer of 1627.[1] From an early age, he had formed powerful connections to leading puritan families, and he enjoyed financial and social patronage from Coke—one of the leading jurists in England and the Chief Justice of the King's Bench. Given this resume and how well-connected he was in London, Williams surely would have anticipated marrying well and preaching from a prominent English pulpit after graduation. So why did he leave England in 1630?*

No texts that document Williams's earliest years remain, aside from one remembrance he wrote much later in 1652 (which we have included below), so it is hard to understand his motivations. Historians suggest that both his experiences as a child—Williams was around eight years old when Bartholomew Legate was burned at the stake in 1612 at Smithfield for heresy[2]—and also as a teenager sitting in the Star Chamber[3] taking notes for Coke, learning from

---

1. Coke paid £140 for Williams to attend Charterhouse school, which converts to approximately £22,956 pounds sterling in 2023 or approximately $28,390 US dollars. That tuition was, as John Barry notes, "more than double the costs of Cambridge University." Barry, *Roger Williams*, 57. For another point of comparison, the physician at Charterhouse earned £20 per year. Camp, *Roger Williams*, 49. Currency conversion: www.nationalarchives.gov.uk/currency-converter; https://www.bankofengland.co.uk/monetary-policy/inflation/inflation-calculator.

2. Legate was the last person burned at Smithfield and among the last in England. Smithfield was also the site of many earlier anti-Protestant executions. Winslow, *Master Roger Williams*, 28–29; Barry, *Roger Williams*, 43–44.

3. The Court of the Star Chamber was established in 1515 and acted as a kind of king's council, made up of judges and members of the Privy Council. It was disbanded

his work in the courts and on the Privy Council, affected him deeply.[4] *Scholars also suggest that Coke's imprisonment by King James I must have been distressing and perhaps served as another early example of state persecution for Williams. Williams's decision to leave Cambridge after completing his undergraduate degree also offers a clue. When Williams graduated with his A.B. from Pembroke, he would have been asked to agree to the Three Articles— something that was required of all graduates beginning in 1623—which means that he accepted the monarch's power over ecclesiastical affairs in the Church of England and that he agreed to use the Book of Common Prayer, among other things.*[5] *His signature indicates that he agreed to these in July 1627. But, sometime in late 1628 or very early 1629, he ended his graduate studies, left Pembroke College, gave up his scholarship, turned down two ministerial posts, and opposed the Book of Common Prayer. Historians suggest that the decision to discontinue his advanced studies illustrates his increased alienation from the established Church.*[6] *Instead of a pulpit, he accepted a job with an elite nonconformist family in Essex, about 30 miles east of London, in very late 1628 or early 1629.*

Williams was part of a much wider reform movement in the Church of England, often referred to as "puritanism." Like most puritans in early seventeenth-century England, Williams was a Calvinist who wanted the English church to rid itself of all remaining vestiges of its Catholic past, even as England's monarchs (James I and Charles I) sought to limit what they saw as excesses in the puritan movement, welcomed the return of some ceremonies, and required complete obedience to the Church of England, which had the monarch as its head.[7] *Anti-Calvinist William Laud was appointed bishop of London in 1628 and then archbishop of Canterbury in 1633; he reintroduced things like altar rails, ministerial vestments, crucifixes, and a Book of Common Prayer—making their use mandatory for all ministers in the Church of England.*[8] *As the 1652 letter below indicates, Williams remembered feeling driven out of England by Bishop Laud. It also seems that following graduation,*

---

by the Long Parliament in 1641 because Charles I had tended to use it to prosecute religious dissenters for nonconformity and other people critical of his policies. It was the king's court and therefore was not bound by common law, nor did it have juries.

4. Barry, *Roger Williams*, 23–25, 43–58; Winslow, *Master Roger Williams*, 19–59; Camp, *Roger Williams*, 1–112.

5. Winslow, *Master Roger Williams*, 70–71, 90. The Long Parliament ended this requirement in 1640.

6. Gilpin, *Millenarian Piety*, 31. Winslow included the statement that proves when Williams withdrew. Winslow, *Master Roger Williams*, 72.

7. Winship, *Hot Protestants*, 60–70.

8. Winship, *Hot Protestants*, 81, 91–113.

Williams increasingly wanted English parish churches to be totally independent or "separate" from an English church that he found insufficiently reformist, which places him at the more radical end of the puritan spectrum. Radical nonconformists like Williams—those people who refused to "conform" to the demands of the English crown and Church of England's practices no matter the consequences—were forced underground, and some even chose to abandon England for the Netherlands or New England. Williams's ideas in this period are not that unusual in this radical puritan underworld, even if he eventually pushed for more separation from the Church of England than did most of his fellow emigrants to Massachusetts Bay.[9]

When Williams boarded the Lyon *in December 1629 and headed for New England, he was a Cambridge-educated, fiercely puritan young minister, who had facility in Latin, Greek, and Dutch, along with experience as a notetaker in the relatively new style of shorthand.[10] Thanks to Coke and the extended Masham family for whom he worked, he was also well connected in the highest circles of elite nonconformists in London. So, it is no surprise that the ministers and magistrates in Boston warmly welcomed him when he emigrated in 1630; the texts below may help illustrate why he left.*

King James I to George Abbott, Archbishop of Canterbury, August 4, 1622[11]

Known as "Directions to Preachers," this text was drawn up by King James I of England in response to the growing power of the puritans in the Church of England, and to what he saw as the rise of "dangerous doctrines" being supported by some Church of England ministers. James had supported puritan-led, Calvinist, reform efforts until the Thirty Years' War pitted Catholic armies against Frederick V's Protestant forces in the Palatinate and other Protestant areas in Germany. Desperate to avoid war, James did not support Calvinist Frederick, but instead sought a Spanish Catholic bride for his son Charles (which failed), and lifted restrictions on Catholics in England. Puritans in England rebelled against James, which led to a change in James's thoughts on several important questions: he increasingly favored Church of England

9. Winship describes him as an "extreme separatist" who "had been a minister in England. But at some point he had taken up decidedly non-puritan, radical convictions that would dissolve the disciplined, unitary Christian commonwealth the puritans were trying to create in Massachusetts." Winship, *Hot Protestants*, 97.

10. For Williams's knowledge of Dutch, see Camp, *Roger Williams*, 19, 22–23; for his shorthand skills, see Fisher et al., *Decoding Roger Williams*, 5–13.

11. James I to the Archbishop of Canterbury, August 4, 1622 in Tanner, *Constitutional Documents of the Reign of James I*, 80–82.

ceremony over preaching, promoted the divine right of Kings, and tried to curry favor from his Catholic subjects.

All of this deeply worried English protestants, especially puritan ministers. The "Directions to Preachers"—written by James and distributed to all bishops in England directly from the Archbishop of Canterbury—sought to severely limit what clergy in England could preach from their pulpits. Point three below prohibits preaching on predestination (a central tenet of Calvinist doctrine); point four warns that no preacher can "meddle with matters of State," which is clearly trying to silence criticism of what became known as "the Spanish match" for Prince Charles; point five prohibits all anti-Catholic preaching. When James I died in 1625 and was replaced by his son, Charles I—"an anti-Calvinist with an intense attachment to bishops and ceremonial religion" who was married to a French Catholic princess—it is no wonder that reformist ministers in the Church of England became very concerned.[12] This text provides a glimpse of what puritan nonconformist ministers were facing, especially someone like Williams, who had independent, Separatist leanings.

Forasmuch as the abuses and extravagances of preachers in the pulpit have been in all times suppressed in this realm by some Act of Council or State with the advice and resolution of grave and learned prelates . . . And whereas at this present divers young students, by reading of late writers and ungrounded divines, do broach many times unprofitable, unsound, seditious, and dangerous doctrines, to the scandal of the Church and disquiet of the State and present government, we upon humble representation unto us of these inconveniences by yourself and sundry other grave and reverend prelates of this Church, as also of our . . . zeal for the extirpation of schism and dissention growing from these seeds . . . do by these our special letters straitly charge and command you to use all possible care and diligence that these limitations . . . concerning preachers be duly and strictly . . . put in practice and observed. . . . send them forthwith copies of these directions, to be by them speedily sent . . . unto every parson, vicar, curate, lecturer, and minister . . . letting them know that we have a special eye unto their proceedings and expect a strict accompt thereof, both from you and every of them. . .

I. That no preacher under the degree and calling of a Bishop, or Dean of a cathedral or collegiate church (and they, upon the King's days and set festivals) do take occasion, by the expounding of any text of Scripture whatsoever, to fall into any set discourse, or commonplace, otherwise than by opening the coherence and division of his text), which shall not be

12. Winship, *Hot Protestants*, 75.

comprehended and warranted in essence, substance, effect or natural inference within some one of the Articles of Religion set forth 1562, or in some of the Homilies set forth by authority of the Church of England, not only for a help of the non-preaching, but withal for a pattern and a boundary (as it were) for the preaching ministers. And for their further instructions for the performance thereof, that they forthwith read over, and peruse diligently, the said Book of Articles, and the two Books of Homilies.

II. That no parson, vicar, curate, or lecturer shall preach any sermon or collation hereafter upon Sundays and holy days in the afternoon, in any cathedral or parish church throughout the kingdom but upon some part of the Catechism or some text taken out of the Creed, Ten Commandments, or the Lord's Prayer (funeral sermons only excepted), and that those preachers be most encouraged and approved of who spend the afternoon's exercise in the examination of children in their Catechism, which is the most ancient and laudable custom of teaching in the Church of England.

III. That no preacher of what title soever under the degree of a Bishop, or Dean at the least, do from henceforth presume to preach in any popular auditory the deep points of predestination, election, reprobation, or of the universality, efficacity, resistibility or irresistibility, of God's grace; but leave those themes rather to be handled by the learned men, and that moderately and modestly by way of use and application, rather than by way of positive doctrines, being fitter for the Schools than for simple auditories.

IV. That no preacher of what title or denomination soever from henceforth shall presume in any auditory within this kingdom to declare, limit, or bound out by way of positive doctrine, in any lecture or sermon, the power, prerogative, and jurisdiction, authority, or duty of Sovereign Princes, or otherwise meddle with matters of State and the differences between Princes and the people than as they are instructed and presidented in the Homilies of Obedience and the rest of the Homilies and Articles of Religion, set forth (as before is mentioned) by public authority, but rather confine themselves wholly to those two heads of faith and good life which are all the subject of the ancient sermons and homilies.

V. That no preacher of what title or denomination soever shall presume causelessly (or without invitation from the text) to fall into bitter invectives and undecent railing speeches against the persons of either Papists or Puritans, but modestly and gravely, when they are occasioned thereunto by the text of Scripture, free both the doctrine and discipline of the Church of England from the aspersions of either adversary, especially when the auditory is suspected to be tainted with one or the other infection.

VI. Lastly, That the Archbishops and Bishops of the kingdom (whom his Majesty hath good cause to blame for their former remissness) be more

wary and choice in their licensing of preachers, and revoke all grants made
to any chancellor, official, or commissary to pass licences in this kind: And
that all the lecturers throughout the Kingdom of England (a new body sev-
ered from the ancient clergy, as being neither parsons, vicars, nor curates)
be licensed henceforward in the Court of Faculties, only upon recommendation of the party from the bishop of the diocese under his hand and seal,
with a *fiat* from the lord Archbishop of Canterbury [and] a confirmation
under the Great Seal of England. And that such as do transgress any one of
these directions be suspended by the Bishop of the diocese, or in his default,
by the Archbishop of the province, *ab officio et beneficio*, for a year and a
day, until his Majesty, by the advice of the next Convocation shall prescribe
some further punishment.

Roger Williams to Lady Joan Barrington, c. April 1629[13]

*New nonconformist ministers struggled to find clerical positions under Arch-
bishop Laud's increasingly restrictive rules, but wealthy puritan families could
hire family chaplains, both for their own edification and to help support and
shelter a puritan minister. Rather than remain at Pembroke College pursuing
further studies after graduation (and agree to the new requirement to swear
that the Church of England service was scripturally-based), Williams accepted
a position at Otes Manor in Essex as chaplain to Sir William Masham and his
family. Along with serving as chaplain, Williams also accompanied Masham
when he returned to London in early 1629 to serve in Parliament.[14] Sir Robert
Barrington and Sir Thomas Barrington were Masham's brothers-in-law, the
three served in Parliament together, and they all trusted Williams to carry
messages and relay news from London to Essex: "Mr Williams who walkes
the city will be able to say more than I can."[15] Lady Barrington, to whom this
letter is addressed, was married to Sir Francis Barrington, who served in Parliament from 1601–1628, and was the mother of Sir Robert and Sir Thomas.
Sir Francis Barrington was imprisoned for refusing a "forced loan" to King
Charles I and died shortly after being released, having been unwell in prison.
Lady Barrington was also aunt to both Oliver Cromwell and Edward Whalley,
one of the men who signed the death warrant for Charles I. The Mashams
and Barringtons were deeply interconnected and nonconformist.[16] At the time*

13. Roger Williams to Lady Joan Barrington, c. April 1629, *Correspondence of Roger Williams* 1:1–4.

14. Barry, *Roger Williams*, 73–74; Gilpin, *Millenarian Piety*, 30.

15. Barry, *Roger Williams*, 78.

16. Winslow describes Otes as "a hotbed of Puritan sentiment of the more militant

Williams wrote this letter, Lady Joan's daughter, Elizabeth, was married to Sir William Masham.

Williams's position at the time brought him into contact with a powerful constellation of nonconformists, many of whom occupied a social position that far exceeded his own. When Williams sought (and failed to secure) Lady Joan's permission to marry her niece, Jane Whalley (who was living with the Barringtons), Williams was reminded of the power that social distinction carried. He refers below to the rumors swirling about his desire to marry above his station, Jane's dowry, and his own admission that he is "unworthy." But he also clearly lays out his personal financial situation in hopes that Lady Barrington will agree to the marriage. Given that Williams was twenty-six years old when he wrote this letter to seventy-seven-year-old Lady Barrington, commenting on her gray hair and imminent death may not have been his best strategy to win her over.

[Otes, Essex, England]

Madame,

Your Ladiship may wonder at this unwonted absence! and also aske what means this paper-deputie? . . . Many and often speeches have long fluttered and flowne abroad[17] concerning your Ladiships neere kinswoman[18] and my unworthy selfe. What litle eare I have given that way (further then I have hearkened after your Ladiships mins) all that know me here, doe know. Yet like A rowling Snowball or some flowing streame, the report extends and gathers stronger and stronger . . . I presume therefore to Consult (as most of right I acknowledge I ought) with the soonest with your Ladiship, especially considering her loving and strong Affection togeather with the report as strong abroad.

Good Madame may it please you then to take notice. I acknowledge my selfe altogeather unworthy and unmeete for such A proposition. The neerenes of her blood to your Ladiship and godly flowrishing branches hath forc't me to confesse her Portion in that regard to be beyond Compare, invalueable. Yet many feares have much possest me. . . . I have receaved some good Testimonialls from mine owne experience more from others, not the least from your good Ladiships selfe.

---

sort, both ecclesiastical and political." The Barringtons were also financial backers of the short-lived Providence Island colony in the West Indies. Winslow, *Master Roger Williams*, 75, 91–92. Camp, *Roger Williams*, 82–85.

17. Around.

18. Jane Whalley, Lady Joan's niece. For Whalley's life after she was prevented from marrying Williams, see Winslow, *Master Roger Williams*, 83–85.

Objections have come in about her Spirit, much accused for passionate and hastie, rash and unconstant. Other feares about her present Condition it being some Indecorum for her to condescend to my low-ebb. There I some thing stick:[19] but were all this cleared, there is one barr not likely to be broken, and that is the present estate of us both. That portion it hath pleased God to allot her (as I heare) is not for present and happily (as things now stand in England) shall never be by us enjoyed.[20]

For mine owne part: It is well knowne (though I would gladly conceal my selfe) how A gracious God and tender Conscience . . . hath kept me back from honour and preferment. Beside many former offers and that late new-England call I have had since 2 severall[21] livings profferd me each of them 100 li[22] per annum: but as things yet stand among us I see not how any great meanes and I shall meete that way. Nor doe I seek nor shall I be drawne on any tearmes to part (even to my last parting) from Oates so long as any Competencie[23] can be raised, and libertie affoorded. . . . Beside this meanes I now from hence enjoy, litle is there that I can call mine. After the death of an aged loving Mother, amongst some other children, I amay expect . . . some 20 li or 20 marck per annum.[24] At hand . . . I have some 7 score pieces[25] and a litle (yet Costly) studie of bookes. Thus possessing all things, I have nothing, yet more then God owes me, or then my blessed saviour had himselfe.

Poore yet as I am I have some few offers at present, one put into my hand, person and present portion worthy.[26] Yet stand they still at dore, and

19. Hesitate.

20. LaFantasie suggests that her dowry is "in jeopardy because her father was being defrauded by unscrupulous relatives." *Correspondence of Roger Williams*, 1:4n8. It is worth asking whether Williams may have thought that her lack of dowry made a match with a clergyman more acceptable.

21. Distinct or particular.

22. Derived from the Latin word "libra"(which translates to "pound"), *li* is the abbreviation for pound. According to online currency converters, £100 in 1630 was equivalent to approximately £15,229 pounds sterling, or $18,848 US dollars in 2023. www.nationalarchives.gov.uk/currency-converter; https://www.bankofengland.co.uk/monetary-policy/inflation/inflation-calculator.

23. Salary or support.

24. Williams's mother, Alice Pemberton Williams, had inherited property on Cow Lane, including a tavern and three "tenements," that supported her in her widowhood. Her will (filed in January 1635) left Williams ten pounds yearly for twenty years, but according to LaFantasie, he never received any of this money. *Correspondence of Roger Williams*, 1:4n11.

25. Probably pieces of silver.

26. According to LaFantasie, unlike earlier in the letter, the offers he refers to here are not jobs, but marriages; apparently there were others, and one in particular, that seemed appropriate. Whether one of these is Mary Bernard—his eventual wife—we cannot be sure.

shall, untill the fairest end the Lord shall please to give to this, shall come to light. I have bene bold to open to your Ladip[27] the whole Anatomie of the busines. To wrong your precious name and answer her kind love with want would be like Gall to all the hony of my life,[28] and marr my marriage joyes. The kind affection of your deare Ladiship and worthy Niece is of better merit and desert. I shall add for the present I know none in the World I more affect, and (had the Lord bene pleased to say Amen in those other regards) should doubtles have fully answered (if not exceeded) her affection.

But, I have learn'd another lesson to still my soule as A weaned childe and give offence to none. I have learn'd to keepe my studie, and pray to the God of heaven (as oft as I doe pray) for the everlasting peace and well-fare of your kind Ladiship, whose soule and Comfort is in the number of my greatest Cares.

The Lord that hath caried you from the wombe to gray heires,[29] crowne out those gray heires by making your last dayes (like the close of some sweet harmonie) your best: fruitfull (like Sarah) in old age, out shining all those starrs that shine about you, going downe in peace, rising in Glory in the armes of your dearest Saviour, To wch everlasting armes, he often commits your Soule and Yours, who is the unworthiest (though faythfull) of all that truely serve and honour you.

Roger Williams

Roger Williams to Anne Sadleir, c. April 1652

Anne Sadleir's endorsement, c. April 1652

While written more than thirty years after his decision to emigrate to Boston, Williams's letter to Anne Sadleir includes important details about why he left, and how at least one elite English woman felt about him long after he departed. Sadleir (1584–c. 1670) was the eldest daughter of Sir Edward

27. Abbreviation for Ladyship.

28. "Putting a little gall in the honey" is a French proverb, and in the Bible, gall is a common metaphor for something very bitter.

29. In another letter, sent May 2, 1629, Williams is even more blunt about her impending death: "when there is but the breadth of A few gray haires, betweene you and your everlasting home, let me deale uprightly with you." Later in the letter, Williams reiterates how little time she has left: "I beseech you, your candle is twinckling and glasse neere run. The Lord only knowes how few minutes are left behind." According to LaFantasie, this letter so enraged Lady Barrington that her "animosity had reached scandalous proportions." Barrington suffered from deep bouts of depression and spiritual doubts, which Williams seemed to want to help with, but this second letter apparently did little to comfort her. *Correspondence of Roger Williams*, 1:4–8.

Coke, the famous jurist for whom Williams worked as a notetaker for about four years when he was a teenager. Coke served as Speaker of the House of Commons, chief justice of the Court of Common Pleas, member of the King's Privy Council, and on the Star Chamber. He also helped draft the charter for the proposed Virginia Company colony in 1606.[30] Coke paid for Williams to attend Charterhouse School; Coke's patronage was key to Williams's entry into elite circles and most biographers suggest that Coke had enormous influence on the person Williams became. This letter also describes Williams's great sadness at leaving England. While Williams may have addressed Sadleir as "My much honoured friend," she clearly did not think of him fondly at all; in fact as the comment below indicates, by 1652, she wished for his hanging due to the "rebel" that he had become (in her mind).

From my Lodging [near] St. Martins, neere the shambles
at Mr Davis his howse, a shoomaker at the Signe of the Swan [London]

My much honoured friend Mrs. Sadler
. . . This last winter I landed (once more) in my Native Country being sent over from some parts of New England with some Addresses to the Parliamt.

My very great Busines and my very great straights of Time, and my very great Journey homeward to my deare Yoakfelow and many children[31] I greatly feare will not permit me to present my ever obliged Dutie and Service to you at Stondon,[32] especially if it please God that I may dispatch my Affaires to depart with the ships within this fortnight[33]. . .

Since I landed I have published 2 or 3 things[34] and have a large Discourse[35] at the presse, but tis Controversiall with wch I will not trouble your Meditations. Only, I crave the Boldnes to send you a plaine and peaceable Discourse of my owne personall Experiments wch in a Letter to my deare wife (upon the Occasion of her great sicknes neere Death) I sent her being absent my selfe amongst the Indians. And being greatly obliged to Sir Henry Vane Junior (once Govr of N. England) and his Lady, I was perswaded to

30. Barry, *Roger Williams*, 23–43.

31. Williams often referred to his wife as his "yoke-fellow." By 1652, he and Mary Bernard Williams had six children.

32. Standon is the name of the Sadleir manor house in Hertfordshire.

33. He did not leave until early 1654.

34. He published *Fourth Paper, Presented by Major Butler, Experiments of Spiritual Life*, and *Hireling Ministry None of Christs* during this trip.

35. This is *Bloody Tenent yet More Bloody.*

publish it[36] in her name and humbly to present Your honourable hands with one or 2 of them. . .

My much honoured friend, That Man of Honour and Wisedome and pietie your deare father, was often pleased to call me his Son and truely it was as bitter as Death to me (when Bishop Laud pursued me out of this Land and my Conscience was perswaded agst the Nationall Church and Ceremonies and [Bishops] beyond the Conscience of your deare Father) I say it was as bitter as Death to me when I rode Windsor way to take ship at [Bristol], and saw Stoke-Howse[37] where that blessed man was and I then durst not acquaint him with my Conscience and my Flight. But how many thouhsand times since have I had honourable and precious remembrance of his person and the Life the Writings the Speeches and Examples of that Glorious Light? And I may truely say that beside my naturall Inclination to studie and Actvitie, His Example Instruction and Incowragemt have spurd me on to a more then ordinarie industrious and patient Course, in my whole Course hietherto. . .

[*Anne Sadleir's Endorsement*[38]] This Roger Williams when he was a youth would in a short hand take sermons, and speeches in the starchamber and present them to my dear father, he seeing him so hopeful a youth, tooke such liking to him that he put him in to suttons hospital[39] and he was the second that was placed there. Full little did he think that he would have proved such a rebel to god the king and his cuntry. I leve his letters that, if ever he has the face to turn into his native cuntry, Tyborn[40] may give his wellcome.

36. This refers to *Experiments of Spiritual Life*, which was dedicated to Lady Vane. We included portions of this publication in chapter 9 below.

37. Stoke House was Coke's country estate, just north of Windsor, where he died in September 1634. *Correspondence of Roger Williams*, 1:360n13.

38. An "endorsement" is a comment written by the recipient of a letter, often detailing when they received it, and by which carriers or means of conveyance it was sent. In this case, Sadleir added much more than those common details.

39. "Sutton's Hospital" was the more common name for Charterhouse School, where Williams attended thanks to Coke's financial support.

40. Tyburn was the place of execution (near central London) from the twelfth century until 1783. The site of the gallows is the current location of the Marble Arch.

Chapter 2

Three Pulpits in
Massachusetts, 1631–1635

JUDGING BY THE SURVIVING *documents, Williams seemed to write very little about his earliest years in New England. He used his prestige as a Cambridge-educated clergyman to advocate for several contentious reforms almost from the day he arrived in Massachusetts: all churches must completely separate from the Church of England; oaths required for political loyalty must be prohibited; and the patent that granted land to the Massachusetts Bay company was fraudulent and must be returned to the King.[1] Williams also denied that the government had any right to punish offenders for ecclesiastical wrongs, or to coerce spiritual practice at all, such as compulsory church attendance. All of this was unpopular with the leaders in Massachusetts Bay for many reasons, not least of which they worried about endangering their position with the English government. Williams moved four times in three years, unable to find a church that supported his antagonism toward state-sponsored religion. The documents in this section from those early years illustrate his restlessness and his growing impatience with the unseparated churches in the Massachusetts Bay and Plimouth colonies. After his arrival in Boston, he spent a few months in Salem, then moved to Plimouth until late 1633. When Salem's minister, Samuel Skelton, died, Williams returned to Salem to assume the role of Teacher. By October 1635, the General Court of Massachusetts ordered him out of the colony. In this chapter, along with a few texts from Williams—some written at the time, and others written in retrospect—the governors of both Massachusetts Bay and Plimouth colonies narrate Williams's uneasy fit in their towns.*

---

1. Gilpin, *Millenarian Piety*, 16.

This chapter and the next are best read as preparation for Williams's fight against state interference in matters of religious practice—a topic that figured in most of his published works and in many of his personal letters. The texts that people traditionally associate with Williams's ideas on "separation of church and state" are in chapter 7, but these two chapters illustrate his developing ideas on why the government cannot meddle in—or even worse, compel— spiritual practice.

Roger Williams to John Cotton Jr., March 25, 1671[2]

Many years after his forced exile, in a letter to John Cotton Jr., Williams describes why he chose not to accept a pulpit in Boston when he first arrived from England—the Boston puritans were not really "seperated" from the Church of England. He also suggests why he refused the Plimouth offer that followed. While the Plimouth churches may have been more "officially" separated from the Church of England than the churches in Massachusetts Bay were, Williams found Plimouth's continued connections to the Church of England troubling. As he explains in this letter, Plimouth residents continued to correspond with neighbors in England and attend Anglican services when visiting England. Plimouth churches also maintained close ties with churches in Massachusetts Bay. All of this indicated to Williams that they were not separated enough.

In New [England] being unanimously chosen Teacher at Boston (before Yor deare Father came divers yeares) I conscientiously refused & withdrew to plymmouth, because I durst not officiate to an unseperated people, as upon Examination & Conference, I found them to be: At plymmouth I spake on ye Lords days & weeke days, & wrought hard at the How[Hoe] for My Bread (& so afterward at Salem) untill I found them both Professing to be a Seperated people in N. E. (not admitting ye most Godly to Communion without a Covenant) & yet out Communicating with ye Parishes in Old, by their members repairing on frequent occasions thether.

Journal of John Winthrop, April 12, 1631[3]

In his journal, Governor John Winthrop recounts Salem's decision to offer a call to Williams in early 1631. Starting in 1629, the Salem church was an

---

2. Roger Williams to John Cotton Jr., March 25, 1671 in *The Correspondence of John Cotton Junior*, 73–78.

3. Winthrop, *Journal*, 50.

autonomous covenanted church, which was clearly separatist.[4] *Williams initially accepted Salem's offer to minister to them, and Winthrop was clearly
unhappy that the Salem church welcomed Williams, especially after Williams
rejected Boston's pulpit. Winthrop was very concerned that Williams denied
the right of civil governments to punish people who broke the first four commandments (the "first table") and that Salem would act without consulting
Boston authorities first. The General Court sent a letter to Salem asking them
to at least delay offering Williams a position, and Winthrop convinced the
Salem elders to withdraw their offer.*

April 12, 1631: At a Court holden at Boston, (upon information to
the Governour that they of Salem had called mr Williams to the office of a
Teacher) a letter was written from the Court to mr Endecott, to this effecte
that wheras mr. Williams had refused to joyne with the Congregation at
Boston because they would not make a public declaration of their repentance for havinge Communion with the Churches of Englande while they
lived there, & besides had declared his opinion that the magistrate might
not punishe the breache of the Sabbath nor any other offence, as it was a
breache of the first table. therefore they mervayled [marveled] they would
chuse him, without advisinge with the Counsell, & withall desiringe him
that they would forbeare to proceede till they had conferred about it.

William Bradford, *Of Plimouth Plantation*, late 1631[5]

*After Salem withdrew their offer of a ministerial post, Williams moved south
to the colony of Plimouth. Below, Governor William Bradford describes Williams's short stay in the Plimouth Colony. Historians suggest that the strange
opinions Bradford describes were really more about his "increasingly vocal
defense of the land rights of Native Americans" than about separatism.*[6] *And
as Narragansett scholar Mack Scott has suggested, it was likely the direct influence of his time among the Wampanoag near Plimouth that first caused*

---

4. While this was troubling to the leaders who arrived in Boston in 1630, the Salem
church simply "implemented principles espoused by a diverse collection of English
congregationalists over the preceding four decades." Gilpin, *Millenarian Piety*, 23.

5. Bradford, *Of Plimouth Plantation*, 398–99.

6. Davis, *On Religious Liberty*, 10; James Warren suggests that John Cotton also
wrote that Williams first articulated concerns about Indigenous land and the King's
patent while in Plimouth. Warren, *God, War, and Providence*, 44–45, 49.

Williams to question the legitimacy of the king's unilateral patent for what was clearly Indigenous land in the first place.[7]

Mr Roger Williams (a man godly & Zealous, having many precious parts; but very unsettled In Judgement) came over first to the Massachusetts, but upon some discontent left that place, and came hither (where he was friendly Entertained, according to their poor ability,) and exercised his gifts amongst them, & after some time was admitted a member of the church. And his teaching well approved, for the benefit whereof I still bless God, and am thankful to him, even for his sharpest admonitions & reproofs, so far as they agreed with truth. He this year began to fall into some strange opinions, and from opinion, to practise; which caused some controversy between the church, & him, and in the end some discontent on his part, by occasion whereof he left them something abruptly. Yet afterwards sued for his dismission[8] to the church of Salem, which was granted, with some caution to them concerning him, and what care they ought to have of him. But he soon fell into more things there, both to their, and the government's trouble & disturbance. I shall not need to name particulars, they are too well known now to all, though for a time, the church here went under some hard censure, by his occasion from some, that afterwards smarted themselves. But he is to be pitied, and prayed for; and so I shall leave the matter, and desire the Lord to shew him his errors; and reduce him into the way of truth, and give him a settled Judgement, and constancy in the same, for I hope he belongs to the Lord, and that he will shew him mercy.

Journal of John Winthrop, September 1633–1635[9]

Williams returned to Salem and served with the settled minister, Samuel Skelton. Winthrop's journal records Williams's second stay in Salem and details Williams's concern that the private ministerial meetings then being held in Boston could devolve into a centralized authority over individual churches in the colony, closer to a Presbyterian synod.[10] *Soon after, Williams questioned*

7. Mack Scott, correspondence with the authors, January 22, 2023.

8. In early New England churches, church members had to request permission to leave one church congregation before joining another. Bradford uses the word "sue," but it essentially means "ask" in this case. Bradford does write that he offered some warning to the Salem church when he sent permission for Williams to move congregations.

9. Winthrop, *Journal*, 102–3, 107–8, 109, 137.

10. Presbyterian churches were overseen by boards of lay and clerical elders (presbyteries) and were subject to more centralized control than Congregational or "Independent" churches in the New England colonies were. What some Boston ministers

the validity of the royal patent, and even the settling of colonies themselves, likely as a result of his time among the Wampanoag and Narragansett.[11] *According to Williams, the land belonged to Native Americans and settling colonies on behalf of "Christendom" suggests that there is a Christendom in the first place—which Williams denied because national churches were illegitimate. Williams clearly struggled in Massachusetts Bay, repeatedly raising concerns about magistrates interfering in questions of religious practice. The excerpts from Winthrop's journal below show Williams trying to raise serious concerns, but then officially retracting them when the Massachusetts Bay Colony leaders rejected his interpretations, and then still persisting in teaching on these same matters in Salem.*

Nov. 1633: The ministers in the Baye & Sagus[12] did meet, once a fortnight, at one of their howses by Course, where some question of moment was debated: mr. Skelton the Pastor of Salem & mr. Williams who was removed from Plimouthe thither (but not in any office thoughe he exercised by way of prophysye[13]) tooke some exception against it, as fearinge it might growe in tyme to a Presbiterye or Superintendancye,[14] to the prejudice of the Churches Libertyes: but this feare was without Cause, for they were all cleere in that pointe that no Churche or person can have power over another Churche, neither did they in their meetinges exercise any suche jurisdiction &c

Dec. 27, 1633: The Governor & Assistantes mett at Boston, & tooke into consideration a treatice which mr Williams (then of Salem) had sent to them, & which he had formerly written to the Governor & Councell of Plimouthe wherein amonge other things, he <questions> disputes their right to the lands

---

saw as an opportunity to discuss "some question of moment" every two weeks, Skelton and Williams saw as something that might be "injurious to the liberty of individual congregations." In this same period, the town of Salem was also bristling at what it saw as increasing centralization of power in Boston. At the very time that Williams and Skelton pushed back against centralizing church polity, the town refused to submit funds to support the building of forts in Boston. Gilpin, *Millenarian Piety*, 39; Winship, *Hot Protestants*.

11. James Warren suggests that Williams's criticism of English settler attitudes toward Indigenous land "was rooted in his radical theology and reinforced by his constantly expanding knowledge of Indian society and culture." Warren, *God, War, and Providence*, 49.

12. Saugus, a town between Boston and Salem, Massachusetts.

13. Within puritanism, the practice of lay exhortation on parts of the Bible was often called "prophesying."

14. Williams is surely thinking about the centralized power of the Church of England, that has the monarch as the head of the church, according to the 1534 Act of Supremacy.

they possessed heere: & concluded that claiminge by the kinges grant they could have no title: nor otherwise except they componded with the natives: for this takinge advise with some of the most juditious ministers (who muche condemned mr willms error & <over> presumption) they gave Order that he should be convented at the next Court, to be Censured &c: There were 3: passages chiefly wherat they were muche offended. 1: for that he Chargeth Kinge James to have tould a solemne publicke lye: because in his Patente he blessed God that he was the first Christian Prince that had discovered this land. 2: for that he chargeth him & others with blasphemy for callinge Europe Christendom or the Christian world: 3: for that he did personally apply to our present Kinge Charles these 3: places in the Revelation viz: [Rev. 16:13–14; Rev. 17: 12–14; Rev. 18:9] mr. Endecott being absent the Governor wrote to him to let him knowe what was doone, & withall added divers Argumentes to confute the said errors. <when> wishinge him to deale with mr wms. to retracte the same &c. wherunto he returned a verye modest & discreet answeare: mr wms. allso wrote to the Governor & allso to him & the rest of the Councell, verye submissively: professinge his intent to have been onely to have written for the private satisfaction of the Governor &c: of Plim: without any purpose to have stirred any further in it, if the Governor heere had not required a Copye of him. withall offering his booke or any parte of it to be burnt &c. At the next Court he appeared privatly & gave satisfaction of his intention [. . .] his loyalty. so it was left & nothinge doone it in.

January 24, 1634: The Governor & Councell mett againe at B[oston]: to consider of mr Williams Lettre &c when with the advise of mr Cotton & mr Willson, & weighinge his Lettre, & further Consideringe of the aforesaid offencive passages in his booke (which beinge written in verye obscure & implicate phrases, might well admitt of doubtfull interpretation) they fonde the matters not to be so evill as at first they seemed: whereupon they agreed that upon his retraction &c. & takinge an oath of Alegeance to the Kinge it should be passed over.

Nov 27, 1634: It was likewise informed that mr williams of Salem had broken his promise to us in teaching publicly against the kings Patente & our great sinne in clayminge right thereby to this contrye &c: & for usuall terminge the Churches of England an Antichristian we granted summons to him for his appearance at the next Court.

Oaths

As documents above illustrate, Williams was increasingly uncomfortable in the Massachusetts Bay Colony, and the colony's leaders were unhappy with his public and repeated criticism of them. Several events led to the final decision to banish Williams in October 1635, including Williams's condemnation of oaths that year. The colony required all men over age sixteen to swear an oath to prove fidelity to the authority of the colony, in addition to the typical requirements of oath-taking before testifying in courts or accepting public office.[15] *John Winthrop described the conflict with Williams over oaths in his journal beginning in April 1635. Williams maintained his unwillingness to swear oaths long after leaving Massachusetts Bay.*[16] *Modern readers may not see oaths as anything more than civic performance, but for Williams, an oath was a prayer, and forcing people to profess an oath when they may not believe in the words they were saying was wrong. It was another example of the civil magistrates forcing spiritual practice. For an "unregenerate" person—or someone who had not experienced God's saving grace—to swear an oath meant they were taking God's name in vain, which is a grievous sin. Of course, the officials in Massachusetts Bay did not see it this way. For government officials in New and Old England, oaths were an important part of running civil society; to challenge them meant dangerously chipping away at the bonds of government.*

Massachusetts Bay Colony Oath of Freemen, May 14, 1634[17]

I, [state your name], being, by Gods providence, an inhabitant & ffreeman within the jurisdiccon of this comonweale, doe freely acknowledge my selfe to be suject to the govermt thereof, and therefore doe heere sweare, by the greate & dreadfull name of the everlyveing God, that I wilbe true & faithfull to the same, & will accordingly yeilde assistance & support thereunto, with my pson & estate, as in equity I am bound, & will also truely indeavr to mainetaine & preserve all the libertyes & previlidges thereof, submitting my selfe to the wholesome lawes & orders made & established by the same; and furthr, that I will not plott nor practise any evill against it nor consent to any that shall soe doe, but will timely discover and reveale the same to

15. Historian Timothy Hall suggested that the colony used oaths to "reinforce almost all social responsibilities" and their "use of oaths to secure truthfulness and loyalty among Massachusetts inhabitants was, by current standards, extravagant." According to Hall, even the colony's leaders began to worry about people being asked to swear oaths too frequently and placed a limit on who could administer them. Hall, *Separating Church and State*, 35.

16. Years after being forced to leave the colony, Williams visited England and had a case dismissed by the chancery court because he refused to swear the oath, which meant that he was forced to forfeit the money he had won in a lawsuit. Gilpin, *Millenarian Piety*, 45.

17. Shurtleff, *Records of the Governor and Company of the Massachusetts Bay*, 1:117.

lawfull authority nowe here established, for the speedy preventing thereof. Moreover, I doe solemnely bynde my myself, in the sight of God, that when I shalbe called to give my voice touching any such matter of this state, wherein ffreemen are to deale, I will give my vote & suffrage, as i shall judge in myne owne conscience may best conduce & tend to the publique weale of the body, without respect of psons, or favr of any man. Soe helpe mee God, in the Lord Jesus Christ.

Journal of John Winthrop, April 30, 1635[18]

The Governor & Assistandes sent for mr williams the occasion was for that he had tought publicly that a magistrate ought not to tendre an Oathe to an unregenerate[19] man: for that we thereby have Comunion with a wicked man in the worshipp of God: & cause him to take the name of God in vaine: he was heard before all the ministers & verye cleerly confuted: mr Endecott was at first of the same opinion: but he gave place to the Truethe

Roger Williams, "An Appendix as Touching Oathes, a Querie," *The Hireling Ministry None of Christs, or a Discourse touching the Propagating the Gospel of Christ Jesus* (1652)[20]

Nearly twenty years later, Williams returned to his concern about oath-taking in his book The Hireling Ministry None of Christs. *In this text, he clearly describes an oath as a prayer, and therefore, he argues that oaths are spiritual practice, not civil speech, and cannot be demanded by civil authorities.*

Although it be lawfull (in case) for Christians to invocate the Name of the most High in Swearing: Yet since it is a part of his holy worship, and sometimes put for his whole worship, and therefore proper unto such as are his true Worshippers in Spirit and Truth: and persons may as well be forced unto any part of the worship of God as unto this, since it ought not to be used, but most solemnly, and in most solemne and weighty cases, and (ordinarily) in such as are not otherwise determinable; since it is the voice of two great Law-givers, from God, Moses and Christ Jesus, that in the mouth of two or three Witnesses (not Swearing) every Word shall stand: Whether the inforcing of Oaths and spiritual Covenants upon a Nation promiscuously,

18. Winthrop, *Journal*, 144. Winthrop is not governor at this time.
19. That is, be fully "saved" by their profession of saving grace.
20. Williams, *Complete Writings of Roger Williams*, 7:188.

and the constant inforcing of all persons to practice this Worship in the most triviall and common cases in all Courts (together with the Ceremonies of Booke, and holding up the hand &c.) be not a prostituting of the Holy Name of the most High to every unclean Lip, and that on slight occasions, and taking of it by Millions, and so many millions of times in vaine, and whether it be not a provoking of the eyes of his jealousie who hath said it, That he will not hold him (what him or them soever) guiltlesse that taketh his name in vaine.

"Modell of Church and Civil Power," 1634

Williams's Replies, from *The Bloudy Tenent* (1644)[21]

In March 1634, the Massachusetts Bay General Court asked "the elders and brethren of every church . . . [to] consult and advise of one uniforme order of dissipline in the churches, agreeable to the Scriptures" and "to consider howe farr the magistrates are bound to interpose for the preservation of that uniformity and peace of the churches."[22] The resulting text—"The Modell of Church and Civil Power"—written in 1634 by several ministers in Massachusetts Bay, was the first attempt by the colony's ministers to articulate their ideas on the proper relationship between church and state. The "Modell" was circulated in manuscript only and made its way to Williams privately. It remained a scribal publication (as opposed to one printed at a press) until Williams incorporated it into The Bloudy Tenent *printed ten years later in 1644 in London.[23] Historians have suggested that Williams probably did not receive it until after his banishment, even though it had been written and sent to Salem earlier. Williams offered his theory about the identity of the anonymous author in the subtitle he added to the text when he included it in* The Bloudy Tenent: *"Composed by Mr. Cotton and the Ministers of New England, and sent to the Church at Salem." Williams devoted nearly half of his* The Bloudy Tenent—204 pages—to reprinting the "Modell" and interleaving responses to each claim the "Modell" made. We have included some excerpts here, rather than in a later chapter that includes* The Bloudy Tenent, *because it sits more comfortably chronologically here, in Williams's earliest years in New England. It also suggests that as early as 1636, Williams had a clear answer to the thorny*

21. "Modell of Church and Civil Power," *Complete Writings of Roger Williams*, 7:221–425.

22. Shurtleff, *Records of the Governor and Company of the Massachusetts Bay*, 1:142.

23. Hall, "Not in Print yet Published," 29–80.

question the General Court posed about the proper relationship between civil and ecclesiastical jurisdictions.

According to historian James Byrd, the "Modell" argued that civil leaders could not allow other faiths to coexist within the colony because they believed that doing so would destroy both the churches and the colony. According to the leaders of Massachusetts Bay, allowing "diverse religions in the state was sheer madness because religious diversity would lead to political and moral divisions and civil peace would degenerate into chaos." But Williams saw this "Modell" as a "violent document—a clear articulation of the 'bloody doctrine of persecution for the cause of conscience.'"[24] We have included a few sections below, labeling them as "Modell" or "Truth/Peace"—the latter of which represent Williams's replies—to indicate who is speaking. Williams used quotation marks in his text to indicate which portions were direct quotations from the "Modell," so we have done the same. We have used Williams's original chapter numbers to indicate where each paired excerpt was drawn from.

Modell: "Seeing God hath given a distinct power to the Church and Common-weale, the one Spirituall . . . the other Civill . . . and hath made the members of both Societies subject to both Authorities, so that every soule in the Church is subject to the higher powers in the Commonweale, and every member of the Commonweale (being a member of the church) is subject to the Lawes of Christs Kingdome, and in him to the censures of the Church; the Question is, how the Civill State and the Church may dispence their severall Governments without infringement and impeachment of the power and honour of the One or of the Other, and what bounds and limits the Lord hath set betweene both . . ." [ch.LXXXII]

Modell: "Whereas divers affecting transcending power to themselves over the Church have perswaded the Princes of the World, that the King-dome of Christ in His Church cannot rise or stand, without the falls of those Commonweales wherein it is set up, we do beleeve and professe the contrary to this suggestion; the government of the one being of this World, the other not; the Church helping forward the prosperity of the Com-monweale by means only Ecclesiasticall and Spirituall; the Commonweale helping forward her owne and the Churches felicity by meanes politicall or temporall; the falls of Commonweales being knowne to arise from their scattering and diminishing the power of the Church, and the flourishing of Commonweales with the well ordering of the people (even in morall and civil virtues) being observed to arise from the vigilant administrations of the holy Discipline of the Church . . ."

24. Byrd, *Challenges of Roger Williams*, 61.

Truth: Ans. From this confession, that the Church or Kingdome of Christ may be set up without prejudice of the Commonweale, according to John 18.36 My Kingdome is not of this World, &c. I observe that although the Kingdome of Christ, the Church and the Civill Kingdome or Government be not inconsistent, but that both may stand together; yet that they are independent according to that Scripture, and that therefore may be (as formerly I have proved) flourishing Commonweales and Societies of men where no Church of Christ abideth; and secondly, the Commonweale may be in perfect peace and quiet, notwithstanding the Church . . . be in distractions . . . [ch.LXXXIII]

In the "Modell's" eighth question, the Massachusetts ministers asserted that religious intolerance was necessary to protect both the church and the colony, partially because purity was the purpose of migrating to Massachusetts Bay in the first place, and that forcing all residents to attend church services is a magistrate's duty. Williams countered with the precedent of history, noting that when governments have tried to control the consciences of their nation's people, it was Christians who were "persecuted." Williams then reminded the "Modell's" authors in a pointed condemnation that they have not separated from the Church of England, and that Massachusetts Bay forced everyone to support the church financially, whether they are members or not. This section ends with a powerful claim: If governments force a religion on people that they may not really believe, and people must silence their own authentic beliefs or face persecution, then they are never able to practice their faith freely. So, then, the government was preventing people from having or practicing any faith at all "in all their dayes."

Modell: ". . . the Magistrate . . . hath power to forbid all Idolatrous and corrupt Assemblies, who offer to put themselves under their patronage, and shall attempt to joyne themselves into a Church-estate, and if they shall not hearken, to force them therefrom by the power of the Sword, Psal. 101.8. For our tolerating many Religions in a State of severall Churches, beside the provoking of God, may in time not only corrupt, leaven, divide, and so destroy the peace of the Churches, but also dissolve the continuity of the State, especially ours whose wals are made of the stones of the Churches; it being also contrary to the end of our planting in this part of the World, which was not only to enjoy the pure Ordinances, but to enjoy them all in purity. Thirdly, He hath power to compell all men within his grant, to heare the Word, for hearing the Word of God is a duty which the light of Nature leadeth even Heathens to . . . Yet he hath no power to compell all men to become members of Churches, because he hath not power to make them fit members for the

Church . . . Nor may he force the Churches to accept of any for members, but those whom the Churches themselves can freely approve of."

Truth: . . . [The] Magistrate should encourage and countenance the Church, yea and protect the persons of the Church from violence, disturbance, &c. it being truly noble and glorious . . . 'Tis true, all Magistrates in the world do this: viz. Incourage and protect that Church and Assembly of worshippers, which they judge to be true and approve of; but not permitting other consciences then their owne. It hath come to passe in all ages, and yet doubtlesse will, that the Lord Jesus . . . [is] driven and persecuted out of the World. [ch.C]

Peace: . . . this appears not to be the bottome, for in Old England the New English joyne with Old in the ministrations of the Word, Prayer, singing, contribution, maintenance of the Ministrie, &c . . . if I say, they should set up Churches after their conscience, the greatnesse and multitudes of their owne Assemblies would decay, and with all the contributions and maintenance of their Ministers, unto which all or most have been forced. [ch.CI]

. . . And however they affirme that persons are not to be compelled to be members of Churches, nor the Church compelled to receive any: Yet if persons be compelled to forsake their Religion which their hearts cleave to, and to come to Church, to the worship of the Word, Prayers, Psalmes, and Contributions, and this all their dayes: I aske whether this be not the peoples Religion, unto which submitting, they shall be quiet all their dayes . . . I aske, Will it not inevitably follow that they . . . enforce people to bee of no Religion at all, in all their dayes? [ch.CII]

Toward the end of his refutation of the "Modell," Williams used the metaphor of a ship at sea, and the proper responsibilities of ship's master/pilot versus the civil magistrate ("Prince") that may be on board.

Truth: The Church of Christ is the Ship, wherein the Prince (if a member . . .) is a passenger. In this ship the Officers and Governours, such as are appointed by the Lord Jesus, they are the chiefe, and (in those respects) above the Prince himselfe, and are to bee obeyed and submitted to in their works and administrations, even before the Prince himselfe . . . In this respect every Christian in the Church, man or woman (if of more knowledge and grace of Christ) ought to be of higher esteeme (concerning Religion and Christianity) then all the Princes in the world, who have either none or lesse grace or knowledge of Christ: although in civill things all civill reverence, honour and obedience ought to be yeelded by all men. [ch.CXXVI]

Truth: A Pagan or Antichristian Pilot may be as skillfull to carry the Ship to its desired Port, as any Christian Mariner or Pilot in the World, and may performe that worke with as much safety and speed: yet have they not command over the soules and consciences of their passengers or mariners under them, although they may justly see to the labour of the one, and the civill behaviour of all in the ship . . . [ch.CXXXII]

Chapter 3

Banishment, 1635

As THE DOCUMENTS IN *the last chapter illustrate, Williams offered persistent criticism of the Massachusetts Bay Colony's leaders: he denied their use of oaths, challenged the charter, and argued that civil leaders cannot interfere with spiritual matters—anything included in the "first table" of the Commandments, or those Commandments that concern a person's relationship to God. This last challenge left Massachusetts Bay authorities little choice but to demand that Williams retract his criticism. At first, Williams was penitent, but by 1635, Williams encouraged his Salem neighbors to begin a letter-writing campaign blaming the Massachusetts government "for their open transgression of the rule of justice." Then Williams stopped attending services in Salem altogether, renouncing the Salem churches as well. The Massachusetts authorities asked him to testify before the General Court to answer their growing concerns. The documents below illustrate attempts by Massachusetts Bay's political and ministerial leaders to reign Williams in, which ultimately failed. The texts also suggest that during his nearly five years in the Massachusetts Bay and Plimouth colonies, both Winthrop and Williams wanted to make things work—there was no sudden rupture, but an earnest back and forth between the two men. The Massachusetts court banished Williams from the colony in October 1635.*

Journal of John Winthrop, July 8, 1635[1]

Winthrop[2] listed Williams's many errors in his Journal on July 8. According to Winthrop, Williams believed the following: that the civil authorities had no right to punish violations of the "first table"; that requiring oaths by men who may not be "saved" was wrong; that regenerate people should not pray with unregenerate people, even if those unregenerate people were their spouses or children. According to Winthrop, churches in the colony had been planning to write letters to Salem warning them about Williams's increasingly danger-ous opinions, and the court was shocked that Salem would offer Williams a ministerial position. It ends with a stern promise to Williams: the "magistrate" would remove anyone who continued to maintain these beliefs after clear cen-sure from the court.

July 8, 1635: mr Williams of Salem was summoned & did appeare. it was layd to his Charge that beinge under Question before the magistrates & Churches for diverse dangerous opinions viz. 1: that the magistrate ought not to punishe the breache of the first table, otherwise then in suche Cases as did disturbe the Civill peace. 2: that he ought not to tender an oathe to an unregener[ate] man. 3: that a man ought not to praye with suche thoughe wife Child &c. 4: that a man ought not to give thankes after the Sacrament nor after meate. &c: & that the other Churches were about to write to the Church of Salem to admonishe him of these errors: notwithstandinge the Churche had since called him to Affirme of a Teacher. muche debate was about these things the said opinions were adjudged by all magistrates & ministers (who were desired to be present) to be erronious & verye danger-ous: & the Callinge of him to office at that tyme was judged a great Con-tempte of authoritye: so in fine tyme was given to him & the Church of Salem to consider of these thinges till the next general Court, & then either to give satisfaction to the Court, or els to expect the sentence. It beinge pro-fessedly declared by the ministers (at the request of the Court to give their advise) that he who should obstinately maintaine suche opinions (whereby <he> a Churche might runne into Heresye, Apostacye or Tiranye, & yet the Civill magistrate could not entermeddle) were to be removed, & that the other Churches ought to request the magistrate so to doe.

---

1. Winthrop, *Journal*, 149–50.

2. Winthrop was not governor at this time; John Haynes was then governor of Mas-sachusetts Bay Colony.

The Church at Salem to the Elders of the Church at Boston, after July 22, 1635[3]

The letter below is the only letter that survives from Williams's turbulent early conflicts with Boston churches. The original copy is worn and mutilated, and as Glenn LaFantasie suggests, "its damaged condition is an apt reminder of the many gaps and holes in the primary sources for this period . . . only a handful of items—some of them biased or written after the fact—contain useful evidence about Williams's expulsion from the colony."[4] Williams co-wrote this letter on behalf of the Salem congregation, and it touches on some of the friction between Williams and the Boston ministers, including questioning the proper authority of the state in ecclesiastical matters.[5] The letters that Williams refers to in the opening lines no longer survive.

[Salem, Massachusetts Bay]

The Church of Jesus Christ at Salem, to our dearly beloved and much Esteemed in Jesus, the Elders of the Church of Christ, at Boston

Your letters (dear and wellbeloved in Christ) dated the 22 of this 5th moneth, have been read openly before us, wherin we understand you see not your way clear before you, for delivering of our humble complaint unto the Church of Christ with you as also your reasons why you dare not publish[6] to the bodie our letters. Our Dear Brethren according to your loving & Christian desire, we dare not but gently & tenderly interpret this your delay as springing from your holy care . . . We give you many & hartie thanks for your loving and f[ai]thfull dealing in returning us a reason of your holie feares & Jealousies.

. . . The church hath the right wch the officers may not assume unto themselves and therefore it hath been questioned whether publick letters sent to a Church of Christ ought not to be delivered publicly to the Elders, in the face of the church met togither according to what is written, Acts 15:30 When they had gatherd the Multitude (that is the Church) together then they delivered the letters . . .

. . . Your reasons of not reading are three; two against reading at all, the third, agst reading it on the Lordes day. The first more expressly concerning

---

3. Our version of this degraded manuscript draws on both of the most recent transcriptions: *Correspondence of Roger Williams*, 1:23–29 and *Correspondence of John Cotton*, 203–10.

4. LaFantasie, "The Road to Banishment" in *Correspondence of Roger Williams*, 1:12–23.

5. James, *Colonial Rhode Island*, 17–18.

6. By "publish," Williams means "announce."

[*torn*] our admonition (You say) is a gift[7] wch shold not be offered up until we have reconciled our selves to our much honoured and beloved the majistrates who are against us.

. . . We doubt not but a peticion may be both delayed & rejected, but we must needs profess our exceeding greif that a church of Christ shall under goe a punishmt before convented, be punished (if there were due cause) before exhorted to repentance in a rule of Christ, and hundreds of innocents punished of the town [torn] as the conceived nocents[8] of the Church.

. . . We hope we shall ever be with the formost in all humble respect & service to all higher powers, according to God, we speak now of our much honoured Brethren as Brethren, whose soules are deer & pretious to us, in holie Covenant, & therin conceive the onely way to honour them in the Lord, is to beseech them to wash away the dishonour of the most high, by true, godly sorrow & repentance, & in this your service we conceive in the end you will finde that most true wch the spirit of God writes, open rebuke is better than secrett love.[9]

Your 3d Argumt is that you dare not upon the Lords day deal in a worldly busines, nor bring a Civill busines in the church. First pleas you to remember (our dear and welbeloved in Christ) that for any Civill matter we open not our mouth. We speak of a spirituall offence against our Lord Jesus, & against the holy Covenent of Brethren, & so we doubt not though uncleannesse [illeg.] oppression be offenses agst the Civil state wch the church meddles not with, yet the church deals with members lawfullie for their breach of covenant & disobedience agst the Lord Jesus.

. . . Now our blessed Christ Jesus who holdeth his starrs in his right hand, & out of whose mouth goes a sharp two-edged sword, & whose countenance shines as the sunne in his strength Rev 1.16. shine mercifully and clearly upon your soules in all holy [directions] consolations and salvations. Your most unworthy Brethren, unfainedly respective and affectionate in Christ Jesus.

Roger Williams
Samuel Sharpe

7. LaFantasie suggests that the Boston elders are calling the letters from Salem "a gift," in the sense of "something given with a corrupting intention" (as in 2 Chr 19:7) or of "something given to gain favor" (as in Prov 18:16). *Correspondence of Roger Williams* 1:29n9.

8. Criminals.

9. Prov 27:5.

Journal of John Winthrop, August 1635[10]

As Winthrop wrote in the journal entry below, Williams had recently told the Salem church that he could no longer join with them or with any congregation in Massachusetts Bay. He suggested elsewhere that his Salem neighbors should not join a church because all churches in Massachusetts Bay were full of "antichristian pollution" since they had not separated from the Church of England[11] and allowed—in fact, required—unregenerate people to attend services with regenerate people.[12] Clearly, Williams refused to abide by what the Massachusetts authorities demanded of him.

August 1635: mr Williams Pastor of Salem beinge sicke & not able to speake wrote to his churche a protestation that he could not communicate with the Churches in the Baye: neither would he communicate with them except they would refuse Communion with the rest: but the wholl Churche was grieved heerewith.

Journal of John Winthrop, October 1, 1635[13]

In this journal entry, Winthrop describes the court's final attempt to bring Williams into line. When they questioned Williams about what they saw as his dangerous positions, Williams stood firm and debated the issues that same day with Thomas Hooker, then minister in Newtown (Cambridge). Hooker was unable to convince Williams to renounce his opinions, and on the following day, the General Court sentenced him to leave the colony. With only one exception, the colony's ministers agreed with the sentence, and the Salem church apologized for the letter they had sent earlier in the summer criticizing the magistrates. Salem had other reasons to distance themselves from Williams. Earlier, in July 1635, Salem had petitioned the General Court for a new land grant at Marblehead Neck, but Massachusetts Bay rejected their petition because of their support for Williams. Salem tried to rally support from other towns

10. Winthrop, *Journal*, 153.

11. Clark Gilpin suggests that Williams was never going to find peace in a Massachusetts Bay church: "for Williams the purity of the separated church was the paramount consideration," and when he realized that Massachusetts leaders "seemed to prize social order above what he believed to be religious purity he followed in disillusionment the well-worn path of the Separatist reformers." Gilpin, *Millenarian Piety*, 47–48.

12. Winthrop, *History*, 1:204; Francis Bremer narrates these conflicts from Winthrop's perspective in *John Winthrop*, 249–52. For a fuller discussion of Williams's extreme Separatism, see Gilpin, *Millenarian Piety*, 14–49.

13. Winthrop, *Journal*, 158.

and criticized what they saw as Boston's civil overreach into church concerns, but had little success, and support for Williams quickly deteriorated. In March 1636, with Williams safely expelled, Salem was granted the Marblehead land.[14]

At this General Court mr Willms the teacher of Salem was again Covenanted,[15] & all the ministers in the Bye beinge desired to be present, he was Charged with the said 2: Lettres, that to the Churches to Complayninge of the magistrates for injustice, extreame oppression &c: & the other to his owne churche, to persuade them to renounce Comunion with all the Churches in the Baye, as full of Antichristian polution &c: he justified both these Letters, & maintained all his opinions: & being offered further Conference or disputation, & a monthes respitt, he chose to dispute presently, so mr Hooker was appointed to dispute with him, but could not reduce him from any of his errors: so the next morninge the Court sentensed him to depart out of our jurisdiction within 6: weekes. all the ministers save one approving the sentence & his owne churche had him under question allso for the same cause & he at his returne home refused Communion with his owne Churche, who openly disclaimed his errors, & wrote an humble submission to the magistrates, acknowledginge their fault in joining with mr williams in that Letter to the Churches against them &c

Banishment Order from the Massachusetts Bay General Court, October 9, 1635[16]

The General Court gave Williams six weeks to leave Massachusetts Bay, allowing the extra time because Williams was ill. Williams's sentence of banishment was not revoked until 300 years later in Massachusetts House Bill #488 (1936).[17]

---

14. LaFantasie, "The Road to Banishment," in *Correspondence of Roger Williams,* 1:19–23; Gilpin, *Millenarian Piety,* 46–48.

15. Covenants are promises made between a believer and a loving God. Church congregations in early New England's puritan colonies agreed to communal covenants, where church members became, in John Cotton's words, "perfectly joined together in one mind and one judgment." Communities in crisis sometimes renewed their covenants as a means of admitting sinfulness and seeking God's forgiveness. By describing Williams as "again Covenanted," Winthrop means that Williams was once again a member of the Salem church. Hall, *Puritans,* 232; Winship, *Hot Protestants,* 247–49.

16. Shurtleff, *Records of the Governor and Company of the Massachusetts Bay,* 1:160–61.

17. Hall, *Separating Church and State,* 33–39.

Whereas Mr. Roger Williams, one of the elders of the church of Salem, has broached and dyvulged dyvers newe & dangerous opinions, against the authoritie of magistrates, as also writ [letters] of defamacion, both of the magistrates & churches here, & that before any conviccon, & yet mainetaineth the same without retraccon, it is therefore ordered, that the said Mr. Williams shall [depart] out of this jurisdiccon within six weekes nowe nexte ensueing, wch if hee neglect to pforme, it shalbe lawfull for the [Governor] & two of the magistrates to send him to some place out of this jurisdiccon, not to returne any more without license from the Court.

Journal of John Winthrop, early January 1635/6[18]

The Massachusetts authorities had allowed Williams extra time to leave the colony, but asked that he remain quiet and stop spreading his ideas to others. Williams refused and continued to teach in his home, something Winthrop describes below as "infection." As the document below illustrates, they finally attempted to arrest him in January 1636, unaware that he had departed the colony a few days earlier. Williams and Winthrop developed an alliance and friendship, and later Williams admitted that Winthrop had assisted his escape before the arrest order.[19] During the January 18 session, the General Court accused Winthrop of "over muche lenytye & remissness" in his dealing with Williams.[20] Winthrop's journal entry also indicates that before his expulsion, Williams had convinced "about 20" people to join him in a settlement at Narragansett Bay. In later retellings, Williams described striking out into the freezing wilderness alone; but it appears that he already had a clear plan of where he was going and a small group of people who planned to join him.

The Governor & Assistantes mett at Boston to consult about mr Williams, for that they were Credibly informed, that notwithstandinge the Injunction layd upon him (upon the libertye granted him to staye till the Springe) not to goe about to drawe others to his opinions, he did use to entertaine companye in his howse & preache to them, even of suche pointes as he has been Censured for: & it was agreed, to send him into England

18. Winthrop, *Journal*, 162–63. Note: Mary Bernard Williams and the other twenty people who intended to join Williams all managed to keep this premeditated plan secret.

19. In a 1670 letter, Williams wrote that the "ever honrd Govr Mr Wintrop privately wrote to me to steer my Course to the Nahigonset Bay and Indians, for many high and heavenly and publike Ends, incowraging me from the Freenes of the place from any English Claims or Pattents." *Correspondence of Roger Williams*, 2:610.

20. Winthrop, *Journal*, 167.

by a shippe then readye to departe: the reason was because he had drawne
about 20: persons to his opinion & they were intended to erecte a plantation
about the Naragansett Baye, from whence the infection would easyly spread
into these Churches (the people being many of them muche taken with the
apprehension of his Godlinesse) whereupon a warrant was sente to him to
come presently to Boston to be shipped &c he returned answeare (and diverse of Salem came with it) that he could not come without hazard of his
life &c: whereupon a pinance was sent with Comission to Capt. Underhill[21]
&c: to apprehende him & carry him aborde the shippe (which then rode at
Natascut) but when they came at his house, they fonde, he had been gone 3:
dayes before, but whither, they could not learne.

John Cotton to Roger Williams, c. early 1636, published in Williams, *Mr. Cottons Letter Lately Printed, Examined and Answered* (1644)[22]

*After he was banished from Massachusetts Bay, Williams began exchanging
letters with John Cotton. Williams's letters to Cotton, now all unfortunately
lost, reflect his trying to come to terms with his banishment (and his anger
and hurt over the sentence) while still trying to defend his doctrinal positions.
Their letter exchange also illustrates Cotton's attempt to convince Williams
that Cotton was not primarily responsible for the forced exile, but that Williams himself was.[23] The letter below contains a particularly heated exchange
where Williams wrote to Cotton that if he had died in the snow during that
first winter of his forced exile, that Cotton would have been responsible for
his death, to which Cotton replied that only Williams was responsible for
the errors that caused his banishment. This led the two men to stop writing
letters to each other at all. Eight years later, in 1643, when Williams was in
London seeking a charter for the colony for the four towns of Rhode Island,
Cotton's letter mysteriously appeared in print. Williams used the opportunity
to debate the central questions that led Massachusetts Bay to send him away.
The publication of Cotton's letter—A Letter of Mr. John Cottons, Teacher of*

---

21. John Underhill was a militia captain, and one of the commanders of the attack
on Block Island and the devastating massacre at the Pequot fort at Mystic during the
Pequot War (1636–1637). Sending Underhill to arrest Williams indicates the serious-
ness of the colony's plan to expel and deport him.

22. Williams, *Mr. Cottons Letter* in *Complete Writings of Roger Williams*, 1:313–96.

23. As a prominent minister, Cotton surely wielded considerable power, but no
ministers served in elected office and Cotton had no vote in the General Court on the
matter of Williams's banishment. Davis, *On Religious Liberty*, 13–22.

the Church in Boston in New England to Mr. Williams a Preacher there *(1644)—and Williams's published "answer"*—Mr. Cotton's Letter Examined and Answered *(1644)—are the first two publications in their debate over New England churches and religious toleration that continued until Cotton's death in 1652. Three years after this letter exchange, Cotton published* Reply to Mr. Williams, His Examination *(1647) where he wrote that he was unhappy that his letter had been made public at all: "But how it came to be put in print, I cannot imagine. Sure I am it was without my privitie: and when I heard of it, it was to me unwelcome news."*[24]

Williams's reply to Cotton's letter, published in 1644, reflected his palpable anger over what he saw as betrayal by Cotton. Even the opening salutation of Cotton's letter—where Cotton addresses Williams as "Beloved in Christ"—led Williams to reply angrily: "I desire it may be seriously reviewed by Himself and Them, and all men, whether the Lord Jesus be well pleased that one, beloved in him, should (for no other cause than shall presently appeare) be denied the common aire to breath in, and a civill cohabitation upon the same common earth; yea and also without mercy and humane compassion be exposed to winter miseries in a howling Wildernes?" Clearly the intervening eight years did nothing to dissipate Williams's anger. In 1644, Williams republished and replied to every line of Cotton's letter, refuting and answering every claim Cotton made. Most importantly, in this text, Williams used his own banishment to prove that church and state are erroneously bound together in Massachusetts Bay. For the modern reader, and perhaps for people in the seventeenth century, this exchange seems needlessly acrimonious. As Niantic and Narragansett educator Chrystal Mars Baker states, "The entire discourse between these two men of religion is so full of judgment, self-righteousness, and disagreement and division that one can scarcely understand how they could see themselves spiritually superior to the Indigenous people of this land."[25]

To the Impartiall Reader:

This Letter I acknowledge to have received from Mr. Cotton (whom for his personall excellencies I truly honor and love.) Yet at such a time of my distressed wandrings amongst the Barbarians,[26] that being destitute of

---

24. Cotton, *Reply to Mr. Williams* in *Complete Writings of Roger Williams,* 2:9.

25. Chrystal Mars Baker, correspondence with the authors, January 24, 2023.

26. In both published texts and personal correspondence, Williams often referred to the kindness and hospitality of his Indigenous neighbors, and while writing this text, he was also writing *A Key,* which deftly explored Native culture and language. So his use of "barbarians" here seems unsettling. It may be his attempt to dramatize the suffering he endured in the early years of exile, especially to an English audience. Narragansett scholar Mack Scott suggests that while "Williams complained of destitution, he was

food, of cloths, of time I reserved it (though hardly, amidst so many barba-rous distractions) and afterward prepared an Answer to be returned.

In the Interim, some Friends being much grieved, that one, publikely acknowledged to be godly and dearely beloved, should yet be so exposed to the mercy of an howling Wildernesse in Frost and Snow, &c. Mr. Cotton to take off the edge of Censure from himselfe, profest both in speech and writing, that He was no procurer of my sorrows.

Some Letters then past bewteen us, in which I proved and exprest, that if I had perished in that sorrowfull Winters flight; only the blood of Jesus Christ could have washed him from the guilt of mine.

His finall Answer was, had you perished, your blood had beene on your owne head; it was your sinne to procure it, and your sorrow to suffer it. Here I confesse I stopt, and ever since supprest mine Answer; waiting if it might please the Father of mercies, more to mollifie and soften, and render more humane and mercifull, the care and heart of that (otherwise) excellent and worthy man.

It cannot now, be justly offensive, that finding this Letter publike (by whose procurement I know not) I also present to the same publike view, my formerly intended Answer. [. . .]

Your most unworthy Countrey-man,

Roger Williams

Mr. Cotton: Though I have little hope (when I consider the uncircum-cision of mine owne lips, Exod.6.12) that you will hearken to my voyce, who hath not hearkened to the body of the whole Church of Christ with you, and the testimony, and judgement of so many Elders and Brethren of other Churches, yet I trust my labour will be accepted of the Lord; and who can tell but that he may blesse it to you also, if (by his helpe) I indeavour to shew you the sandinesse of those grounds, out of which you have banished yours from the fellowship of all the Churches in these Countries.

Mr. Cotton endeavoureth to discover the sandines of those grounds out of which (as he saith) I have banished my selfe, &c. I answere, I ques-tion not his holy and loving intentions and affections, and that my ground seem sandie to himselfe and others . . . Mr. Cotton endeavours to prove the firm rock of the truth of Jesus to be the weak and uncertain sand of mans invention . . . The rockie strength of those grounds shall more appeare in the Lords season, and himselfe may yet confesse so much, as since he came

---

able to pen this response because of the charity he received from the Narragansett. In fact, support from Indigenous persons sustained all of Williams's critiques, rumina-tions, and writings from 1636 through 1676." Mack Scott, correspondence with the authors, January 22, 2023.

into New England he hath confest the sandines of the grounds of many of
his practices in which he walked in Old England . . .

After my publike triall and answers at the generall Court, one of the
most eminent Magistrates . . . stood up and spake:

Mr. Williams (said he) holds forth these 4 particulars;

First, That we have not our Land by Pattent from the King, but that
the Natives are the true owners of it, and that we ought to repent of such a
receiving it by Pattent.

Secondly, That it is not lawfull to call a wicked person to Sweare, to
Pray, as being actions of Gods Worship.

Thirdly, That it is not lawfull to heare any of the Ministers of the Parish
Assemblies in England.

Fourthly, That the Civill Magistrates power extends only to the Bodies
and Goods, and outward state of men, &c.

I acknowledge the particulars were rightly summ'd up, and I also hope,
that, as I then maintained the Rockie strength of them to my own & other
consciences satisfaction so (through the Lords assistance) I shall be ready
for the same grounds, not only to be bound and banished, but to die also, in
New England, as for most holy Truths of God in Christ Jesus.

Yea but (saith hee) upon those grounds you banished your selfe from
the society of the Churches in these countries.

I answer, if Mr. Cotton mean my owne voluntary withdrawing from
those Churches resolved to continue in those evils, and persecuting the witnesses of the Lord presenting light unto them, I confesse it was my owne
voluntary act . . . if he mean this civill act of banishing, why should he call a
civill sentence from the civill State, within a few weeks execution in so sharp
a time of New Englands cold. Why should he call this a banishment from
the Churches, except he silently confesse, that the frame or constitution of
their Churches is but implicitly National . . . for otherwise why was I not yet
permitted to live in the world, or Common-weale, except for this reason,
that the Common weale and Church is yet but one, and hee that is banished
from the one, must necessarily bee banished from the other also . . .

I doubt not but that what Mr. Cotton and others did in procuring
my sorrowes was not without some regret and reluctancie of conscience
and affection . . . Yet to the particular that Mr. Cotton consented not, what
need he, being not one of the civill Court? But that hee councelled it (and
so consented) . . . I shall produce a double and unanswerable testimony.
First, hee publickly taught, and teacheth . . . that body-killing, soule-killing,
and State-killing doctrine of not permitting, but persecuting all other consciences and wayes of worship but his own in the civill State . . . Secondly,
as at that sentence divers worthy Gentlemen durst not concurre with the

rest in such a course, so some that did consent, have solemnly testified, and with tears . . . that they could not in their soules have been brought to have consented to the sentence, had not Mr. Cotton in private given them advice and counsell . . .

Mr. Cotton: And yet it may be they passed that sentence against you not upon that ground, but for ought I know, upon your other corrupt doctrines, which tend to the disturbance both of civill and holy peace, as may appeare by that answer which was sent to the Brethren of the Church of Salem, and to your selfe . . . I speake not these things (the God of Truth is my witnes) to adde affliction to your affliction but (if it were the holy will of God) to move you to a more serious sight of your sin, and of the justice of Gods hand against it. Against your corrupt Doctrines, it pleased the Lord Jesus to fight against you with the sword of his mouth (as himselfe speaketh, Rev. 2. 16.) in the mouthes and testimonies of the Churches and Brethren. Against whom, when you overheated yourselfe in reasoning and disputing against the light of his truth, it pleased him to stop your mouth by a suddaine disease, and to threaten to take your breath from you. But you in stead of recoyling . . . chose rather to persist in your way, and to protest against all the Churches and Brethren that stood in your way: and thus the good hand of Christ that should have humbled you, to see and turne from the errour of your way, hath rather hardned you therein, and quickned you onely to see failings (yea intolerable errours) in all the Churches and brethren, rather than in your selfe.

. . . I acknowledge the Land of England, the civill Laws, Government and people of England, not to be inferiour to any under heaven. Only 2 things I shall humbly suggest unto my deare Countrymen . . . as the greatest causes, fountaines and top roots of all the Indignation of the most High, against the State and Countrey: First that the whole Nation and Generations of Men have been forced (though unregenerate and unrepentant) to pretend and assume the name of Christ Jesus, which only belongs . . . to truely regenerate and repenting soules. Secondly, that all others dissenting from them . . . have not been permitted civil cohabitation in this world with them, but have been distressed and persecuted by them.

Mr. Cotton: The second stumbling blocke or offense which you take at the way of these Churches is, that you conceive us to walke betwixt Christ and Antichrist. First, in practising separation here, and not repenting of our preaching and printing it in our owne country. Secondly, in reproaching your selfe at Salem and others for separation . . .

Answ 1. Instead of halting betwixt Christ and Antichrist, wee conceive the Lord hath guided us to walke with an even foote betweene two extreames; so that we neither defile our selves with the remnant of pollutions in other Churches, nor doe wee for the remnant of pollutions renounce the Churches themselves, nor the holy ordinances of God amongst them, which our selves have found powerfull to our salvation. This moderation, so farre as we have kept it in preaching or printing, wee see no cause to repent of, but if you shew us cause why we should repent of it, wee shall desire to repent that we repented no sooner.

. . . I desire Mr. Cotton and every soule to whom these lines may come, seriously to consider, in this Controversie, if the Lord Jesus were himself in person in Old or New England, what Church, what Ministry, what Worship, what Government he would set up, and what persecution he would practice toward them that would not receive him? FINIS.

Roger Williams to John Winthrop, October 24, 1636[27]

Williams wrote this letter in reply to Winthrop's letter (now lost) in which Winthrop asked Williams to reflect on how his recent banishment had affected him spiritually. Earlier scholars have suggested that Winthrop might have been trying to convince Williams of the errors of his ways, perhaps even to elicit a public apology from Williams. However, more recent interpretations suggest that Winthrop's letter was closer to an official condemnation of Williams's positions.[28] After a respectful—even friendly—opening, Williams's reply turned Winthrop's questions back onto the settlers of Massachusetts Bay; rather than ask about the state of Williams's soul, he wrote, they should be examining their own. As he did in many later writings, Williams saw his banishment as a way of serving God: "I have gained the honor of one of his poore witnesses." When Williams calls himself a "witness," he is referring to the two witnesses in the book of Revelations (11:3–12) who defended Christ for 1,260 days, and were then executed by "the beast." His use of the term "witness" is synonymous with "martyr."[29] Williams believed that being forced into exile allowed him to challenge what he saw as spiritual errors in the New England churches.[30] There are also powerful hints of ideas he will develop later in published tracts. Most importantly, he referred to the ancient Apostolic church as the only pure church; because the Papacy destroyed that ancient church, only Christ's return can begin the regathering of true churches. He also gently, but clearly, reminded

27. *Correspondence of Roger Williams*, 1:65–72.

28. See LaFantasie, "Reply to John Winthrop," in *Correspondence of Roger Williams*, 1:57–65.

29. Lemons, "Roger Williams Not a Seeker," 711; Williams often referred to himself as a "witness," as he did in other letters later in this chapter.

30. Gilpin, *Millenarian Piety of Roger Williams*, 80–95.

*Winthrop of his personal role in banishing Williams by retelling the mytho-
logical story about Hercules and the tunic of Nessus. Williams concluded the
letter with news about the death of a shady English trader named John Stone
near the Connecticut River and fears of a Mohawk attack (one of the early
incidents that helped spark the Pequot War in 1637–1638).*

Sir, Providence, the 24th of the 8th.[31]

Worthy and wellbeloved.

I was abroad about the Pequt[32] business when your letter arrived and
since [since then] Messengers have not fitted etc.

I therefore now thanckfully acknowledge your wisedome and Gen-
tlenes in receaving so lovingly my late rude and foolish Lines. You beare
with Fooles gladly because you are wise . . .

Your 6 Quaeries I welcome my love forbidding me to surmise that a
Pharisee a Sadduce a Herodian etc. wrote them: but rather that your Love
and pitie framed them as a phycitian to the Sick etc . . .

Your first Quaerie then is this:

What have you gained by your newfound practices etc.?

I confess my Gaines cast up in mans Exchange are Losse of Friends,
Esteeme, maintenance, etc. but what was Gaine in that respect I desire to
count losse for the excellancie of the Knowledge of Christ Jesus my Lord etc.

To all his glorious name I know I have gained the honour of one of his
poore witnesses, though in Sackcloth[33]

To your beloved selves and others of Gods people yet asleepe this witness in the Lords season at your waking shall be prosperous, and the seed
sowne shall arise to the greater puritie of the Kingdome and Ordinances of
the Prince of the Kings of the Earth.

To my selfe (through his rich grace) my Tribulacion hath brought some
Consolacion, and more Evidence of his Love Singing Moses his Song and

31. The date of this letter is unclear, but LaFantasie suggests that the contents indicate it was written about a year after Williams was exiled from Massachusetts Bay, so he
has dated it as "1636?" See *Correspondence of Roger Williams*: 1:60–62.

32. Williams had been meeting with the Pequot in the fall of 1636 to try to discourage them from joining with the Narragansett against the English settlers. There are
other letters where Williams describes his efforts including Williams to General Court
of Massachusetts Bay, before October 14, 1651 and Williams to Mason and Prence,
June 22, 1670. We have included the October 14, 1651 letter in this chapter. As we have
mentioned before, Williams often described his diplomatic work to Winthrop to reaf-
firm his commitment to their shared colonizing objectives and to highlight his work
with Indigenous neighbors.

33. "Sackcloth" is a coarsely woven, scratchy fabric worn in mourning; God's witnesses wear sackcloth in Rev 11:13. Lemons, "Roger Williams not a Seeker," 711.

the Lambs in the weake victorie wch through his Helpe I have gotten over the Beast his Picture, his Marke, and Number of his Name. Revel. 15.2.3 . . .

To your 2nd: viz: Is your Spirit as even as it was 7 yeares since?

I will not follow the Fashion either in Commending or Condemining of my selfe. You and I stand at one dreadfull Dreadfull Tribunall. Yet what is past I desire to Forget and to press forward, towards the marke, for the price of High Calling of God in Christ.

And for the Evennes of my spirit

Toward the Lord I hope I more long to know and doe his holy pleasure only: and to be ready not only to be Banished, but to Die in New England for the name of the Lord Jesus.[34]

Towards your Selves I have hitherto begd of the Lord an Even Spirit, and I hope ever shall as

First Reverently to esteeme of and tenderly to respect the persons of many hundreths of you etc.

2ndly To rejoice to spend and be Spent in any service (according to my Conscience) for Your Wellfares.

3rdly To rejoice to find out the least Swarving in Judgment or practice from the helpe of any even the least of you.

Lastly to mourne dayly, heavily uncessantly til the Lord looke downe from Heaven, till the Lord look downe from Heaven and bring to all his precious living stones in to one New Jerusalem.

To your third viz: Are you not grieved that you have grieved so many?

I say with Paul I vehemently Sorrow, for the Sorrow of any of Zions Daughters . . . Yet I must (and O that I had not cause) grieve because so many of Zions daughters see not and grieve not for their Soules Defilements, and that so few beare John Companie in weeping after the unfoulding of the seales wch only weepers are acquainted with.

You thereupon propound a 4th. Doe you thinck the Lord hath utterly forsaken us?

I answere Jehovah will not forsake his people for his great names Sake I Sam. 12. The fire of his love towards those whome once he loves is aeternall like himself: and thus farr be it from me to question his aeternall Love towards You etc. Yet if you graunt that ever you were as Abraham among the Chaldees, Lot among the Sodomites, the Kenites among the Amalekites as Israell in Egipt or Babell, and that under paine of their plagues and Judgments you were bound to leave them, to flie out, (not from the places as in

---

34. James Byrd argues that this letter shows that Williams "had found a biblical means of interpreting his banishment in the New Testament record of the life and words of Paul. Indeed, in his letter to Winthrop and the Bay Colony, Williams presented himself as a seventeenth-century Paul." Byrd, *Challenges of Roger Williams*, 129.

the Type) but from the Filthines of their Sinns etc. and if it prove as I know it assuredly shall, that though you have come farr, yet you never came out of the wilderness to this Day[35] . . . And this Sir I beseech you doe more Seriously then ever and abstract your selfe with a holy violence from the Dungheape of this Earth, the Credit and Comfort of it, and cry to Heaven, to remoove the Stumbling blocks, such as Idolls after wch Sometimes the Lord will give his owne Israell an Answere.

Sir You request me to be free with you, and therefore blame me not if I answere your Request, desiring the like Payment from your owne deare hand at any time in any thing.

And let me add, that amongst all the people of God wheresoever scattered about Babells Bancks either in Rome or England etc. your case is the worst by farr: because while others of Gods Israell tenderly respect such as desire to feare the Lord your very Judgment and Conscience leads you to Smite and beate your fellow Servants, expel them [from] your Coasts etc. and therefore, though I know the Elect shall never finally be forsaken yet Sodomes Egypts Amaleks Babells Judgments ought to drive us out to make our Calling out of this world to Christ, and our Election sure in him.

Sir, your 5t[h] is From what Spirit and to what End doe you drive?

Concerning my Spirit as I said before I could declaime agst it, but whether the Spirit of Christ Jesus, for whose visible Kingdome and Ordinances I witness etc. or the spirit of Antichrist (I John 4) agst. whome only I contest doe drive me, let the Father of Spirits be pleased to Search and (worthy Sir) be you also pleased by the word to Search: and I hope you will find that as you Say you doe, I also Seeke Jesus who was nayled to the Gallowes. I aske the way to lost Zion, I witness what I believe I See patiently (the Lord assisting) in Sackcloth, I long for the bright Appearance of the Lord Jesus to consume the Man of Sinn. I long for the appearance of the Lambes wife also New Jerusalem. I wish heartily prosperitie to you all Govr and people in your Civill way, and mourne that you see not your povertie, Nakednes etc. in Spiritualls, and yet I rejoice in the hopes that as the way of the Lord to Apollo so within a few yeares, (through I feare many tribulacions) the way of the Lord Jesus the first and most ancient path shall be more plainely discovered to you and me.

35. Williams uses the example of the captivity of the Israelites to criticize the churches of Massachusetts Bay; while the settlers may have left England and even established their own churches, they are still too connected to the Church of England, according to Williams. So, while they may believe themselves to be in the "wilderness," they have not come nearly far enough. Williams refers to the wilderness purposefully to refer again to his banishment.

Lastly You aske whether my former condition would not have stood with a gracious Heart etc.?

At this Quaerie sir I wonder much because you know what Sinnes yea all manner of Sinnes (the sinn unto Death excepted) a Child of God may lye in. Instance I neede not . . . Doe you not judge that your owne Heart was gracious even when (with the poysened shirt[36] on your back) you Etc.?

. . . Now worthy Sir I must call up your wisedome, your love your Patience your Promise and Faythfullness, Candid Ingenuitie etc. My hearts desire is abundant, and exceedes my pen . . .

Where I err Christ be pleased to restore me . . . If you please I have also a few Quaeries to your self. Without your leave I will not: but will ever mourne (the Lord assisting) that I am no more (though I hope ever) Yours.

R. Will

Sir Concerning Natives: the Pequts and Nayantaquits[37] resolve to live and die togeather and not yeald up one.[38] Last night Tiding came that the Mauquauags[39] (the Caniballs)[40] have slaine some of our Countrimen at Qunnihticut.[41] I hope it is not true.

36. Williams refers here to the Greek myth of the tunic of Nessus, the Centaur. Hercules put on a shirt, given him by his wife, that became poisoned because it was dipped in the blood of the Centaur. Sickened while wearing this poisoned shirt, Hercules threw Lichas into the sea.

37. Niantic.

38. This is probably referring to two Pequot accused of killing Stone; neither the Pequot nor the Niantic accepted blame for his death.

39. Mohawk.

40. Williams, like many English colonists, indulged in wild rumors about Mohawk ferocity, including cannibalism. Many recent scholars suggest that colonizers used the trope of cannibalism to further justify violence against Indigenous people. *Correspondence of Roger Williams*, 1:71.

41. Connecticut.

Letter to Governor John Winthrop, May 2, 1639.
Courtesy of Rhode Island Historical Society.

Roger Williams to the General Court of Massachusetts Bay, before October 14, 1651[42]

Williams wrote about his banishment throughout his life, and this letter reflects the emotional and practical problems his exile caused. In this letter, he is simply asking the General Court of Massachusetts Bay for permission to sail out of Boston. In 1643, when Williams sailed to England, he had to sail out of Dutch-controlled New Amsterdam (now New York City), because when he was banished, he was prohibited not just from living in Massachusetts Bay, but he was not allowed to set foot in the colony for any reason. (In 1644, when he returned from his first trip to London, he had a letter of safe passage from Parliament asking the Massachusetts government to allow him to land and travel safely out of the colony.) Before requesting permission to reenter Massachusetts Bay just long enough to catch his boat bound for England, Williams reminds the Court of all the ways he had been a helpful ally—especially during the Pequot War—despite their decision to banish him. In the process, as Narragansett and Niantic tribal educator Chrystal Mars Baker has noted, Williams reveals his true agenda here: not a "friend" of Indigenous people, but simply an extension of the larger colonialism of which all English people were a part. Williams boasts that he has been "instrumental to the peace and the spreading of the English plantings in this Countrey." This included the campaign against the Pequot, which led to a genocidal war and English settlement on unceded lands. In the end, Mars Baker suggests, Williams acted "selfishly and untruthfully . . . his allegiance was to his own people."[43]

To help make his case for departing from Boston, Williams mentions the name of the relatively recently deceased former governor, John Winthrop. He also informs them that this trip to England was sponsored by the colony of Rhode Island and the towns of Providence and Warwick; he had been dispatched on official business as an agent of the colony. There was an immediate need for Williams to plead his case before Parliament: In April 1651, William Coddington returned to Rhode Island with a commission as governor of Aquidneck Island (also called Rhode Island, where the towns of Newport and Portsmouth were located), which granted him full control for life, including military power, over the island. The residents of Providence, Newport, and Warwick were distraught over Coddington's takeover, and Williams feared that this commission might invalidate the patent he received in 1644. The chaos created by Coddington's control over Aquidneck was the main cause of Williams's trip to London. As Williams did in many of his writings, in this letter

---

42. *Correspondence of Roger Williams*, 1:353–55.
43. Chrystal Mars Baker, correspondence with the authors, January 24, 2023.

he anticipates the negative reactions his request may elicit, and he provides
answers for each possible problem that this may cause. The General Court
consented, allowing Williams to enter Massachusetts Bay before he sailed from
Boston in November 1652.

[Providence]

To the honoured Generall Court of the Massachuset Colonie now assembled at Boston.

The humble peticion of Roger Williams.

Although it be true that it pleased this honoured Govrment now many
Yeares since to pass a Sentence of Banishmt upon me, wch sentence and
the Consequences (bitter Aflictions and miseries, Losses Sorrowes and
Hardships,) I have humbly desired (through the helpe of the most High) to
endure with a quiet and patient mind:

Yet, may it please You favorable to remember that at my last Arrivall
from my Native Countrey I presented this honoured Govrmt with Letters[44]
from many of your noble and honble [honorable] Friends then of the Parliamt of England, lamenting Differences, and perswading Moderation, if not
Reconcilemt and pacification.

Please You to remember that ever since the time of my Exile I have
bene (through Gods helpe) a professed and knowne Servant to this Colonie
and all the Colonies of the English in peace and War so that scarce a weeke
hath passed but some way or other I have bene used as instrumental to the
peace and spreading of the English plantings in this Countrey.[45]

In the Pequt Troubles, receaving Letters from this Govermt I hazarded
my Life into extreame danger, by labouring to prevent the League betweene
the Pequts and the Narigansets, and to worck a League betweene the English
and the Narigansetts, wch worck as an Agent from this Colonie, and all the
English in the Land I (through helpe from God) effected. The fruit thereof
(as our much honoured Mr Winthrop deceased wrote to me) hath bene
peace to the English ever since.

At present let me not offend you in saying that I pass not only as a
private passenger, but as a Messenger and Agent to the high Court of the
parliamt of England, in the name of my neighbours the English, occasioned
by the late Graunt obtained by Mr Codington for Roade Iland.

44. LaFantasie suggests that Williams is exaggerating here, as he could only find
one letter that Williams delivered to the General Court from friends in Parliament.
Correspondence of Roger Williams, 1:354.

45. This is a telling window into some of Williams' activity and mentality—as a
facilitator of English colonialism, despite what many Narragansett and Wampanoag
people today see as his pretentions towards friendship with Natives.

In all wch respects I humbly pray, that (notwithstanding the former sentence) I may find that Civilitie and Courtesie from the English of the Massachusets Colonie, that I (inoffencively behaving my selfe,) may inoffencively and without molestacion pass through Your Jurisdiction as a stranger for a night to the ship and [so] (if God so please) may land againe, from the land of our Nativitie.

But some may say You are an opposite to the Way of our Worship, and beside You goe as an Adversaries with Complaint agst us for the Towne of Warwick.[46]

To the first I humbly pray it may be remembred that not only I but the many millions of millions of our Father Adams children (wch are as the Sand upon the Seashoare) are not of your perswasion.[47] Yea and many thoughsands of that poore Remnant of Gods children abroad, are at lamentable difference with you and Themselves as to the Worship of God in Christ Jesus. I add who knowes but upon humble and Christian debatemts and Agitations not only I but Your honoured Selves, may yet see cause to put our mouths in the dust togeather, as touching the present Controversies about the Christian [Worship].

To the second, I humbly and truely answere that if it please this honoured Court to depute 2 or 3 of your selves to receave and debate mine Answer to this objection I hope (through Gods assistance) to make it apparant that I goe not as [an] Enemie to the Massachusets but as a professed Instrumt of a peaceable and honble end of that sad Controvseries and as an humble Servant rather then an Enemie to this honoured Goverment of the Massachusetts.

I am unworthy Yet desire to be your humble Servant.

Roger Williams

Roger Williams to John Cotton Jr., March 25, 1671[48]

John Cotton's son, John Cotton Jr., wrote Williams a letter that tried to reignite his father's epistolary and pamphlet debate with Williams over religious

46. In the early 1640s, a debate erupted over the purchase of the land that became Warwick. The Massachusetts Bay Colony tried to use this purchase to extend their influence into Rhode Island, which partially motivated Williams's trip to London. See chapter 4 for more on Samuel Gorton, William Arnold, and the Shawomet purchase.

47. Here, Williams reminds Winthrop that most people on the earth—all of whom he describes as God's children—are not Nonconformist puritans living in Massachusetts Bay. And that even some of those Massachusetts Bay puritans do not agree with Winthrop's policies.

48. Roger Williams to John Cotton Jr., March 25, 1671 in *Correspondence of John*

toleration, something that had ended more than twenty years earlier when the elder Cotton died in 1652. Historians are unsure what prompted the younger Cotton to initiate this exchange and Cotton's letter to Williams is now lost. It may be that new troubles with Baptists in Cotton's own part of Plimouth Colony led him to attack Williams anew, since Williams, while not officially a Baptist, staunchly defended adult, or believer's, baptism.[49] *Williams's reply offers an opportunity to see how an older Williams remembered his banishment and his debate with Cotton decades later. His tone is still fierce—he reminds the younger Cotton that his father "was not God, but man"—and he questions the son's motives. Some of Williams's assertions in this letter are problematic, especially the idea that Oliver Cromwell's religious advisor, Reverend John Owen, supported Williams, and that King Charles I agreed with the arguments Williams made in* The Bloudy Tenent of Persecution. *As Glenn LaFantasie suggests, there is no evidence that King Charles I even read it, although he did favor religious toleration more generally.*[50] *Williams mentions other names, including his successor at Salem, Hugh Peter, who returned to England in 1641 and supported the beheading of Charles I, for which he was executed himself during the Restoration. Most of Williams's arguments had not changed in the intervening years, and he offers to debate the leaders of Plimouth, Connecticut, and Massachusetts Bay colonies over compulsory religious adherence, among other things. In his letter, Cotton must have suggested that Williams was excommunicated, something Williams denies, writing instead that he left the church of his own choice and later ceased his ministry so that he could "keepe my soule undefiled." Cotton was bold to bring up excommunication, especially since Cotton himself was briefly excommunicated from his father's own church as a young man following an adultery scandal in 1662.*

Providence 25 March 1671 (so calld)

SR,

Lo: respects premised. About 3 Weeks since I recd Yors dated in 10br [December]:& wonder not yt Præjudice, Interest & passion have lift up Your Feete thus to trample on me as on . . . Some Common Thiefe or Swearer, Drunckard or Adulterer, imputing to me ye Odious Crimes of Blaspheamies, Reproaches, Slanders Idolatries . . . And all this with out any Scripture, Reason or Argumnt wch might inlighten my Conscience, as to any Error, or offense to God or Yor deare Father . . .

Cotton Junior, 73–77; LaFantasie provides additional context for this letter in *Correspondence of Roger Williams*, 2:627–33.

49. For Williams's attitudes toward baptism, see: Fisher et al., *Decoding Roger Williams*, 18–32.

50. Haefeli, *Accidental Pluralism*, 1–16, 201–20.

My great offense (you So often repeate) is My Wrong to Yor dear Father Yor glorified Father &c But ye truth is, ye Love & Honor wch I have alwayes shewed (in Speech & writing) to yt Excellently learned & holy Man Yor Father, have bene so great yt I have bene censured by divers for it. God knowes yt for Gods Sake I tenderly loved & honoured his pson (as I did the psons of ye Magistrates, Ministers & Members whome I knew in old England, & knew their holy Affections & upright Aimes & great Selfe deniall to enjoy more of God in this wildernes) . . .

Tis true, my first booke ye bloudy Tenent was burnt by ye Presbiterian Partie[51] (then prevailing): But this booke, whereof We now speake (being my Reply to Yor Fathers Answere,) was recd with Applause & Thancks by ye Armie by ye Parlmt, professing yt of Necescity, Yea of Christian Equity, there Could be no Reconciliation, Pacification or Living togeather but by pmitting of Dissenting Consciences to live amongst them: In So much yt yt excellent Servant of God mr John Owen (Calld Dr. Owen) told me before ye Generall, (who Sent for me about yt very busines) yt before I Landed, Himselfe & many others had answered mr Cottons booke allready.[52]

The first booke, & ye Point of Permitting Dissenters his Maties Royall Father assented too,[53] & how often hath ye Son our Soveraigne[54] declared himselfe indulgent toward Dissenters notwithstanding ye Clamors & Plottings of his Selfe Seeking [Bishops]? . . .

Sr I Pray forget not yt Yor Father was not God but man Sinfull & failing in many things as we all doe saith ye Holy Scripture . . .

Sr You Call my 3 Proposalls &c abominable, false & wicked . . You are pleased to Count me Excommunicate . . . But Sr, ye truth is (I will not say I excommunicated you but) I first withdrew Communion from Yor Selves for halting betweene Christ & Antichrist, ye Parish Churches & Christian

51. During the English Civil War, Parliament was divided between Presbyterians (who largely favored ending the war quickly, even if it meant working with Charles I, and maintaining some central control over church congregations) and the Independents (who were willing to continue the war against a totally deposed Charles I and were pushing for more autonomy for Nonconformist churches). When Williams published *The Bloudy Tenent*, the Presbyterians dominated Parliament and ordered it burned.

52. Williams's memory does not fit with what John Owen did. A Presbyterian earlier in life, Owen had become a "staunch Independent" after reading John Cotton's *The Keyes of the Kingdom* (1644), not Williams's *Bloody Tenent Yet More Bloody* (1652). As LaFantasie explains, Owen completed a book Cotton left unfinished when he died and is "unlikely" to have disagreed with Cotton's reply to Williams. *Correspondence of Roger Williams*, 2:631.

53. Williams suggests here that King Charles I read and agreed with *The Bloudy Tenent*, which seems highly unlikely. *Correspondence of Roger Williams*, 2:632.

54. King Charles II.

Congregations: Long after when you had Consultations of killing me, but
Some rather advised a Drie Pyt of Banishmnt: mr Peters advised an Excommunication to be Sent me (after ye manner of Popish Bulls &c) But the same
man in London embraced me, & told me he was for Liberty of Conscience[55]
& preacht it & Complaind to me of Salem for excommunicating his distracted wife & for wronging him in his Goods wch he left behind him.

Sr, You tell me my Time is Lost &c because (as I conceave you) not in
ye function of Ministrie . . . God knowes I have much & long & Conscientiously & mournfully waighed & digd into ye Differences of ye Protestants
themselvs about ye Ministry: He knows what Gains & Præfermnts I have
refused in Universitie, City Countrey & Court in Old Eng, & Something
in N. E. &c to keepe my Soule undefiled in this Point, & not to act with a
douting Conscience &c

God was pleased to shew me much of this in Old Engl:[56] And in New
being unanimously chosen Teacher at Boston (before Yor deare Father
came divers yeares) I conscientiously refused & withdrew to plymmouth,
because I durst not officiate to an unseperated people, as upon Examination
& Conference, I found them to be: At plymmouth I spake on ye Lords days
& weeke days, & wrought hard at ye [Hoe] for My Bread (& so afterward at
Salem) untill I found them both Professing to be a Seperated people in N.
E. . . . & yet out Communicating with ye Parishes in Old, by their members
repairing on frequent occasions thether . . .

Sr I am unworthy (though desirous to be)

Your Friend & Servant

Roger Williams

55. Hugh Peter (1598–1660) was the pastor of the Salem church after Williams left.
In fall 1638, Peter excommunicated ten church members, including Roger and Mary
Williams, because they had been re-baptized in Providence. Peter issued a letter to the
other churches in the colony informing them of this, which is the letter Williams is
referring to here. In two letters to John Winthrop Jr., Williams described Peter's friendly
reception in England: Williams to John Winthrop Jr., April 20, 1652 and July 12, 1654;
Lemons, "Roger Williams not a Seeker," 698.

56. Williams offers this comment forty years after leaving England. He certainly
arrived in Boston in 1631 with clear ideas on the need for liberty of conscience. But
his banishment by a civil government for what he believed were religious beliefs and
the four decades following his arrival—much of it spent in Indian country—surely
strengthened, clarified, and deepened those ideas. Narragansett scholar Mack Scott
suggests that Williams came to many of his more enlightened views because of his time
with Natives. Mack Scott, correspondence with the authors, January 22, 2023.

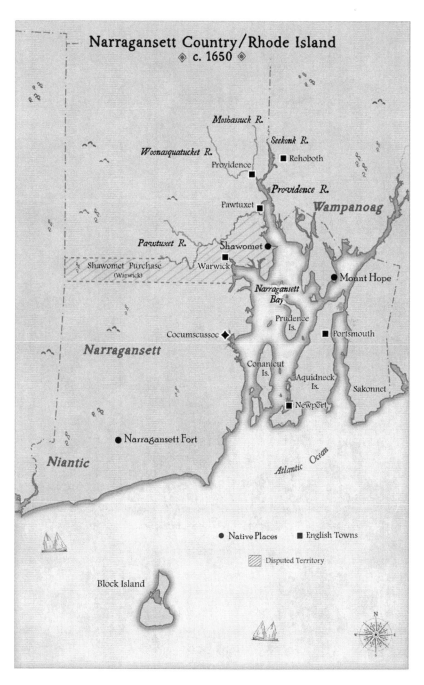

Narragansett Country/Rhode Island
◈ c. 1650 ◈

Moshassuck R.

Seekonk R.

Woonasquatucket R.

■ Rehoboth

Providence ■

Providence R.

Pawtuxet ■

Wampanoag

Pawtuxet R.

Shawomet ●

Shawomet Purchase
(Warwick)

Warwick ■

● Mount Hope

Narragansett Bay

Prudence Is.

Cocumscussoc ◆

● Portsmouth ■

Conanicut Is.

Narragansett

Aquidneck Is.

Sakonnet

■ Newport

● Narragansett Fort

Niantic

Atlantic Ocean

● Native Places   ■ English Towns

▨ Disputed Territory

Block Island

N

Narragansett Country / Rhode Island c. 1650.
Map by Lynn Carlson, Compass Cartographic, ©2023.

Chapter 4

Establishing Providence, 1635–1682

FORCED INTO A WINTER *exile from Massachusetts Bay, Williams found safety with the Wampanoag sachem Ousamequin, who first allowed him to settle along the east side of the Seekonk River, near present-day Rumford, Rhode Island. Documents in chapter 3 suggest that Williams, along with about twenty supporters, had decided on Narragansett Bay as the site of a new settlement well before Williams left Massachusetts in January 1636. According to historian Julie Fisher, Williams "did not relocate to Narragansett Bay in spite of the presence of Narragansett, Niantic, Wampanoag, Pequot, and Mohegan communities but because of its proximity to them," largely because of beneficial trade opportunities with both the Wampanoag and Narragansett.[1] Within a few months, Plimouth authorities informed Williams and his group that he was still in territory they claimed, forcing them to abandon their newly planted gardens and move a few miles west, into Narragansett territory, at the confluence of the Moshashuck and Woonasquatucket Rivers, at the head of the Narragansett Bay. Narragansett sachems Canonicus and Miantonomo allowed Williams to settle on their land most likely because they saw him as a potential trading partner. In doing so, the Narragansett sachems were extending to Williams the hospitality that they had offered to other colonists and Native clans and tributaries,[2] as Narragansett scholar Mack Scott has noted.[3] Although it is possible that the Narragansett saw Williams as a buffer between themselves and the Wampanoag, Williams had fully entered*

---

1. Fisher, "Roger Williams and the Indian Business," 364.

2. Among Indigenous nations, a tributary was a subordinate entity from whom an annual payment or gift is owed for protection.

3. Mack Scott, correspondence with the authors, January 22, 2023.

Native territory and space, was there as a guest, and was expected to abide by Narragansett codes of hospitality and reciprocity.[4] *Williams later called the sachems' conveyance of land a "sale" but it was far more involved than a single financial transaction. Rather, the transfer was based on reciprocal and mutual responsibilities. As he explained to John Winthrop, "What was paid was only a gratuity, though I choose, for better assurance and form, to call it a sale."*[5]

What modern readers know as "Rhode Island" began as a collection of three (and eventually four) towns—Newport, Providence, Portsmouth, and, later, Warwick. These towns often guarded their independence and sought outside allies, including Massachusetts Bay, Plimouth, the monarch, and Parliament, during disputes with other Rhode Island proprietors. Williams is often remembered as the person who "founded" the colony, but other English colonizers—including William Aspinwall, William and Anne Hutchinson, William Coddington, John Clarke, and Samuel Gorton, some of whom were banished from other colonies as well—settled parts of what would later become the Colony of Rhode Island and Providence Plantations.[6] *The Narragansett sachems extended hospitality to most of these other groups as well.*

The early years in the Narragansett Bay settlements were marked by conflict and turmoil. In part, this was because Rhode Island quickly became known as a place of refuge for other political and theological outcasts, many of whom brought with them strong and opposing opinions that had to be managed in some way. Myriad political and religious controversies erupted, including unauthorized land purchases, political disagreements, disunity, and—perhaps most alarmingly to Rhode Island residents—the efforts of the Massachusetts Bay colony to claim jurisdiction over the large tract of land called Warwick in the 1640s and 1650s. While the Charter of 1663 meant that they all lived together under a single government—whether they wanted to or not— rancor and fighting continued.[7]

For more than a decade, Williams spent much of each year at his Cocum-scussoc trading post away from his family until he sold the post to Richard Smith in 1651. This active trade with regional Natives was Williams's main source of income. Despite this successful trading post, he complained bitterly about financial hardship. Documents in this chapter illustrate that he had to convince Rhode Island's residents that while there was certainly no mandatory enforced religious practice, they still had to pay taxes to support the colony's

4. Fisher, "Roger Williams and the Indian Business," 366.

5. Roger Williams to John Winthrop, June 14, 1638, *Correspondence of Roger Williams*, 1:165.

6. James, *Colonial Rhode Island*, 13–32.

7. James, *Colonial Rhode Island*, 13–32, 48–94.

administration and he expected to be reimbursed when he traveled to England to seek Parliamentary support and royal patents. Whether Williams was really suffering financially or whether he was just simply aware of how much money he was losing by not selling alcohol to his Indigenous neighbors is debatable, of course.[8] *Williams moved in and out of city and colony leadership, serving as Rhode Island's governor, chief officer, or president for more than fifteen years. The letters and documents that follow give a sense of Williams's attempts to establish and sustain not only Providence amidst the chaos and "ugly incidents," but the entire colony of Rhode Island and Providence Plantations over the course of his lifetime.*[9]

Roger Williams to John Winthrop, before August 25, 1636[10]

The letter below illustrates some of the pragmatic challenges Williams faced as the head of a new colony, as well as his willingness to reach out to Winthrop for guidance, despite his banishment. Williams did not have an official patent or charter from the Crown, so the heads of household in the new settlement met informally (but regularly) to craft their own civil authority—a process he described for Winthrop. The arrival of single men quickly challenged this arrangement of authority vested in heads of households. Williams wondered what right he personally had to control who moved into the new settlement, given that he received the original land, and offered some of his own money to the sachems. Given the communal nature of their civil authority, Williams wondered whether the original settlers must all agree before a new person moves into New Providence. It is striking that Williams is asking Winthrop for advice about how to establish a civil government. Does this signal that Williams is aware of the challenges that lie ahead for him or even that he is floundering a little? Writing from deep in Indian country—the "dens of Lyons" Williams refers to below—Williams concludes the letter by mentioning

8. Chapter 6 includes a 1669 letter from Williams to John Winthrop Jr. where he discusses the alcohol trade.

9. Sydney James wrote that "the role and conduct of the colony's government had to be thrashed out in a series of ugly incidents." *Colonial Rhode Island*, 56; Williams's letters from early March 1641 to late June 1645 are all lost. Those years cover his first trip to London, the publication of several of his most important books, the securing of the colonial charter for Providence Plantations, and the first year after his return from London. The archival silence in this tumultuous period means that we have little certainty about what Williams was doing, where he was traveling, or what his thoughts were on the swirl of activity around him. LaFantasie, "Lost Correspondence and Incomplete Records, 1641–1645," *Correspondence of Roger Williams*, 1:217.

10. *Correspondence of Roger Williams*, 1:53–57.

his fears of war with the large Pequot nation to the west, which only height-
ened his sense of insecurity.

Much honoured Sir

The frequent experience of your loving eare ready and open toward
me (in what your Conscience hath permitted) as allso of that excellent spirit
of wisdome and prudence wherewith the Father of Lights hath endued you,
embolden me to request a word of private advise with the soonest Convenience if it may be, by this messenger.

The Condicion of my selfe and those few families here planting with
me; you know full well. We have no pattent: nor doth the face of Magistracie
suite with our present Condicion. Hietherto, the masters of Families have
ordinarily mett once a fort night and consulted about our common peace,
watch, and planting: and mutuall consent hath finished all matters with
speede and peace.

Now of late some Young men single persons (of whome we had much
neede) being admitted to freedome of Inhabitation, and promising to subject
to the Orders made by the Consent of the Howse holders, are discontented
with their estate, and seeke the Freedome of Vote allso, and aequalitie etc.

Beside, our dangers (in the midst of these dens of Lyons) now especially, call upon us to be Compact in a Civill way and power.

I have therefore had thoughts of propounding to my neighbours a
double subscription, Concerning wch I shall humbly crave your helpe.

The first Concerning our selves the masters of families: thus

We whose names are here under written, late Inhabitants of the Massachusetts (upon occasion of some difference of conscience) being permitted
to depart from the Limits of that pattent, under the wch we came over into
these parts, and being cast by the providence of the God of Heaven, remote
from others of our Countriemen amongst the Barbarous in this towne of
New Providence, doe with free and joynt consent promise each unto other,
that, for our common peace and Wellfare (untill we heare further of the
Kings royall pleasure concerning our selves) we will from time to time
subject our selves in Active or passive obedience to such orders and Agreements, as shall be made by the greater number of the present Howseholders, and such as shall be hereafter admitted by their consent into the same
priviledge and Covenant in our ordinarie meeting. In witnes whereof we
hereunto subscribe etc.

Concerning those few young men, and any who shall hereafter (by
your favourable Connivence [i.e., permission]) desire to plant with us: this

We whose names are here under written being desirous to inhabite in
this Towne of New Providence, doe promise to subject our selves in active

or passive Obedience to such Orders and Agreements as shall be made from time to time, by the greater number of the present Howseholders of this Towne, and such whome they shall admit into the same fellowship and priviledge. In witnes where of etc.

Hietherto we chose one (named the officer) to call the meeting at the appointed Time. Now it is desired by some of us that the Howseholders by course performe that worcke, as allso gather Votes and see the Watch goe on etc.

I have not mencioned these things to my neigbours but shall as I see cause upon your lo. [loving] Councell.[11]

As allso, since the place I have purchased 2ly at mine owne charge and engagements the inhabitants paying, (by consent) 30s a piece as they come untill my charge be out for their particular lots[12]: and 3rdly, that I never made any other Covenant with any person, but that if I got a place, he should plant there with me. my quaerie [query] is this

Whither I may not lawfully desire this of my neighbours, that as I freely subject my selfe to Common Consent and shall not bring in any person to the Towne without their consent: so allso that agst my consent no person be Violently [i.e., improperly] brought in and receaved.

I desire not to sleep in securitie and dreame of a Nest wch no hand can reach. I can not but expect changes, and the change of the last Enemie Death, yet dare I not despise a Libertie, wch the Lord seemeth to offer me if for mine owne or others peace: and therefore have I bene thus bold to present my thoughts unto you.

The Pequts heare of your preparations etc. and Comfort them selves in this that a witch[13] amongst them will sinck the pinnaces[14] by diving under water and making holes etc. as allso that they shall now enrich themselves with store of guns but I hope their dreames through the mercie of [the] Lord shall Vanish, and the Devill and his Lying Sorcerers shall be Confounded.

---

11. This implies that Williams wanted Winthrop to see—and maybe even approve—this draft before sharing it with the other English residents of Providence.

12. Williams suggests here that he wants to recoup his initial expenses on the Providence land; it also raises the question of whether he profited from land sales as they increased over time.

13. This is not a word Indigenous people would use to refer to their shaman, paw-waw, or other spiritual guides. As Kathleen Bragdon notes in the most recent edition of the *Key*, "the purpose and religiosity of these practices was frequently misunderstood." Williams, *Key Into the Language of America: The Tomaquag Museum Edition* (2019), 111–12; 111n7.

14. Pinnances were small boats that were carried on larger ships; they were used to bring people and goods to shore from the ship that remained anchored in deeper water.

You may please, sir to take notice that it is of maine Consequence to take some course with the Wunnashowatuckoogs and Wusquowhananawkits,[15] who are the further most Neepnet men for the Pequts driven from the sea coast with Ease, yet there secure and strengthen themselves and are then brought downe so much the neerer to you. Thus with my best respects to your [loving] selfe and Mrs Winthrop I rest your worps [worship's] un-feigned, praying to meete you in this Vale of Teares of hills of mercie above.

R. Williams

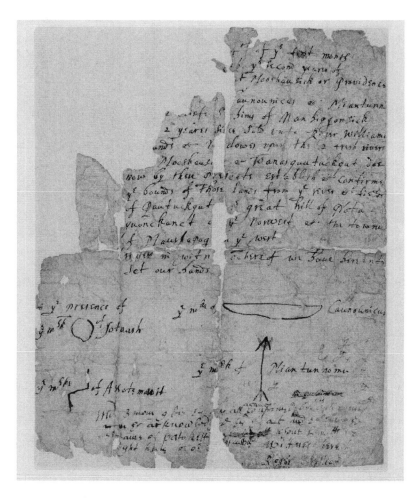

1638 Deed to Providence Land. Vault Collection, Providence City Archives, Providence, Rhode Island.

15. The Wunnashowatuckoog and Wusquowhananawkit were part of the Nipmuc.

Deed from Canonicus and Miantonomo to Roger Williams, March 24, 1637/1638[16]

The document below is the oldest surviving copy of the original deed of the city of Providence, which was the first parcel of land of what became the colony of Rhode Island. It is an incredibly complicated document; even the use of the word "deed" is fraught. Narragansett sachems gifted the land in 1636, but there was no written record of it until 1638, which is the date on this document (as a confirmation of the earlier transaction). But this 1638 document was only entered into the official town records in 1658, after what seems to have been some changes to the original (by William Arnold and William Harris, proprietors of Pawtuxet, who wished to expand their land holdings). Rhode Island officials soon realized that someone had altered the deed, and so re-entered it again into the town records in 1662, with the added sections omitted (which is noted below in a footnote). Accusations of general forgery plagued the document back then and have continued to vex historians in the centuries since that time.

The rather uncertain and dubious history of this document points to the complicated nature of land sales and purchases in the seventeenth century, and why Indigenous people have generally mistrusted land sales and deeds over time. Additionally, scholars continue to debate the meaning of land deeds from Native leaders in general, and of this document in particular. Was it a sale? Was it a gift? What meanings did Narragansett and English signatories read into this document? Narragansett sachems likely saw this as primarily a gift to someone they viewed as a tributary or subordinate group of sorts—someone entering their jurisdiction. Such a gift/deed was never final in the sense of a European sale, and it also came with reciprocal obligations from both parties, which Williams likely did not fully understand. Still, Williams continually pointed to this deed (or a version of it) to claim the right to sell parcels of land to other Providence residents over time. Even so, internal land disputes erupted periodically, from inconsistent deed registration for plots of land and fights over unpenned livestock destroying crops leading in 1640 to Providence residents arming themselves with clubs and going after each other on the streets—"Brawling Continually in mr williams medow," as one observer noted.[17]

[At Nanhiggansick, the 24] of ye first month
[commonly called March in] the second yeare of

---

16. The existing document of this deed is mutilated. Fortunately, the Rhode Island State Archives possesses a transcription that was made when the document was still whole. Kenneth Carlson graciously provided us with this complete transcription. Bracketed items indicate parts that are now illegible.

17. LaFantasie, "Editorial Note," 1:210–11.

[our plantation or planting at] Mooshausick or Providence
[Memorandum, that we C]announicus & Miantunno-
[the two chief s[ac]hims of Nanhiggonsick
[having] 2 yeares since sold unto Roger Williams
[the l]ands & [Mea]dows upon the 2 fresh rivers
Moshaus[ick] & Wanasquatuckqut doe
now by then presents establish & confirme
the bounds of those lands from ye river & fields
of Pautuckqut the great hill of Nota—
quonckanet [on] the norwest & the towne
of Maushapog[ue on] ye west
[As also, in consideration of the many kindnesses &
services he hath continually done for us, both with our
friends at Massachusetts, as also at Quininkicutt &
Apaum or Plymouth, we doe freely give unto him all that
Land from those rivers reaching to Pautuxett river as
Also the grass & meadows upon ye said Pautuxett][18]
river in wit[ness] whereof we have here unto
set our hands

in the presence of the mrke of Caunounicus
the mrke. of Sotaash

the mrke of Assotemawit the marke of Miantunnomi

Md. 3 mon 9 day [this wa]s all again confirmed by Miantunnomi
he acknowled[ged] this by act & hand up the
streams of Patuckett [& Pawt]uxet without limits we
[mi]ght have for use of cattell
witness hereof
Roger Williams
[Benedict Arnold]

Roger Williams to John Winthrop, April 16, 1638[19]

Williams often exchanged correspondence with Winthrop that contained broad and friendly news sharing. Both men were leaders of colonies and seemed to look

18. This bracketed section was seemingly not part of the original land deed from 1636/1638.

19. *Correspondence of Roger Williams*, 1:149–52.

*to each other for advice and support. This letter came at a particularly difficult
time for Winthrop. Williams's letter offers a brief window into many challenges
Winthrop faced and illustrates Williams's wish to empathize with his friend.
Williams refers to several stories that need a little explanation: John Greene first
emigrated to Salem in 1635, but moved to Providence probably by late summer
1636. Greene criticized the Massachusetts General Court for forcing residents to
attend Sabbath services among other church practices, and the Court banished
him, as they had done to Williams. In this letter, Williams reminds Winthrop
that while he had nothing to do with Greene's letter to the Court, he agrees with
Greene's ideas on matters of conscience. (Williams and Winthrop had previously
corresponded about Greene.) John Smith was also banished from Massachusetts
Bay and settled in Providence in 1636. However, Williams reassures Winthrop
that he defended Winthrop against Alice and John Smith's verbal attacks.*

*In this letter, Williams also offers his version of Anne Hutchinson's role
in the birth of Mary Dyer's "monster." Dyer, a woman who was later executed
for being a Quaker in Massachusetts Bay, gave birth to a severely deformed
baby in October 1637. The seventeenth-century Atlantic world used the term
"monster" to describe such births. Hutchinson helped Dyer deliver the baby,
and then helped dispose of the body, at least according to Winthrop. John Cotton told Hutchinson to keep the birth a secret. In this letter, Williams reminds
Winthrop of his friendship with Hutchinson, but also reasserts support for
Cotton, by suggesting that he did not actually say what Hutchinson suggested
he had said (even though Cotton himself later admitted his role to Winthrop).
Hutchinson was accused of the heresy of Antinomianism[20] and was banished
from Massachusetts Bay in November 1637, but was held under house arrest
in Roxbury until March 1638. She then joined her husband and friends on
Aquidneck Island (then known as "Rhode Island") after spending some time
with Williams in Providence and Portsmouth. Hutchinson herself also gave
birth to a "monster" shortly after settling on Aquidneck. Williams and Winthrop were still struggling with the fallout from the Pequot War and what to do
with Native captives. (See chapter 5 for more on Pequot captives.) In the final
paragraphs, Williams reflects on one of the practical problems his banishment
has caused: getting his letters safely to correspondents in Massachusetts Bay.*

20. Antinomianism emphasized the inner experience of God's grace rather than
obedience to ecclesiastical laws and was considered a heresy by Massachusetts Bay
authorities. Hutchinson also believed that most ministers in Massachusetts Bay were
preaching "a covenant of works" rather than "free grace," and during her trial, she said
that she had heard God speak directly to her. Colonial leaders saw Hutchinson as a direct and dangerous challenge to their authority and to the civil order in Massachusetts
Bay. Hall, *Antinomian Controversy*.

Providence 16th of this 2nd

Much honoured Sir

I kindly thanck you for your loving inclination to receave my late protestation concerning my selfe ignorant of Mr Greenes letter etc. I desire unfeignedly to rest in my Appeal to the most high, in what we differ as I dare not but hope you doe: it is no small griefe that I am otherwise perswaded, and that Some times you say (and I can say no lesse) that we differ. The fire will try your works and mine, the Lord Jesus helpe us to make sure of our persons that we seeke Jesus that was Crucified: however

It is and ever shall be (the Lord assisting) my endeavor to pacifie and allay where I meete with rigid and censorious spirits who not only blame your actions but doome your persons: and indeede it was one of the first grounds of my dislike of John Smith the miller and especially his wife viz: their judging of your persons as Divills etc.

I also humbly thanck you for that sad relation of the monster etc. The Lord speakes once or twice: he be pleased to open all our Eares to his Discipline.

Mrs Hutchinson (with whome and others of them I have had much discourse) makes her Apologie for her concealement of the monster that she did nothing in it without Mr Cottons advice, though I can not believe that he subscribes to her Applications of the parts of it. The Lord mercifully redeeme them, and all of us from all our delusions and pitie the desolations of Zion and the stones thereof.

I find their longings great after Mr. Vane[21] although they thinck he can not return this yeare. The eyes of some are so earnestly fixt upon him that Mrs Hutchinson professeth if he come not to New England she must [go] to Old Engl.

I have endeavoured by many Arguments to beate [off] their desires of Mr Vane as G.G. [General Governor] and the chiefe are satisfied unles he come so for his Life but I have endeavoured to discover the snare in that allso.

---

21. Sir Henry Vane emigrated to Massachusetts Bay in 1635 and was elected governor in May 1636 at the young age of twenty-two. Vane's "unorthodox" puritanism led him to support Anne Hutchinson, among other radical puritans, and he even considered establishing a splinter colony in early 1637. Vane's governorship was turbulent and short-lived; he sailed back to England after the elections of May 1637 ousted him and he never returned to New England. He served in several Parliaments, was the Commissioner of the Admiralty under Cromwell, was chosen as a Parliamentary member to the Westminster Assembly, advocated religious toleration, and helped Williams lobby the crown for Rhode Island's charter in 1644. He was beheaded in 1662 during the Restoration. Williams often stayed with the Vane family during his trips to England. See chapter 9 for more about the Vane family. Winship, *Hot Protestants*, 104–9; Barry, *Roger Williams*, 248–49; 303–9; 360–80.

Sir concerning your intended meeting for reconciling of these Natives our friends and dividing the Pequts our enemies I have imagined your name, and mine owne, and if no course be taken the name of that God of Truth whome we all profess to honour will suffer not a little, it being an ordinary and common thing with our neighbours if they apprehend any shew of breach of promise in my selfe thus to object: doe you know God and will you lye? etc.

The Pequts are gathered into one, and plant their old fields, Wequash and Okace[22] carrying away the people and their treasure wch belong to your selves. I should be bold to presse my former Motion or else that with the next convenience they might be sent for other parts etc.

I hope it will never be interpreted that I press this out of feare of any revenge upon my selfe by any of them. I ever yet (in point of reason to say no more) conceaved this place the Safest of the land and can make it appeare etc. but out of desire to cleare your name and the name of the most High wch will be ill reported of in case (according to so many promises) an honorable and peaceable Issue of the Pequt warr be not established.

Sir the bearer hereof (not daring either to bring my letter or attend for an Answere) I must request you send your letter to Rich. Collicuts that so a native many convey it: or [else] to Nicholas Upshalls. And I should be bold humbly to propound to the Countrey whether in case there be a necessitie of keeping leauge with the Natives and so consequently many occasions incident, (and some wch I will not write of) as allso a conveniencie of Informacion this way how matters may stand with you on the Sea shoare, as I say whither it be not requisite so farr to dispence with the late Order of Restraint as to permit a Messenger freely.

Tis true I may hire an Indian: yet not always, nor sure, for these 2 things I have found in them: Sometimes long keeping of a letter: 2ndly if a feare take them that the letter concernes themselves they Suppresse it, as they did with one of special Informacion wch I sent to Mr Vane.[23]

Sir there will be a new Heavens and a New Earth shortly but no more Sea (Revel. 21.2). The most holy God be pleased to make us willing now to beare up the Tossings Dangers and calamities of this Sea and to Seale up to us upon his owne grounds, a great Lot in that glorious state aproaching. So Craving pardon for Prolixitie with mine and [wife's] due respect to Mrs Wintrop Mr Deputie [Thomas Dudley] Mr Bellingham etc. I rest Your [Worship's] desirous to be ever Yours unfeigned

Roger Williams

22. Uncas was the Mohegan sachem; Wequash was a Pequot captain during the Pequot War. For more information and context on Uncas and Wequash, see chapter 5.

23. Katherine Grandjean explores Native letter-carrying and Williams's use of Indigenous letter bearers in *American Passage*, 1–5, 45–75.

Roger Williams to John Winthrop, March 8, 1640/1641[24]

*Samuel Gorton's arrival in Providence posed serious problems for Williams.[25]
Gorton (c. 1592–1677) arrived in Boston with his family in 1637 and quickly
moved to Plimouth. Historians uniformly describe him as difficult and contentious, and his religious ideas readily earned him enemies in Massachusetts.
The Plimouth General Court charged him with "stirring up the people to mu-
tinie in the face of the Court" and the church elders accused him of heresy for
his lay preaching; he was banished from Plimouth colony in December 1638.
When Gorton arrived on Aquidneck Island (Rhode Island), he immediately
sparred with William Coddington, which led to a splintering of settlements
on Aquidneck as Coddington and his allies moved south, founding Newport.
Coddington worked to reunite the warring settlements on Aquidneck, which
he accomplished in March 1640 when he wooed Pocasset (Portsmouth) residents back into an alliance, leaving Gorton somewhat isolated. Gorton refused
to accept the new government of Aquidneck Island, calling the magistrates
"Just Asses." Those "asses" threw him in jail and ultimately banished him from
the island. By early 1641, Gorton landed in Providence with a small group of
settlers. As the letter below illustrates, Williams was worried about Gorton
from the beginning. Gorton did not cause the divisions that Williams describes
below, but surely made them worse. By November 1641, thirteen residents in
Providence even appealed to Governor John Winthrop, seeking help from the
Massachusetts Bay Colony—an intervention Winthrop admitted he could not
provide, but the chaos Gorton caused offered the Bay colony a chance to try to
bring Narragansett Bay land under their control. Gorton moved further south,
acquiring a piece of land from local Native sachems, then called Shawomet,
later Warwick. Documents following this one pick up Gorton's story, as two sachems rejected Gorton's "purchase" of Shawomet and turned to Massachusetts
Bay for help in getting their stolen land back. Later in this chapter, documents
indicate that Gorton's followers refused to compensate Rhode Island's agent in
London as well.*

*Gorton's religious ideas in Providence also troubled Williams, as the letter
below illustrates. Gorton's later publications reflect his belief in the "indwelling
of the spirit" in all believers—something Williams dismisses as "Familisme"—
and Gorton rejected churches as impediments to direct experiences of grace*

24. *Correspondence of Roger Williams*, 1:215. LaFantasie contextualizes and interprets this letter: "Samuel Gorton in Providence, 1640/4" in *Correspondence of Roger
Williams*, 1:208–15.

25. For more on Gorton, see documents later in this chapter and in chapter 6. Gura,
Glimpse of Sion's Glory, 276–303; James, *Colonial Rhode Island*, 28–31; Barry, *Roger
Williams*, 265–73, 293–96, 313–15, 350–55.

*between believers and God. Scholars have described Gorton as a "mystic"
who drew on ideas of prominent English radicals such as Robert Towne, John
Eaton, and Tobias Crisp, and he joined a Baptist church after he returned to
England in the mid-1640s.[26] By all accounts, his lay preaching style in both
old and New England was passionate, compelling, anti-authoritarian, and
anti-clerical, which made him popular in Providence and a big problem for
Williams. Williams and Gorton shared a belief that civil governments had
no role to play in matters of conscience, but Gorton went much further. He
argued that civil governments could not punish believers for breaches of civil
law—a rejection of civil authority that Williams did not accept.[27]*

Providence 8. 1st. 1640.

Master Gorton having foully abused high and low at Aquednick, is
now bewitching and bemadding poore Providence, both with his uncleane
and foule censures of all the Ministers of this Country, (for which my selfe
have in Christs name withstood him) and also denying all visible and externall Ordinances in depth of Familisme,[28] against which I have a little
disputed and written,[29] and shall (the most High assisting) to death: As
Paul said of Asia, I of Providence (almost) All suck in his poyson, as at first
they did at Aquednick. Some few and my selfe withstand his Inhabitation,
and Towne-priveledges, without confession and reformation of his uncivill
and inhumane practices at Portsmouth: Yet the tyde is too strong against
us, and I fear (if the framer of Hearts helpe not) it will force mee to little
Patience, a little Isle next to your Prudence.[30] Jehovah himselfe bee pleased

26. Gura, *Glimpse of Sion's Glory*, 282–96.

27. Gura, *Glimpse of Sion's Glory*, 295–99.

28. According to Michael Winship, Gorton was not a "Familist," or follower of the
"Family of Love," which was a "small, secretive religious movement whose adherents believed that Christians could eventually enjoy perfect union with God . . . and that their
own revelations superseded those of the Bible." Williams is using it here as a derogatory
term, lumping Gorton in with others who believed in the direct infusion of the Holy
Spirit. Winship, *Hot Protestants*, 294. See also *Correspondence of Roger Williams*, 1:216n2.

29. None of Williams's published texts specifically address Gorton, but the doctrinal
differences that set the two men apart are well explored in many of Williams's works. If
he drafted any texts specifically to debate Gorton, they did not survive. *Correspondence
of Roger Williams*, 1:216n3.

30. Patience Island is west of the northern tip of Prudence Island in Narragansett
Bay. Williams sold Patience Island in 1651 to his neighbor and friend, Richard Scott, to
help cover the costs of his second trip to London. (That friendship had soured by 1658.)
According to Sydney James, Canonicus and Miantonomo gave Prudence Island to both
Winthrop and Williams, although Williams uses "your" to refer to Prudence Island
here. *Correspondence of Roger Williams*, 1:186n3; James, *Colonial Rhode Island*, 8.

to bee a Sanctuary to all whose hearts are perfect with him In Him I desire unfainedly to be Your Worships true an affectionate

Roger Williams.

Parliamentary Patent, 1644[31]

In 1643, Williams went to England to seek a patent to combine the settlements of Providence, Portsmouth, and Newport. Prior to this patent, Williams and the founders of Portsmouth and Newport were all operating without official English royal backing. This became a more pressing matter in 1642 and early 1643 when Samuel Gorton purchased a large tract of land south of Providence (later called Warwick) and submitted himself to the Massachusetts Bay Colony, thereby inviting their claim to the region. Massachusetts Bay was seeking a grant to parts of the Narragansett Bay as well, and as historian Sydney James suggests, that colony "had many more influential friends than Williams could muster."[32] Williams's lobbying efforts in London—in the midst of the English Civil War—were intense and ultimately successful. The excerpts from the patent below focus on land boundaries, relations with Indigenous neighbors, and the nature of government in the new colony. Note the repeated use of the term "civil," which suggests that the patent referred only to civil government, with no mention of religious requirements. Scholar Jonathan Beecher Field argues that the patent, coupled with A Key *and* The Bloudy Tenent, *were all part of an "integrated political campaign to preserve Providence Plantations from the Bay Colony's territorial ambitions" and presented "a vision of the new American world" to Parliament: the patent "authorizes Williams's dissenting view of America in both its racial and religious dimensions."[33] Once the patent was granted, Gorton's land (Warwick) seemed to be included, but after Williams returned with this patent, Gorton sailed to England to defend his claim, setting off another dispute.[34]*

. . . And whereas there is a Tract of Land in the Continent of America aforesaid, called by the Name of the Narraganset-Bay; bordering Northward and Northeast on the Patent of the Massachusetts, East and Southeast on Plymouth Patent, South on the Ocean, and on the West and Northwest by the

31. "Parliamentary Patent for Providence Plantations, March 14, 1643." This website uses the old-style calendar date instead of 1643/1644. https://avalon.law.yale.edu/17th_century/rio3.asp.

32. James, *Colonial Rhode Island*, 57.

33. Field, *Errands into the Metropolis*, 27.

34. James, *Colonial Rhode Island*, 57, 60.

Indians called Nahigganneucks, alias Narragansets; the whole Tract extending about Twenty-five English Miles unto the Pequot River and Country . . .

And whereas divers well affected and industrious English Inhabitants, of the Towns of Providence, Portsmouth, and Newport in the tract aforesaid, have adventured to make a nearer neighborhood and Society with the great Body of the Narragansets, which may in time by the blessing of God upon their Endeavours, lay a sure foundation of Happiness to all America. And have also purchased, and are purchasing of and amongst the said Natives, some other Places, which may be convenient both for Plantations, and also for building of Ships Supply of Pipe Staves and other Merchandize. And whereas the said English, have represented their Desire to the said Earl, and Commissioners, to have their hopeful beginnings approved and confirmed, by granting unto them a free Charter of Civil Incorporation and Government; that they may order and govern their Plantation in such a Manner as to maintain Justice and peace, both among themselves, and towards all Men with whom they shall have to do.

In due Consideration of the said Premises, the said Robert Earl of Warwick, Governor in Chief, and Lord High Admiral of the said Plantations, and the greater Number of the said Commissioners, whose Names and Seals are here under-written and subjoined, out of a Desire to encourage the good Beginnings of the said Planters, Do, by the Authority of the aforesaid Ordinance of the Lords and Commons, give, grant and confirm, to the aforesaid Inhabitants of the Towns of Providence, Portsmouth, and Newport, a free and absolute Charter of Incorporation, to be known by the Name of the Incorporation of Providence Plantations, in the Narraganset-Bay, in New-England. Together with full Power and Authority to rule themselves, and such others as shall hereafter inhabit within any Part of the said Tract of land, by such a Form of Civil Government, as by voluntary consent of all, or the greater Part of them, they shall find most suitable to their Estate and Condition; and, for that End, to make and ordain such Civil Laws and Constitutions, and to inflict such punishments upon Transgressors, and for Execution thereof, so to place, and displace Officers of Justice, as they, or the greater Part of them, shall by free Consent agree unto.

Submission of the Chief Sachem of the Narragansett to Charles I, April 19, 1644[35]

This document was not penned by Roger Williams, but it is an important part of the Native world he inhabited, and it reveals the complicated political

35. Native Northeast Portal Transcription, https://nativenortheastportal.com/anno

maneuverings by both English and Natives. On the surface, this document is an astonishing relinquishing of Narragansett land, possessions, and sovereignty to King Charles I. Given the strength of the Narragansett nation in the 1640s, this seems entirely unnecessary (and unlikely). As Narragansett and Niantic educator Chrystal Mars Baker states, "It shall forever be my conviction that my ancestors, the great and powerful sachems of the Narragansett would never have 'chosen' to subject themselves to any English king or laws of 'protection' . . . they had existed within their own form of government and protections from time immemorial and never needed the help of any colonizers or settlers."[36] Another interpretation, therefore, is that this document was written by ill-meaning colonists and signed by unsuspecting Narragansett sachems. And indeed, this "submission" was seemingly orchestrated by Rhode Island residents who potentially benefited from positioning themselves as the arbitrators of Narragansett diplomacy. This included Samuel Gorton, who was at odds with Williams and other Rhode Island leaders, as documents earlier in this chapter illustrate.

But a third and more probable interpretation exists: that the Narragansett sachems, working within the realm of international diplomacy and treaty-making, strategically used King Charles I to accomplish their own goals closer to home. In this reading, then, the Narragansett sachems knew precisely what they were doing: by "submitting" directly to the king of England, they protected themselves from local colonial machinations on their land. To "submit" in this way was a strategy of preserving their own autonomy. There is no evidence that the Narragansett actually saw themselves at a point of weakness or submission to the King of England. Instead, they opened up diplomatic channels between two sovereign nations, thereby forcing accountability regarding local colonial actions. And this submission came with mutual obligations, which they state plainly as the primary condition of their "submission": "upon condition of his Majesty's royal protection and righting of us in what wrong is, or may be done onto us, according to his honorable laws and customs, exercised amongst his subjects. . ." The Narragansett were seemingly exasperated by the multiple claims to authority within and outside of Rhode Island, and determined to go straight to the king for justice.

If this is the case, both Roger Williams and the Narragansett sachems appealed to King Charles I within a year for protection from enterprising colonists. Each one had different purposes, perhaps, but both sought to preserve their own society and to bring some order and stability to the region through diplomatic means.

---

tated-transcription/digcoll3983.

36. Chrystal Mars Baker, correspondence with the authors, January 24, 2023.

Know all men, colonies, peoples, and nations, unto whom the same hereof shall come, that we, the chief sachems, princes or governors of the Narragansett (in that part of America now called New England) together with the joint and unanimous consent of all our people and subjects, inhabitants thereof, do upon serious consideration, mature and deliberate advice and counsel, great and weighty grounds and reasons moving us thereunto, whereof one most effectual unto us is that noble fame we have heard of, that great and mighty prince, Charles, King of Great Britain, in that honorable and princely care he hath of all his servants and true and loyal subjects, the consideration whereof moveth and bendeth our hearts with one consent, freely, voluntarily, and most humbly, to submit, subject, and give over our selves, peoples, lands, rights, inheritances, and possessions whatsoever, in our selves and our heirs, successively forever, unto the protection, care, and government of that worthy and royal prince, Charles, King of Great Britain and Ireland, his heirs and successors forever, to be ruled and governed according to those ancient and honorable laws and customs established in that so renowned realm and kingdom of Old England.

We do, therefore, by these presents confess, and most willingly and submissively, acknowledge ourselves to be the humble, loving, and obedient servants and subjects of his Majesty, to be ruled, ordered, and disposed of, in ourselves and ours, according to his princely wisdom, counsel, and laws of that honorable state of Old England, upon condition of his Majesty's royal protection and righting of us in what wrong is, or may be done onto us, according to his honorable laws and customs, exercised amongst his subjects, in their preservation and safety, and in the defeating and overthrow of his and their enemies; not that we find ourselves necessitated hereunto, in respect of our relation, or occasion we have or may have with any of the Natives in these parts, knowing ourselves sufficient defense, and able to judge in any matter or cause in that respect, but have just cause of jealousy and suspicion, of some of his Majesty's pretended subjects; therefore,

our desire is to have our matters and causes heard and tried according to his just and equal laws in that way, and order His Highness shall please to appoint; nor can we yield over ourselves unto any that are subjects themselves, in any case, having ourselves been the chief sachems, or princes, successively, of the country, time out of mind, and for our present and lawful enacting hereof, being so far remote from his Majesty, we have by joint consent, made choice of four of his loyal and loving subjects, our trusty and well-beloved friends, Samuel Gorton, John Wickes,[37] Randall Holden, and

---

37. A neighbor and ally of Samuel Gorton at Warwick. He died in 1676 during King Philip's War.

John Warner, whom we have deputed and made our lawful attorneys or commissioners, not only for the acting and performing of this, our deed, in the behalf of his Highness but also for the safe custody, careful convey-ance, and declaration hereof unto his Grace, being done upon the lands of the Narragansett at a court or general assembly called and assembled together of purpose for the public enacting and manifestation hereof. And for the further confirmation and establishing of this, our act and deed, we, the abovesaid sachems, or princes, have, according to that commendable custom of Englishmen, subscribed our names and set our seals hereunto, as so many testimonies of our faith and truth, our love and loyalty to that, our dread Sovereign, and that according to the Englishmen's account, dated the 19th day of April, 1644,

Pessicus, his mark, chief sachem and successor of that late deceased Miantonomo

The mark of that ancient Canonicus, protector of that late deceased Miantonomo during the time of his nonage

The mark of Mixan,[38] son and heir of that abovesaid Canonicus

Witness:	Witnessed by two of the chief counsellors to Sachem Pessicus, Awashaw,[39] his mark, Tomanick,[40] his mark, Indians
Certifica-tion:	Sealed and delivered in the presence of these persons, Christopher Helme, Robert Potter, Richard Carder, English
Copy:	A true copy of the act and deed of the voluntary and free submis-sion of the chief sachem and the rest of the princes, with the whole people of the Narragansetts unto the government and protection of that honorable state of Old England, set down here verbatim

38. The eldest son of the Narragansett sachem Canonicus I. He was also the hus-band of the Niantic sachem Ninigret's sister Quaiapen.

39. Awashaw was an important Narragansett diplomat. He acted as a counselor to Narragansett sachems such as Pessicus and Ninigret.

40. Tomanick was a chief counselor to the Narragansett sachem Pessicus.

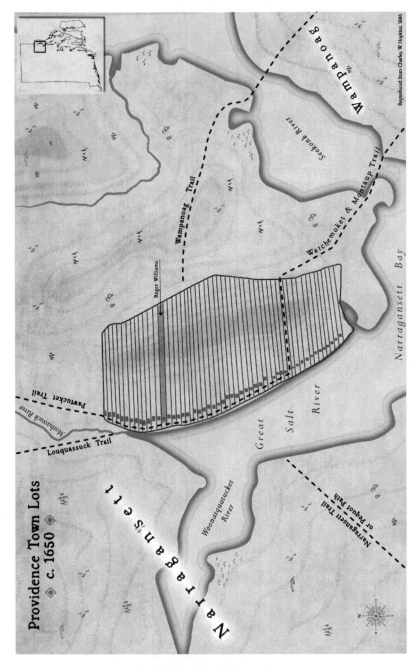

Providence Town Lots, c. 1650.
Map by Lynn Carlson, Compass Cartographic, ©2023.

This map indicates the location of each household lot in Providence in 1650 according to that year's tax list. The lots are equal in size and placement, with each having access to the Great Salt River leading to Narragansett Bay and a steep uphill in the backyard. By 1650, a small handful of householders had acquired two adjoining lots, often by moving. The residents of each lot are listed below, with lot one starting at the top (the North end of Providence) and ending with lot fifty-two at the South end just above Mile End Cove. The year following each name indicates the year they purchased the lot. Roger Williams's own parcel (highlighted on the map) is lot fourteen. If a lot changed hands before 1650, we have indicated both the former and current resident. It appears that some house lots were unowned as of the 1650 tax list, although they had been owned at an earlier point. As the map illustrates, some women owned home lots and there was considerable movement within Providence, within the colony, and to outside the colony before 1650.

1. Gregory Dexter 1644

2. Gregory Dexter (formerly Matthew Waller 1643)

3. Pardon Tillinghast 1649 (formerly Thomas Painter 1643, moved to Newport)

4. formerly Edward Manton 1640 (moved to lot 18)

5. formerly John Greene Jr. 1637 (moved to Warwick in 1642)

6. formerly Benedict Arnold 1636 (moved to Pawtuxet in 1638)

7. formerly Francis Weeks 1636

8. Benedict Arnold (formerly William Arnold 1636, moved to Pawtuxet in 1638)

9. John Elderkin (formerly Thomas James 1637, moved to Pawtuxet in 1639)

10. John Greene Jr. (formerly John Greene Sr. 1636, moved to Warwick in 1642)

11. John Throckmorton (formerly John Smith 1636, moved in 1646)

12. Richard Scott (formerly Widow Reeve 1638, left colony)

13. Richard Scott (formerly Joshua Verin 1636, left colony)

14. Roger Williams 1636

15. formerly John Throckmorton 1637 (moved to lot 11)

16. Henry Wright (formerly Williams Harris 1636, moved to Pawtuxet in 1638)

17. Peter Greene (formerly Alice Daniels 1637, wife of W. Greene Sr., moved to Warwick)

18. Edward Manton (formerly John Sweet 1637, moved to Warwick)

19. formerly William Carpenter 1636 (moved to Pawtuxet in 1638)

20. formerly Robert Coles 1637 (moved to Pawtuxet in 1638)

21. Thomas Olney Sr. 1637

22. formerly Thomas Angell 1636 (moved to lot 23)

23. Thomas Angell (formerly Francis Weston 1637, moved to Warwick)

24. Richard Waterman 1637

25. Hugh Bewitt before 1650 (formerly Ezekiel Holiman 1637, moved to Pawtuxet in 1640; this lot served as the Town House lot from 1644–1647)

26. Stukeley Westcott 1638

27. Robert Williams (formerly William Reynolds 1637, left the colony)

28. Robert Williams (formerly Daniel Abbott Sr. 1639, died 1647)

29. Chad Brown 1639

30. George Richards (formerly John Warner 1639, moved to Warwick in 1642)

31. formerly George Richards 1639 (moved to lot 30)

32. formerly Richard Scott 1639 (moved to lot 13)

33. William Field 1639

34. John Field 1639

35. George Shepard (formerly Joshua Winsor 1630, moved to lot 46)

36. Thomas Harris Sr. 1639

37. Adam Goodwin 1639

38. William Barrows 1639

39. William Mann

40. Nathaniel Dickens (formerly William Wickenden 1639, moved to Fox Point)

41. Nicholas Power 1639

42. Nicholas Power (formerly Joan Tyler 1641, who married Nathaniel Dickens and moved to lot 40)

43. Jane Sears 1641

44. Thomas Hopkins 1636

45. Robert West (formerly Edward Hart 1641, left the colony)

46. Joshua Winsor (formerly Matthew Weston 1643, moved to Warwick)

47. formerly John Lippitt 1641

48. John Ashton (formerly Hugh Bewitt 1641, moved to lot 25)

49. William Hawkins (formerly Robert West 1640, moved to lot 45)

50. William Hawkins 1641

51. Thomas Roberts (formerly Christopher Unthank 1642, moved to Warwick)

52. formerly Robert Williams 1644 (moved to lot 28)

Mary Bernard Williams to Roger Williams, June 1650[41]

Roger's wife, Mary Bernard Williams, was raised in a powerfully dissenting ministerial family, served as a lady's maid to Lady Masham at Otes Manor in Essex (where Roger was employed as chaplain), and emigrated to Boston with him after their marriage in December 1629. She joined him on each of his many moves during their first years in Massachusetts Bay, and settled in Providence with him when she was twenty-seven, remaining there until she died. Only nine words written by her have survived. We include this tiny text partly to illustrate the archival silences that frustrate our ability to fully describe Williams's life, and also to draw attention to the fact that what documents remain in no way reflect what once was. This single address sheet proves that Mary wrote to Roger—probably frequently given his long absences from Providence, both at his trading post and abroad. That none of her letters survive does not mean that she did not write any. Roger used the address sheet from a letter that Mary never mailed as scrap paper to write down some comments about proper punishments for adultery—a fact that perhaps ensured that this document was kept.

my deare & loueing huband [Roger Williams] att [narragansett] thes

41. Roger Williams to John Winthrop Jr, 22 June 1650, Winthrop Papers Special Collections, P-350, Box 8, Massachusetts Historical Society, Boston, MA. We are grateful to Charlotte Carrington-Farmer for her work on Mary Bernard Williams; "More than Roger's Wife: Mary Williams and the Founding of Providence." *New England Quarterly*, forthcoming 2024. This text introduction draws on that work.

Roger Williams to the Town of Providence, c. January 1654/1655[42]

According to historian Glenn LaFantasie, the letter below "is one of Williams's most famous and most celebrated writings." First printed in 1756, the letter—usually called the "Ship of State letter"—is compelling both for its content and its style. Despite how often it has been reprinted in the 350 years since Williams wrote it, historians know very little about what prompted it, or even its exact date. Williams biographer Samuel Brockunier offered the most convincing interpretation of the letter's context: in November 1654, the town of Providence tried to establish a compulsory militia muster. When some residents balked at being forced to serve in the militia, the town set fines to punish non-compliance. The threat of punishment unleashed a full-blown protest, led by Robert Williams (Roger's brother), who drew on Roger Williams's ideas when he confronted the town authorities. The letter below is Roger Williams's clarification that his ideas on liberty of conscience did not apply to the protestors' refusal to serve in the militia. Does this letter illustrate a Williams who had grown suspicious of his neighbors claiming that individual liberties always trump communal cooperation?[43] Scholars Chris Benecke and Christopher Grenda argue that Williams believed "being forced to support someone else's church or submitting to a religious test for office constituted an unjust burden on conscience; paying to support the civil functions of the commonweal or bearing arms when the colony was under attack did not."[44] Williams was clearly struggling with contention in the colony and was "dismayed by his fellow Rhode Islanders' unwillingness to submit to civil authority."[45] As the documents in this chapter illustrate, the 1640s and 1650s were marked by dissention, including challenges by religious radicals like the Gortonists (and anti-Gortonist efforts to silence them) and land disputes both from neighbors in Massachusetts Bay and from within the colony itself, including one led by William Coddington. Coddington received a royal commission in 1651 naming him governor of Aquidneck for life, and at times had sought military help from the Dutch in New Netherland.[46] This chaos threatened Williams's efforts to prove that a healthy and prosperous colony did not require religious enforcement.

42. *Correspondence of Roger Williams*, 2:419–25.

43. For a full discussion of this letter, its provenance and context, and its place among Williams's texts, see "The Ship of State Letter, ca. January 1654/5: Editorial Note," in *Correspondence of Roger Williams*: 2:419–25.

44. Beneke and Grenda, *Lively Experiment*, 4.

45. Murphy, "'Livelie Experiment' and 'Holy Experiment,'" 41.

46. James, *Colonial Rhode Island*, 63.

[Providence?]

Loving Friends and Neighbours,

It pleaseth GOD, yet to continue this great Liberty of our Town-Meetings, for which, we ought to be humbly thankful, and to improve these Liberties to the Praise of the Giver, and to the Peace and Welfare of the Town and Colony, without our own private Ends.—I thought it my Duty, to present you with this my impartial Testimony, and Answer to a Paper sent you the other Day from my Brother,—That it is Blood-Guiltiness, and against the Rule of the Gospel, to execute Judgment upon Transgressors, against the private or public Weal.—That ever I should speak or write a Tittle that tends to such an infinite Liberty of Conscience, is a Mistake; and which I have ever disclaimed and abhorred. To prevent such Mistakes, I at present shall only propose this Case.—There goes many a Ship to Sea, with many a Hundred Souls in one ship, whose Weal and Woe is common; and is a true Picture of a Common-Wealth, or an human Combination, or Society. It hath fallen out sometimes, that both Papists and Protestants, Jews, and Turks, may be enbarqued into one Ship. Upon which Supposal, I do affirm, that all the Liberty of Conscience that ever I pleaded for, turns upon these two Hinges, that none of the Papists, Protestants, Jews, or Turks, be forced to come to the Ships Prayers or Worship; nor, secondly, compelled from their own particular Prayers or Worship, if they practice any. I further add, that I never denied, that notwithstanding this Liberty, the Commander of this Ship ought to command the Ship's Course; yea, and also to command that Justice, Peace, and Sobriety, be kept and practised, both among the Seaman and all the Passengers. If any Seamen refuse to perform their Service, or Passengers to pay their Freight;—if any refuse to help in Person or Purse, towards the Common Charges, or Defence; —if any refuse to obey the common Laws and Orders of the Ship, concerning their common Peace and Preservation;—if any shall mutiny and rise up against their Commanders, and Officers;—if any shall preach or write, that there ought to be no Commanders, nor Officers, because we are all equal in CHRIST, therefore no Masters, nor Officers, no Laws, nor Orders, no Corrections nor Punishments—I say, I never denied, but in such Cases, whatever is pretended, the Commander or Commanders may judge, resist, compel, and punish such Transgressors, according to their Deserts and Merits. This, if seriously and honestly minded, may, if it so please the Father of Lights, let in some Light, to such as willingly shut not their Eyes.—I—remain, studious of our common Peace and Liberty, —

Roger Williams

Charter of Rhode Island and Providence Plantations, July 15, 1663[47]

The continued chaos in the four towns of Rhode Island and the 1660 restora-
tion of the English monarch provide important context for this Charter. The
1644 Patent had been granted to Williams by Parliament, not the crown, so in
1661, Rhode Island's agent in London, John Clarke,[48]*was instructed to seek a*
charter from King Charles II. Connecticut Colony got there first and received
a very favorable land boundary with Rhode Island that caused problems for
Rhode Island for years.[49] *In London, Clarke spent six months waiting for funds*
from Rhode Island and trying to limit Connecticut's land grab, watching out
for potential land takeover by Massachusetts Bay, all the while looking to take
land then under Plimouth's control.[50] *Ultimately Clarke drafted and ensured*
acceptance of the charter, which gave the colony legal standing from the crown
and articulated Williams's vision for a government that remained unentan-
gled in spiritual matters. In the 1663 charter, the king allowed "liberty in the
worship of God" (even if it meant not conforming to the Church of England)
despite the 1662 Act of Uniformity that required all Englishmen and women
who lived outside the colonies to adhere to the practices of the Church of Eng-
land. Rhode Island's charter counted on King Charles II's "religious and po-
litical vision that favored religious diversity over uniformity." Historian Evan
Haefeli goes further and suggests that the king "endorsed Rhode Island's lively
experiment" because he could not permit that amount of religious diversity at

47. "Charter of Rhode Island and Providence Plantations, 15 July 1663." https://ava-
lon.law.yale.edu/17th_century/ri04.asp#1. Sydney James offers a brief overview of the
Charter's many provisions in *Colonial Rhode Island*, 68–70. This Charter later served as
the Constitution of the State of Rhode Island until 1843.

48. John Clarke (1609–1676) was educated as a physician in England, emigrated to
Massachusetts Bay in 1637, moved with William and Anne Hutchinson to Aquidneck,
and signed the Portsmouth Compact in March 1638. Unhappy in Portsmouth, in 1639
Clarke joined William Coddington who moved south and established the town of Newport. Clarke founded the Baptist church in Newport in 1644. Clarke's and Coddington's
alliance did not last long, and Clarke was sent to London to challenge Coddington's
1651 Commission for Aquidneck Island. In London in 1652, he published *Ill Newes from
New-England*, which defended believer's baptism (rather than infant baptism), described
what he believed to be religious persecution in Massachusetts Bay, and promoted liberty
of conscience. Clarke stayed in London as the colonial agent for Rhode Island until 1664,
which left him deeply indebted. He served in the assembly and as Deputy Governor of
Rhode Island. Lemons, "John Clarke"; James, *John Clarke and His Legacies*, 43–84.

49. James, *Colonial Rhode Island*, 67–68.

50. In 1663, Clarke got Connecticut Governor John Winthrop Jr. to agree to the
Pawcatuck River as Connecticut's eastern border, which Connecticut denied, and
fought against until 1727. Conflict between Plimouth and Rhode Island over towns east
of the Blackstone River and Narragansett Bay lasted until the Privy Council intervened
in 1747. James, *Colonial Rhode Island*, 67–68.

home.[51] *The English crown supported this new charter, in part, to also keep the Massachusetts Bay colony in check.*[52] *Even with that broader English context in mind, this charter acknowledges the religious nonconformity of Rhode Island residents with stunning clarity.*

Given Williams's refusal to take oaths, it is noteworthy that the 1663 Charter required elected officials in the colony's government to "give their solemn engagement, by oath or otherwise,[53] *for the due and faithful performance of their duties in their several offices and places, before such person or persons as are by these presents hereafter appointed to take and receive the same." Along with describing the structure of the colony's government and elections, its land and sea boundaries, taxation, and military expectations, the charter also defended Rhode Islanders' right to go whaling and plant vineyards. The excerpts below focus on questions of religious adherence and Indigenous relations. No one would be coerced into any particular religious practice and Native conversion may happen, but only because the settlers' "good life and orderlie conversations. . . invite" them to do so. As Narragansett scholar Mack Scott reminds us, the charter somewhat jarringly also reserves the right of the colonists to, with just cause, "invade and destroy the native Indians, or other enemyes of the sayd Collony."*[54] *This is a sharp reminder that Rhode Island and all of Williams's idealism were part of a larger English invasion of Indigenous land, and that, as King Philip's War would later show, English colonists (no matter their religious persuasion) saw themselves unified against Natives in times of war.*

. . . they, pursueing, with peaceable and loyall mindes, their sober, serious and religious intentions, of godlie edifieing themselves, and one another, in the holie Christian ffaith and worshipp as they were perswaded; together with the gaineing over and conversione of the poore ignorant Indian natives,[55] in those partes of America, to the sincere professione and obedience of the same ffaith and worship, did, not onlie by the consent and good encouragement of our royall progenitors, transport themselves out of this kingdome of England into America, but alsoe, since their arrivall there, after their first settlement amongst other our subjects in those parts, Nor

51. Haefeli, "How Special was Rhode Island?" 23–27.

52. James, *Colonial Rhode Island*, 66–70.

53. The "or otherwise" is important here, allowing residents to sign a pledge, for example, rather than be forced to take an oath.

54. Mack Scott, correspondence with the authors, January 22, 2023.

55. This represents crown aspirations more than colony ones, since by 1663 neither Williams nor other Rhode Islanders had a program of any sort in place to convert Natives to Christianity.

the avoideing of discorde, and those manic evills which were likely to ensue
upon some of those oure subjects not beinge able to beare, in these remote
parties, theire different apprehensiones in religious concernements, and in
pursueance of the afforesayd ends, did once againe leave theire desireable
stationies and habitationes, and with excessive labour and travell, hazard
and charge, did transplant themselves into the middest of the Indian natives, who, as wee are informed, are the most potent princes and people of
all that country; where, by the good Providence of God, from whome the
Plantationes have taken their name, upon theire labour and industrie, they
have not onlie byn preserved to admiration, but have increased and prospered, and are seized and possessed, by purchase and consent of the said
natives, to their ffull content, of such lands, islands, rivers, harbours and
roades, as are verie convenient, both for plantationes and alsoe for buildings
of shipps, suplye of pypestaves, and other merchandise . . .

And whereas, in theire humble addresse, they have ffreely declared,
that it is much on their hearts (if they may be permitted), to hold forth
a livlie experiment, that a most flourishing civill state may stand and best
bee maintained, and that among our English subjects, with a full libertie in
religious concernements; and that true pietye rightly grounded upon gospell principles, will give the best and greatest security to sovereignetye, and
will lay in the hearts of men the strongest obligations to true loyaltye: Now
know bee, that wee beinge willinge to encourage the hopefull undertakeinge
of oure sayd lovall and loveinge subjects, and to secure them in the free
exercise and enjovment of all theire civill and religious rights, appertaining
to them, as our loveing subjects; and to preserve unto them that libertye, in
the true Christian ffaith and worshipp of God, which they have sought with
soe much travaill, and with peaceable myndes, and loyall subjectione to our
royall progenitors and ourselves, to enjoye; and because some of the people
and inhabitants of the same colonie cannot, in theire private opinions, conform to the publique exercise of religion, according to the litturgy, formes
and ceremonyes of the Church of England, or take or subscribe the oaths
and articles made and established in that behalfe;[56] and for that the same,
by reason of the remote distances of those places, will (as wee hope) bee
noe breach of the unitie and unifformitie established in this nation: Have
therefore thought ffit, and doe hereby publish, graunt, ordeyne and declare,
That our royall will and pleasure is, that noe person within the sayd colonye,
at any tyme hereafter, shall bee any wise molested, punished, disquieted,
or called in question, for any differences in opinione in matters of religion,

56. Here is a clear example of the king's acceptance that Rhode Island colonists
would not be expected to follow the practices of the Church of England or even take
oaths.

and doe not actually disturb the civill peace of our sayd colony; but that all and everye person and persons may, from tyme to tyme, and at all tymes hereafter, freelye and fullye have and enjoye his and theire owne judgments and consciences, in matters of religious concernments throughout the tract of land hereafter mentioned . . .

[The elected government of the colony has the right to] direct, rule, order and dispose of, all other matters and things, and particularly that which relates to the makinge of purchases of the native Indians, as to them shall seeme meete; whereby oure sayd people and inhabitants, in the sayd Plantationes, may be soe religiously, peaceably and civilly governed, as that, by theire good life and orderlie conversations, they may win and invite the native Indians of the countrie to the knowledge and obedience of the onlie true God, and Saviour of mankinde . . .[57]

[The elected government of the colony has the right to] assemble, exercise in arms, martiall array, and putt in warlyke posture, the inhabitants of the sayd collonie, For theire speciall defence and safety; and to lead and conduct the sayd inhabitants, and to encounter, expulse, expell and resist, by force of armes, as well by sea as by land; and alsoe to kill, slay and destroy, by all fitting wayes, enterprises and meaner, whatsoever, all and every such person or persons as shall, at any tyme hereafter, attempt or enterprize the destruction, invasion, detriment or annoyance of the sayd inhabitants or Plantations; and to use and exercise the lawe martiall in such cases only as occasion shall necessarily require; and to take or surprise, by all wayes and meanes whatsoever, all and every such person and persons, with theire shipp or shipps, armor, ammunition or other goods of such persons, as shall, in hostile manner, invade or attempt the defeating of the sayd Plantations, or the hurt of the said Company and inhabitants; and upon just causes, to invade and destroy the native Indians, or other enemyes of the sayd Collony. Neverthelesse, our will and pleasure is, and wee doe hereby declare to the rest of oure Collonies in New England, that itt shall not bee lawfull ffor this our sayd Collony of Rhode-Island and Providence Plantations, in America, in New-England, to invade the natives inhabiting within the bounces and limitts of theire sayd Collonies without the knowledge and consent of the said other Collonies. And itt is hereby declared, that itt shall not bee lawfull to or ffor the rest of the Collonies to invade or molest the native Indians,[58] or

57. These kinds of idealistic aspirations to evangelize Natives were common in early English colonial charters (including the one for Massachusetts Bay in 1629). But it feels a bit more surprising here, given Williams's general stance on the evangelization of Natives, and the very little that had been done to that point within Rhode Island.

58. This clause became much more relevant during King Philip's War, although ultimately Rhode Island leaders did allow the United Colonies (a confederation

any other inhabittants, inhabiting within the bounds and lymitts hereafter
mentioned (they having subjected themselves vnto vs. and being by vs taken
into our speciall protection),[59] without the knowledge and consent of the
Governour and Company of our Collony of Rhode-Island and Providence
Plantations . . .

. . . and that itt shall bee lawfull to and for the inhabitants of the sayd
Colony of Providence Plantations, without let or molestation, to passe and
repasse with freedome, into and thorough the rest of the English Collonies,
vpon their lawfull and civill occasions, and to converse, and hold commerce and trade, wit: such of the inhabitants of our other English Collonies
as shall bee willing to admits them thereunto, they behaveing themselves
peaceably among them; any act, clause or sentence, in any of the sayd
Collonies provided, or that shall bee provided, to the contrary in anywise
notwithstanding . . .[60]

Roger Williams to the Town of Warwick, January 1665/1666[61]

*Williams was no longer president of the colony when he wrote this letter, and
while he was an elected assistant at the time, Glenn LaFantasie suggests that
Williams wrote the letter simply as a private individual, not as a representative
of the colony. The Town of Warwick balked at paying its share of the expenses
for John Clarke's lobbying work in London securing a charter for Rhode Island
in 1663.[62] Clarke went into deep personal debt to cover his costs while serving
as the colony's agent in London, but Warwick's representatives were not present in the General Assembly when they voted for £600 in compensation—a
number Warwick found exorbitant—and Warwick's representatives disliked
the centralization of power that this request represented. Gorton's followers
in Warwick even suggested that they might prefer inclusion in Connecticut's*

Massachusetts, Connecticut, Plimouth, and New Haven formed in 1643) to enter
Rhode Island and attack Narragansett towns, especially the fort in the Great Swamp in
December 1675.

59. See the 1644 Narragansett submission to King Charles I earlier in this chapter.
This shows the diplomatic importance of that "submission."

60. The ability to travel freely into other colonies was essential for trade and commerce; as a banished person, Williams would have had special interest in this part of
the charter, perhaps.

61. *Correspondence of Roger Williams*, 2:534–43.

62. Warwick, like the other original towns in the colony, "cherished localism and,
far from parting with it in accord with the charter, insisted that it be further honored by
the central government." James, *Colonial Rhode Island*, 72–74.

charter.[63] *Williams reminds his neighbors that the new charter negotiated by Clarke protects privileges unheard of elsewhere in the world, including liberty of conscience and taxation based on the votes of elected representatives. Scholars have long suggested that by 1663 Rhode Islanders were living in one of the most religiously free places in the western world, but this letter shows Williams himself saying that repeatedly. He compares Warwick's unwillingness to help cover Clarke's costs to people who eat good food and "call for the best wine" at a tavern, and then leave without paying their bill. He also suggests that Warwick's Native American neighbors treat their official representatives far more generously. Despite Williams's dire predictions about what could befall a colony that denied basic compensation to its agents, Warwick did not pay their share until the 1670s. For Warwick's side of the story, see "From the Town of Warwick," February 20, 1665/1666 in* Correspondence of Roger Williams, *2:543–50.*

Providence 1. Jan 1665/6. (so calld)

Beloved Friends and Countrimen

My due respects presented with heartie desires of Your present and eternall prosperitie when this short Life is over. I was resolved to have visited you my selfe this winter and to have perswaded with Argumts of Trust and Love the finishing of the paymts relating to his Maties Royall Graunt and Charter to us. But it pleased God to visit me with old pains and Lamenesses, so that sometimes I have not bene able to rise nor goe to stand.

I pray Your Courteous Leave (therefore) of Saluting You with these few Lines, and Your favorable Attention to them.

On 2 hinges my discourse shall turne: First the Fairnes and Equity of the Matter: 2. The damage and Hazard if not performed.

As to the first: the Fairnes of the Matter, please You to heare 2 or 3 witnesses. The first is Common Honestie and Common Justice in Common dealings between Man and Man. This gives to Every Man his Due, a pennyworth for a peny: and will cry shame upon us that Mr Clarke should be undone Yea destroy'd and ruind (as to this World) for his so great and so long paines, Faythfullnes and Diligence, for wch he ought in Common Justice, to be faithfully satisfied and honbly rewarded, although it should have pleased God to have granted him no Successe, no Charter, no Favour in the Eyes of our Soveraigne Lord the King.

These very Barbarians when they send forth a publike messenger they furnish him out, they defray all paymts, they gratifie him with Rewards, and if he prove lame and sick and not able to returne, they visit him and bring

---

63. James, *Colonial Rhode Island*, 91–92.

him home upon their shoulders (and that many Scores of miles) with all Care and Tendernes.[64]

At the first Rode Iland, but afterward the whole Colony requested, employed, and sent to Mr Clarke a Commission and Credentialls sealed, with wch the King was satisfied, and owned him for our publike Agent. . .

At our Gen Assembly when Mr Clarkes accounts were fairly brought in of what he had recd and what he had borrowed (upon the Mortgage of his howse and Land) to goe through out Worke, the Assembly appointed a Committee of able and judicious men to Examine the accounts: upon whose Report and upon their owne further Examinacion and Consideracion they saw cause to agree upon a Very moderate and Equall Summe to be raised throughout the Colony, to be discharged unto him.

Worthy friends it is Easy to find Cloaks and Coulours for Denyalls or Delais to any Busines We have no mind to. I have visited most of my Neighbours at Providence this winter. Some say they are Sory and ashamed of the Delay and promise to finish it with Speede. Some few say they have done it. Some say they like not Some Words in the Charter. Some say they will pay if all doe. Some are agst all Govrmt and Charters and Corporacions. Some are not so and Yet cry out agst Thieves and Robbers who tale any Thing from them agst their Wills. Some say they will see what became of their former paymts before they will part with any more. Some will see the Charter first because they hear that Col. Cartwright caried the Charter into Engl. with him. Some say let those that sent Mr Clarke into Engl. at first pay him. And some say other things, but none say ought (in my Judgmt) wch answers the witnes of Common Honesty. For the whole Summ and Scope of his Maties Royal graunt and charter to us is to bestow upon us 2 inestimable Jewells.

The first is peace, commonly calld among all men the Kings Peace, among our selves and among all the Kings subjects and Friends in this Countrey and wheresoever. And further at our Agents most seasonable peticion the King prohibites all his Subjects to act any Hostilitie toward our Natives inhabiting with us without our Consent, wch hath hietherto bene otherwise practiced to our Continuall and great grievance and disturbance.

The 2 Jewell is Libertie: the first of our Spirits wch neither Old nor N. Engl knowes the like, nor no part of the World a greater.

2   Libertie of our persons: No Life nor Limbe taken from us: No Corporall punishmt no Restraint, but by knowne Lawes and Agreemts of our owne making.

---

64. As he often did in his correspondence and publications, Williams used Natives as a foil to criticize English practices.

3   Libertie of our Estates Howses Catle, Lands, Goods, and not a peny to be taken by any rate from us, without Every Mans free debate by his Deputies, chosen by himselfe and Sent to the Gen. Assembly.

4   Libertie of Societie or Corporacion: of Sending or being sent to the Gen. Assembly: of choosing and being chosen to all offices, and of making and repealing all Lawes and Constitutions among us.

5   A libertie (wch other Charters have not) to wit of attending to the Laws of Engl. with a favourable mitigacion Viz: not absolutely but respecting our Willdernes Estate and Condicion.

I Confesse it were to be wished that these Dainties might have fallen from God and the King like Showers and Deawes and Manna from Heaven, gratis and free, like a joyfull Harvest or vintage without any paine of our Husbandry. But since the most holy God the first cause hath ordained Second Causes, and Means and Agents and Instrumts: it is not more honest for us to withdraw in this case then for Men to come to an Ordinary and to call for the best wine and Liquors, the best Meats Rost and bak't, the best Attendance etc. and to be able to pay for all and yet most unworthily steale away and not discharge the Reckoning. [. . .]

Shall we say we are Christians Yea but ingenious or just men, to ride Securely (in a troublous Sea and time) by a New Cable and Anckor of Mr Clarks procuring and to be so far adrift to langwish and sinck, with his Back broke for putting under his shoulder to Ease us.

Wch of you (said Christ Jesus to his Enemies) will see an Ox or a sheepe fall into a pit and not pull it out on the Sabbath day? What Beast can labour harder in plowing, drawing or carying then Mr Clark hath done so long a time and with so litle provender? Shall we now when he looks for Rest at night, tumble him (by our Neglects) into a Ditch of Sadnes, Grief Povertie and Ruine? . . .

If we wholy neglect this Busines what will become of our Credits: Will not our stinck reach the nostrills of our Neighbours yea of all the Inhabitants of the World that hear of us?. . . Who will not here after be fearfull to trust us, when like false marchants our Bills shall be protested that all men may take heed how they deale with us?[65]

. . . What a worme and sting of Bitternes will it be to us, to rememb (like Jerusalem in the dayes of Afliction) all our pleasant things? Such peace, such Security, such liberties for Soule and Body as were never enjoyed by an

65. Williams reminds Warwick that colonies need international trade and trade requires maintaining good credit with those outside the colony. Ultimately, credit is built on trust, and he worries that potential trading partners will look unfavorably on a colony that does not even pay its own agents.

English men, nor any in the World that I have heard of? If now for our Un-thanckfullnes, it should please God to turn the Wind, and bring the Wheele over us, and to clap on our Necks those iron Yokes wch so many thouhsands and millions of mens necks are under in all Nations of Mankind. will it not then be as Gall to our minds to Call to mind how free we were . . .

With what Indignation (must we needs imagine) will the King him-selfe Entertaine the Thought of such a people, that shall so undervalue and slight the rich and Extraordinary Favours wch it pleased God to put into his Royall Heart to bestow upon this Colony? . . .

Worthy friends, the changes of the Heavens and the Earth have bene great and sudden and seen and felt by us all this Winter. Let us not Sooth and Sing our Selves asleep with murthering Lullabies. Let us provide for Changes and by timely Humiliation, prevent them. For my selfe, seeing what I see over all N. Engl. I can not but say with David Psal. 119. My flesh trembleth for feare of thee and I am afraid of thy Judgmts.

I remain longing after Your present and Eternall peace.

R.W.

Roger Williams to the Town of Providence, January 15, 1681/1682[66]

The struggle to ensure that towns pay what Williams saw as their fair share continued, so Williams sent the request below to the town of Providence, a letter that one historian described as a "homily on taxes and good citizenship." Williams reminds his fellow Rhode Islanders that all men in the world "Submit to Govrment" and that good government costs money. In number 11 below, Williams indicates that the expenses he incurred while traveling to England to secure the 1644 patent were never fully repaid. In number 13, he reminds the men and women of Providence that their charter was unlike any other in New England in that it allowed freedom of conscience. In number 20, Williams refers to Newton's Comet that appeared in 1680 as a "blazing Herauld from Heaven," and perhaps as a providential warning to pay taxes.

Providence 15 Jan, 1681 (so calld)

Considerations presented, touching Rates.

1   Govrment and Order in Families Towns etc. is the Ordinance of the most High (Rom. 13) for the peace and Good of Mankind.

---

66. *Correspondence of Roger Williams*, 2:774–76.

2　Six things are written in the hearts of all Mankind yea even in Pagans: First that there is a Deitie, 2 that Some Actions are naught 3 that the Deitie will punish 4 that there is another Life 5 that Mariage is [honorable] 6 that Mankind can not keepe together without some Government.

3　There is no English Man in his [Majesty's] Dominions or elsewhere, who is not forced to Submit to Govrment.

4　There is not a Man in the World (except Robbers Pyrates, Rebells) but doth Submit to Govrment.

5　Even Robbers, Pyrates and Rebells themselvs can not hold togeather but by Some Law among themselvs and Govrment.

6　One of these 2 great Lawes in the World must prevaile, either that of Judges and Justices of peace, in Courts of peace: Or the Law of Arms, the Sword and Bloud.

7　If it Come from the Courts of Trialls in Peace, to the Triall of the Sword and Bloud, the Conquerour is forced to Setle Law and Govrment.

8　Till matters come to a Setled Govrment, No man is ordinarily sure of his Howse, Goods Lands Catle Wife Children or Life.

9　Hence is that Ancient Maxime: It is better to live under a Tirant in peace, then Under the Sword, or Where Every man is a Tirant.

10　His [Majesty] sends Governrs to Barbados Virginia etc. but to us he shews greater favour in our Charters, to choose Whom We please[67]

11　No Charters are obtaind without great Suit, Favour or Charges. Our first Cost an hundreth pound (though I never recd it all): Our second about a thousand, Conecticuts above Six thousand.[68]

12　No Govrment is maintaind without Tribute Custome, Rates, Taxes etc.

13　Our Charter Excells all in N. Engl. or the World, as to the Souls of Men.

---

67. It is more likely that the English crown knew that a royal governor would help ensure that proper taxes and duties were returned from the far more profitable plantation colonies of Barbados and Virginia, than those expected from Rhode Island.

68. As he did in the document prior to this one, Williams reminds the town of Providence that charter negotiations are expensive and that neither he nor John Clarke had been reimbursed for their expenses. Connecticut's bill of £6000 seems very high in comparison to Rhode Island's. It is not clear what Williams means by "Favour," but perhaps Connecticut offered extra money on the side to ease charter negotiations.

14 It pleaseth God (Rom. 13) to command Tribute Custome and Conse-
    quently Rates etc. not only for feare, but for Conscience Sake.

15 Our Rates are the least (by far) of any Colony in N. Engl.

16 There is no man that [hath] a vote in Towne or Colony, but he hath a
    hand in making the Rates by himselfe or his Deputies.

17 In our Colony the Gen. Assembly, Govr, Magistrates, Deputies, Towne
    Clerkes, Raters, Constable etc. have done their duties, the failing lies
    upon particular persons.

18 It is but Folly to resist (one or more and if one why not more). God
    hath stirred up the Spirit of the Govr, Magistrates and officers (driven
    to it by necessitie) to be Unanimously resolved to see the Matter fin-
    ished: and it is the dutie of every man to maintayne Encowrage and
    strengthen the hand of Authoritie.

19 Black Clouds (some Yeares) have hung over Old and N. Engl. heads.[69]
    God hath bene wonderfully patient and long suffering to us? But who
    sees not Changes and Calamities hanging over us.

20 All men feare that this blazing Herauld from Heaven denounceth from
    the most High, Wars pestilences, famines.[70] Is it not then our Wise-
    dome to make and keepe peace with God and Men?

Your old unworthy Srvant   R.W.

---

69. Williams, now close to seventy-nine years old, is probably referring to a long list
of calamities, including the Pequot War, the English Civil War, the chaos of the 1640s
and 1650s in his own colony, the fall of Cromwell and the tumultuous period between
the execution of King Charles I in 1641 and the return of the monarchy in 1661 with
King Charles II, among other "black clouds."

70. Alexandra Walsham explores the way people in the seventeenth-century Atlantic World interpreted celestial events, such as comets: Walsham, "Sermons in the Sky."

Chapter 5

Native Relations

Aspirations and Betrayals, 1632–1643

WILLIAMS'S RELATIONSHIPS WITH INDIGENOUS *nations in southern New England are challenging to interpret. Many scholars of Williams have seen him as one of the most sympathetic and engaged English colonists—a clear foil for other English New England residents who did not bother to purchase land or learn Native languages. And Williams himself uses the language of "friend" and "friendship" with regard to Natives, at least in the early years. Yet, a careful and more holistic consideration of Williams's activities in the first decade of his time in New England reveals deep cultural biases, self-interest, and inconsistencies.*

The readings below try to capture some of the range of Williams's aspirations and activities in all of their chaotic and damaging rawness. Yes, he learned Native languages and spent time with Natives in their wetus, learning about their cultures and communities. And he published one of the earliest ethnographies of Narragansett culture and linguistic phrasebook, A Key Into the Language of America *(1643). But* A Key *is saturated with English assumptions and misunderstandings of Narragansett culture, and Williams ultimately leveraged the publication of the book in London for his own political survival and that of his colony. During this time, Williams also attempted to directly influence the outcome of the Pequot War in 1636–1637 by discouraging an alliance between the Pequot and Narragansett. His intention was to redirect any Narragansett support away from the Pequot to English forces because he knew Narragansett involvement in the war could be a deciding factor.*

85

After the war, Williams also supported the enslavement of Natives, requested a Pequot captive for himself, and served as a slave catcher in Providence by sending runaway Pequot back to Boston.

Through this all, Williams managed to cultivate working relationships through trade and diplomacy with Narragansett sachems, who likely saw Williams as a political pawn of sorts that they could use for their own purposes. In this way, both Williams and Narragansett leaders tried to use each other to accomplish their own goals. This intimate familiarity with regional Native individuals, communities, customs, and cultures was an important part of who Williams was in this world. And yet, despite this, he sometimes wrote about them in derogatory terms and continued to do so for the rest of his life. This only reaffirms, in the words of Niantic and Narragansett tribal educator Chrystal Mars Baker, that Williams's "allegiance was to his own people; his true intentions were to help the English, not 'friend' the Natives. He helped them stay and develop this place after their English fashion, rather than encourage the English to learn from the Indigenous and accept their practices of living, especially as it pertains to land 'ownership' and use."[1]

For readers who are used to only hearing a more romanticized view of Williams's relationships with Natives or his views on religious liberty and the separation of church and state, his direct involvement in the very worst and cruelest aspects of settler colonialism can come as a surprise. In this way, despite his lofty ideals, he shows himself to be a man of his times—fully part of an invasive colonial presence and invested in ensuring that the English colonial experiment succeeded at any cost.

Evangelization

Roger Williams to John Winthrop, July–December 1632[2]

This letter contains one of the few instances in which Roger Williams privately communicates his ambitions regarding Native evangelization. The reference is fleeting, but he states that his desire is for "Native soules," which is a clear reference to converting Natives to Christianity. When Williams wrote this letter, he was in Plimouth Colony, where he had frequent contact with Wampanoag and—likely—Narragansett. The rest of the letter is about an entirely different topic, namely, a larger conversation taking place in Boston about the appropriate age of church elders and (in the postscript) whether individuals could serve

---

1. Chrystal Mars Baker, correspondence with the authors, January 24, 2023.

2. This letter is undated, but dating is inferred based on content. LaFantasie, *Correspondence of Roger Williams*, 1:9.

as church elders and civil magistrates at the same time. Williams references Native evangelization in this context seemingly as a way to explain why he will not ever be an elder of a church, namely, that he is focused on attempting to convert Natives instead. But as chapter 8 illustrates, this early optimism about Native evangelization was tempered over time by the vitality of Wampanoag and Narragansett religious and cultural traditions.

Plymmouth:[3]

Much honour'd & beloved in Christ Jesu

Your Christian acceptation of our Cup of Cold water is a blessed Cup of wine, strong & pleasant to our wearied spirits: Only let me crave a word of Explanation: among other pleas for a young Councellour (which I feare will be too light in the ballance of the holy One) you argue from 25 in a church Elder:[4] Tis a riddle as yet to me, whether you meane any Elder in these New English churches, or (which I believe not) old English, disorderly, functions, from whence our Jehovah of armies more & more redeem his Israell,[5] or the Levites who served from 25 to 50: Numb: 8. 24:[6] or my selfe, but a child in every thing (though in Christ, called, & persecuted even in & out of my fathers house these 20 yeares). I am no Elder in any church,[7] no more nor so much as your worthy selfe nor, ever shall be if the Lord please to graunt my desires, that I may intend what I long after, the Natives soules:[8] & yet if I at present were, I should be in the dayes of my Vanitie nearer upwards of 30

3. After arriving in Boston in 1631, Williams briefly spent time in Salem, Massachusetts, before moving to nearby Plimouth Colony. (He later returned to Salem before his exile in 1635/1636.) See chapter 1 for texts regarding this period in Williams's life.

4. Winthrop seems to suggest that church elders should be at least twenty-five years old.

5. Williams here sounds like a committed Separatist, suggesting God was saving more people from out of the English church context.

6. Numbers 8:24: "This is it that belongeth unto the Levites: from twenty and five years old and upward they shall go in to wait upon the service of the tabernacle of the congregation" (KJV).

7. Williams is perhaps being modest, since he turned down a prominent pastoral position at the First Church in Boston upon his arrival in 1631.

8. Williams showed great interest in Native language, religion, and culture shortly after his arrival in New England, but there is not much, if any, evidence that he pushed Natives towards conversion in a typically Protestant Christian sense. Later in life he recalled that he spent time "in their filthy Smoakie holes (even while I lived at Plymmouth and Salem, to gaine their Toung etc.)." See Roger Williams to the Assembly of Commissioners, November 17, 1677?, below.

then 25:⁹ ffor whether Timothie or Titus¹⁰ be in thought, etc. at your leasure I crave interpretation. Sorry I am since Rationalls so much circumround & trouble you that bestiale quid¹¹ (& mine especially) should come neere you: but since the Lord of heaven is Lord of Earth allso & you follow him as a deare child I thanckfully acknowledge your care & love about the cattell & further entreate if you may (as you give me in couragement) procure the whole of that second & Let me know how & how much payment will be here accepted, or in mony in England.¹² The Lord Jesus be with your Spirit & your dearest One (& mine) in their extremities to you both & all the Sts [Saints] our due remembrances

Yours in all unfeyned & brotherly affections.

Roger Williams

The brethren salute you¹³

Sr You lately sent musick to our Eares, when we heard, you perswaded (& that effectually & successfully) our beloved Mr Nowell to surrender up one sword:¹⁴ & that you were preparing to seeke the Lord further: a dutie not so frequent with Plymouth as formerly: but Sperom eliora¹⁵

Pequot War (1636–1637)

Although the 1629 charter of the New England Company stated a desire to "wynn and incite the Natives of Country, to the Knowledg and Obedience of the onlie true God and Savior of Mankinde, and the Christian Fayth," within six years of the founding of Boston the Massachusetts Bay Colony waged a

9. Williams's own vague reference to his age is one of the few clues we have regarding his date of birth. As Glenn LaFantasie has suggested, this places his birthdate sometime between 1603 and 1605.

10. Here Williams means the New Testament books of 1 and 2 Timothy and Titus (all traditionally ascribed to the Apostle Paul).

11. Latin: perhaps "something beastly" or "relating to animals."

12. Williams here shifts the letter from spiritual topics to more earthly things, namely, some cattle that Winthrop apparently had a hand in purchasing for Williams.

13. That is, in Plimouth.

14. Increase Nowell was elected a ruling elder at the First Church in Boston in August 1630; Nowell resigned this church post in 1632 when he was elected to serve as secretary of Massachusetts Bay. Williams here is affirming the view of Winthrop and others that Nowell should not hold both a civil and a church office at the same time. The idea that the church and civil state constitute the "two swords" of God date back to medieval Christianity: the sword of the spirit and the temporal sword. Therefore, for Nowell to "surrender up one sword" was to give up one office. Smyth, *Complete Works of Rev. Thomas Smyth*, 4: 97.

15. Latin: "I hope for better things."

vicious, genocidal war against the Pequot nation. The English justified the war due to two murders—of a Dutch trader and an English trader—in two separate incidents. The Pequot, however, were beginning to resent the increasing presence of the English in their territory, especially with at least four English towns founded nearby in 1635, and may well have wanted to send a message. But nothing could justify the fury of violence of the English against the Pequot in the months that followed. English magistrates became obsessed with completely eradicating the Pequot, even hunting down refugee bands of women and children in Connecticut swamps. The absolute nadir of the war was the Mystic Massacre of May 26, 1637, when in the early morning hours the English and their Native allies murdered between 500 and 700 Pequot, most of whom were children, women, and the elderly. As Narragansett elder Dawn Dove has noted, the Narragansett were distraught by this "unmerciful killing of non-combatants" and left the battlefield in disgust.[16] And yet, the carnage continued. As Massachusetts and Plimouth soldiers systematically hunted down remaining Pequot who had not already fled the area, they gathered up any captives they could take and shipped them to Boston to be sold as slaves, between 200 and 300 total. Many additional Pequot men were systematically executed. In the Hartford Treaty of 1638, the terms stipulated that even the name Pequot could not be used in the future. Fortunately, however, within a few years, even the colonial records used the name Pequot again because some Pequot communities had survived.

Throughout, English colonists leaned on Native allies in their attempts to eradicate the Pequot as a people. Williams, too, had an important role in this war, as he helped persuade the Narragansett to fight with the English against the Pequot (the Narragansett had their own reasons for fighting the Pequot, however). Williams served as a vital conduit of information for the allied Massachusetts Bay and Plimouth forces, and in many ways facilitated the redistribution of Pequot refugees and helped balance the power dynamics in the months that followed. But Williams also profited personally from the war, requesting and receiving an enslaved Pequot boy re-named Will to serve in his household. Despite his prominent role in the war and the enslavement of Pequot captives that followed, Williams's letters are a bit tortured, as someone who materially participated in and benefitted from the attempted genocide of the Pequot and yet was quixotically trying to suggest that the Massachusetts Bay residents should not hold Pequot captives for life. Nonetheless, he stopped short of suggesting that all Pequot should be freed, as his own ongoing enslavement of Will clearly illustrates.

16. Dawn Dove, correspondence with the authors, January 14, 2023.

Roger Williams to John Winthrop, June 30, 1637[17]

This letter is an important window into the treatment of Pequot captives during the Pequot War, as well as the key diplomatic role Williams played throughout the conflict. Despite his appreciation for Native cultures and the Narragansett surrounding Providence, Williams repeatedly shows himself to be especially partisan during times of warfare. As is rather consistent throughout Williams's life, he had conflicted views of Natives. On the one hand, he uses derogatory language typical of English colonists at the time ("miserable drove of Adams degenerate seede"); on the other hand, he consistently recognizes their human-ity ("our brethren by nature"). Similarly, Williams suggests that the remaining Pequot be hunted down and captured, even as he in the same breath counsels mercy and the sparing of women and children. Williams participated in the enslaving of the Pequot captives, even requesting a very specific Pequot boy "with the red about his neck," showing Williams's intimate knowledge of the Pequot captives. This letter also shows the important diplomatic and informa-tional roles Williams played in the region. The Massachusetts Bay Colony may have exiled him, but when it came to war with Natives, Williams largely sided with the English (although he occasionally critiqued the actions of soldiers and leaders of the Massachusetts Bay colony).

New Providence[18] this 6t[h] instantis

Much honoured Sir

It having againe pleased the most High to put into your hands another miserable drove of Adams degenerate seede, and our brethren by nature:[19] I am bold (if I may not offend in it) to request the keeping and bringing up of one of the children.[20] I have fixed mine eye on this litle one with the red about his neck, but I will not be peremptory in my choice but will rest in your loving pleasure for him, or any etc.[21]

17. *Correspondence of Roger Williams*, 1:88–90.

18. That is, Providence, Rhode Island.

19. Williams here represents a rather dour outlook regarding Natives, followed im-mediately with a more optimistic one. This is consistent with Williams's views of Na-tives through most of his life, namely, that he expressed admiration of and appreciation for Natives and their culture while at other times he specifically stated how he believed their practices were "barbarous" and misguided.

20. During the Pequot War, English soldiers took hundreds of Pequot captive. Eng-lish magistrates sold these captive men, women, and children (many of whom were non-combatants) locally in New England as servants and slaves. Additionally, a few dozen were sold into the wider Atlantic slave market.

21. Williams here is requesting a specific Pequot child as his slave, one with an apparent red birthmark on his neck (or possibly some sort of inked marking or tattoo,

Sir Capt. Patrick[22] gives me a hint of the likely returne of most of your forces (Sasacous[23] and about a score of men with him and other companies, 4 score in one, surviving). I shall humbly propound whether it be not considerable, that better now then hereafter the Pursuit be continued.[24]

1st Because it may stop a conglutination betweene them and the Mowhauogs,[25] wch longer time is like to make.

2ndly Longer time will put many opportunities of occasionall revenge into their hand, as we see in the 3 last cut of [off] upon Qunnihticut river, after the fort cut of.[26]

Capt Patrick allso informes me of a great Itch upon the Souldiers to fall fowle upon our neighbours [i.e., the Narragansett]. Litle sparkes prove great fires. The God of Peace, who is only wise be pleased to guide us. Capt Patrick confesseth that they were the chiefe Actors in the last Captives, and had taken all by a wile and slaine 2 before the English came.[27] I heare no speech at present about inaequalitie, but Content and affection toward us.

I much rejoice that (as he sayth) some of the chiefe at Qunnihticut[28] Mr Heynes[29] and Mr Ludlow[30] are almost averse from killing women and children.[31] Mercie outshines all the worckes and Atributes of him who is the

---

or maybe even a scarf). We know from other documents this Pequot boy was given the English name, Will. See also, Zimmermann, "This litle one with the red about his neck."

22. Captain Daniel Patrick, one of the commanders of the Massachusetts Bay troops sent to fight against the Pequot.

23. Sassacus was a Pequot sachem who survived the attacks and fled the region with a company of Native men.

24. Williams here suggests immediately pursuing Sassacus and other remaining Pequot soldiers.

25. The Mohawk were part of the Five Nations (later Six) of the Haudenosaunee (Iroquois) Confederacy and controlled much of the trade and commerce surrounding present-day Albany, New York. The Mohawk were a powerful and large nation that exerted much influence in the region. Williams and others were concerned the Pequot might team up with the Mohawk to fight against the English.

26. Williams warns that to leave Pequot bands roaming around would open up the English to later raids of retaliation.

27. The Massachusetts Bay and Plimouth forces wanted to widen the war and attack the Narragansett, in part because the Narragansett apparently tried to keep approximately one hundred Pequot captives for themselves (which the English soldiers felt they had a right to instead).

28. That is, Connecticut.

29. John Haynes, who served as governor of Connecticut.

30. Roger Ludlow, the deputy governor of Connecticut.

31. After the senseless killing of Pequot women, children, and noncombatants, the Connecticut leaders seemed more willing to spare them, which Williams praises in his indirect way.

Father of mercies: unto whome with earnest supplications for you and yours I rest Your wops [worship's] unfained.

Roger Williams

My best respects to good Mrs Wintrop, Mr Deputie [Thomas Dudley] Mr Bellingham[32] and theirs.

Roger Williams to John Winthrop, July 15, 1637[33]

In this fascinating letter to Massachusetts Governor John Winthrop, Williams continues to process ongoing issues and challenges in the aftermath of the Pequot War. Williams seems especially bothered by the unjust treatment of the Pequot and the hypocrisy of waging a war against them instead of converting them. In the latter part of the letter, Williams guardedly processes some of the events and the consequences of what was perhaps an even bloodier affair than he anticipated. He hints at possible wrongdoing by the English and looks to the Old Testament for parallel examples, in particular the example of the Israelite king Amaziah, who killed the servants who murdered his father, King Josiah, but spared the children of the murderers (2 Kings 14). In the end, Williams was burdened and somewhat chastened, as his statement "God wash away Iniquitie and receave us graceously" indicates. He laments in his postscript that the war makes it seem like the English have forgotten their professed intentions of converting Natives (and have instead killed them).

Williams's letter additionally gives insights into the complicated relationships between local nations, tribes, and bands. A Pequot Native named Wequash turned on his own people to help the English; two Nipmuc bands found themselves fighting each other over how to deal with Pequot refugees; Pequot allies fled west to Mohawk country in what is now New York; and the Narragansett sachems continually tried to maintain control over an incredibly complex and challenging situation (elsewhere they indicated they were shocked by the ruthlessness of the English soldiers). Williams remained indispensable for the colonial leadership in Plimouth and Massachusetts that had officially turned their backs on him.

New Providence this 15th of the 5t[h]

Sir

For the Captives and bootie I never heard any of these Natives question the Acts of the English, only that Native who brought letters to you

32. Presumably Richard Bellingham, a colonial magistrate and lawyer who also periodically served as the governor of Massachusetts Bay.

33. *Correspondence of Roger Williams*, 1:101–3.

from Capt Patrick and was twice at Boston, related so much as I wrote of in my former, at his returne to the Nanhiggonsick viz. that your selfe should (be angry) with the English etc. I met since with him and he sayth (he) had it not from your selfe but an English man at Roxbury. (I) thought good to cleare your name and remoove suspicions from Mr Stoughton etc.[34]

Wequash is alive.[35] So is allso the other like to recover of his wound.[36] I never heard, that Miantunnomu[37] was displeased with Wequash for any service to the English but that Wequash was suspected to deale falsely when he (went) to hunt for the Pequts at the rivers mouth.[38] Tis true there is no feare of God before their eye, and all the Cords that ever bound the Barbarous to Forreiners were made of Selfe and Covetuousnes.[39] Yet if I mistake not I observe in Miantunnomu some sparkes of true Friendship. Could it be deeply imprinted in to him that the English never intended to despoile him of the Countrey I probably Conjecture his friendship would appeare in attending of us with 500 men (in Case) agst any forreigne Enemies.[40]

34. Williams here is referring to a prior letter with Winthrop. Williams seems to be responding to Winthrop's apparent concern that Indigenous peoples felt the English were not justified in their war against the Pequot. Williams assures Winthrop that the Narragansett, at least, were not openly critical, from what he heard. But other sources reveal that the Narragansett were dismayed by the senseless violence against the Pequot at the Mystic Fort Massacre.

35. Wequash was a Pequot captain who was allied with the English. As described in the 1643 pamphlet New England's First Fruits, Wequash joined the English during the war and greatly aided the English in their horrific slaughter of the Pequot at Mystic Village in May 1637. New England's First Fruits held him up as a successful convert to Christianity, and Williams revealed in his introduction to A Key that he had many conversations about religion with Wequash, although he could not be certain of the authenticity of his conversion. New Englands First Fruits, 11–14.

36. Wequash had earlier injured another Pequot, Sosoa, who was also loyal to the English.

37. Miantonomo, a Narragansett sachem.

38. Some English leaders suspected that Wequash was still loyal to the Pequot.

39. Despite his relative respect for Indigenous cultures, Williams often used degrading language regarding Natives in his correspondence with other English officials and friends.

40. After the Pequot War, the Narragansett surely looked to extend and preserve their power against the English. Williams recognized the central role the Narragansett would play in regional power dynamics, and he hoped—for personal and practical reasons—they could be persuaded to be allies of the English. Notably, Williams recognizes that concerns for retaining their lands was at the center of Narragansett concerns.

The Neepmucks[41] are returnd with 3 heads of the Wunnashoatuckoogs.[42] They slue 6, wounded many, and brought home 20 Captives.[43]

Those Inlanders are fled up toward the Mowhauogs.[44] So they say (is) Sasacous.[45] Our friends at Qunnihticut[46] are to cast a jealous eye at that people. They say (unles they are belied) that (they are) to warre with the English etc.

Truly sir to speake my thoughts in your eare freely, I blesse the Lord for your mercifull dealing etc. but feare that some innocent blood cryes at Qunnihticut.[47] Many things may be spoken to prove the Lords perpetuall warr with Amalek[48] extraordinary and misticall: but the 2 Kings 14.5.6. is a bright Light discovering the Ordinary path wherein to walke and pleas him.[49] If the Pequts were Murtherers (though pretending revenge for Sasacous his Fathers Death wch the Dutch affirmed was from Mr Govr) yet not comparable to those treacherous servants that slue their Lord and King Joash K. [King] of Judah, and tipe[50] of Jesus, yet the Fathers only perish in their sinn in the place quoted etc.[51] The blessed Lambe of God wash

41. Nipmuc, a nation in what is now northwestern Connecticut and southern Massachusetts.

42. Also Wunnashowatuckoog, a Nipmuc band in central Massachusetts, south of what is now Worcester, who were accused of sheltering Pequot warriors and refugees. See Hodge, *Handbook of American Indians*, 976.

43. This is a reminder of the complicated nature of Indigenous relations and alliances. The Nipmuc and Narragansett fought with the English against the Pequot and their tributaries (including a band of Nipmuc) in the Pequot War. Here another band of Nipmuc brought in three heads and twenty captives of these Pequot-allied Nipmuc.

44. Mohawk, one of the nations part of the Haudenosaunee Confederacy in what is now New York.

45. Sassacus was a Pequot sachem who Williams reports as having fled west to the Haudenosaunee.

46. Connecticut.

47. This is a stunning admission that the Pequot War was perhaps not so justified, and that war crimes had taken place.

48. The Amalekites, located near the Egyptian border, and the Israelites were constantly at war in the Old Testament.

49. The story Williams refers to in 2 Kgs 14:5–6 is when the Israelite king Amaziah consolidated power and executed those who had murdered his father, King Josiah. Amaziah followed the Mosaic Law, which states that children should not be put to death for the sins of their fathers, by sparing the children of the murderers. Williams seems to hold up this story as an example for Massachusetts Bay regarding the Pequot, especially the children.

50. That is, type. Roger Williams and other puritans had a "typological" approach to the Old Testament, in which certain people were "types" of Jesus or other people or events, prefiguring him or them in some way.

51. Williams rejects an equivalence between the Old Testament murderers of King

away Iniquitie and receave us graceously. Thus with best salutes to your lo. [loving] selfe and yours[,] Mr Deputie [Thomas Dudley] Mr Bellingham and other lo. friends with them and dayly cryes to the Father of Mercies for (you) I rest Your worps [worship's] unfaigned Roger Williams

Postscript

Sir to yours brought by Juanemo[52] on the Lords day I could have litle speech with him: but concerning Miantunnomu I have not heard as yet (of any) unfaythfullnes toward us. I know they bely each other: and I observe our Country men have allmost quite forgotten our great pretences to K. [King] and state and all the world concerning their soules etc. I shall desire to attend with my poore helpe to discover any perfidious dealing: yet shall desire the revenge of it for a common good and peace though my selfe and mine should perish by it. Yet I feare the Lords Quarrell is not ended, for wch the warr began viz. the litle sence (I speake for the generall that I can heare of) of their soules Condicion and our large protestations [i.e., affirmations] that way etc.[53] The general speech is, all must be rooted (out, etc. The) body of the Pequin men yet live, and are only remooved from (their dens) if the good Lord grant that the Mowhaugs[54] and they, and the (whole at) the last unite not. For mine owne pt [part] (I can not be) without suspicions of it.[55]

Sir I thanckfully expect a litle of your (helpe (in a) way of Justice and aequitie) concerning another (unjust debtour of mine, Mr. Ludlow,[56] from whome allso (in mine absence) I have) much (suffered. The good Lord) smile upon you and yours in the face of his annointed. Your wops [worship's] unworthy

R.W.

Josiah and the Pequot, implying that the Pequot survivors are even more deserving of mercy than were the children of King Josiah's assassins.

52. Ninigret.

53. Williams here interprets the Pequot War as sent by God to punish the English colonists for not evangelizing Native Americans. Viewing trials and hardships as a warning or lesson from God was a common interpretive trope among Puritans.

54. The Mohawk.

55. Williams's comments here reveal the post-war prejudice against the Pequot as well as the ongoing fear that they might join with the Mohawk and retaliate.

56. George Ludlow, who owed Roger Williams money from his time in Plimouth. In a prior letter, Williams asked Winthrop for help getting payment from Ludlow, since it was apparently further stressing Williams's own finances to have the debt still outstanding.

Roger Williams to John Winthrop, July 31, 1637[57]

In this brief letter, Williams once again takes up a topic he had addressed in his June 30, 1637, and July 15, 1637, letters to Winthrop (above). The pressing issue continued to be what to do with the Pequot captives taken during the Pequot War. It is evident Williams is trying to find a practical solution based on biblical (Old Testament) principles and yet rooted in a basic humanity. Two aspects of this letter stand out. First, Williams continues to monitor the progress of his request from June 30 that Winthrop send one particular Pequot boy to him in Providence. Williams gives a bit of family information about the boy—who he asks Winthrop to name—and tries to justify keeping a non-combatant Pequot slave by stating that it will be for his own and the public good. Second, Williams once again weighs in on the question of what to do with Pequot captives. Williams moves beyond what English magistrates widely accepted—that adult male Natives in known rebellion deserve death, according to the Old Testament—to state that even non-combatant Pequot deserved "perpetual slaverie" instead. Still, he once again counsels a relatively charitable (by English standards) approach, namely, to let them go after a certain number of years. There is no indication that the last part of his recommendation was adhered to. And Williams also seemingly disregards how monumentally disruptive it was to separate families on a large scale, and how destabilizing the war was in terms of Pequot survival. As Narragansett and Niantic tribal educator Chrystal Mars Baker notes, this is a moment when Williams's hypocrisy and self-interest are on full display, yet again using religion to justify his actions.[58]

New Providence the 2nd of present weeke

    Much honoured Sir

    . . . Sir I here yet not of any of the runnaway Captives at amongst our neighbours.[59] Yesterday I heard that 2 scapt[60] from them to the Pequt. If any be or doe come amongst them I suppose they shall be speedily returned, or I shall certifie where the default is.

    Sir I desire to be truely thanckfull for the Boy intended. His Father was of Sasquaukit[61] where the last fight was: and fought not with the English as

---

57. *Correspondence of Roger Williams*, 1:108–10.

58. Chrystal Mars Baker, correspondence with the authors, January 24, 2023.

59. As English colonists found out, it was difficult to keep Pequot enslaved. Those who could, ran away, often returning to their homelands or joining with other local Native nations. In referencing "our neighbors," Williams is likely speaking of the Narragansett.

60. Escaped.

61. Susquakit was a Pequot town on the edge of the Pequot (Munnacommock) Swamp. It was the site of one of the last major battles of the Pequot War, in July 1637.

his mother (who is with you and 2 children more) certied [certified] me.[62] I shall endeavour his good, and the more common [good], in him. I shall appoint some to fetch him: only I request that you would please to give a name to him.[63]

Sir concerning Captives (pardon my wonted boldnes) the Scripture is full of mysterie, and the Old Testament of Types.[64]

If they have deserved Death, tis Sinn to spare.

If they have not deserved Death, then what punishment? Whether perpetuall slaverie.[65]

I doubt not but the Enemie may lawfully be weakned and despoiled of all comfort of wife and children etc.:[66] but I beseech you well weigh if after a due time of trayning up to labour, and restraint, they ought not to be set free: yet so as without danger of adjoyning to the Enemie.[67] Thus earnestly looking up to heaven for you and all yours I rest your Worps [Worship's] unfaigned

Roger Williams

My best respect to Mrs Wintrop Mr Deputie[68] Mr Bellingham[69] etc.

Naumec et al., "Battle of Pequot (Munnacommock) Swamp."

62. Williams freely admits that no member of this boy's family was fighting against the English. But still, they were scooped up and enslaved, something Williams does not protest. Williams also reveals that Winthrop himself has retained at least three Pequot captives: the boy's mother and two additional children.

63. Most English colonists gave Natives English names, or at least shortened or corrupted Indigenous names, whether enslaved or not. This was partly because Indigenous names were hard to pronounce for the colonists. But in this case it was more ideological—Williams wanted to give his enslaved Indian a fresh start down the road of civilization and evangelization.

64. Most English colonists looked to the Old Testament for justifications of exploration, colonization, and conquest (using the Israelites and their divinely sanctioned taking of the Promised Land).

65. Williams raises "perpetual slaverie" as a justifiable punishment for non-combatants, even as he in the same breath suggests a more charitable approach.

66. This is a candid acknowledgement of the family and personal disruption enslavement caused.

67. New England magistrates worried that if Natives were released, they would simply join with other Native nations and plan revenge against English settlements. Williams acknowledges this, but suggests (rather idealistically) a sustained time among the English would prevent this from happening.

68. Thomas Dudley, the deputy governor of Massachusetts.

69. Richard Bellingham, a Massachusetts magistrate.

Roger Williams to John Winthrop, February 28, 1637/1638[70]

Written in the aftermath of the Pequot War in 1636–1637 (but before the Treaty of Hartford in 1638), in this letter Williams sends a detailed report to Massachusetts Governor John Winthrop on the negotiations and news from Rhode Island and Connecticut. Like many of his letters to Winthrop and other Massachusetts Bay correspondents, Williams imagines himself to be a critical ongoing ally with an ear to the ground in Native country. Williams states that he used his relationships with the Narragansett sachems Canonicus and Miantonomo to keep the Narragansett out of the war with the Pequot (the Pequot were trying to get the Narragansett to join forces against the English, which would have been devastatingly effective). But as Narragansett scholar Mack Scott notes, Williams likely vastly overstated his influence in Narragansett affairs, here and elsewhere.[71] In this letter, Williams reports that Uncas, the Mohegan sachem, is positioning himself as a regional power broker, taking in Pequot families and warriors and shoring up his own power and wealth.

Importantly, however, Williams also weighs in on the fate of the Pequot taken captive by the English during the war. As before, Williams's views are a bit muddled. He counsels mercy for those who were not directly involved in the fighting and killing. But for Williams, mercy means dispersal and servitude among English and non-Pequot Native nations. Williams recommends dividing the Pequot Natives among the English in Massachusetts Bay and Connecticut—presumably as slaves and servants. But, given the requests by the Narragansett and Mohegan sachems, Williams also understands that some Pequot should either be sent to these Nations or that, over time, enslaved Pequot will run away to and seek shelter among other Native nations. Either way, Pequot who are dispersed but not enslaved should be required to pay a tribute. Williams very practically suggests a tribute of wolves' heads, which would also serve to reduce a pesky problem for the colonists.

At the end of the letter, Williams also returns to an early favorite topic of his, namely, the evangelization of Native Americans. Although he sounds rather optimistic in this letter, and although within five years he would publish his remarkable A Key Into the Language of America *(1643), by 1645 he was far less optimistic, as his book* Christenings Make Not Christians *published in that year shows. Scholars have recognized that, despite early professions of desires to convert Natives to Christianity, and despite his relatively high level of linguistic fluency in Narragansett and Wôpanâak, Williams really never claimed any converts and seems to have made far fewer efforts after 1645. This*

---

70 *Correspondence of Roger Williams,* 1:145–149.

71. Mack Scott, correspondence with the authors, January 22, 2023. See also Scott, "From a 'Great Tree' to a New Dawn."

was also partly due to his more general skepticism about the proper apostolic authority for much of anything regarding religion, including forming churches and evangelizing Natives.

Providence 28th of the 12th.[72]

Sir

Some few dayes since I receaved letters from Mr Hooker[73] who had Safely receaved your packet with thancks etc. . . .

Visiting Caunounicus[74] lately recovered from the pits brinck this winter, he asked how Mr Governour[75] and the English did, requesting me to send [for] him 2 words: 1st That he would be thanckfull to Mr Govr for some Sugar (for I had sent him mine owne in the depth of the winter and his sicknes).

2ndly he called for his Sword wch said he Mr Governour did send me by you and others of the English, saying Mr Govr protested he would not put up his Sword, nor would he have us put up ours, till the Pequt[76] were subdued, and yet Sayth he at Monahiganick[77] there are neere 300, who have bound and robd our men (even of the very covering of their Secret parts)[78] as they have past from Qunnticut[79] hether.[80] After much more to this purpose I told him that Mr Govr had promised him to set all in order this Spring.

Sir I understand that Okace the Monahigon[81] hath Sasacous his sister to wife and one of the wives of Sasacous his Father Tattaopame, and thats one reason beside his ambition and neerenes that he hath drawne all the

72. February 28 (1638). February was the last (twelfth) month of the year in the Julian Calendar.

73. Likely Thomas Hooker in Hartford, Connecticut.

74. Canonicus, a Narragansett sachem.

75. That is, John Winthrop, the governor of the Massachusetts Bay Colony.

76. That is, the Pequot, against whom the English, Mohegan, some Nipmuc, and Narragansett fought in 1636–1637.

77. Mohegan, the principal residence of the Mohegan Natives, in southeastern Connecticut.

78. Meaning, they were stripped naked, even of their most basic undergarments.

79. Connecticut.

80. The Narragansett sachem Canonicus seems to be requesting permission to protect and retaliate for some of his men who were being harassed by Pequot refugees at Mohegan.

81. Uncas the Mohegan. Uncas was the sachem of the Mohegan, who had recently split off from the Pequot.

scattered Pequts to himselfe and drawne much wealth from them. More I could trouble you with etc.[82]

Caunounicus and Miantunnomu both desired that there might be a division made of these Surviving Pequots (except the Sachims and murtherers) and let their share be at your owne Wisedomes.[83]

I shall be humbly bold to present mine owne thoughts concerning a division and disposall of them. Since the most high delights in mercy, and great Revenge hath bene allready taken what if (the murtherers being Executed) the rest be divided and dispersed, (according as their numbers shall arise and division be thought fit) to become subject to your selves in the Bay and at Qunnticut[84] wch they will more easily doe in case they may be Suffred to incorporate with the Natives in either places: as also that, as once Edgar the Peaceable did with the Welsh in North Wales, a tribute of wolves heads be imposed on them etc. wch (with Submission) I conceave an incomparable way to Save much Cattell alive in the land.[85]

Sir I hope shortly to send you good newes of great hopes the Lord hath sprung up in mine Eye of many a poore Indian soule enquiring after God. I have convinced hundreths at home and abroad that in point of Religion they are all wandring etc.[86] I find what I could never heare before, that they have plenty of Gods or divine powers: the Sunn, Moone, Fire, Water,

82. Almost a decade prior, Uncas married the sister of the Pequot leader Sassacus. Sassacus was also the daughter of the then Pequot sachem, Tatobam. The marriage illustrates two important realities about Native marriages, namely, that they were often about strengthening kinship ties and alliances between the Native nations (in this case, the Pequot and Mohegan), and secondly, it was common for Native leaders to have multiple wives as a result of such alliance-building.

83. As a reward for their participation in the war against the Pequot, the Narragansett expected—as was common—to receive Pequot captives, who would largely be incorporated into the Narragansett community and be treated virtually as equals. This varied greatly from how the English treated Pequot captives (the English enslaved them to work in their households and on farms).

84. Notably, Williams is not challenging the enslavement of Natives in Massachusetts Bay; he is here suggesting a more equitable distribution between Massachusetts Bay colonists and Mohegan and Narragansett communities.

85. Edgar the Peaceable was a tenth-century king of England who, as Williams noted, demanded the heads of three hundred wolves as an annual tribute. This only lasted for three years, until the king of Wales insisted he could not find enough wolves. Penrose [Mrs. Markham], History of England, 27. Williams's suggestion was practical, given the wolves that repeatedly raided the livestock of colonists. William Wood in his description of New England in 1634 called wolves the "greatest annoyance" because they killed livestock and attacked humans. Wood, New-England's Prospect, 22.

86. Williams believed he had successfully communicated to hundreds of Natives that they were sinners and lost, according to his own English Christianity.

Snow, Earth, the Deere, the Beare etc. are divine powers.[87] I brought home lately from the Nanhiggonsicks the names of 38 of their Gods all they could remember and had I not with feare and caution withdrew they would have fallen to worship O God (as they speake one day in 7). But I hope the time is not long that Some shall truely blesse the God of Heaven that ever they saw the face of English men.[88] So waiting for your pleasure and advice to our neighbours concerning this intended meeting for the establishing of peace through all the bowells of the Countrey and beseeching the most high to vouch safe his Peace and Truth through all your Quarters, with my due respects to Mrs Winthrop, Mr Deputie [Thomas Dudley], Mr Bellingham etc. I rest Your Wops [Worship's] in all true respect and affection

Roger Williams

Sir I heard no more as yet from Charlstowne men coming this way. Mr Coxall and Mr Aspinwall have sent to me about some of these pts [parts], and in case for shelter for their wives and children.

87. Williams elucidates more of what his understanding was of Narragansett cosmology in *A Key Into the Language* (1643), in his chapter on religion.

88. Williams believed that the time was not yet right (in terms of God's authority given) for the conversion of Native Americans.

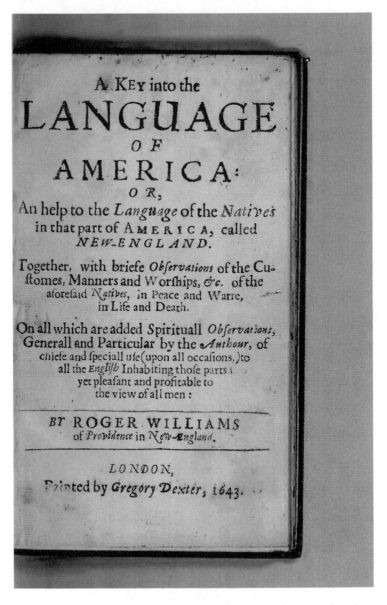

Title page to Roger Williams, *A Key into the Language of America* (London: Gregory Dexter, 1643). Courtesy of John Carter Brown Library.

Native Cultures

Roger Williams, *A Key into the Language of America* (1643)[89]

What follows is a small selection from Williams's first publication, A Key into the Language of America, *often simply referred to as* A Key. *Part Narragansett language phrasebook, part spiritual debate, and part cultural observations (with a sprinkling of poetry as only a puritan could compose), this work meant and continues to mean different things to different readers. Williams believed it was an entry point—or "key"—into many more conversations and topics, and in that he somewhat succeeded. For those interested in a unique, if filtered, view of Narragansett society,* A Key *is a rich source of observations, even if Williams did not always entirely understand what he was seeing and continually presented his own interpretational biases.*

Divided into thirty-two chapters that describe various aspects of Narragansett life, Williams covers elements of everyday life, things like greetings, food, and family, to more complicated topics such as warfare, justice, and of course, spiritual beliefs. Explaining how Williams learned about Narragansett communities also explains his skill in the Narragansett language. By the time Williams published his Key, *he had been in North America for over a decade. During this time, he had spent days, nights, even weeks, in Narragansett and Wampanoag homes and communities speaking with Narragansett and Wampanoag men, women, and children. Today, we might describe his language learning efforts as an "independent immersive language program." It is important to remember, however, that his education was far from over. Another forty years in Narragansett country awaited Williams and if he had published a second edition of* A Key, *he undoubtedly would have made changes.*

There is a larger political context for Williams's Key *as well. Williams published this while he was in London, and he was there for a specific purpose: to secure a charter from royal authorities in order to defend Rhode Island from Massachusetts Bay puritans, who saw Williams's colony as illegitimate. In* A Key, *Williams positioned himself as the greatest linguist in New England, and the one that was best positioned to both serve as a diplomat and to convert Natives to Christianity. These were powerful considerations for officials in London, and in the end, they were part of what allowed Williams to secure his charter. For some contemporary Indigenous readers, these ulterior motives taint the entire project. As Narragansett and Niantic tribal educator Chrystal Mars Baker has noted, "I will never be convinced of his 'friendship' to the Natives.* A Key *is filled with judgment and condemnation and personal opinion as written from his perspective and presented in England to secure something*

---

89. Williams, *Key* in *Complete Writings of Roger Williams,* 1:61–284.

benefitting his 'agenda.'"[90] *Even so,* A Key *stands as an important, even if faulty, publication, a rare look at Indigenous cultures through the eyes of a somewhat sympathetic—even if self-serving—English colonist. What comes through are echoes of conversations, debates, and questions that continue to help readers hear other voices from early America. In 2019, the Tomaquag Museum published an edition of* A Key *that combines linguistic expertise with Indigenous cultural knowledge and insights. While our annotations below draw from these insights at times, we would point readers to that edition in its entirety, since it contains an important modern-day perspective from a variety of Narragansett knowledge keepers, educators, and elders.*[91]

To my Deare and Wellbeloved Friends and Countreymen in old and new ENGLAND.

I Present you with a Key; I have not heard of the like, yet framed, since it pleased God to bring that mighty Continent of America to light:[92] Others of my Countreymen have often, and excellently, and lately written of the Countrey (and none that I know beyond the goodnesse and worth of it.)

This Key, respects the Native Language of it, and happily may unlocke some Rarities concerning the Natives themselves, not yet discovered.[93]

I drew the Materialls in a rude lumpe at Sea,[94] as a private helpe to my owne memory, that I might not by my present absence lightly lose what I had so dearely bought in some few yeares hardship, and charges among the Barbarians; yet being reminded by some, what pitie it were to bury those Materialls in my Grave at land or Sea; and withall, remembering how oft I have been importun'd by worthy friends, of all sorts, to afford them some helps this way.

I resolved (by the assistance of the most High) to cast those Materialls into this Key, pleasant and profitable for All, but specially for my friends residing in those parts:[95]

90. Chrystal Mars Baker, correspondence with the authors, January 24, 2023.

91. Spears et al., *Key Into the Language of America: The Tomaquag Museum Edition.*

92. Meaning, since Europeans became aware of the Americas in 1492.

93. Williams vastly simplifies the linguistic complexity of Indigenous languages in the Americas. He may have oversimplified things to a London audience, but as he later admits a few paragraphs later, within a few hundred miles, in New England alone, Native languages differed enough to be almost incomprehensible.

94. Williams suggests he wrote most of *Key* while sailing to London in 1643, from the Dutch city of New Amsterdam (after 1664 renamed New York), which is notable because he was not permitted to travel to Boston after his banishment.

95. Williams imagined *Key* to be used by colonists in New England, which may in fact have been the case, given that the actual book itself is quite small, presumably meant to be tucked into a coat pocket.

A little Key may open a Box, where lies a bunch of Keyes

With this I have entred into the secrets of those Countries, where ever English dwel about two hundred miles, betweene the French and Dutch Plantations; for want of this, I know what grosse mis-takes my selfe and others have run into.[96]

There is a mixture of this Language North and South, from the place of my abode, about six hundred miles; yet within the two hundred miles (aforementioned) their Dialects doe exceedingly differ; yet not so, but (within that compasse) a man may, by this helpe, converse with thousands of Natives all over the Countrey: and by such converse it may please the Father of Mercies to spread civilitie, (and in his owne most holy season) Christianitie; for one Candle will light ten thousand, and it may please God to blesse a little Leaven to season the mightie Lump of those Peoples and Territories.[97]

It is expected, that having had so much converse with these Natives, I should write some litle of them.

Concerning them (a little to gratifie expectation) I shall touch upon foure Heads:

First, by what Names they are distinguished.

Secondly, Their Originall and Descent.

Thirdly, their Religion, Manners, Customes, &c.

Fourthly, That great Point of their Conversion.

To the first, their Names are of two sorts: First, those of the English giving: as Natives, Salvages, Indians, Wild-men, (so the Dutch call them Wilden) Abergeny men, Pagans, Barbarians, Heathen.

Secondly, their Names, which they give themselves.

I cannot observe, that they ever had (before the comming of the English, French or Dutch amongst them) any Names to difference themselves from strangers, for they knew none; but two sorts of names they had, and have amongst themselves.

---

96. The Dutch had established colonies in what is now Connecticut and New York in the 1610s and 1620s, and the French had done the same farther to the north along the St. Lawrence River in what is now Canada. English colonization nestled between these two other European colonies, as well as among vast and numerous Indigenous nations.

97. Williams again likely overstates the utility of the Narragansett language for adequately conversing with a large number of Natives in the region. But his reason is clear: he is trying to convince a London audience that he has the ability through his linguistic knowledge to "civilize" and evangelize Natives in New England. In the wake of the Pequot War (1636–1637) in New England, and other conflicts with Natives elsewhere (as in Virginia in 1622), this was an especially pressing concern for officials in London.

First, generall, belonging to all Natives, as Nínnuock, Ninnimissinnû-wock, Eniskeetompaûwog, which signifies Men, Folke, or People.

Secondly, particular names, peculiar to severall Nations, of them amongst themselves, as, Nanhigganêuck, Massachusêuck, Cawasumsêuck, Cowwesêuck, Quintikóock, Qunnipiêuck, Pequttóog, &c.[98]

They have often asked mee, why wee call them Indians Natives, &c. And understanding the reason, they will call themselues Indians, in opposition to English, &c.[99]

For the second Head proposed, their Originall and Descent.

From Adam and Noah that they spring, it is granted on all hands.[100]

But for their later Descent, and whence they came into those pars, it seemes as hard to finde, as to finde the wellhead of some fresh Streame, which running many miles out of the Countrey to the salt Ocean, hath met with many mixing Streames by the way. They say themselves, that they have sprung and growne up in that very place, like the very trees of the wildernesse.[101]

They say that their Great God Cawtántowwit created those parts, as I observed in the Chapter of their Religion. They have no Clothes, Bookes, nor Letters, and conceive their Fathers never had;[102] and therefore they are easily perswaded that the God that made English men is a greater God,

98. That is, Narragansett, Massachusett, Cawsumsett, Connecticut, [*Quintikóock*], Quinnipiac, and Pequot. The Cawsumsett were likely Pokanoket or Wampanoag who lived in what is now Warren, Rhode Island, whose principal town was Sowams. We cannot be certain which nation Williams was referring to with the term "Quintikóock." Williams, *Key*, in *Complete Writings of Roger Williams*, 1:22n6–10.

99. This is a fascinating commentary on how English lumped all Natives together in ways that defied Indigenous notions of self-identity. Natives use—then and now—specific tribal designations, and desire non-Natives to do the same.

100. In this short statement, Roger Williams makes an important point: English men and women generally were not questioning the basic shared humanity of Indians. Indians and English alike were descended from Adam and Noah, just like the rest of the human race. In later centuries, European and American racism led them to consider Africans and Indians as separate races, and perhaps even created separately (and not coming from Adam). Some Indian leaders believed this, too, over time, and promoted it as a way to keep Indians separate from the negative influences of European religion and culture. See, for example, the Nativist movements from the mid-eighteenth century through the early nineteenth century as just one manifestation of this.

101. This continues to be an important corrective to non-Indian theories of where they came from and how they arrived in their lands. Natives almost universally have origin stories in which they were placed or created on their own lands.

102. European conceptions of what it meant to be properly clothed differ from our own contemporary sensibilities. Natives did have clothes, of course—skins, hides, and other items for various seasons, along with moccasins. Williams is once again painting a starker picture for his London readers than what he knew to be true.

because Hee hath so richly endowed the English above themselves:[103] But when they heare that about sixteen hundred yeeres agoe, England and the inhabitants thereof were like unto themselves, and since have received from God, Clothes, Bookes, &c. they are greatly affected with a secret hope concerning themselves.

Wise and Judicious men, with whom I have discoursed, maintaine their Originall to be Northward from Tartaria: and at my now taking ship, at the Dutch Plantation,[104] it pleased the Dutch Governour, (in some discourse with mee about the Natives), to draw their Line from Iceland, because the name Sackmakan (the name for an Indian Prince, about the Dutch) is the name for a Prince in Iceland.

Other opinions I could number up: under favour I shall present (not mine opinion, but) my Observations to the judgement of the Wise.

First, others (and my selfe) have conceived some of their words to hold affinitie with the Hebrew.[105]

Secondly, they constantly annoint their heads as the Jewes did.

Thirdy, they give Dowries for their wives, as the Jewes did.

Fourthly (and which I have not so observed amongst other Nations as amongst the Jewes, and these:) they constantly seperate their Women (during the time of their monthly sicknesse) in a little house alone by themselves foure or five dayes, and hold it an Irreligious thing for either Father or Husband or any Male to come neere them.

They have often asked me if it bee so with women of other Nations, and whether they are so separated: and for their practice they plead Nature and Tradition. Yet againe I have found a greater Affinity of their Language with the Greek Tongue.[106]

103. As Williams surely knew, many Natives did not see themselves as inferior to Europeans with regard to religion or culture, but this was a common trope in the early contact literature of the time that served Europeans' sense of their own self-superiority.

104. That is, New Netherland, in what later became New York Colony in 1664. Williams was still banned from Massachusetts Bay, so he had to leave for London from New Amsterdam (New York City).

105. Some English theologians and linguists (including the missionary John Eliot) believed they had found similarities between Indigenous languages in New England and the Hebrew language of the Old Testament/Hebrew Bible. In fact, some writers believed that Native peoples more generally came from the so-called ten lost tribes of Israel from the eighth century BCE. Williams's analysis suggests several observed points of supposed similarities between New England First Nations and biblical Israelites, such as anointing the head, giving dowries for their wives, and separating the women during their monthly period (something required by the Levitical Code in the Old Testament).

106. Williams also found some similarities between the Narragansett language and the Greek language, although he does not give any concrete examples.

2. As the Greekes and other Nations, and our selves call the seven Starres (or Charles Waine the Beare,) so doe they Mosk or Paukunnawaw the Beare.[107]

3. They have many strange Relations of one Wétucks, a man that wrought great Miracles amongst them, and walking upon the waters, &c. with some kind of broken Resemblance to the Sonne of God.[108]

Lastly, it is famous that the Sowwest (Sowaniu) is the great Subject of their discourse. From thence their Traditions. There they say (at the South-west) is the Court of their great God Cautántouwit: At the South-west are their Forefathers soules: to the South-west they goe themselves when they dye; From the South-west came their Corne, and Beanes out of their Great God Cautántowwits field: And indeed the further Northward and Westward from us their Corne will not grow, but to the Southward better and better. I dare not conjecture in these Vncertainties, I believe they are lost, and yet hope (in the Lords holy season) some of the wildest of them shall be found to share in the blood of the Son of God.

To the third Head, concerning their Religion, Customes, Manners &c. I shall here say nothing, because in those 32. Chapters of the whole Book, I have briefly touched those of all sorts, from their Birth to their Burialls, and have endeavoured (as the Nature of the worke would give way) to bring some short Observations and Applications home to Europe from America.

Therefore fourthly, to that great Point of their Conversion so much to bee longed for, and by all New-English so much pretended, and I hope in Truth.

For my selfe I have uprightly laboured to suite my endeavours to my pretences: and of later times (out of desire to attaine their Language) I have run through varieties of Intercourses with them Day and Night, Summer and Winter, by Land and Sea, particular passages tending to this, I have related divers, in the Chapter of their Religion.

Many solemne discourses I have had with all sorts of Nations of them, from one end of the Countrey to another (so farre as opportunity, and the little Language I have could reach.)[109]

Your unworthy Country-man
R O G E R W I L L I A M S.

Directions for the use of the LANGUAGE.

107. The Big Dipper, or Ursa Major (Latin for "Greater Bear").

108. Williams is here suggesting that the Narragansett traditions relating to Wetucks have some echoes of the Christian stories of Jesus in the New Testament.

109. This is a good reminder that Williams's knowledge is drawn from multiple New England Native nations.

1. A Dictionary or Grammer way I had consideration of, but purposely avoided, as not so accommodate to the Benefit of all, as I hope this Forme is.

2. A Dialogue also I had thoughts of, but avoided for brevities sake, and yet (with no small paines) I have so framed every Chapter and the matter of it, as I may call it am Implicite Dialogue.

3. It is framed chiefly after the Narrogánset Dialect, because most spoken in the Countrey, and yet (with attending to the variation of peoples and Dialects) it will be of great use in all parts of the Countrey.

4. Whatever your occasion bee either of Travell, Discourse, Trading &c. turne to the Table which will direct you to the Proper Chapter.

5. Because the Life of all Language is in the Pronuntiation, I have been at the paines and charges to Cause the Accents, Tones or sounds to be affixed, (which some understand, acoording to the Greeke Language, Acutes, Graves, Circumflexes) for example, in the second leafe in the word Ewò He: the sound or Tone must not be put on E, but wò where the grave Accent is.

In the same leafe, in the word Ascowequássin, the sound must not be on any of the Syllables, but on quáss, where the Acute or sharp sound is.

In the same leafe in the word Anspaumpmaûntam, the sound must not be on any other syllable but Maûn, where the Circumflex or long sounding Accent is.

6. The English for every Indian word or phrase stands in a straight line directly against the Indian: yet sometimes there are two words for the same thing (for their Language is exceeding copious, and they have five or six words sometimes for one thing) and then the English stands against them both: for example in the second leafe,

Cowáunckamish &	*I pray your Favour.*
Cuckquénamish.	

CHAP. I. Of Salutation.

Observation.

The Natives are of two sorts, (as the English are.) Some more Rude and clownish, who are not so apt to Salute, but upon Salutation resalute[110] lovingly. Others, and the generall, are sober and grave, and yet chearfull in a meane, and as ready to begin a Salutation as to Resalute, which yet the English generally begin, out of desire to Civilize them.

What cheare Nétop? is the general salutation of all English toward them, Nétop is friend.

---

110. Meaning to return salutations or greetings.

| Netompaûog | *Friends.* |

They are exceedingly delighted with Salutations in their own Language.

| Neèn, Keèn, Ewò, | *I, you, he.* |
| Keén ka neen | *You and I.* |

| Asco wequássin, | *Good morrow.* |
| Asco wequassunnúmmis | |

Askuttaaquompsìn?	*Hou doe you?*
Asnpaumpmaûntam	*I am very well.*
Taubot paumpmaúntaman	*I am glad you are well.*

. . .

Tawhich neepouweéyean,	*Why stand you?*
Pucqúatchick?	*Without dores.*
Tawhítch mat petiteáyean?	*Why come you not in?*

Observ. In this respect they are remarkably free and courteous, to invite all strangers in; and if any come to them upon any occasion, they request them to come in, if they come not in of themselves.[111]

Awássish	*Warme you.*
Máttapsh yóteg	*Sit by the fire.*
Tocketúnnawem	*What say you?*
Keén nétop?	*Is it you friend.*
Peeyàush nétop,	*Come hither friend.*
Pétitees.	*Come in.*

. . .

Observ. I have acknowledged amongst them an heart sensible of kindnesses, and have reaped kindnesse against from many, seaven years after, when I my selfe had forgotten, &c hence the Lord Jesus exhorts his followers to doe good for evill: for otherwise, sinners will do good for good, kindnesse for kindnesse, &c.[112]

111. Note Williams's repeated portrayal of Narragansett hospitality, both in the phrases and observations, that define this opening section. First-hand experience taught Williams that Narragansett communities and their neighbors put a premium on being gracious hosts.

112. This exchange of kindness, or favors, was part of the wider cultural practice that anthropologists today would describe as "gifting." In a gifting economy, relationships

Cowàmmaunsh	*I love you.*[113]
Cowammaûnuck	*He loves you.*
Cowámmaus	*You are loving.*
Cowáutam?	*Understand you?*
Nowaûtam	*I understand.*
Cowâwtam tawhitche nippeeyaûmen,	*Doe you know why I come.*
Cowannantam?	*Have you forgotten?*
Awanagusantowosh	*Speake English.*[114]
Eenàntowash	*Speake Indian.*
Cutehanshishaùmo	*How many were you in Company?*
Kúnnishishem?	*Are you alone?*
Nníshishem	*I am alone.*
. . .	
Kukkowêtous	*I will lodge with you.*
Yò Cówish	*Do lodge here.*
Hawúnshech	*Farewell.*
Chénock wonck cup peeyeâumen?	*When will you be here againe?*
Nétop tattà	*My friend I cannot tell.*

From these courteous Salutations Observe in general: There is a favour of civility and courtesie even amongst these wild Americans, both amongst themselves and towards strangers.

---

between leaders relied on the practice of giving gifts, that is, the exchange of gifts or services between parties. A leader gave a gift with the expectation of an eventual return of a gift or favor from the recipient. This exchange and expectation of future reciprocity had the expressed goal of building and maintaining a relationship between parties. A gift today was an investment in the future of the relationship.

113. Williams often presented phrases in a logical order so a reader could, theoretically, follow the back and forth of a natural conversation. Other exchanges, like this one, suggest the vast unspoken subtexts—such as cultural norms, political agendas, and recent events—that shaped these conversations.

114. Even in these early chapters, Williams includes the negotiation English and Narragansett speakers might use to decide which language would be used during encounters.

Mortar and pestle with Flint maize.
Courtesy of Tomaquag Museum Collections.

Chap. II. Of Eating and Entertainment.

Ascúmetesímmis?	*Have you not yet eaten?*
Matta niccattuppúmmin,	*I am not hungry.*
Niccàwkatone,	*I am thirstie.*
Mannippêno?	*Have you no water?*
Nip, or nipéwese	*Give me some water.*
Namitch, commetesímmin,	*Stay, you must eat first.*
. . .	
Necáwni mèich teàqua.	*First eat something.*
Tawhitch mat me chóan.	*Why eat you not?*
Wussaúme kusópita.	*It is too hot.*
Teâguunnumméitch	*What shall I eate?*
. . .	

Whomsoever commeth in when they are eating, they offer them to eat of that which they have, though but little enough prepar'd for themselves. If any provision of fish or flesh[115] come in, they make their neighbours partakers with them.

If any stranger come in, they presently give him to eate of what they have; many a time, and at all times of the night (as I have fallen in travell upon their houses) when nothing hath been ready, have themselves and their wives, risen to prepare me some refreshing.

The observation general from their eating, &c.

It is a strange truth that a man shall generally finde more free entertainment and refreshing amongst these Barbarians, then amongst thousands that call themselves Christians.[116]

More particular:[117]

1. Course bread and water's most their fare;
O Englands diet fine;
Thy cup runs ore with plenteous store
Of wholesome beare and wine.

2. Sometimes God gives them Fish or Flesh,
Yet they're content without;
And what comes in, they part to friends
and strangers round about.

3. God's providence is rich to his,
Let none distrustfull be;
In wildernesse, in great distresse,
These Ravens[118] have fed me.

115. Meat.

116. While Williams writes in general terms, he is clearly criticizing his New England puritan peers. After Massachusetts Bay officials expelled him from the colony, Wampanoag and Narragansett communities offered resources and refuge.

117. Williams ended each chapter with a poem that he composed to pick up on themes from the chapter. This poem carries over the theme of Narragansett hospitality from the first chapter.

118. Williams's choice of a raven to represent Native peoples here hints at his cultural knowledge. While he may have chosen this bird due to English associations, it is more likely that Williams knew it played a prominent role in Narragansett creation stories.

Wetu built by Redwing, at the original Tomaquag Museum in Tomaquag Valley, Ashaway, Rhode Island, ca. 1960. Courtesy of the Tomaquag Museum Archives.

Chap. III. Concerning Sleep and Lodging.

Nsowwushkâwmen	*I am weary.*
Nkàtaquaum.	*I am sleepie.*
Kukkovetoùs.	*Shall I lodge here?*
Yo nickowémen?	*Shall I sleepe here?*
Kukkowéti.	*Will you sleepe here?*
Wunnégin, cówish.	*Welcome, sleepe here.*
Nummouaquômen.	*I will lodge abroad.*
Puckquátchick nickouêmen.	*I will sleepe without the doores,*

Which I have known them contentedly doe, by a fire under a tree, when sometimes some English have (for want of familiaritie and language, with them) been fearefull to entertaine them.[119]

In Summer-time I have knowne them lye abroad often themselves, to make roome for strangers, English, or others.

Mouaquómitea,	*Let us lye abroad.*
Cowwêtuck,	*Let us Sleepe.*
Kukkóuene?	*Sleepe you?*
Cowwêke,	*Sleepe, sleepe.*
Cowwêwi,	*He is asleepe.*
Cowwêwock,	*They sleepe.*
Askukkówene?	*Sleepe you yet?*
Takitíppocat,	*It is a cold night.*
Wekitíppocat,	*It is a warme night.*
Wauwháutaw ánawat, and Wawhautowâvog,	*There is an alarme, or, there is a great shouting:*

Howling and shouting is their Alarme; they having no Drums nor Trumpets: but whether an enemie approach, or fire breake out, this Alarme passeth from house to house; yea, commonly, if any English or Dutch come amongst them, they give notice of Strangers by this signe; yet I have knowne them buy and use a Dutch Trumpet, and knowne a Native make a good Drum in imitation of the English.

Mattannauke, or	*A fine sorte of mats*
Mattannoukanash,	*to Sleep on.*
Maskítuash,	*Straw to ly on.*
Wuddtúckqunash, ponamáuta,	*Let us lay on wood.*

This they doe plentifully when they lie down to sleep winter and summer, abundance they have and abundance they lay on: their Fire is instead of our bedcloaths. And so, themselves and any that have occasion to lodge

119. The Narragansett practice of expecting, and often welcoming, visitors into their homes became an ongoing source of tension when English families, including leaders, proved less inclined to return the courtesy. Given that Williams's trading business and political career depended on his on-going relationship with local Narragansett, it is not surprising that his letters mention various occasions where he and his family hosted individuals and even large groups of Narragansett and Wampanoag visitors.

with them, must be content to turne often to the Fire if the night be cold, and they who first wake must repaire the Fire.[120]

Mauataúnamoke	*Mend the fire.*
Mauataunamútta,	*Let us mend the fire.*
Tokêtuck,	*Let us wake.*
As kuttokémis	*Are you not awake yet*
Tókish Tókeke	*Wake wake.*
Tókinish,	*Wake him.*
Kitumyái tokéan,	*As soone as I wake.*
Ntunnaquômen	*I have had a good dream.*
Nummattaquômen	*I have had a bad dream.*

When they have had a bad Dreame, which they conceive to be a threatening from God, they fall to prayer at all times of the night,[121] especially early before day: So David's zealous heart to the true and living God: At midnight will I rise &c. I prevented the dawning of the day, &c. Psal. 119, &c.

CHAP. XXI. Of Religion, the soule, &c.

Manìtmanittówock.	God, Gods.

Obs.[122] He that questions whether God made the World, the Indians will teach him.[123] I must acknowledge I have received in my converse with them many Confirmations of those two great points, Heb. 11. 6. viz:

1. That God is.
2. That hee is a rewarder of all them that diligently seek him.[124]

120. Williams's early visits with Narragansett and Wampanoag communities often included intimate surroundings. He is most likely describing these nightly routines based on his own experiences. While it is tempting to picture him sleeping separately in his own accommodations, he would have shared the common area in a wetu (the Narragansett word for their homes) for sleeping. A wetu, depending on its size, could accommodate a single or multiple families.

121. While sleeping in a wetu, Williams would have slept close to, even next to, someone. More than once he was probably awakened by other sleepers who were singing or "praying" themselves back to sleep during the night.

122. An abbreviation for "observation," here and throughout.

123. Throughout *Key*, Williams uses Native Americans (generically) to critique English Christians, as he does here. But there is an important reality here that some other colonists overlooked, namely, that the Narragansett and other southern New England Natives did have religious ideas and practices, as this section of *Key* intends to illustrate.

124. Hebrews 11:6, from the Christian Bible, likely from the authorized King James

They will generally confesse that God made all: but then in speciall, although they deny not that English-mans God made English Men, and the Heavens and Earth there! yet their Gods made them and the Heaven, and Earth where they dwell.[125]

| Nummusquaunamúckqun manìt. | God is angry with me?[126] |

Obs. I have heard a poore Indian lamenting the losse of a child at break of day, call up his Wife and children, and all about him to Lamentation, and with abundance of teares cry out! O God thou hast taken away my child! thou art angry with me: O turne thine anger from me, and spare the rest of my children.

If they receive any good in hunting, fishing, Harvest &c. they acknowledge God in it.[127]

Yea, if it be but an ordinary accident, a fall, &c. they will say God was angry and did it, musquàntum manìt God is angry. But herein is their Misery.[128]

First they branch their God-head into many Gods.[129]

Secondly, attribute it to Creatures.[130]

First, many Gods: they have given me the Names of thirty seven which I have, all which in their solemne Worships they invoke: as

version (1611), which Williams's quotation most closely follows (strangely, perhaps, since puritans often preferred the Geneva version). Williams here continues themes from the introduction to *Key* regarding the inherent religiosity of Native Americans and, by implication, the possibility of converting them to Protestant Christianity.

125. It is fascinating to see Williams's Native interlocutors articulating a theory of separate creations, since scholars usually associate it more with later Nativist movements in the eighteenth century.

126. Trying to understand the loss of a child is a universal human quandary, although it is hard to know how much Williams is reading his own puritan perspective into these mourning rituals and verbalizations.

127. Williams rightly notes the close relationship with and orientation of thankfulness toward the natural and animal world.

128. In the early seventeenth century, "misery" could refer to one's abject position. This is, of course, Williams's perspective, not Native people's perspective of themselves.

129. See the discussion of this section in the Tomaquag Museum's edition of *A Key*. It is likely Williams, while recognizing the central and singular role Kautantowwit played in Narragansett cosmology, misinterpreted various powers and spirits as "deities." Spears, *Key into the Language of America: The Tomaquag Museum Edition*, 109–10.

130. As Williams shows below, by "creatures" he does not (at least primarily) mean animals, but rather celestial and earthly bodies and forces.

Kautántowwìt the great South-West God, to to whose House all soules goe, and from whom came their Corne, Beanes, as they say.

Wompanand	*The Easterne God.*
Chekesuwànd.	*The Westerne God.*
Wunnanaméanit.	*The Northerne God.*
Sowwanànd.	*The Southerne God.*
Wetuómanit.	*The house God.*

. . .

Squáuanit.	*The Womans God.*
Muckquachuckquànd.	*The Childrens God,*

. . .

Secondly, as they have many of these fained Deities[131]: so worship they the Creatures in whom they conceive doth rest some Deitie:

Keesuckquànd.	*The Sun God.*
Nanepaûshat.	*The Moone God.*
Paumpágussit.	*The Sea.*
Yotáanit.	*The Fire God,*

Supposing that Deities be in these, &c.

When I have argued with them[132] about their Fire-God: can it say they be, but this fire must be a God, or Divine power, that out of a stone will arise in a Sparke, and when a poore naked Indian is ready to starve with cold in the House, and especially in the Woods, often saves his life, doth dresse all our Food for us, and if it be angry will burne the House about us, yea if a spark fall into the drie wood, burnes up the Country, (though this burning of the Wood to them they count a benefit, both for destroying of vermin, and keeping downe the Weeds and thickets?)[133]

131. Language like "fained Deities" reminds us that Williams sees Native Americans through his western Christian bias.

132. Williams reveals himself to be more evangelistic than he comes across in other sections.

133. New England Natives routinely burned out the underbrush of sections of forests in a controlled way for the benefits that Williams mentioned, in addition to making

Prasentem narrat quaelibet herba Deum.[134]

Every little Grasse doth tell,

The sons of Men, there God doth dwell.

Besides there is a generall Custome amongst them, at the apprehen-sion of any Excellency in Men, Women, Birds Beasts, Fish, &c. to cry out Manittóo, that is, it is a God, as thus if they see one man excell others in Wisdome, Valour, strength, Activity &c. they cry out Manittóo A God: and therefore when they talke amongst themselves of the English ships, and great buildings, of the plowing of their Fields, and especially of Bookes and Letters, they will end thus: Manittôwock They are Gods: Cummanitiôo, you are a God, &c[135] A strong Conviction naturall: in the soule of man, that God is; filling all things, and places, and that all Excellencies dwell in God, and proceed from him, and that they only are blessed who have that Jehovah their portion.[136]

| Nickómmo. | A Feast or Dance.[137] |

Of this Feast they have publike, and private and that of two sorts.

First in sicknesse, or Drouth, or Warre or Famine.

Secondly,

After Harvest, after hunting, when they enjoy a caulme of Peace, Health, Plenty, Prosperity, then Nickómmo a Feast, especially in Winter, for then (as the Turke saith of the Christian, rather the Antichristian,[138]) they run mad once a yeare in their kind of Christmas[139] feasting.

---

it easier to hunt deer and small game.

134. Latin for "Every plant tells about God."

135. Here, Williams is drawing upon a dubious trope in which Europeans believed that Indigenous peoples saw them as gods due to their supposedly superior technology and firepower.

136. This is a reflection of a common Christian articulation (with a reformed/Cal-vinistic slant) of natural theology, namely, that a basic understanding of God is possible from the natural world alone.

137. Feasts, dances, and other kinds of community ceremonies were important mo-ments in communal life. Williams mentions two main reasons for gathering, but other sources reveal a greater diversity. In particular, a Nikommo was a community feast of thanksgiving, one that continues among the Narragansett to this day. Spears, *Key into the Language of America: The Tomaquag Museum Edition*, 110n5.

138. This is Williams's subtle but sharp critique against usual European Christians, whom he sees rather as "anti-Christian."

139. Native Americans did not observe Christmas, of course. Williams is making the interesting analogy as an outsider to a religion, like Muslims or Christians.

Powwáw.	*A Priest.*
Powwaûog	*Priests.*

Obs. These doe begin and order their service, and Invocation of their Gods, and all the people follow, and joyne interchangeably in a laborious bodily service, unto sweatings,[140] especially of the Priest, who spends himselfe in strange Antick Gestures, and Actions even unto fainting.

. . .

They have an exact forme of King, Priest, and Prophet,[141] as was in Israel typicall of old in that holy Land of Canaan, and as the Lord Jesus ordained in his spirituall Land of Canaan his Church throughout the whole World: their Kings or Governours called Sachimaüog, Kings, and Atauskowaûg Rulers doe govern: Their Priests, performe and manage their Worship: Their wise men and old men of which number the Priests are also, whom they call Taupowaüog they make solemn speeches and Orations, or Lectures to them concerning Religion, Peace, or Warre and all things.

. . .

They have a modest Religious perswasion not to disturb any man, either themselves English, Dutch, or any in their Conscience, and worship,[142] and therefore say:

Aquiewopwaúwash.	*Peace, hold your peace.*
Aquiewopwaúwock.	
Peeyaúntam.	*He is at Prayer.*
Peeyaúntamwock.	*They are praying.*
Cowwéwonck.	*The Soule,*

Derived from Coweene to sleep, because say they, it workes and operates when the body sleepes. Mìchachunck the soule, in a higher notion

140. Although Williams here is likely speaking of a ritual performance that causes the leader to break into a sweat, Natives also sweated ritually, in a sweat lodge made specifically for this purpose.

141. Williams here resonates with many English puritan theologians in finding Hebrew/Old Testament parallels between the ancient Israelites and Native Americans. He was clearly imposing his own biblical framework on Native leadership structures, which naturally had their own logic quite apart from the Christian Bible or Israelite history.

142. Williams, who himself was against coercion in terms of individual belief and practice, clearly identifies with a different but parallel practice among the Narragansett and Wampanoag. As the present-day Narragansett commentators rightfully note in their edition of *Key*, Williams did not always extend this respect to Narragansett beliefs and practices. Spears, *Key into the Language of America: The Tomaquag Museum Edition*, 112n9.

which is of affinity, with a word signifying a looking glasse, or cleere re-semblance, so that it hath its name from a cleere sight or discerning, which indeed seemes very well to suit with the nature of it.

Wuhóck.	*The Body.*
Nohòck: cohòck.	*My body, your body.*
Awaunkeesitteoúwicohòck:	*Who made you?*
Tunna-awwa com-mítchichunck-kitonckquèan?	*Whether goes your soul when you die?*
An. Sowánakitaúwaw.	*It goes to the South-West.*

Obs. They believe that the soules of Men and Women goe to the Sou-west, their great and good men and Women to Cautàntouwit his House, where they have hopes (as the Turkes have of carnall Joyes[143]): Murtherers thieves and Lyers, their Soules (say they) wander restlesse abroad.

. . .

Nétop Kunnatótemous.	*Friend, I will aske you a Question.*
Natótema:	*Speake on.*
Tocketunnântum?	*What thinke you?*
Awaun Keesiteoûwin Kéesuck?	*Who made the Heavens?*[144]
Aûke Wechêkom?	*The Earth, the Sea?*
Míttauke.	*The World.*

. . .

Besides, they will say, Wee never heard of this before:[145] and then will re-late how they have it from their Fathers, that Kautántowwit made one man and

143. This seems like an unfair comparison, as nothing in Native cosmology sug-gests that virgins are waiting for them in Cautantawit's house (as Williams implies by mentioning "carnal Joyes" and Muslims). Instead, Narragansett oral tradition refers to the southwest as a "Happy Hunting Grounds" where "all will be as it was once before." Spears, *Key into the Language of America: The Tomaquag Museum Edition*, 113n16.

144. Williams is giving a small window into his evangelistic conversations with Narragansett and Wampanoag individuals.

145. In an omitted section, Williams relays the story of creation as described in Gen 1–3, in abbreviated form.

woman of a stone, which disliking, he broke them in pieces, and made another man and woman of a Tree, which were the Fountaines of all mankind.[146]

. . .

Obs. After I had (as farre as my language would reach[147]) discoursed (upon a time) before the chiefe Sachim or Prince of the Countery, with his Archpriests, and many other in a full Assembly; and being night, wearied with travell; travell and discourse, I lay downe to rest; and before I slept, I heard this passage:

A Qunníhticut Indian (who had heard our discourse) told the Sachim Miantunnōmu, that soules went up to Heaven, or downe to Hell; For, saith he, Our fathers have told us, that our soules goe to the Southwest.

The Sachim answered, But how doe you know your selfe, that your soules goe to the Southwest; did you ever see a soule goe thither?

The Native replyed; when did he (naming myselfe) see a soule goe to Heaven or Hell?

The Sachim againe replied: He hath books and writings, and one which God himselfe made, concerning mens soules, and therefore may well know more than wee that have none, but take all upon trust from our forefathers.

. . .

CHAP. XXII. Of their Government and Justice

| Sâchim-maûog. | King, Kings.[148] |
| Sachimaûonck, | A Kingdome or Monarchie.[149] |

Obs. Their Government is Monarchicall, yet at present the chiefest government in the Counrey is divided betweene a younger Sachim,

146. This is a reference to Native creation stories, which parallel the Christian Genesis creation account, although Europeans never saw Native origin stories on the same level.

147. This is a fascinating (and rare) admission of linguistic limitations on the part of Williams, especially when it comes to the evangelization of Natives (which is one of the main framings of *Key*). In other places, he implies that he has the ability to converse theologically at a high level.

148. The identification by Europeans of Native sachems and leaders as "kings" is common, although not accurate. As Niantic and Narragansett educator Chrystal Mars Baker notes, "This is the common practice of defining Native ways using English thought/likeness/interpretation. This is what has been done by Roger Williams and others and continues to be done today. We were sovereign nations with systems which may not ever be known." Chrystal Mars Baker, correspondence with the authors, January 24, 2023.

149. Williams is here imposing on the Narragansett a political structure that felt familiar to him, namely, a monarchy, which was not accurate. The Narragansett in particular had a head sachem with sub sachems that functioned in much more democratic modes. Spears, *Key into the Language of America: The Tomaquag Museum Edition*, 119n2.

Miantunnômu, and an elder Sachim Caunoúnicus, of about foure score yeeres old this young mans Uncle; and their agreement in the Government is remarkable:

The old Sachim will not be offended at what the young Sachim doth; and the young Sachim will not doe what hee conceives will displease his Uncle.

Saunks.	*The Queen, or Sachims Wife.*
Sauncksquûaog.[150]	*Queenes.*
Otán,-nash.	*The towne, townes.*
Otânick.	*To the towne.*
Sachimmaacómmock	*A Princes house,* which

according to their condition, is farre different from the other house, both in capacity or receit; and also the finenesse[151] and quality of their Mats.[152]

Ataúskawaw-wáuog.	*Lord, Lords.*
Wauôntam.	*A Wise man or Counsellour.*
Wauóntakick.	*Wise men.*
Enátch or eàtch Keèn anawáyean.	*Your will shall be law.*
Enàtch neèn ánowa.	*Let my word stand.*
Ntínnume.	*He is my man.*
Ntacquêtunck ewò.	*He is my subject.*
Kuttáckquêtous.	*I will subject to you.*[153]

Obs. Beside their generall subjection to the highest Sachims, to whom they carry presents: They have also particular Protectors, under Sachims,

150. Often rendered as sunksquaw.

151. Fineness.

152. Southern New England Algonquian wetus were made of bent saplings covered with bark. Handwoven mats often lined the floor and walls and could be used for other decorative purposes.

153. The language of subjection here is likely in reference to tributary relationships, in which subordinated, smaller tribes, paid tribute in the form of material goods to the dominant tribe. This tribute is the "presents" Williams references in the next paragraph.

to whom they also carry presents, and upon any injury received, and complaint made, these Protectors will revenge it.[154]

Ntannôtam.	*I will revenge it.*
Kuttannótous.	*I will revenge you.*
Miâwene.	*A Court or meeting.*
Wèpe cummiâwene.	*Come to the meeting.*
Miawêtuck.	*Let us meet.*
Wauwháutowash.	*Call us a meeting.*
Miawêmucks.	*At a meeting.*
Miawéhettit.	*When they meet.*

Obs. The Sachims, although they have an absolute Monarchie over the people;[155] yet they will not conclude of ought that concernes all, either Lawes, or Subsides, or warres, unto which the people are averse, and by gentle perswasion cannot be brought.

. . .

Obs. I could never discerne that excesse of scandalous sins amongst them, which Europe aboundeth with. Drunkennesse and gluttony, generally they know not what sinnes they be; and although they have not so much to restraine them (both in respect of knowledge of God and Lawes of men) as the English have, yet a man shall never heare of such crimes amongst them of robberies, murthers, adulteries, &c. as amongst the English: I conceive that the glorious Sunne of so much truth as shines in England, hardens our English hearts; for what the Sunne softeneth not, it hardens.[156]

Tawhìtch yò enêan?	*Why doe you so?*
Tawhìtch cummootóan?	*Why doe you steale?*

154. Protection was the primary benefit of a tributary relationship.

155. This was likely an overstatement of the power of the sachem; although he held real power, counselors and even tribal elders, including women, held great sway.

156. Williams is here presenting a fairly idealized depiction of Native communities (as his translations immediately following reveal), but for a purpose: to critique English Christianity. Natives know less about God and sin, Williams is saying, and yet they sin less in all areas than the supposedly Christian English. However, it is surely true, as the Narragansett commentators of the Tomaquag edition note, that Europeans brought with them alcohol and other negative influences that adversely impacted Native communities. Spears, *Key into the Language of America: The Tomaquag Museum Edition*, 121n17.

Tawhìtch nanompaniêan?	*Why are you thus idle or base?*
Wewhepapúnnoke.	*Bind him.*
Wèpe kunnishaûmis.	*You kild him.*
Wèpe kukkemineantín.	*You are the murtherer.*
Sasaumitaúwhitch.	*Let him be whipt.*
Upponckquittáúwhitch.	*Let him be imprisoned.*[157]
Níppitch ewò.	*Let him die.*
Níphéttitch.	*Let them die.*
Nìss-Nìssòke.	*Kill him.*
Púm-púmmoke.	*Shoot him.*

Obs. The most usuall Custome amongst them in executing punishments, is for the Sachim either to beat, or whip, or put to death with his owne hand, to which the common sort most quietly submit: though sometimes the Sachim sends a secret Executioner, one of his chiefest Warriours to fetch of a head, by some sudden unexpected blow of a Hatchet, when they have feared Mutiny by publike execution.

Kukkeechequaûbenitch.	*You shall be hanged.*[158]
Níppansínnea.	*I am innocent.*
Uppansìnea-ewo.	*He is innocent.*
Matmeshnowaûwon.	*I knew nothing of it.*
Nnowaûntum.	*I am sorry.*
Nummachiemè.	*I have done ill.*
Aumaúnemoke.	*Let it passe, or take away this accusation.*
Konkeeteatch Ewó.	*Let him live.*
Konkeeteáhetti	*Let them live.*

157. There is no evidence that the Narragansett had anything like English prisons.
158. Once again, Williams is here reflecting English practices more than Native ones.

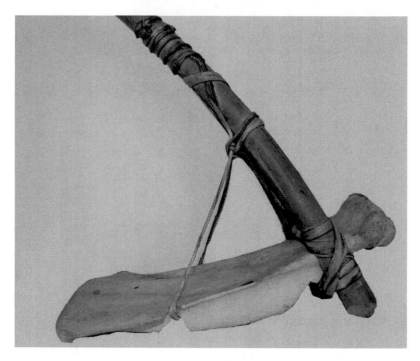

Deer Shoulder Blade Hoe. Courtesy of Tomaquag Museum Collections.

Roger Williams to an Assembly of Commissioners, c. November 17, 1677[159]

This letter is an example of how historians find valuable sources in many, even unexpected, places. While Williams wrote this letter near the end of his life, he is reflecting on his experiences much earlier in life. On the one hand, this account has the benefit of hindsight. On the other hand, given that he is defending himself in a Rhode Island court, it is evident that Williams is casting himself and his actions in the best light possible. Though clearly it contains its biases, there are still valuable insights into Williams's earlier life and activities in Narragansett Country.

In his letter to a special commission in Providence, Williams countered charges levied at him by William Harris, a colonist who had left Salem and followed Williams to Narragansett Bay in 1639. These old acquaintances were in a heated dispute about the boundaries of Pawtuxet, an area of land just south of Providence, and neither party was backing down. In addition to

159. *Correspondence of Roger Williams,* 2:749–54.

lobbing degrading terms at Williams, Harris accused him of using Providence land sales to profit off his English neighbors. Williams quickly fired back and, in defending himself, offered a rare glimpse into the early activities that made his language skills and consequent relationship with Native leaders possible.

Williams's rebuttal to Harris also provides another view into Narragansett culture and how that culture shaped early Narragansett land arrangements with colonists. Williams emphasized that his entrance into Narragansett Bay was not the result of one monetary exchange but rather a series of gift exchanges with Narragansett, exchanges that preceded his arrival and continued well after his relocation. Central to Native diplomacy, including Williams's own relationships with neighboring sachems, was the practice of giving gifts (or gifting). As Williams was at pains to explain to the court and his critics, the value in gifting derived partly from the gift itself, but equally importantly, also from the belief that exchanging gifts built ongoing relationships. Williams was adamant that gifting made the English entrance into Narragansett Bay possible and that, as he financed these gifts, they came at his expense.

[Providence]

To the much honrd Assembly of Commissioners, and also the Inquest or Jury, sent From the respective Colonies to Providence etc. 9br [November] 1677 (so called)

The answere of Roger Williams apart to the Declaration of W. Harris against the Towne of Providence, in what particularly by name the said W. H. falsely and simply accuseth the said Roger Williams.

First he [William Harris] chargeth R. Williams for taking the lands of Providence in his owne name which should have bene taken in the names of those that came up with him. 2 He sold the Land of Providence for more then it Cost him . . .

It is no new thing for me to beare all sorts of Reproaches Slanders etc. from W. Har. about Fortie Years together.

His language of me (and all that displease him) hath bene a Foole an Asse, a simple Dunce, a knave, a lyar a Thiefe, a cheater an hyocrite [hypocrite], a Drunckard, a Traitour, a whore monger with Indian Women etc.[160] To all which I can humble appeale to the Father of Spirits that through his infinite Mercy I have now many Years (above three score) abhord the Appearances and occasions of any of these Evills and am not such a foole to think much to be cald with the Prince of Life Christ Jesus Deceaver, Mad man, Drunckard, Glutton, Blaspheamer Traitour etc. . . . .

160. Harris was alone in accusing Williams of being a "drunckard" or having sexual relations with any Native woman, let alone multiple women.

For first it is not true that I was imployed by any, made Covenant with any, was supplied by any, or desired any to come with me into these parts. My Soules desire was to doe the Natives good, and to that End to learne their Langwage (which I afterward printed) and therefore desired not to be troubled with English Company. Yet out of Pity I gave leave to W. Harris then Poor and destitute to Come along in my Company. . . . I promised W. Har. land and others if it Pleased God to vouchsafe it me. But God furnished my selfe with, or by advantages wch W. Har. nor Scarce any in N. Engl. Had.

1st A Constant Zealous desire to dive into the Natives language.

2 God was pleased to give me a Painfull, Patient spirit to lodge with them in their filthy Smoakie holes (even whiles I lived at Plymmouth and Salem,) to gaine their Toung etc.

3 I spared no Cost toward them and in Gifts to Ousamaquin Yea and all his, and to Cawnounicus and [his?] tokens and Presents etc. many years before I came in person to the Nahiganset; and therefore when I came I was welcome: to Ousamaquin and that old Prince Canounicus who was most shie of all English to his last breath.[161]

4 I was knowne to all the Wompanoogs and the Nagisosiks [Narragansett] to be a publike speaker and at Plymmouth and Salem and therefore with them held as a Sachim.[162] 5 I could debate with them (in a great Measure) in their owne Language. 6 I had the favour and Countenance of that noble Soule Mr Winthrop[163] who all Indians respected. 7 I mortgaged my howse and Land at Salem (worth some hundreths) for Supplies to goe through [etc.?] and therefore was it a simple busines for me to put in any with my Selfe. All that came with me and afterwards were not ingaged, but Came and went at pleasure but I was forced to goe through and Stay by it. . . .

As to that and simple charge that I bought Cheap and Sold deare W. Harris can not be ignorant that Caunownicus whom he calls (in the Declaration) the Conquerour of all these parts: He was not I say to be stird with mony to sell his land to let in Foreignrs. Tis true he recd presents and Gratuities many of me: but it was not thouhsands nor ten thoughsands of mony could have bought of him an English Entrance into this Bay. Thouhsands

---

161. Ousamequin, also known as Massasoit, was the well-known Pokanoket sachem who began conducting diplomacy with the English of Plimouth shortly after their arrival. Canonicus was a powerful Narragansett sachem. By the time Williams wrote this letter, both leaders had died.

162. Indigenous society valued public speaking and expected their leaders to be skilled orators.

163. That is, John Winthrop the elder, the Massachusetts Bay governor, who had died in 1649.

Could not have bought of him Providence or Pawtuxit or Aquedenick or any other Land I had of him.

I made him and his Youngest brother's Son Miantunnomu[164] gifts of 2 Sorts: First formr Presents from Plymmouth and Salem. 2 I was here their Councellour and Secretary in all their Wars with Pequts Monhiggins Long Ilanders Wompanoogse. They had my person my shallop and Pinnace and hired servant at etc. Command on all occasions, transporting 50 at a time, and lodging 50 at a time at my howse. I never denyed them ought [i.e., aught] [lawfully?] they desired of me. Caunounicus laid me out Ground for a trading howse at Nahigonset with his owne hand but he never traded with me, but had freely what he desird Goods Mony etc. so that tis simple to imagine that many hundrets excused me to the last of that mans breath whom (dying) sent for me and desired to be buried in my cloth of Free gift and so he was. My trading howse which yielded me 100 li profit per annum God knowes that for the publike Peace sake I left and lost it above 20 year since when I went last for England.[165] ...

So Will not the Judge of the World be a Terror to you in the day of your Trial but be a Bosome of Consolation to your souls for which earnestly cries to Heaven Your most unworthy Servant

R.Williams

Postscr: Sirs If there be any Difference between W. Harris and me, I humbly offer to End it by Arbitracion wch I humbly conceave also will be the only Medecine for this long and multiplied Disease now before you: and best answer his Maties [Majesty's] and all Desires in this Busines.[166] By this meanes the Countrey will be inhabited and with Joy and Speed.

164. An influential Narragansett sachem and cousin of Canonicus.

165. In approximately 1639, Williams opened a trading house at Cocumscussoc, located about twenty miles due south of Providence on the water. Williams later sold it to his trading partner, Richard Smith, in 1651.

166. In the end, Williams lived out the remainder of his life in Providence while the Pawtuxet matter, in a manner of speaking, proved the death of Harris. In the winter of 1679–1680, Harris, determined to make his case before King Charles II himself, sailed for England. Enroute, Barbary pirates captured the ship and took the passengers, including Harris, to Algiers as prisoners. After a year, Harris's family was finally able to arrange his ransom. A weakened Harris made it to England but died three days later.

Chapter 6

Navigating Native Politics and Relationships, 1648–1669

NATIVE POLITICS, THAT IS, *the range of activities and beliefs that Indigenous communities engaged to govern at home and away, played a significant role in Roger Williams's life. They shaped his travel, compelling him to journey to different communities to act as a translator or interpreter. They impacted his finances because his presence in political activities required giving gifts to and hosting numerous Indigenous leaders. Just as Narragansett sachems hosted Williams by housing him and feeding him on visits, Williams's political activities also required his family to marshal their time and resources to host visiting tribal leaders and their parties at his home. For both parties, these activities were never "one and done" affairs but rather a series of ongoing conversations and visits that stretched over the course of his lifetime. The finances of this arrangement were such that Williams supported himself and his family from profits derived from trading, yet what benefits Narragansett leaders and their communities received at times could prove more elusive. As Narragansett scholar Mack Scott asks, did Narragansett communities experience the same financial benefit that Williams and his family enjoyed from Narragansett contributions?[1] It is a question worth asking.*

Centuries later, Williams's letters remain valuable, despite his biases, because they offer insights into Native politics at the time. Even if he only grasped one part of the complexity of each situation, he still gives readers a sense of how dynamic and far-reaching inter- and intratribal politics were in practice. While Williams was not the only Englishmen providing this intelligence

---

1. Mack Scott, correspondence with the authors, January 22, 2023.

during the century, he was an important one owing to his language skills, the working relationships he cultivated in Indian Country, and his own position of leadership in the Rhode Island colony. His insights, in turn, provide a sobering reminder. Sometimes English colonists (political leaders, religious leaders, civic leaders) were operating with incomplete and grossly distorted views of explosive situations. Yet there were other times that they had an understanding of Native politics and chose to use this knowledge to exploit and even exacerbate divisions within Native communities to advance English aims.

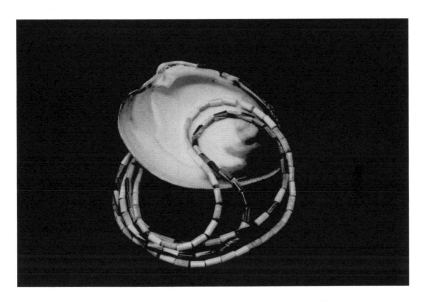

Quahaug and contemporary Wampumpeage beads.
Courtesy of Tomaquag Museum Collections.

Roger Williams to John Winthrop Jr., October 10, 1648[2]

In this letter, Williams describes an important meeting between himself, a delegation sent by the United Colonies from Boston, and Narragansett sachems. (The United Colonies was a confederation of Massachusetts Bay, Connecticut, New Haven, and Plimouth formed in 1643.) This gathering took place at Williams's trading post in Cocumscussoc, rather than Boston (Boston officials often required Native leaders to travel to them). His letter is a glimpse into the complicated intertribal politics he sifted through on a regular basis. Of note are the number of Native places, people, and communities he refers to by name.

2. *Correspondence of Roger Williams,* 1:250–52.

This is not a letter of stereotypes or generalized references; rather, the details he includes, such as names and family connections which the Native speakers themselves probably provided, introduce readers to a rich Indigenous world.

In this instance, Williams and the other English authorities were investigating whether Narragansett sachems had ordered the assassination of Uncas, a neighboring Mohegan sachem. The Narragansett had spent almost a decade trying to hold Uncas ("Onkas") accountable for his role in the execution of a powerful Narragansett sachem named Miantonomo in 1643. Their efforts continued into 1648 because colonial authorities from Massachusetts Bay and Connecticut colonies had spent that entire time working against Narragansett efforts. Williams, and indeed most of the Englishmen present, were nervous that the Narragansett had finally made arrangements to counter this English obstruction of justice by bringing Mohawk warriors (men with a fierce reputation from what is now New York) to help the Narragansett in their struggles with the Mohegan. Even as Williams looked for answers, his letter shows his knowledge of the issues at hand. In particular, it is interesting to note where and how Williams gathered his information.

Deserving an explanation for modern readers is Williams's references to "peag" or sometimes "fath." "Peag" was short for for wampumpeag, or wampum, and its importance at the time for both Narragansett and English communities cannot be overstated. As Aquinnah Wampanoag Artist Elizabeth Perry explains, "Wampum is a traditional and contemporary coastal Algonquian artform from the longer Wampanoag term wampumpeak—meaning 'shell beads.' Carved from thick, slow-growing ocean bivalves called the quahog, striking purple and white contrasts afford the ability to sculpt abstract geometrics and animal effigy forms and beads in a variety of sizes."[3] Together, craftsmen and women from many First Nations in the Northeast strung them together into belts, headbands, necklaces, or other adornments. While the beads themselves are beautiful, they were spiritually significant as well and, because of that, were central items of exchange in Native diplomacy well before the arrival of the English. The English and Dutch, in turn, commodified wampum and began using it in New England as a form of currency, going as far as to standardize units of fathoms (hence references to "fath") to measure it.

Caucaumqussick 10.8.48 (so called)

Sir,

Best salutacions to Your deare selves and loving sister. In my last I intimated a promise of presenting You with what here passeth. Capt. Atherton,

---

3. Elizabeth James Perry, "About Wampum," https://elizabethjamesperry.com/pages/about-wampum.

Capt. Hugh Prichard, Rich. Wood and Strong Furnell[4] have bene with me (as allso Wm Arnold instead of his Sonn Benedict,[5] who withdrew him selfe though sent unto) these 6 or 7 dayes. They are at Nayantaquit[6] 2 nights. Capt. Atherton purposed to visit you, but they appointing their meeting with all the Sachims at my howse they came back,[7] and this morning (the 4th day of the weeke) they are departed with good content toward the [Massachusetts] Bay. From the Commissioners they brought severall Articles but the Maine were 3: 1. Concerning the Mauguawogs[8] etc. 2. The Payment. 3. Onkas,[9] his future safetie.

To the first they Sent answer, (and that they confirmed with many Asseverations[10] that and one of them voluntarily tooke the English mans God to witness) that they gave not a peny to hire the Mauquawogs agst the Monhiggins,[11] but that it was wholy wrought by Wussooankquassin[12] (which they discovered as a Secret) who being bound by Onkas: and Wuttouwuttaunum Onkas his cozen having attempted to shoote a Mauquaw Sachim at that time, resolved with the Mauquawogs (to whome he also gave peag) to take revenge upon Onkas. Wussoonkquassin sent them word and desired Peag of them in the Spring but they professe they consented not nor sent not a peny. Afterwards they sent Waupinhommin up to enquire to Paucomtuckqut and however they have given some of the Mauauawogs Peag this Yeare (as they have allwayes done) Yet they say they are cleare from giving a peny to hire etc. They confesse their Enmitie against Onkas, and they (to the 2.) will not rest until they have finished their payments that they may presente their complaints agst Onkas, who (they say) and others Indians within these 3 yeare have Committed 13 Murthers impune

4. A delegation sent by the commissioners of the United Colonies.

5. Benedict Arnold, future governor of Rhode Island, spoke Algonquian languages and acted as a translator for English authorities on a number of occasions.

6. Niantic, a Native nation related to the Narragansett, southwest of Narragansett.

7. Sachems and other Indigenous leaders learned to be wary when meeting with English envoys after a number of tense and even violent encounters over the years. In this case, the Narragansett sachem Pessicus initially removed himself to Aquidneck Island before finally returning to attend this meeting.

8. Williams is most likely referring to the Mohawk, the easternmost nation of the Haudenosaunee or the Iroquois Confederacy, located on the Mohawk River just west of modern-day Albany.

9. The Mohegan sachem, also identified as Uncas.

10. Meaning to solemnly affirm or positively declare.

11. That is Mohegan, the community led by Uncas.

12. Or Sequassen, a sachem within the Wangunk communities, located in present-day central Connecticut.

being out of their reach in the English protection.[13] This last yeare they pleaded they were neer starved and therefore sent but a small quantity.[14] Now they promise upon return of their men from hunting this winter to make a Contribution, the next spring another and so according as they can draw the people to it will not cease to finish, and if they die their children shall fulfill and that it is their sore griefe etc. with much to this purpose. For Onkas they professe neither directly nor indirectly to have to doe with him, yet hope the English will not deale partially [i.e. favorably] with him. They desired the English receipt of their Peag. I produced the note You sent me, which because it was not signed with Your Fathers hand or the Treasurers etc. the Messengers promised to send them one from the Bay.

Nenekunat[15] made great Lamentation that you had entertained hard thoughts of him in this busines, and all the Sachims here profest their Sorrow and that you had hearkened to Wequashcuck,[16] who they say never contributed nor joined in the Pequt wars, and now flatters to draw his neck out of the Paymts to the English. They hope you will not Countenance him to rob Nenekunat of those hunting places which the Commissioners gave him leave to make use of and he with the English had fought for with the Expence of much treasure and hazard of his life. They desire that he may and Causasenamon[17] and the rest of the Pequots be as Your Litle dogs but not as Your Confederates, which they say is unworthy Your selfe etc. Sir I perceive the English about the Bay enquire after new places. Capt Atherton prayes me shortly to convey a letter to you.

I forgot one passage that the Sachims discovered that Wussoonckquassin gave peag to the Mauquawogs to retreat. It seems they are (Switzer like) mercenarie,[18] and were hired on and off. These Sachims I believe desire Cordially to hould friendship with both the English and the Mauquawogs

13. Meaning, unnamed English authorities were protecting Native men (from unidentified tribal communities) that the Narragansett had accused of murder and were preventing the Narragansett from bringing these men to justice.

14. Food stores were depleted in the region for both Indigenous and English communities for related reasons. An overtrading of corn to the English had shrunk Narragansett corn stores. Meanwhile, the English were, ironically, relying heavily on Narragansett trading because English farmers were exporting so much of their corn for profit to the West Indies.

15. Also Ninigret, an increasingly powerful sachem to the Niantic community.

16. Also spelled Wequashcook, an Eastern Niantic sachem.

17. Also Cassacinamon, a sachem who led a Pequot community that neighbored Uncas' Mohegan community, Ninigret's Niantic community, and John Winthrop Jr.'s New London community. Ninigret made clear in his words to Williams that he did not see Cassacinamon as his equal.

18. Comparing them to Swiss mercenary or for-hire soldiers.

togeather. I am confident (whether they lye or not about Wussoonckquassin) that they never intended hurt against the English, nor your selfe and
yours especially to home they professe great respect and jointly they desire
that Wequashcuck may come back to Quawnecontaukit from whence he
went for if he joyne with Onkas they suspect he will secretly be a means
of some of their Death. Lastly wheras they heard that the women with you
were something fearfull, Nenekunat prayes Mrs Winthrop to be assured
that there never was nor never shall be to his knowledge the least offence
given to her or her neighbours by any of his (though he hath learnt it partly
by your just abhorring of Onkas his outragious carriage among you and of
which I have not softly told these messengers and the admired partialitie in
the Case.) For a token of his fidelitie to Mrs Winthrop, Nenekunat he prayes
me to write that all the women of his towne shall present Mrs Winthrop
with a present of Corne[19] at Pawcatuck if she please to send in any Convey-
ance to Pawcatuck for it. Sir to gratifie them I am thus bold with you and
desiring Your eternal peace I rest your worships unworthy

Roger Williams

Sir I formerly writ to you and now still crave your helpe with Wequashcuck who keeps basely frome me for 5 or 6 coats and I can neither get peag
nor cloth.[20]

Roger Williams to John Winthrop Jr., c. mid-November 1648[21]

*By the late 1640s, Rhode Island was a small collection of four towns—Provi-
dence, Warwick, Newport, and Portsmouth—with a total population of no
more than a thousand colonists. The neighboring Narragansett, however,
numbered some eight thousand by conservative estimates, but as Narragansett
scholar Mack Scott urges, the number was likely between ten and twenty thousand. Williams and the nascent colony he represented needed, at the very least,
a working relationship with Narragansett sachems if the small and struggling
towns were to survive. The Narragansett sachems, however, assumed more
from Williams. As Scott emphasizes, they would have expected an even more
intimate relationship with him that would include assistance on a regular
basis. This assistance included a range of actions but this letter highlights his*

19. Within local Indigenous communities, corn was a special gift, something one
gave to family and friends, not strangers.

20. Sachems valued English coats for the status they conveyed and often wore them
during diplomatic meetings as material reminders to their English audience of their
past assistance or status.

21. *Correspondence of Roger Williams*, 1:258–60.

language skills in the form of interpreting and translating services. Sometimes that was interpreting for other English authorities as he had the month before, or in this instance by conveying Ninigret's words with a letter.[22]

In this case, the Niantic and Narragansett sachem Ninigret (Nenekunat) visited Williams because he wanted him to write two letters on his behalf. One regarded English settlement while the other concerned accusations that Mohegan and Pequot leaders had made against him. Williams understood that, as a way of building a working relationship, it was his responsibility to write the letters. Writing this letter helped to fulfill the exchange that Narragansett leadership expected after allowing Williams to establish his trading post and then nascent towns in the first place. Important to keep in mind is that this is Williams's translation of Ninigret's message, not a transcription. Williams tailored his phrasing for an English audience just as he made translation choices to better communicate to Narragansett leaders, such as using the phrase "English Sachims" with Ninigret. Small details in this note make it clear this was not his first time writing for Ninigret as Williams anticipates the sachem's request for a response.

Nar. [Narragansett]

Sir

Loving respects to yourselfe and dearest and Mrs. Lake premised. 2 days since Nenekunat came to me, and requested me to write 2 letters, the one in answere to Capt. Athertons motion for some English planting on Block Iland and on a neck at Nayantaquit,[23] the other to your Selfe, in both protesting his Innocencie as to the death of his son in Law, with which Onkas[24] and the Pequts charge him. He prayes you (as of your Selfe) to signifie (as much as you can) Items to the Pequts that they be quiet and attempt nothing (at least treacherously) against him which he suspects, from words from Onkas, that it will be pleasing to the English. He prayes you allso to be mindfull of endeavouring to remove Wequashcuck,[25] so constant a provocation before him: and at present he prayes you to send for some skins which lately as Lord of the place he hath received. I hope the English Sachims[26] as

22. Mack Scott, correspondence with the authors, January 22, 2023.

23. Block Island, a small island off the coast of (what is now) Rhode Island and Niantic, a coastal community where Ninigret's Niantic lived (and Narragansett still live) near Charlestown, Rhode Island.

24. The Mohegan sachem Uncas.

25. Or Wequashcook, also Harmon Garrett, a nephew of Ninigret, sachem to a Pequot community near Ninigret in Pawcatuck.

26. That is, English authorities, often referring to an English governor or commissioner from the United Colonies.

I tell him in the Spring will heare and gratifie him in his just desires the want of which I guess is the cause that he is not free as yet for Block Iland etc. but expresseth much if the English doe him Justice against his Enemies. Oh sir how far from Nature is the Spirit of Christ Jesus that loves and pities prayes for and doth good to Enemies? Sir it is like he will request a line of Answer, which if you please to give, I pray Sir write when either of those ships you write of are for England and by which you write your selfe. . . . Sir, yours

R.W.

Roger Williams to John Winthrop Jr., October 9, 1650[27]

To his English peers, Williams often cast his interpreting work between English and Indigenous leaders as indispensable. Were his descriptions of his inter-preting self-serving promotion, objective observations, or something more complicated? Here, Williams shows how his interpreting could temper a tense situation and yet lead to a final outcome that might disappoint all parties involved. The key events that led up to this moment stem from 1645 when the commissioners of the United Colonies had attempted to extort money from Narragansett sachems. The commissioners threatened Narragansett leader-ship with war if they did not pay a large fine and agree to a list of other outra-geous and demeaning demands. Narragansett leaders, as they later described it, agreed for the simple reason that Englishmen with weapons had them sur-rounded. Now, the commissioners had decided to send an armed expedition into Narragansett country and force payment of this fine with instructions to seize the payment (paid in wampum) and even take sachems as hostages. Not only that, but the armed expedition, led by the Humphrey Atherton that Williams names, was launching their hostilities at the same time that this community was holding a burial for the son of a highly regarded Narragansett leader. Consider the outcome: What do the Massachusetts Bay men gain and lose by the end of these events? What do the Narragansett gain and lose?

There is a larger story emerging here as well: Wealthy Englishmen in Massachusetts Bay Colony were trying yet again to expand the colony's border into Narragansett country and even the neighboring colony of Rhode Island. Note that the commissioners, acting for the Massachusetts Bay Colony, are sending armed forces into Narragansett Country, an area well outside the bounds of their authority. In the years after this event, Massachusetts Bay leaders, including the Captain Humphrey Atherton who led this expedition, used debt and payments of fines to coerce Narragansett leaders into land sales—sales that Bay officials hope will bring Narragansett country and even

27. *Correspondence of Roger Williams*, 1:322–24.

parts of Rhode Island under the jurisdiction of Massachusetts Bay. The Bay colony's plans failed, but a much larger threat to Narragansett homelands arrived in the form of regional war twenty-five years later; the tensions that drove it—egregious breaches of Native jurisdiction and calculated methods aimed at defrauding Native communities of land—were evidently part of colonial strategy by 1650.

Nar[ragansett] 9.8.50 (so called)

Sir

Best respects and love present to Your selfe and dearest. My howse is now filled with Souldiers and therefore in hast[e] I write in an Indian howse. It hath pleased God to give me, and the English, and the Natives that were met together and the whole land I believe a gracious deliverance from the plague of Warr.

On the last day last [month] came to my howse Capt. Atherton with above 20 souldiers and 3 horse. The Capt requested me presently to travel to the Sachims (met together in mourning for Wepitieammocks dead son within 3 or 4 mile of my howse) and to demaund the rest of pay 308 fath[om] and 200 more for these charges etc. I went alone and drew them out of the mourning howse who answered they were ever resolved to pay but they were distracted by that Peace broke by the Monhiggins[28] in that Hostilitie begun upon them at Pequt[29] which they answered not because of the English: but expected Satisfaction, but receive none etc. Yet they refused not to pay. I returned and the Capt with me went to them and 2 or 3 souldiers as was agreed and after a little discourse we agreed in the same place to meete on the second day. We did and all day till night. The Capt. demaunded the peag or 2 Sachims, the Natives promised peag within alitle time. The Capt. would have one or 2 present and in the Evening drew up his men (unkowne to me Sent for) round about the Sachims in a hole and the Indians (20 for one of us) armed and ready with guns and bowes about us. The Capt. desired me to tell the Sachims he would take by force Nenekunat and Pesiccosh.[30] Then I protested to the Capt: before Indians and English I was betrayed for first I would have hazarded Life or blood for a little money: 2 if my cause and call were right I would not be desperate with so few men to assault Kings in the midst of such Guards about us, and I had not so much as a knife or stick about me. After long Agitacion upon the ticklist point

28. Mohegan.

29. An area slightly inland on coastal Connecticut, southwest of Cocumscussoc, the site of Williams's trading post, named after the Pequot communities that lived and still live there.

30. That is, the Niantic sachem Ninigret and the Narragansett sachem Pessicus.

of a great slaughter (as all the souldiers now Confesse) the God of mercy appeared. I perswauded the Capt to stay at my howse 4 days and the Natives within 4 dates to bring in the peag and I would lay down 10 fath[om] (as formerly I had done 20 God knowes beyond my Ability).

Sir to morrow, the peag is to come. I hope such a quantitie as will stop proceedings. I tould the Capt. he had desperately betraied me and himself. He tells me he will give me good Satisfaction before he depart.[31] I presume he Feares God in the maine but feare he can never satisfy me nor his own Conscience, which i hope the Lord will shew him and shew the Countrey what dangerous Councells the Commissioners[32] produce: which makes me feare God is preparing Warr in the Countrey. Just now a letter from Rhode Island comes for my voyage to Engl[and] but as yet I resolve not.[33] God graciously be pleased to set our Affections on another Countrey and him selfe above in his deare Son.

Sir Yours in him I desire to be unfeigned

R.W.

Roger Williams to the General Court of Massachusetts Bay, October 5, 1654[34]

When Williams wrote this letter, the Massachusetts Bay Colony was considering launching an attack against the powerful Narragansett. The commissioners of the United Colonies believed that the sachem Ninigret was in league with the Dutch governor of New Netherland (after 1664 New York) and, with his newfound support from the Dutch, was preparing to launch a surprise attack against English colonies. English conversations with the sachem failed to allay suspicion, after which the commissioners rather rashly ordered a combined force of 300 men to invade Niantic (Ninigret's home near Charlestown, Rhode Island) in early October. Once there, troops intended to force the Niantic sachems to meet English demands, even if that required taking hostages to force Narragansett compliance. This was a disconcerting thought for Williams and other Rhode Islanders who lived, as Williams put it, "amongst" Narragansett communities. Or as Narragansett scholar Mack Scott suggests, Williams might have judged such actions to be a serious miscalculation on the part of the United Colonies and he was trying to prevent an embarrassing or costly loss

---

31. Meaning that Atherton would pay Williams back or settle his debt with him.
32. The commissioners of the United Colonies.
33. Williams sailed almost a year later in November 1651.
34. *Correspondence of Roger Williams,* 2:408–16.

to English forces.[35] Ultimately, there was no bloodshed, no hostage-taking, and the crisis passed.

Practically speaking, this letter had little, if any, effect on the course of events, for reasons that had more to do with mail delivery problems than Williams's arguments. Rather, the letter's value lies in its ability to show readers today what Williams's advocacy for the Narragansett, or any Native community, might have looked like. In particular, this letter highlights Williams's frequent balancing act, the one where he advocated for Native peoples on the one hand while he acknowledged, even espoused, English concerns and religious beliefs on the other. For example, he acknowledged English reasons for war but argued for peace. He referred to Native peoples generally as "barbarians" and "treacherous," yet described the Narragansett sachem Canonicus as a "Prudent and Peaceable Prince." One moment, Williams makes wide, generalized statements about Native politics, the next he delves into specifics, including references to intertribal conflicts.

Providence 5.8.54 (so calld)

Most honoured Sirs

I truely wish Your peace and pray Your gentle acceptance of a Word I hope not unseasonable.

We have in these parts a Sound of Your Meditations of War agst These Natives amongst whome we dwell. I consider that War is one of those 3 Great, Sore plauges, with which it pleaseth God to afflict the Sons of men. I consider allso that I refused lately many offers in my Native Countrey, out of a Sincere desire to seeke the good and peace of this.

. . . I humbly pray Your Consideracion whether it be not: not only possible but very easie for the English to live and die in peace with all the Natives of this Countrey.[36]

For 2ndly are not all the English of this Land (generally) a persecuted people from their Native Soile, and hath not the God of peace and Father of Mercies made these Natives more friendly in this Wildernes then our Native Countrimen in our owne land to us? Have they not entred Leagues of Love, and to this day continued Peaceable Commerce with us? Are not our Families and Townes growne up in peace amongst them?[37] Upon which I hum-

---

35. Mack Scott, correspondence with the authors, January 22, 2023.

36. Williams's response to some rumors of Massachusetts Bay Colony's possible war against Ninigret and the Narragansett is rather fascinating here. It is, of course, partly out of self-interest that he tries to persuade the General Court of Massachusetts to not start a war, but there is seemingly something deeper here, too, that Williams outlines in the points that follow.

37. Williams's description of settler-Native relations is pretty idealized, but it does point

bly aske how it can Suite, with Christian Ingenuitie to Take hould of some seeming Occasions for their Destructions, which (though the Heads be only aimed at) Yet all Experience tells us, falls on the Body and the innocent.

Thirdly I pray it may be remembered, how greatly the name of God is Concerned in this Affaire; for it Can not be hid, how all England and other nations ring with the glorious Conversion of the Indians of New England. You know how many bookes are dispersed throughout the nation of the subject (in some of them the Nariganset Chiefe Sachims are publikely branded for refusing to pray and be converted): how have all the pulpits in Engl. bene commanded to sound of this Glorious Worck and that by the highest Command and Authoritie of Parliament, and the Churchwardens went from House to house to gather up supplies for this Worck. (I speak not Ironically but only mention what all the printed books mention.)[38]

Honored Sirs Whether I have bene and am a friend to the Natives turning to Civilitie and Christianitie, and whether I have bene instrumental and desire so to be (according to my Light) I will not trouble You with, only I beseech You consider how the name of the most holy and jealous God may be preserved betweene the clashings of these Two: Viz: The Glorious Conversion of the Indians in New England and the Unnecessary Warrs and cruel Destructions of the Indians in New England.[39]

4thly I beseech You forget not, that although we are apt to play with this plauge of War more then with the other 2 Famine and Pestilence, yet I beseech you consider, how the present Events of all Wars that ever have bene in this world, have bene wonderfully Tickle [i.e., risky], and the future Calamities and Revolucions wonderfull in the latter end.

. . .

Now with Your Patience a Word to these 2 Nations[40] at War, (occasion of Yours) the Narrigansetts and Long Ilanders,[41] I know them both experimentally [i.e., through experience] and therefore pray you to remember

---

toward the general peace and relationships he tried to establish with the Narragansett.

38. Williams here is referring to the so-called "Eliot Tracts"—a series of pamphlets published in London that promoted the work of John Eliot and other missionaries among the Nipmuc, Massachusett, Wampanoag, and Pennacook nations. In at least one place, Eliot and other authors describe the resistance to Christianity they encountered among the Narragansett, which implicitly casts Williams in a negative light.

39. Again, a strong statement against wars with Natives in light of the supposed evangelization aims the English professed.

40. Referring here to Indigenous nations, the Narragansett and the Montaukett.

41. Long Island had a number of Native communities but in this case, Williams was specifically referring to the Montaukett who lived directly across from Ninigret's community on the other side of Long Island Sound, near the English at Easthampton.

First that the Narigansetts and the Mauquawogs[42] are the 2 great Bodies of Indians in this Countrey: and they are Confederates and long have bene, and they both yet are friendly and peaceable to the English. I doe humbly conceave that if ever God call us to a just War with either of them he calls us to make sure of the one to friend. Tis true some distast was lately here amongst them, but they parted friends and some of the Narigansets went home with them, and I feare that both these and the Long Ilanders and Monhiggins and all the Native of the land may upon the sound of a defeat of the English be induced easily to joyne each with other agst us.[43]

2 The Narigansets as they were the first, so they have bene long Confederates with You, they have bene true in all the Pequt Wars to You, they occasioned the Monhiggins to come in too, and so occasioned the Pequts downfall.[44]

3 I can not Yet learne that ever it hath pleased the Lord as Yet to permit the Narrigansets to staine their Hands with any English Bloud neither in open Hostilities nor secret murthers as both Pequts and Long Ilanders did and Monhiggins allso in the Pequt Wars. Tis true they are Barbarians but their greatest offences against the English have bene matters of money or pettie revengings of themselvs on some Indians upon Extreame provocations, but God hath kept them cleare of our Bloud.

4. For the people many hundreth English, have long experimented them to be inclined to peace and Love with the English Nation.[45]

Their late famous long lived Caunounicus[46] so lived and died and in the same most honorable manner and sollemnitie (in their Way) as You laid to sleepe Your Prudent Peacemaker Mr Wintrop,[47] did they honour this their Prudent and Peaceable Prince, mine eyes beheld it. His Son Meiksah[48]

42. Mohawk.

43. Williams warns that a war against the Narragansett may draw in the Mohawk and other Native nations to destroy the English. In a way, Williams anticipates a war that started two decades later, often called King Philip's War.

44. Although none of the Massachusetts Bay leaders reading this letter were likely to have forgotten the Pequot War (which at this point had taken place almost twenty years prior), Williams is correct in reminding them of the way the Narragansett both fought as allies to the English and rallied Mohegan warriors as well.

45. The prior sentence combined with this one illustrates Williams's inconsistent approach to the Narragansett. On the one hand, he calls them "Barbarians," and in the next sentence he praises them for being peaceable towards the English.

46. A powerful and much respected Narragansett leader (and uncle to Miantonomo) whom Williams had known for many years before his death in 1647.

47. John Winthrop, deceased by this point, but an important Massachusetts Bay Colony leader and governor.

48. Mixan, the eldest son of Canonicus.

inherites his Spirit. Yea through all their Townes and Countries, how frequently doe many and ofttimes one English man travell alone with safetie and loving kindnes?

The Cause and Roote of all the present mischiefe is the pride of 2 Barbarians Ascassasotick the Long Iland Sachim, and Nenekunat[49] of the Nariganset. The former is proud and foolish, The later proud and fierce. I have not seene him these many Yeares, Yet from their sober men I heare he pleads.

First that Ascassasotick a very inferiour Sachim (bearing himselfe upon the English) hath slaine 3 or 4 of his people, and since that sent him Challenges and Darings to fight and mend himselfe.

2ndly He Nenekunat consulted by sollemne Messangers with the chiefe of the English Govrnours, Major Endicot, then Governor of the Massachusets, who sent him an implicite Consent to right himselfe, upon which they all plead, that the English have [not?] just occasion of Displeasure.

3 After he had taken Revenge upon the Long Ilanders and brought away about 14 Captives (divers of their chiefe Women,) Yet he restored them all againe upon the mediation and desire of the English.

4 After this peace made, the Long Ilander pretending to visit Nenekunat at Block Iland, slaughtered of his Narrigansets neere 30 persons at midnight: 2 of them of great note, especially Wepiteammocks Sonn, to whom Nenekunat was uncle.

5 In the prosecution of this War, although he had drawne downe the Inlanders to his Assistance, Yet upon protestation of the English against his proceeding he retreated and dissolved his Armie.[50]

Honoured Sirs I know it is said the Long Ilanders are subjects. But I have heard this greatly questioned, and indeed I question whether any Indians in this Countrey, remayning Barbarous and pagan may with Truth or Honour be cald the English subjects.

2 But graunt them Subjects, what capacitie hath their late massacre of the Narrigansites (with whome they had made peace) without the English consent, though still under the English name, put them into?[51]

---

49. Ninigret.

50. Williams here is describing a complicated series of violent exchanges between the Montaukett on Long Island and the Narragansett of Rhode Island: a raid by Ascassasotick, a counter raid by Ninigret, and a counter-counter raid by Ascassasotick. English magistrates got involved at several points, but Williams is essentially imploring them to stay out of it.

51. This is a somewhat radical position. Williams is questioning whether Indigenous peoples can be subjects of the crown if they are still "Barbarous and pagan." But in this case, he may be using the point to argue against war and English intervention.

3 All Indians are Extremely treacherous,[52] and if to their owne Nation for private ends revolting to strangers, what will they doe upon the Sound of one defeate of the English, or the trade of killing English cattle and persons, and plunder, which will most certainly be the trade if any Considerable partie escape alive as mine eyes beheld in the Dutch War.

But I beseech you say Your Thoughts, and the Thoughts of Your Wives and Litle ones, and the Thoughts of all English, and of Gods people in England and the Thoughts of his Highnes and Councell (tender of these parts) if for the Sake of a few inconsiderable Pagans and Beasts wallowing in Idlenes, stealing, lying, whoring, Treacherie, Witchcrafts, Blaspheamies and Idolatries: all that the gracious hand of the Lord hath so wonderfully planted in this Wildernes should be destroyed.[53]

How much more noble were it, and glorious to the name of God and your owne that no Pagan should dare to use the name of an English subject, who comes not out (in some degrees) from Barbarisme to Civilitie, in forsaking their filthy nakednes, in keeping some kind of Cattell etc. which your Councells and Commands may tend to, and as (prudent and pious Mr Wintrop deceased said) that Civilitie may be a leading step to Christianitie is the humble desire of your most unfaigned in all Services of Love

Roger Williams of Providence Colony President

Roger Williams to Robert Carr, March 1, 1665/1666[54]

This letter, almost overwhelming with its bullet list of items, thrusts readers into the tense political struggles between competing sachems, Massachusetts Bay and Rhode Island officials, and royal representatives from England. At stake here were the Shawomet homelands, or more accurately, at stake again. A leader within this community, Pomham, had fought off an earlier effort to displace his community in the 1640s when a Narragansett sachem, Miantonomo, had tried to sell the land to their English neighbor Samuel Gorton of Warwick.[55] Twenty years later, Gorton and Warwick men again tried to force Pomham out, this time by appealing to visiting representatives of King Charles II, who were currently in the area, in hopes of an intervention by the crown.

52. Another instance of Williams's anti-Indian colonial bias.

53. The language Williams uses is inflammatory and derogatory, but his point is a weighty one: Is English intervention in the intertribal disputes of some minor sachems worth risking the downfall and destruction of the currently (mostly) peaceable English settlements? Williams thinks not.

54. *Correspondence of Roger Williams*, 2:550–51.

55. For more on Gorton, see chapter 4; James, *Colonial Rhode Island*, 30–32.

This letter also encapsulates the gap between what Williams said about the Indigenous ownership of land, his role as mediator, and his involvement in the face of English land grabs. Williams begins by acknowledging Pomham's "ancient" relationship to this land, underscored by the community's fierce defense to remain on it. Williams then speaks of his promises to "the Natives in this Bay" to keep the peace. Yet all of this would have been outrageous to Pomham. Williams is lobbying, not for the Shawomet to stay on their land, but for the Warwick men to delay in forcing them out until after harvest season. Equally, the deal that was on the table from the king's commissioner, Sir Robert Carr, demanded that Pomham's community subject themselves to Narragansett authority. So, Williams was advocating—but on behalf of the English and the Narragansett, not the Shawomet. (William's description of what the Shawomet would do to defend their home is strikingly close to what they did do during King Philip's War.) Williams urged a little peace, and in the end, that is all he got.

Providence 1. March 1665 (ut vulg.)

Sir,

My humble, and hearty respects presented with humble, and hearty desires of your present and eternal felicitie. Haveing heard of a late confederacy amongst great numbers of these Barbarians to assist Pumham etc. I thought it my duty to wait upon your Honour with these humble salutacions, and apprecacions of the safety of your person, not to be easily hazarded amongst such a Barbarous scum, and offscouring of mankind. Besides, Sir this is an old ulcerous busines, wherein I have been many years engaged, and have (in the behalf of my loving Friends of Warwicke) pleaded this cause, with the whole [General] court of the Massachusits Magistrates, and Deputies; and prevailed with them to yield, that if I and Pumham could agree, they would ratifie our agreement. But Pumham would not part with that Neck, on any terms. I crave leave to add (for the excuse of this boldniss) that the Natives in this Bay doe (by my promise to them, at my first breaking of the ice amongst them) expect my endeavours of preserving the publike peace, which it hath pleased God, merfically to help me to doe many times (with my great hazard, and charge,) when all the Colonies and the Massachusits, in especiall, have meditated, prepared, and been (some times many hundreds) upon the march for war against the Natives in this Colony. Of this my promise, and duty, and constant practise, mine owne heart, and conscience before God; as also some Natives put me in mind at present.

1. First then (although I know an other claim laid to this land, yit) Pumham being the ancient possessor of this Lordship, I humbly query, whither it be just to dispossiss him (not only without consent, which feare

may extort, but without some satisfying consideration.) I had a Commission from my friends of Warwicke to promise a good round value, and I know some of them have desired the Natives I though it cost them some hundreds of Pounds.

2. Your Honour will never effect by force a safe, and lasting conclusion, until you first have reduced the Massachusits to the obedience of his [Majesty] and then these appendants (towed at their stern) will easily (and not before) wind about also.

3. The business as circimstantiated will not be effected without bloudshed, Barbarians are Barbarians. There be old grudges betwixt our country men of Warwick and them. They are a Melancholy people, and judg themselves, (by the former Sachim and these English) oppressed, and wronged.[56] You may knock out their braines, and yet not make them peaceably to surrender; even as some oxen will die before they will rise; yet with patience, and gentle meanes will rise, and raw, and doe good service.

4. These Barbarians know that it is but one partie in Warwick which claim this Neck. The greatest part of the towne cry out against the other, to my knowledg and the Natives also.

5. The Natives know that this party in Warwick are not only destitute of help, from their owne Townesmen, but of the other townes of this Colony also.

6. They know it would please the Massachusetts, and most of the other Colonies, that Mr Gorton, and his friends had been long ere this destroyed.[57]

7. They know that Ninicroft, and Pessicus are Barbarians, and if it come to bloud, and that at the first, the worst be to the English (in any appearance) they will joyne to further the prey: How ever if King Phillip keepe his promise, they will be too greate a party against those two Sachims.[58]

8. Lastly, Sir We profess Christianity, which commends a little with peace: a dinner of green herbes with quietness: and if it be possible, commandes peace with all men. I therefore humbly offer, if it be not advisable

56. That is, Pomham judged himself and the Shawomet oppressed and wronged and was most likely referring to the earlier attempt by Narragansett sachem Miantonomo to sell Shawomet land to Warwick men against the Shawomet objections and claims to the land.

57. Translating for the Shawomet leaders, Williams is writing to say that the Shawomet know that Massachusetts Bay authorities had long clashed with Samuel Gorton and other Warwick men.

58. Pomham, as translated by Williams, is referencing intertribal politics that Williams himself could not see. In this case, the sachem's suggestion here is that the increasingly influential Wampanoag sachem Pumetacom (later called "King Philip" by the English) was offering to aid Pomham in his struggle to remain independent from Narragansett and Niantic powers.

(in this juncture of time) to lay all the blame on men, and on my intercession, and mediation, for a little further breathing to the Barbarians until Harvest, in which time a peaceable and loveing agreement may be wrought, to mutual content, and satisfaction.

Sir I humbly crave your Honours gracious pardon to this great boldness of Your most humble, and bounden Servant

Roger Williams

Roger Williams to John Winthrop Jr., August 19, 1669[59]

Though this letter begins with a discussion about a runaway dog, it ends on a far more serious subject than English pets: the alcohol trade in New England. Alcohol was a scourge to Native communities and community leaders, including sachems, who found themselves in an impossible situation. English traders showed little hesitation in selling alcohol to Native buyers and they showed even less regard for the damage it wrought within Indigenous homes. At the same time, Indigenous leaders struggled to cut off consumer demand. Narragansett sachems went as far as petitioning the king of England himself to stop the flow of alcohol into Narragansett country and they made their reasons plain enough. In his complaint, the Narragansett sachem Pessicus described how thirty-two of his men had "dyed by drinking of it."[60] On ending alcohol sales into Indian Country, Williams and Narragansett sachems agreed. Williams railed against the damage that English traders created by plying alcohol.

Providence Aug. 19 1669 (so called)

Sir

Lo[ving] respects to Your Selfe and Your dearest and other

Friends etc. I have no Tidings (upon my Enquiry) of that poore Dog (about which you sent to me). I feare he is runwild into the Woods, though tis possible English or Indians have him. Oh Sir what is that word that Sparrowes and Hairs are provided for and Beasts etc. how much more Mankind. (He Saveth Man and Beast.) How much more his Sons and Daughters and Heirs of his Crowne and Kingdome?

Sir I have encouraged Mr Dexter to send you a Limestone and to salute You with this inclosed. He is an intelligent man, a master Printer of London, and Conscionable (though a Baptist) there maligned and traduced by Wm Harris (a dolefull Generalist). Sir if there be any occasion of Your Selfe (or others) to use any of this stone, Mr Dexter hath a lusty Team and lustie Sons

---

59. *Correspondence of Roger Williams*, 2:591–92.
60. Bartlett, *Records of the Colony of Rhode Island*, 2:128.

and a very wiling heart being a Sangwine Cheerful Man to doe Your Selfe
or any (at Your Word especially) any service upon very honest and cheap
Considerations: and if there be any occasion, Sir you may be confident of all
Ready Service from Your old unworthy Servant.

R.W.

While you were at Mr. Smiths that bloudie Liquor trade (of which
Rich. Smith hath of old driven) fired the Countrey about Your Lodging.[61]
The Indians would have more Liquours etc. [;] it came to Blowes. The Indians Complaind to Rich. Smith, he tould them he was busie with Your De-
partures. Next day the English Complaint of Some hurte and went 28 (and
more men) to fetch in the Sachim. The Indians quickly with a shout routed
the horse and Caused their Returne and are more insolent by this Repulse
and Yet are willing to be peaceable were it not for that Divell of Liquors. I
might have gaind thousands (as many as any) by that Trade but God hath
graciously given me rather to choose a drie morsell etc.

Sir Since I see you I read Mortons Memorialls[62] and rejoice at the
Encomiums upon Your Father and other precious Worthies, though I be a
Reprobate. Comtempta vilior alga.[63]

61. Richard Smith is the trader who took over Williams's former trading post at
Cocumscussoc, and his son continued the trade after him. In addition to alcohol, ar-
chaeological records suggest Smith was also active in selling firearms to local Native
customers.

62. Nathaniel Morton's then recently published New Englands Memoriall (1669),
which included references to Roger Williams.

63. Translated as, "Cheaper than despised seaweed," a line that appears in ancient
texts by the first-century Roman poet Virgil.

Chapter 7

Liberty of Conscience, 1637–1671

WILLIAMS'S IDEAS ON WHAT *will later be known as the "separation of church and state" served as the focus of most of his published works and figured in much of his correspondence as well. When Williams founded Providence Plantations, as scholar Teresa Bejan reminds us, he did not simply allow residents to avoid participating in a state-sponsored church or to express their beliefs privately, he created a "society with no established church at all."*[1] *Christopher Grenda argues that the most fervent supporters of toleration, like Williams, "found early seventeenth-century England inhospitable because the English state made dissent from the Protestant Episcopal Church of England illegal."*[2] *English men and women were required to attend church services, and only members of the church of England could hold public office.*[3] *The Massachusetts Bay colony was even more intolerant of religious dissent: Throughout nearly all of the seventeenth century, all residents in the Massachusetts Bay Colony were legally obligated to live within a set distance from a church, attend church services on Wednesdays and Sundays, and pay tithes to support their local church. The Massachusetts Bay Colony also tied religious membership to voting rights as only men who had given testimony of saving grace (thereby becoming full church members) could vote in civil elections. Before the crown required religious toleration in all English colonies in 1689, people in Massachusetts Bay could not join a different church or choose to be part of no church at all—whether they believed themselves converted or not. Williams was deeply committed to protecting the freedom of individual conscience, even*

1. Bejan, "When the Word of the Lord Runs Freely," 65.
2. Grenda, "Faith, Reason, Enlightenment," 27.
3. Winship, *Hot Protestants*, 3.

if that meant allowing people to remain outside a gathered church altogether. (Williams himself withdrew from all church membership in 1639.) The texts in this section encourage readers to see those ideas develop over time, as Williams confronted the reality of building and maintaining a peaceful settlement without an established church, in a world filled with state-sponsored churches that wielded considerable power. While Williams wrote thousands of pages describing and defending his position, political scientist Andrew Murphy summarized it very simply: Williams argued that "human magistrates had authority over people's bodies, while God governed their souls."[4]

Williams had complicated reasons for believing in a liberty of conscience. Intellectually, he argued that New England churches were not pure and were not fully separate as they were still attached to the Church of England, so therefore they should not exclude anyone on the basis of a purity test, nor should they demand adherence.[5] But the bigger practical concern for Williams was that forcing non-believers into attending church with believers puts everyone's souls at risk. Williams wanted an even purer version of the church than other puritans did, and he worried that requiring everyone—even the unregenerate—to participate in churches polluted churches and the regenerate people who attended them. There are other influences, though: Williams grew up seeing dissenters being imprisoned, exiled, and sometimes even executed, and his own banishment loomed large in his writings on freedom of conscience. Williams was part of a transatlantic group of writers in the reformed Protestant, Calvinist world. As the documents below and in chapter 4 illustrate, after his initial migration to Boston, he made two extended trips back to England as a representative of the colony, first in 1643 to request a charter from Parliament, and again in 1652 to solidify that charter. He published his most well-known texts during his fifteen-month stay in London starting in the summer of 1643, including his first work on liberty of conscience, The Bloudy Tenent of Persecution. And given his deep, personal involvement with his Native neighbors, and how frequently he wrote about Indigenous culture as a way of criticizing English practice, his life in Indian country likely influenced his thinking on liberty of conscience as well.

*The parable of the wheat and tares served as the central biblical text for Williams's most important publication on liberty of conscience—*The Bloudy Tenent. *"Tares" are a particular type of weed that look very much like wheat, especially early in their growth, which makes them more damaging to the wheat because they are often left to grow among the healthy crop. Enemies*

4. Murphy, "'Livelie Experiment' and 'Holy Experiment,'" 45.

5. Like many reformed Protestants, he believed that the Apostolic succession had been broken by Constantine's nationalization of the church in the fourth century, and that their churches were not, therefore, true churches.

sow tares in their neighbor's fields to threaten their yields, but pulling tares can damage the wheat as well. Using the same metaphor, historian David Hall suggests that Williams was simply "willing to let the weeds alone . . . because the world was a wilderness and would be until God decided that it should be otherwise, the scattered godly seedlings from the garden had no business tormenting the ungodly weeds."[6]

Roger Williams to John Winthrop, July 21, 1637[7]

Many of Williams's early writings and correspondence are now lost. This letter hints at some of his later thoughts on the ministry and state churches, as well as on liberty of conscience. In 1637, Williams drafted a reply to John Robinson's A Treatise of the Lawfulnesse of Hearing of the Ministers in the Church of England, *published in Amsterdam in 1634 after Robinson's death. Williams shared his draft reply with other ministers in New England, circulating his ideas in manuscript. He refers below to two Massachusetts Bay ministers who read and commented on the draft: Peter Bulkley, then minister at Concord, and Hugh Peter, minister at Salem, both of whom arrived in Massachusetts Bay in 1635. Robinson's tract claimed that Separatist puritans could safely listen to Church of England ministers preach without being harmed by the general sinfulness of the Church of England. Williams disagreed, increasingly vehemently. According to his thinking in 1637, listening to Anglican clergy preaching the Word was a form of worship, and therefore puritans could not attend Anglican services at all. In this letter to Winthrop, he also warns that Massachusetts Bay had gone too far towards establishing a state church, including requiring the obedience of all Massachusetts residents, practices he calls "misguidings." As with most of his correspondence, even this short letter reflects his wide-ranging concerns; he added a postscript regarding the Pequot War, then still raging—a war he describes here as one of many "barbarous distractions."*

New Providence 21 of the 5t[h] month

  Much honoured Sir

  My unfeigned love and respect to your soules eternall comfort, and firme perswasions of your Levelling at the highest white[8] have imboldened me once more to tell you some poore thought of mine owne pend and sent to some Friends amongst you: wch happily (if the good Lord so please)

---

6. Hall, *Puritans*, 25–33.

7. *Correspondence of Roger Williams*, 1:103–8.

8. Williams is using an archery metaphor here; the "highest white" is the bulls-eye.

may some way conduce to your soules satisfaction in the midst of all your troubles.

I have bene long requested to write my grounds agst the English preaching etc. and especially my answeres to some reasons of Mr Robinsons for hearing.

In the midst of a multitude of barbarous distractions I have fitted something to that purpose: and being not able at present to transcribe the whole: yet having bene long solicited by Mr Buckley (from whome I received some Objections) and by many others, and of late by my worthy friend Mr Peters [who had] sight of them: I have thought good to send so much as [I] have transcribed to the hand of my [loving] friend Mr Buckly.

Sir I am bold to give you this Intimacion because in these first loose leaves, handling the state of a national church from the 38 page[9] I have enlarged the differences between Israell and all other states. I know and am perswaded that your misguidings are great and lamentable, and as the further you pass in your way, the further you wander, and have the further to come back, and the end of one vexation, will be but the beginning of another, till Conscience be permitted (though Erronious) to be free amongst you.

I am sorry my straights are such that I can not transcribe the remainder and especially, what concernes the matter, most concerning your deare selfe, and there is especially the [assailing] of some objections. But if the Lord please I live I shall endeavor the rest and thanckfully receave any Intimacion from your selfe yea from the least, whereby I might my selfe returne from any wandrings. The Lord Jesus be to you and me the Way, the Truth, and he will be the Life also. So prayers Your [Worship's] most unfained

Roger Williams

I have no newes but from Qunnihticut, the receaving of Sasacous, his present and company by the Mawhauogs, and some promises of theirs to him to setle him againe at Pequt. This weeke Souwonckquawsin[10] old Sequins Sonn cut [off] 20 Pequt women and children in their passage to the Mowhauogs also one Sachim who 3 yeares ago was with you in the Bay with a present.

9. Williams is referring to the "Modell of Church and Civill Power," written by ministers in Massachusetts Bay in 1636 and his draft response to it, later published in 1644 as *The Bloudy Tenent*. We have included some excerpts from the "Modell" in chapter 3.

10. Souwonckquawsin (Sequassen) was a leader of the Wangunk from nearby Hartford, and was vehemently opposed to the Pequot. His father, Sequin (Sowheag), was also a sachem among the Wangunk, but was once allied with the Pequot and aided them in raiding Wethersfield in April 1637. It is unclear which sachem visited Winthrop, and Winthrop's own description of the visit does not suggest that any sachem traveled to meet him. *Correspondence of Roger Williams*, 1:108–9.

Roger Williams, *Queries of Highest Consideration* (1644)[11]

While still in London, and shortly after publishing Mr. Cottons Letter Lately Printed, Examined and Answered, *Williams contributed to the debate about whether the Church of England should adopt the Presbyterian structure or the Independent, autonomous church as its model. In the midst of the English Civil War, disputes between Independents and Presbyterians were particularly charged. Independents in England believed that each church congregation stood alone, with no overarching structure maintaining control over clergy or congregations. On the other hand, Presbyterian writers, many from Scotland, believed that each congregation was part of a larger synod that could exercise some control over an individual church's autonomy. A pamphlet war followed, with the "Five Dissenting Brethren" publishing an attack on Presbyterian polity, and Presbyterians publishing attacks on what they saw as the lax control in Independent churches. Williams saw this debate as an opportunity to challenge both Independents and Presbyterians, and instead argues that there should be no state church at all. As James Calvin Davis suggests, "both biblical precedent and recent English history testified to the futility of trying to maintain religious orthodoxy or civic morality through the punishment of minority religions."[12] Williams was especially eager to prove that no state church should impose a single orthodoxy by persecuting people who did not accept it. Williams addresses this text to the Five Dissenting Brethren (Williams refers to them as "the five Holland Ministers"):* Thomas Goodwin, Philip Nye, William Bridges, Jeremiah Burroughs, *and* Sidrach Simpson *and "To the Commissioners from the Generall Assembly (so called) of the Church of Scotland." Note the reference to Matthew's parable of wheat and tares in the 12th Querie; this parable figures prominently in Williams's later publications on religious persecution, including* The Bloudy Tenent.

Right Honorable,

It is a wofull Priviledge attending all great States and Personages, that they seldome heare any other Musick but what is Known will please them. Though our Musick sound not sweet but harsh, yet please you first to Know, it is not fitted to your Eares, but to your Hearts, and the bleeding Heart of this afflicted Nation . . .

Most Renowned Patriots, You sit at Helme in as great a Storm, as ere poor England Common-wealth was lost in: Yet be you pleased to remember, that (excepting the affaires of Heaven, of Religion, of Soules, of Eternity) all

11. Williams, *Queries of Highest Consideration* in *Complete Writings of Roger Williams*, 2:241–75.

12. Davis, *On Religious Liberty*, 16.

your Consultations, Conclusions, Executions, are not of the Quantity, of the value of one poor drop of water, or the little dust of the Ballance . . .

Yet concerning Soules, we will not (as most doe) charge you with the loads of all the Soules in England, Scotland, Ireland: we shall humbly affirme, and (by the help of Christ) maintaine, that the Bodies and Goods of the subject is your charge: Their Soules and yours are set on account to those that professe to be the Lights and Guides, the Messengers and Embassadors sent from Heaven to them.

You will please to say: We are constantly told and we believe it, that Religion is our first Care, and Reformation of that our greatest Taske.

Right Honourable, your Wisdomes Know the Fatall Miscarriages of Englands Parliaments in this point . . . if hee that eates and drinkes the Body and blood of Christ unworthily, eateth and drinketh his owne judgement, and all English soules are bound by Law to eate that Body and Blood at sixteene, who sees not, since (as tis confest scarce one of a thousand but is found ignorant, Impenitent, Unregenerate at those yeeres) that the Body of the People are compelled by Law, to eat and drink at sixteen their own judgment . . . for Non-conforming to these any other practices, the English Masse-Booke, &c. what heavy Persecution have thousands felt and that by Law established? . . . It shall never be your Honour to this or future Ages, to be confined to the Patterns of either French, Dutch, Scotch, or New-English Churches . . .

Querie I. what Precept or Pattern hath the Lord Jesus left you in his last Will and Testament for your Synod or Assembly of Divines, by vertue of which you may expect his presence and assistance . . . we also cause to pray you tell us, Where Christ Jesus hath given you power to assume and appropriate such a Title to your selves, which seems in Scripture to be common to all the Children of God? . . .

Querie II. Whereas you both agree (though with some difference) that the Civill Magistrate must Reform the Church, establish Religion, and so consequently must first Judge, and Judicially Determine which is True, which is False: or else must implicitly beleeve as the Assembly beleeves, and take it upon trust, and so consequently is he the Head, Root and Fountain of the Supremacie of all Spirituall power and hath the power of the Keyes of opening and shutting heaven gates, &c. Of which power upon a grudge (as tis said) about his Wife, King Henry despoiled the Pope, and with consent and Act of Parliament, sate down himselfe in the Popes Chaire in England as since his Successors have done?[13] . . . And oh! since the Common-weale

13. The 1534 Act of Supremacy declared King Henry VIII (1491–1547) to be the supreme head on earth of the Church of England, officially separating the English church from the pope's control. Williams is referring to the common understanding that Henry

cannot without a spirituall rape[14] force the consciences of all to one Worship, oh that it may never commit that rape, in forcing the consciences of all men to one Worship, which a stronger arme and Sword may soon (as formerly) arise to alter.

Querie III. Whether since you professe to be Builders, you have not cause to feare and tremble, least you be found to reject the Corner stone, in not fitting to him only living stones? 1 Pet. 2. Of these living stones, (true Beleevers) the costly Stones of the Temple were types: and without true matter, which (as it is in all works in the World) it is impossible to build a spirituall House unto God?

Querie IV. Whether in your consciences before God, you be not perswaded (notwithstanding your promiscuous joyning with all) that few of the People of England and Scotland, and fewer of the Nobles and Gentry are such spirituall matter, living stones, truely regenerate and converted; and therefore, Whether it be not the greatest Courtesie in the world . . . to acquaint them impartially with their conditions and how impossible it is for a dead Stone to have Fellowship with the living God, and for any man to enter into the Kingdome of God, without a second Birth? John 3.

Querie V . . . we Querie how possible that a person or persons, visibly in a state of nature, dead in sinne, in a state of enmitie and opposition against God (Ephes. 2. Rom. 8.) can ever please God, be visibly maried to God, fight for him under the Banner of Love &c.

Querie VI . . . have there not been as excellent and heavenly Reformers as your selves and Fathers, whose professed Reformation you now dislike?

Querie VII. Since the Law was given by Moses, but Grace and Truth came by Jesus Christ, by whom . . . he hath now revealed his councell in these last times, Heb. 1. We Querie, where you now find one footstep, Print or Pattern in this Doctrine of the Son of God, for a Nationall holy Covenant, and so consequently . . . a National church? Where find you evidence of a whole Nation, Country or Kingdom converted to the Faith and of Christs appointing of a whole Nation or Kingdome to walk in one way of Religion? . . . Again, we aske, Whether in the Constitution of a Nationally Church, it can possibly be framed without a racking and tormenting of the Soules, as well as

---

sought independence from the Catholic church because he wanted to divorce his wife, Catherine of Aragon, who had not given him a male heir, and the pope refused to grant an annulment.

14. For modern readers, Williams's comparing forced religious adherence to rape is shocking. It is not uncommon for him to use this analogy in texts focused on the liberty of conscience, and it may seem hyperbolic now, but it reflects how powerfully he disagreed with state-sponsored religion, and how much he wanted his readers to understand that it was dangerous to their souls.

of the Bodies of persons, for it seems not possible to fit it to every conscience
. . . Lastly, Whether it be not the cause of a world of Hypocrites, the Sooth-
ing up of People in a Formall State Worship to the ruine of their Soules: the
ground of Persecution to Christ Jesus in his Members, and sooner or later,
the Kindling of the devouring flames of Civill Warres, as all Ages justifie?

Querie VIII. . . . We readily grant the Civill Magistrate armed by God
with a civill Sword (Rom. 13.) to execute vengeance against Robbers, Murtherers, Tyrants, &c. Yet where it meerly concerns Christ, we find when his
Disciples desire vengeance upon Offenders, Luke 9, he meekly answers,
You know not what spirit you are of, I came not to destroy Mens Lives,
but to save them . . . we Querie, Whether the blood of so many hundreth
thousand Protestants, mingled with the blood of so many hundreth thousand Papists,[15] as was spilt some hundreth yeares since in the Waldensian
warres,[16] when all the Protestant partie that took the Sword perished with it,
be not a warning to us their offspring?

Querie X. . . . [you] both confesse the Government, Governours, and
the Common Prayer (the Service and Worship of it) to be abominable. Yet
it is confessed that Englands false Nationall Church with her Bishops, Common Prayer, ceremonies, &c., had more evidence of the power of Godlines in
her Children, then was to be found amongst the Scotch, French, Dutch, who
pretend a Reformation purer. It seems therefore evident that neither opposing of Heresies, nor successe in Victories Deliverances, nor power of godlinesse in some persons, can evidence and prove their State and Worship to
be right and pleasing unto God, according to his Ordinance in Christ Jesus.

Querie XI. Since you both seem to magnifie the Scales of Baptisme
and the Lords Supper with a difference and excellency above other Ordinances, We Querie where the Lord Jesus appointed such a difference and
distinction? . . . Furthermore, since a true Baptisme giveth Right to all the
Ordinances of Christ Jesus, we Querie, how any Protestant or Papist, whose
Baptisme you acknowledge to be true, can be denied Communion in the
Supper also . . . and if so, we Querie how farre off Rome and the Pope himselfe is from our bosomes?

15. "Papist" is a common (derogatory) term Protestants used as shorthand to describe followers of the Roman Catholic Church.

16. The Waldensian movement started in the twelfth century in France and spread
throughout Europe in the Middle Ages. The Roman Catholic Church labeled them her-
etics because they denied central tenets of Catholicism, including most sacraments, and
they allowed women to preach. In the sixteenth century, they fit well with the Reformation because they disputed many of the rituals of the Catholic Church. Williams is likely
referring here to the Mérindol Massacre of 1545 in which 3,000 Waldensians were killed.

Querie XII. Since you both professe to want more Light, and that a greater Light is yet to be expected; yea, that the Church of Scotland may yet have need of a greater Reformation &c., we Querie, how you can professe and Sweare to Persecute all others as Schismatiques,[17] Hereticks, &c., that beleeve they see a further Light and dare not joyn with either of your Churches? . . . whether the States of Holland who tolerate, though not owne (as you say) the several Sects amongst them which differ from them, & are of another conscience & worship, whether or no their com not neerer the holy Pattern & command of the Lord Jesus, to permit the tares to have a civil being in the field of the world, untill the harvest the end of it. Mat. 13 . . .

[it is] directly opposite to the very Testament and coming of the Lord Jesus . . . Opposite to the very tender Bowels of Humanity, (how much more of Christianity?) abhoring to poure out the blood of Men meerly for their Soules beliefe and worship. Opposite to the very Essentialls and Fundamentals of the Nature of a Civill Magistracie, a Civil Common weal or combination of Men, which can only respect civill things . . . Opposite to the civill Peace, and the lives of Millions, slaughter'd upon this ground, in mutuall persecuting each other Conscience, especially the Protestant and the Papist. Opposite to the Souls of all Men, who by persecutions are ravished into a dissembled Worship, which their Hearts imbrace not . . . All this in all Ages experience testifies, which never saw any long liv'd Fruit of Peace of Righteousnesse to grow upon that fatall Tree. FINIS.

Roger Williams, *The Bloudy Tenent, of Persecution, for cause of Conscience, discussed, in A Conference between Truth and Peace* (1644)[18]

Recent scholars have described Williams's pivotal text on the separation of church and state as "four hundred scripturally soaked pages" in which he defends the radical idea that churches are solely responsible for spiritual matters and civil governments are only responsible for earthly ones. Using the metaphor of wheat and weeds ("tares") from Matthew, Williams argues that civil governments cannot properly distinguish the saved from the damned, and therefore everyone must be "free to pray, worship, argue, and proselytize as they see fit." Williams does not limit this inclusion to Protestants, but applies it to all faiths, including Catholics, Jews, Muslims, and even people who followed no faith tradition at

17. Schismatics.

18. Williams, *The Bloudy Tenent* in *Complete Writings of Roger Williams*, 3:1–425. Footnotes at the end of each section refer to the pages from which transcriptions were taken.

all.[19] *Readers may see a preview of cultural pluralism, but Williams does not promote anything close to that. While he argues vehemently that no one should be punished for their beliefs or forced into adherence to a particular faith, that does not mean that Williams was willing to entirely leave them alone. Williams describes the eternal punishment that awaited the wicked. As Lisa Gordis argues, "though it does not fit well into his popular images as the father of religious liberty, Williams took comfort and even perhaps joy in his faith that the wicked would be burned up by the angels, while the righteous 'shine as the sun.'"[20]*

It is also important to remember the context of The Bloudy Tenent's *publication; Williams was in London, trying to secure a charter for the colony. He published A* Key into the Language of America *when he first arrived, which the Committee for Foreign Plantations praised. Because he was writing while traveling, and also busy lobbying for his colony's charter, modern readers may find* The Bloudy Tenent *even more challenging to understand than other Williams texts. While Williams wrote this text during his fifteen-month visit, he published it only after he left London. He clearly knew the book would meet with far less favor than the other pieces he published during his visit, and he was right: Parliament ordered it to be burned. According to historian Edwin Gaustad, given how radical this book was "some would have been happy to burn not only the book, but its author as well."[21] But David Hall suggests that there were many others in England who "endorsed toleration or liberty of conscience, some for tactical reasons and others as a matter of principle."[22]*

The text opens with a clear listing of twelve propositions that the rest of the book seeks to defend. For a writer who struggled to stick to his outlines, these twelve propositions are admirably clear, and powerfully challenging to the idea that governments can require any kind of religious observance at all.

First, That the blood of so many hundred thousand soules of Protestants and Papists, spilt in the Wars of Present and former Ages, for their respective Consciences, is not required nor accepted by Jesus Christ the Prince of Peace.

Secondly, Pregnant Scripturs and Arguments are throughout the Worke[23] proposed against the Doctrine of persecution for the cause of Conscience.

19. Beneke and Grenda, *Lively Experiment*, 2–3.

20. Gordis, *Opening Scripture*, 131.

21. Gaustad, "Historical Introduction," Graves, *The Bloudy Tenent*, xxx.

22. Hall, *Puritans*, 266. For more on English supporters of religious toleration, see Coffey, *Persecution and Toleration*.

23. Williams is referring to this book, *The Bloudy Tenent*.

Thirdly, Satisfactorie Answers are given to Scriptures, and objections produced by Mr. Calvin,[24] Beza,[25] Mr. Cotton,[26] and the Ministers of the New English Churches and others former and later, tending to prove the Doctrine of persecution for cause of Conscience.

Fourthly, The Doctrine of persecution for cause of Conscience, is proved guilty of all the blood of the Soules crying for vengeance under the Altar.

Fifthly, All Civill States with their Officers of justice in their respective constitutions and administrations are proved essentially Civil, and therefore not Judges, Governours or Defendours of the Spirituall or Christian state and Worship.

Sixthly, It is the will and command of God, that (since the comming of his Sonne the Lord Jesus) a permission of the most Paganish, Jewish, Turkish, or Antichristian consciences and worships, bee granted to all men in all Nations and Countries: and they are onely to bee fought against with that Sword which is only (in Soule matters) able to conquer, to wit, the Sword of Gods Spirit, the Word of God.[27]

Seventhly, The state of the Land of Israel, the Kings and people thereof in Peace & War, is proved figurative and ceremoniall, and no patterne nor president[28] for any Kingdome or civill state in the world to follow.[29]

Eightly, God requireth not an uniformity of Religion to be inacted and inforced in any civill state; which inforced uniformity (sooner or later) is the greatest occasion of civill Warre, ravishing of conscience, persecution of Christ Jesus in his servants, and of the hypocrise and destruction of millions of souls.

24. John Calvin (1509–1564) was a French Protestant theologian, one of the most powerful writers of the Reformation, and the author of *Institutes of Christian Religion*, among many other texts central to the Reformation. Hall, *Puritans*, 19–28; Winship, *Hot Protestants*, 21–25.

25. Theodore Beza (1519–1605) was a French Protestant theologian who worked with Calvin and succeeded him at the church in Geneva. Like Calvin's works, Beza's texts in translation were steady sellers among English Protestants. Hall, *Puritans*, 17–18.

26. John Cotton.

27. Note that Williams indicates that it is his duty—and the duty of all regenerate people—to try to convince non-believers and followers of other faiths that they are mistaken. They cannot use a civil "sword," but can use the "Sword of God's spirit."

28. Precedent.

29. According to historian James Byrd, Massachusetts Bay ministers argued that the kings of Israel were typological models for civil leaders, so the "leaders of Israel in the Old Testament became authoritative guides for the leaders of the Bay Colony." But Williams denies that Israelite kings can serve as true models because they are only examples, not "types." Byrd, *Challenges of Roger Williams*, 58–59.

Ninthly, In holding an inforced uniformity of Religion in a civill state, wee must necessarily disclaime our desires and hopes of the Jewes conversion to Christ.

Tenthly, An inforced uniformity of Religion throughout a Nation or civill state, confounds the Civill and Religious, denies the principles of Christianity and civility, and that Jesus Christ is come in the Flesh.

Eleventhly, The permission of other consciences and worships then a state professeth, only can (according to God) procure a firme and lasting peace, (good assurance being taken according to the wisdome of the civill state for uniformity of civill obedience from all sorts.)

Twelfthly, lastly, true civility and Christianity may both flourish in a state or Kingdome, notwithstanding the permission of divers and contrary consciences, either of Jew or Gentile.[30]

The preface continues with Williams addressing the text to Parliament. He implores them to set aside matters of conscience, which would be a departure from what previous Parliaments had always done: "All former Parliaments have changed these yoakes according to their consciences, (Popish or Protestant) 'Tis now your Honours turne at helme, and as your task, so I hope your resolution, not to change (for that is but to turne the wheele, which another Parliament, and the very next may turne againe:) but to ease the Subjects and Your selves from a yoake (as was once spoke in a case not unlike Act. 15.) which neither You nor your Fathers were ever able to beare." In a series of direct requests, Williams tells the sitting Parliament that forcing a particular religion on English subjects was "a greater rape, then if they had forced or ravished the bodies of all the women in the World" and that a state religion damages their own souls "by Civill force and violence to their Consciences." His use of the rape metaphor is certainly jarring to modern readers who might rightly question whether requiring adherence to certain church practices is equal to sexual assault. But as we have noted before, his sometimes aggressive language reflects the depth of his convictions, even as it surely offended readers (then and now).

The third prefatory piece directly addresses "every Courteous Reader." Williams laments the "bloody irreligious and inhumane oppressions and destructions under the maske or vaile of the Name of Christ." He also warns his readers that they, too, may suffer persecution: "While I plead the Cause of Truth and Innocencie against the bloody Doctrine of Persecution for cause

---

30. Williams, *The Bloudy Tenent* in *Complete Writings of Roger Williams*, 3:3–4.

of conscience, I judge it not unfit to give alarme to my selfe, and all men to
prepare to be persecuted or hunted for cause of conscience."[31]

The book itself begins with a lengthy excerpt from a book entitled An
Humble Supplication to the King's Majesty, *as it was presented, 1620.*[32] *Wil-*
liams indicates that it was written by John Murton[33] *while he was imprisoned,*
but the author was anonymous. Like Williams, this author also relied on Mat-
thew's tares and wheat parable, and suggests that some who appear to be tares
may actually be wheat. Religious persecution, Williams argues, contradicts the
apostolic foundations of the church and many published writings on doctrine.
Most importantly, only God has the right to rule over a person's soul.

Because Christ commandeth that the Tares and Wheat (which some
understand are those that walke in the Truth, and those that walke in Lies)
should be let alone in the World, and not plucked up until the Harvest,
which is the end of the World, Matth. 13. 30. 38 &c.

The same commandeth Matth. 15. 14. that they that are Blinde (as
some interpret, led on in false Religion, and are offended with him for
teaching true Religion) should be let alone, referring their punishment unto
their falling into the Ditch.

Againe, Luke 9. 54, 55. hee reproved his Disciples who would have had
Fire come downe from Heaven and devoure those Samaritanes who would
not receive Him, in these words: Ye know not of what Spirit ye are, the son
of Man is not come to destroy Mens lives, but to save them.

Paul the Apostle of our Lord teacheth, 2 Tim. 24. 2 That the servant of
our Lord must not strive, but must be gentle toward all Men, suffering the
Evill Men, instructing them with meeknesse that are contrary minded, prov-
ing if God at any time will give them repentance, that they may acknowledge
the Truth, and come to amendment out of that snare of the devill, &c ... And
the Reason seemes to bee, because they who now are Tares, may hereafter
become Wheat ... Some come not untill the 11. houre, Matth 20.6. if those

31. Williams, *The Bloudy Tenent* in *Complete Writings of Roger Williams*, 3:11–13.

32. Williams renamed this book *Scriptures and Reasons Written Long Since by a*
Witness of Jesus Christ, Close Prisoner in Newgate, Against Persecution in Cause of Con-
science, and Sent Some While Since to Mr. Cotton.

33. John Murton/Morton (1585–1626) was one of the founders of the Baptist
church in England. He joined John Smyth's and Thomas Helwys's Separatist congregation in Holland in 1608. After returning to England in 1612, he advocated for complete
liberty of conscience and was imprisoned for nonconformity from 1613 until his death.
He prepared three treatises for the press during his time in Newgate prison, including
the one Williams included in the *The Bloudy Tenent.*

that come not until the last houre should be destroyed, because they come not at the first, then should they never come but be prevented . . .[34]

The Church now, which formerly by induring misery and imprisonment was knowne to be a true Church, doth now terrifie others by imprisonment, banishment, and misery, and boasteth that she is highly esteemed of the world, when as the true Church [she] cannot but be hated of the same . . .[35]

The Lawes of the Civil Magistrates government extends no further then over the body or goods, and to that which is externall: for over the soule God will not suffer any man to rule: onely he himselfe will rule there. Wherefore whosoever doth undertake to give Lawes unto the Soules and Consciences of Men, he usurpeth that government himselfe which appertaineth unto God . . .[36]

The majority of The Bloudy Tenent *is structured as a conversation or "conference" between Truth and Peace, but John Cotton is often referenced in this piece as well, as this book continues their ongoing dispute over freedom of conscience. In the dialogue, Truth and Peace lament that they are both seemingly banished from the earth: "The Gates of Earth and Hell have conspired together to intercept our joyfull meeting and our holy kisses." Peace mourns that conscience has so often led to war, and reminds the reader that both sides in wars claim that God is on their side: "Yea, if they kindle coals, and blow the flames of devouring Warres, that leave neither Spirituall nor Civill State, but burns up Branch and Root, yet how doe all pretend an holy War? He that kills, and hee that's killed, they both cry out, It is for God, and for their conscience." But Truth reassures Peace that violence is not necessary to pursue faith, and that "it is the expresse command of God that Peace be kept, Rom. 13." Peace and Truth agree that the apostolic church no longer exists, so there is no true church until Jesus returns to rebuild it. Therefore, keeping cities peaceful was a civil concern.[37] Again, Williams tries to distinguish between civil concerns and concerns of conscience.*

Peace: Hence it is that so many glorious and flourishing Cities of the World maintaine their Civill peace, yea the very Americans[38] & wildest Pagans keep the peace of their Towns or Cities; though neither in one nor the other can any man prove a true Church of God in those places, and

---

34. Williams, *The Bloudy Tenent* in *Complete Writings of Roger Williams*, 3:29–31.

35. Williams, *The Bloudy Tenent* in *Complete Writings of Roger Williams*, 3:34–35.

36. Williams, *The Bloudy Tenent* in *Complete Writings of Roger Williams*, 3:36.

37. Williams, *The Bloudy Tenent* in *Complete Writings of Roger Williams*, 3:54–67.

38. Williams means Native Americans here.

consequently no spirituall and heavenly peace: The Peace Spirituall (whether true or false) being of higher and farre different nature from the Peace of the place or people, being meerly and essentially civill and humane.

Truth: O how lost are the sonnes of men in this point? To illustrate this: The Church or company of worshippers (whether true or false) is like unto a Body or Colledge of Physitians in a Citie; like unto a Corporation, Society, or Company of East-Indie or Turkie-Merchants, or any other Societie or Company in London: which Companies may hold their Courts, keep their Records, hold disputations; and in matters concerning their Societie, may dissent, divide, breake into Schismes and Factions, sue and implead each other at the Law, yea wholly breake up and dissolve into pieces and nothing, and yet the peace of the Citie not be in the least measure impaired or disturbed; because the essence or being of the Citie, and so the well-being and peace thereof is essentially distinct from those particular Societies; the Citie-Courts, Citie-Lawes, Citie-punishments distinct from theirs. . . .[39]

For ten chapters of the book, Williams uses the parable of the wheat and tares from Matthew (13: 24–30, 36–43) to defend religious liberty, even though many writers had used it to argue for religious persecution. (John Cotton also used this parable.) But writers like Cotton had, according to Williams, fundamentally misinterpreted the parable.[40] Williams argues that the field is the world ("Field of the World"), not the "Garden of the Church." Most importantly, according to Williams, civil authorities can play no role in churches, whether plucking or planting tares or wheat. Before turning to this parable, Williams offers a kind of segue, where he reaffirms the right of governments to punish disturbers of the civil peace, but not punish "breaches" of spiritual matters.

Peace: I shall now trouble you (deare Truth) but with one conclusion more, which is this: viz. That if a man hold forth errour with a boysterous and arrogant spirit, to the disturbance of the civill Peace, he ought to be punished &c.

Truth: . . . But if the matter be of another nature, a spirituall and divine nature, I have written before in many cases, and might in many more, that the Worship which a State professeth may bee contradicted and preached against, and yet no breach of Civill Peace . . . So commonly the meeke and peaceable of the earth are traduced as rebells, factious, peace-breakers,

---

39. Williams, *The Bloudy Tenent* in *Complete Writings of Roger Williams*, 3:72–73.
40. Byrd, *Challenges of Roger Williams*, 89.

although they deale not with the State or State-matters, but matters of divine and spirituall nature.

First, Matth. 13. 30, 38. because Christ commandeth to let alone the Tares to grow up together with the Wheat, untill the Harvest. Unto which he[41] answereth: That Tares are not Bryars and Thornes, but partly Hypocrites, like unto the godly, but indeed carnall (as the Tares are like to Wheat, but are not Wheat,) or partly such corrupt doctrines or practices as are indeed unsound, but yet such as come very near the truth (as Tares do to the Wheat) and so neer that good men may be taken with them, and so the persons in whom they grow cannot bee rooted out, but good Wheat will be rooted out with them. In such a case (saith he) Christ calleth for peaceble toleration, and not for penall prosecution, according to the third Conclusion.

Truth: The substance of this Answer I conceive to be first negative, that by Tares are not meant persons of another Religion and Worship, that is (saith he) they are not Briars and Thornes. Secondly, affirmative, by Tares are meant either persons, or doctrines, or practices; persons, as hypocrites, like the godly: doctrines or practices corrupt, yet like the truth . . . But alas, how darke is the soule left that desires to walke with God in holy feare and trembling, when in such a waighty and mighty point as this is, that in matters of conscience concerneth the spilling of the bloud of thousands, and the Civill Peace of the World in the taking up Armes to supresse all false Religions! when I say no evidence or demonstration of the Spirit is brought to prove such an interpretation, nor Arguments from the place itselfe or the Scriptures of truth to confirme it; but a bare Affirmation that these Tares must signifie persons, or doctrines and practices. . . .[42]

Williams draws a clear distinction between people who commit crimes against civil laws and people who are simply worshiping or practicing their faith differently. Williams also does not suggest that sinners will escape divine punishment; instead, he suggests that civil authorities cannot mete out the punishments that only God can deliver in final judgment.

Truth: First, I answer that as the civill State keepes it selfe with a civill Guard, in case these Tares shall attempt ought against the peace and welfare of it, let such civill offences be punished, and yet as Tares opposite to Christs Kingdome, let their Worship and Consciences be tolerated . . . the Lord

---

41. John Cotton.

42. Williams, *The Bloudy Tenent* in *Complete Writings of Roger Williams*, 3:96–98.

himself knows who are his & his foundation remaineth sure, his Elect or chosen cannot perish nor be finally deceived.

Lastly, the Lord Jesus here in this Parable layes downe two Reasons, able to content and satisfie our hearts, to beare patiently this their contradiction and Antichristianity, and to permit or let them alone . . . if such combustions and fightings were, as to pluck up all the false professours of the name of Christ, the good wheat also would enjoy little peace, but be in danger to bee pluckt up and torne out of this world by such bloody stormes and tempests . . .

The second Reason noted in the Parable which may satisfie any man from wondring at the patience of God is this: when the world is ripe in sinne . . . then those holy and mighty Officers and Executioners, the Angels with their sharpe and cutting sickles of eternall vengeance, shall downe with them, and bundle them up for the everlasting burnings. Then shall that Man of Sin . . . drink of the Wine of the wrath of God which is poured out without mixture into the Cup of his indignation, and he shall be tormented with fire and brimstone in the presence of the holy Angels, and in the presence of the Lambe, and the smoake of their torment shall ascend up for ever and ever, Rev. 14: 10. 11 . . .[43]

Williams often refers to hundreds of years of religious persecution and "holy" wars to remind the reader about what happened when nations did not practice toleration.

Peace: Oh how contrary unto this command of the Lord Jesus have such as have conceived themselves the true Messengers of the Lord Jesus, in all ages, not let such Professours and Prophets alone, whom they have judged Tares, but have provoked Kings and Kingdomes (and some out of good intentions and zeale to God) to prosecute and persecute such even unto death? Amongst whom Gods people (the good wheat) hath also beene pluckt up, as all Ages and Histories testifie, and too too oft the World laid upon bloody heapes in civill and intestine desolations on this occasion. All which would bee prevented, and the greatest breaches made up in this peace of our owne or other Countries, were this command of the Lord Jesus obeyed, to wit, to let them alone untill the Harvest.[44]

Truth: I shall conclude this controversie about this Parable in this briefe sum and recapitulation of what hath beene said. I hope by the evident demonstration of Gods Spirit to the conscience I have proved, Negatively,

---

43. Williams, *The Bloudy Tenent* in *Complete Writings of Roger Williams*, 3:111–13.
44. Williams, *The Bloudy Tenent* in *Complete Writings of Roger Williams*, 3:117.

First, that the Tares in this Parable cannot signifie Doctrines or Practices ... but Persons.

Secondly, the Tares cannot signifie Hypocrites in the Church either undiscovered or discovered.

Thirdly, the Tares here cannot signifie Scandalous Offenders in the Church.

Fourthly, nor scandalous offenders in life and conversation against the Civill state.

Fifthly, The field in which these Tares are sowne, is not the Church.

Againe affirmatively: First, the Field is properly the World, the Civil State or Common-wealth.

Secondly, The Tares here intended by the Lord Jesus are Antichristian idolaters, opposite to the good seed of the Kingdome, true Christians.

Thirdly, the ministers or messengers of the Lord Jesus ought to let them alone to live in the world, and neither seeke by prayer or prophesie to pluck them up before the Harvest.

Fourthly, this permission or suffering of them in the field of the World, is not for hurt, but for common good, even for the good of the good Wheat, the people of God.

Lastly, the patience of God is, and the patience of Men ought to be exercised toward them, and yet nothwithstanding their doome is fearfull at the harvest, even gathering, bundling, and everlasting burnings by the mighty hand of the Angels in the end of the World.[45]

Peace asks Truth about the responsibilities of magistrates and ecclesiastical leaders, as Williams wrestles with the fact that the monarch of England is also the head of the English state church.

Peace: It is said true that Titus and Timothy,[46] and so the Officers of the Church of Christ are bound to prevent soule infection: But what hinders that the Magistrate should not be charged also with this duty?

Truth: I answer, many things I have answered, and more shall; at present I shall only say this: If it be the Magistrates duty or office, then is he both a Temporall and Ecclesiasticall officer; contrary to which most men will affirme; and yet we know the policie of our owne Land and Country hath established to the Kings and Queens thereof, the supreme heads or governours of the Church of England. . . . woe were it with the civill Magistrate

---

45. Williams, *The Bloudy Tenent* in *Complete Writings of Roger Williams*, 3:118–19.

46. Titus and Timothy were two of Paul's missionary companions and were leaders of the early church in Ephesus and Crete.

(and most intolerable burthens do they lay upon their backs that teach this doctrine) if together with the common care and charge of the Commonwealth (the peace and safety of the Towne, City, State or Kingdome) the bloud of every soule that perisheth should cry against him, unlesse he could say with Paul, Acts 20 (in spirituall regards) I am clear from the bloud of all men, that is the bloud of soules, which was his charge to look after, so far as his preaching went, not the bloud of bodies which belongeth to the civill Magistrate.

I acknowledge he ought to cherish (as a foster father) the Lord Jesus in his truth, in his Saints, to cleave unto them himselfe, and to countenance them even to the death, yea also to breake the teeth of the Lions, who offer Civill violence and injury unto them.

But to see all his Subjects Christians, to keepe such Church or Christians in the purity of worship, and see them doe their duty, this belongs to the Head of the Body of Christ Jesus, and such spirituall Officers as he hath to this purpose deputed . . .[47]

Williams refers to examples from Europe's recent past to illustrate how wrong it is for civil powers to punish people for religious differences. In the examples that follow, he refers to both the French bishops and England's Queen Mary, both of whom used "the civill sword in spirituall cases," ordering the persecution and death of Protestants.

It is indeed the ignorance and blind zeale of the second Beast, the false Prophet, Rev. 13. 13 to perswade the civill Powers of the earth to persecute the Saints, that is, to bring fiery judgements upon men in a judiciall way, and to pronounce the such judgements of imprisonment, banishment, death, proceed from Gods righteous vengeance upon such Hereticks. So dealt divers Bishops in France, and England too in Queene Maries days with the Saints of God at their putting to death, declaiming against them in their Sermons to the people, and proclaiming that these persecutions even unto death were Gods just judgements from heaven upon these Heretickes . . .[48]

What a most wofull proofe hereof have the Nations of the Earth given in all Ages? And to seeke no further than our native Soyle,[49] within a few scores of yeeres, how many wonderfull changes in Religion hath the whole Kingdome made, according to the change of the Governours thereof, in the severall Religious which they themselves imbraced! Henry the 7. finds and

47. Williams, *The Bloudy Tenent* in *Complete Writings of Roger Williams*, 3:128–29.
48. Williams, *The Bloudy Tenent* in *Complete Writings of Roger Williams*, 3:132–33.
49. England.

leaves the kingdome absolutely Popish. Henry the 8. casts it into a mould half Popish halfe Protestant. Edward the 6 brings forth an Edition all Protestant. Queene Mary within a few yeares defaceth Edwards worke, and renders the Kingdome . . . all Popish. Maries short life and Religion ends together: and Elizabeth reviveth her Brother Edwards Modell, all Protestant. . .[50]

[Peace]: It hath been Englands sinfull shame, to fashion & change their Garments and Religions with wondrous ease and lightnesse, as a higher Power, a stronger Sword hath prevailed; after the ancient pattern of Nebuchadnezzars bowing the whole world in one most solemne uniformitie of worship to his Golden Image.[51]

In a brief marginal note to chapter XL, Williams summarizes an essential problem of civil governments punishing people for religious differences, namely, anyone who converted to avoid civil punishments was not truly converted, and any religion that demanded adherence from the unconverted was not a "true Religion."

The danger & mischiefe of a civill sword in Soule matters, which makes the civill Magistrate deeply guilty of all those evils which he aims to suppresse. That cannot be a true Religion, which needs carnall weapons to uphold it. Persecutors beget a perswasion of their crueltie in the hearts of the persecuted.[52]

50. Williams offers a brief accounting of the English monarchs and the shifts they caused in the church in England: Henry VII (1485–1509) was the first Tudor monarch and Catholic; Henry VIII (1509–1547) officially separated the Church of England from the Vatican-controlled Roman Catholic Church and by act of Parliament was declared head of the Church of England; Edward VI (1547–1553) became king at age nine when Henry died and was known as a zealous Protestant; Queen Mary (1553–1558) tried to restore the English church to Catholicism and persecuted English Protestants, executing hundreds for heresy; Queen Elizabeth I (1558–1603) rededicated the Church of England to Protestantism and was given title of Supreme Governor of the Church of England, although recent historians acknowledge that she allowed some vestiges of Catholic ritual to remain. Williams skipped over Lady Jane Grey, who was proclaimed queen after Edward VI's death in 1553, but never assumed the throne. She was known to be a devout Protestant.

51. Williams, *The Bloudy Tenent* in *Complete Writings of Roger Williams*, 3:136–37. This story about Nebuchadnezzar, King of Babylon, comes from the third book of Daniel: "Nebuchadnezzar the King made an image of gold, whose height was three score cubits, and the breadth thereof six cubits: he set it up in the plain of Dura, in the province of Babel." (KJV) He required that everyone worship this golden image, threatening to throw anyone who refused into the fire. Three men (Shadrach, Meshach and Abednego) refused and were thrust into the fire, but saved from death by God.

52. Williams, *The Bloudy Tenent* in *Complete Writings of Roger Williams*, 3:138–39.

Williams suggests that Cotton forgave some persecution, but condemned others, depending on who is doing the persecuting, when according to Williams no government had the right to challenge any person's conscience.

Peace: He ends this passage with approbation of Q. Elizabeth for persecuting the Papists, and a reproofe to King James for his persecuting the Puritans, etc.

Truth. I answer, if Queene Elizabeth according to the Answerers Tenent and Conscience, did well to persecute according to his conscience, King James did not [do] ill in persecuting according to his: For Mr. Cotton must grant that either King James was not fit to be a King, had not the essentiall qualifications of a King, in not being able rightly to judge who ought to be persecuted, and who not, or else he must confesse that King James and all Magistrates must persecute such whom in their Conscience they judge worthy to be persecuted. . .

Therefore (lastly) according to Christ Jesus his command, Magistrates are bound not to persecute, and to see that none of their subjects be persecuted and oppressed for their conscience and worship, being otherwise subject and peaceable in Civill Obedience.[53]

. . . A false Religion out of the Church will not hurt the Church, no more then weedes in the Wildernesse hurt the inclosed Garden, or poyson hurt the body when it is not touched or taken, yea and antidotes are received against it.

Secondly, a false Religion and Worship will not hurt the Civill State, in case the worshippers breake no civill Law: and the Answerer (elsewhere) acknowledgeth that the civill Lawes not being broken, civill Peace is not broken: and this only is the Point in Question.[54]

Along with scriptural references, Williams also relies on theologians and other writers to defend his position. In this chapter, he employs Martin Luther to respond to Cotton, referred to here as "the Answerer."

Truth: I answer, in this joynt confession of the Answerer with Luther, to wit, that the government of the civil Magistrate extendeth no further then over the bodies and goods of their subjects, not over their soules: who sees not what a cleare testimony from his own mouth and pen is given, to wit, that either the Spirituall and Church estate, the preaching of the Word, and the gathering of the Church, the Baptisme of it, the Ministry, Government

---

53. Williams, *The Bloudy Tenent* in *Complete Writings of Roger Williams*, 3:187–88.
54. Williams, *The Bloudy Tenent* in *Complete Writings of Roger Williams*, 3:197–98.

and Administrations thereof belong to the civill body of the Common-weale? That is, to the bodies and goods of men, which seemes monstrous to imagine: Or else that the civill Magistrate cannot (without exceeding the bounds of his office) meddle with those spirituall affaires.[55]

In nearly the final chapter of The Bloudy Tenent, *Williams directly addresses his New England neighbors who left England rather than conform to the dictates of the Church of England, suggesting that many differences in doctrine persist among them, and that crossing an ocean did not magically wash those differences away. How can those same New Englanders demand conformity?*

Truth: Alas, who knowes not what lamentable differences have beene betweene the same Ministers of the Church of England, some conforming, others leaving their livings, friends, country, life, rather then conforme; when others againe (of whose personall godlinesse it is not questioned) have succeeded by conformity into such forsaken (so called) Livings? How great the present differences even amongst them that feare God, concerning Faith, Justification, and the evidence of it? concerning Repentence and godly sorrow, as also and mainly concerning the Church, the Matter, Forme, Administrations and Government of it?

Let none now thinke that the passage to New England by Sea, or the nature of the Countrey can doe what onely the Key of David[56] can do, to wit, open and shut the Consciences of men.

Beside, how can this bee a faithfull and upright acknowledgement of their weaknesse and imperfection, when they preach, print, and practice such violence to the soules and bodies of others, and by their Rules and Grounds ought to proceed even to the killing of those whom they judge so deare unto them, and in respect of godlinesse far above themselves?[57]

"A Model of Church and Civil Power" is the final portion of The Bloudy Tenent. *We have included parts of that text in chapter 3.*

55. Williams, *The Bloudy Tenent* in *Complete Writings of Roger Williams*, 3:202.

56. The "Key of David" refers to God's authority over his people, as the house of David symbolizes the kingdom of God. The phrase appears in both Rev 3:7: "These things saith he that is Holy, and True, which hath the key of David, which openeth and no man shutteth, and shutteth and no man openeth" and Isa 22:22: "And the key of the house of David will I lay upon his shoulder: so he shall open, and no man shall shut: and he shall shut, and no man shall open." (KJV)

57. Williams, *The Bloudy Tenent* in *Complete Writings of Roger Williams*, 3:217.

Chapter 8

Native Evangelization, 1635–1680

ONE OF THE GRAND *(if hypocritical) justifications of European colonization of the Americas was the evangelization of Indigenous populations. This must have seemed farcical to Natives, who saw the Spanish, English, and French enslave, dispossess, and kill as often or even more than they evangelized. As Narragansett and Niantic tribal educator Chrystal Mars Baker has noted, Williams and other Europeans could not conceive that Natives had their own legitimate religious traditions, and that maybe they even worshiped the same God.*[1]

The conversion of Native Americans to Christianity sporadically occupied Williams's attention, writings, and activities in his early years. More than most colonists, Williams showed an interest in Native language, religion, and culture from the time of his arrival in Boston in 1631. He had voiced his interests in converting Natives in private correspondence and spent time among the Wampanoag and the Narragansett, even staying in their wetus (bark and sapling houses). This continued after his banishment and flight to found Providence and the eventual colony of Rhode Island in 1635–1636. In 1643, Williams published A Key Into the Language of America, *an important phrasebook of the Narragansett language with additional insights on Narragansett culture, including religion. In the introduction to* A Key, *Williams suggests that his linguistic facility would be a key component of evangelizing Natives.*

But something changed within Williams's thinking at some point along the way. Likely prior to his trip to London in 1643–1644, Williams began to doubt whether Native Americans could be and even should be converted to Christianity for reasons that were practical, linguistic, and theological. Some small part of Williams's reticence was rooted in his growing belief that no one

---

1. Chrystal Mars Baker, correspondence with the authors, January 24, 2023.

had been given a proper commission to convert Natives. He also doubted they could be fully instructed in their own language to completely understand Christianity. But perhaps the most powerful reason, as Narragansett scholar Mack Scott has noted, was a result of his own experiences among Natives and observing the richness of their culture, lifeways, and rituals.[2] *This change of mind may have been the result of the frustration of his own missionary attempts, since most Narragansett and Wampanoag were not inclined to adopt what was an entirely foreign religion. Natives were not sitting around waiting to be converted to Christianity, despite the fantasies conjured up by the 1629 Massachusetts Bay Colony seal, in which a Native says "Come over and help us."*

Furthermore, English requirements for a true conversion were not just theological; they were cultural as well, and involved a rigorous religious and cultural reorientation. Convincing Natives to pray to the Christian God and adopt European cultural habits regarding dress, gender norms, and religious practice was not easy, as the Massachusetts Bay missionary John Eliot found out over the course of the seventeenth century. Just as Roger Williams was largely giving up on converting Natives to Christianity, Eliot and some other ministers (including Thomas Mayhew on Martha's Vineyard) began their own efforts, eventually learning Wôpanaâk and founding so-called "praying towns" for christianized Natives. The founding of a London-based missionary society in 1649, often called the New England Company, poured resources into Eliot's and others' efforts to found praying towns (fourteen such towns in Massachusetts Bay and Connecticut by 1675, with more in Plimouth and on Martha's Vineyard) and produce an indigenous translation of the entire Bible in 1663, in addition to other primers and manuals for Natives' consumption.

Williams, on the other hand, did next to nothing regarding Native evangelization after the early 1640s, despite virtually bragging that he could have brought thousands of Natives to baptism. Williams clearly disagreed with Eliot's intense evangelistic efforts, as his Reply to Eliot *below illustrates. But it is not the case that Williams embraced Indigenous religion or believed they were fine as they were in some sort of modern sense. Williams still saw Natives as "heathens" and in need of conversion, and yet did not believe that they should be coerced or pressured. Later in life, Williams stated that he continued to preach to the Narragansett and other nations, although he never claimed a single conversion. The selections below (combined with the 1632 letter to John Winthrop in chapter 5) show an evolution in Williams' thinking over time.*

---

2. Mack Scott, correspondence with the authors, January 22, 2023.

Roger Williams to Thomas Thorowgood, December 20, 1635[3]

The following is an excerpt of a letter from Williams to Thomas Thorowgood, a puritan minister in England. This excerpt was later printed in a book by Thorowgood in 1650, titled The Jewes in America, or Probabilities, that those Indians are Judaical, *in which he argues (as the subtitle suggests) that Native Americans were descendants of the ten "lost tribes" of Israel in the Hebrew Bible.[4] Thorowgood quotes from two letters that Williams had sent to him in the 1630s, but the originals of these letters have not survived. The idea that Native Americans were somehow related to Jews started in the sixteenth century under the Spanish (a theory the Spanish advocate for Natives Bartolomé de las Casas also espoused) and became popular in the early seventeenth century as English theologians and pastors struggled to fit Natives (who are not mentioned in the Bible) into their biblically based sense of history and humankind. As evidence of the possible connections between Jews and Native Americans, Williams highlights cultural and religious components, as well as linguistic factors—that there were some similarities between Native languages and Hebrew (something the English minister and missionary John Eliot later speculated about as well). Thorowgood was not the only person to write about these supposed connections; in 1650 the respected Dutch scholar Menasseh ben Israel published* The Hope of Israel, *which also speculated on such historical connections from a Jewish perspective. Williams later doubted that Natives were descended from the lost tribes of Israel, and although wider belief in this also waned in the seventeenth century, in the nineteenth century these theories were once again revived as part of a global linguistic and ethnographic interest.*

[Salem, Massachusetts Bay]

Three things make me yet suspect that the poore natives came from the southward, and are Jewes or Jewish quodammodo,[5] and not from the Northern barbarous as some imagine. 1. Themselves constantly affirme that their Ancestors came from the southwest, and thither they all goe dying.[6] 2. They constantly and strictly separate their women in a little Wigwam by themselves

---

3. *Correspondence of Roger Williams*, 1:30–31.

4. Cogley, "Ancestry of the American Indians: Thomas Thorowgood's 'Iewes in America,'" 304–20.

5. Latin, meaning "to a certain extent."

6. New England Natives believed that their origins were from the southwest, towards where the sun set, and that when they died, their souls would return to the southwest, to Cautantowwit's house, as Williams later noted in *Key into the Language of America*, 116.

in their feminine seasons.[7] 3. And beside their God Kuttand to the south-west, they hold that Nanawitnawit (a God over head) made the Heavens and the Earth, and some tast of affinity with the Hebrew I have found.[8]

. . . For the Government of the Common-wealth from the King, as supreme, to the inferiour and subordinate Magistrates, my heart is on them, as once Deborah[9] spake, and as the Governours and assistants[10] doe them-selves take the oath of Allegiance, so they have power by their Charter to give the same to all that shall at any time passe to them, or inhabite with them; But, Tempora mutantur, and it may be tis with them, as with us, & nos mutamur in illis.[11]

Roger Williams, *Christenings Make Not Christians* (1645)[12]

In this rather surprising tract published only two years after A Key into the Language of America, *Williams's rhetoric takes a markedly pessimistic tone. The treatise tackles an enormous topic—namely, the nature of "true" Christianity, especially as it relates to the conversion of Indigenous populations to Christianity—and places it in an appropriately large hemispheric and even global framework. In this text, Williams is far less hopeful about Natives converting to Christianity compared to the optimism of* A Key *only two years earlier. But part of Williams's hesitance was rooted in his theology regarding the true church. He increasingly doubted that God had ordained and given authority for the gathering of true churches or the conversion of American Natives. This made him obsess over the possibility of false conversions to Christianity—conversions that were incomplete, but also not done with proper apostolic authority. This short twenty-two-page tract, then, represents a stunning reversal of his views about Native Americans and their convertibility. To make his point about the danger of false conversions, he uses as examples Catholic*

---

7. Williams is here suggesting that the reported practice of Native women to retire to a separate wigwam or wetu during their monthly period was similar to purity laws in the Hebrew Bible in which women were required to separate themselves during their period (see, for example, Lev 15:19).

8. English colonists such as Williams and John Eliot initially found some linguistic similarities between local Native languages and biblical Hebrew.

9. Deborah was a prophet in the Hebrew Bible who led the Israelites (see Judges chapters 4–5).

10. That is, of the colony of Massachusetts Bay. The governor and assistants were the primary political leaders of that colony.

11. Latin, meaning "times change, and we with them."

12. Williams, *Christenings Make not Christians* in *Complete Writings of Roger Williams*, 7:26–41.

missionaries in the Americas who, as Protestants liked to point out, baptized
Natives in large numbers, often without significant religious instruction to the
adults (many of whom were on their deathbeds) or, more commonly, infants.
Nonetheless, as he did in A Key, *Williams uses Natives as a positive foil for*
European Christians, which likely jolted and even incensed his readers.

Now Secondly, for the hopes of CONVERSION, and turning the
People of America[13] unto God: There is no respect of Persons with him, for
we are all the worke of his hands; from the rising of the Sunne to the going
downe thereof, his name shall be great among the nations from the East
& and from the West &c.[14] If we respect their [s]ins, they are far short of
European sinners: They neither abuse such corporall mercies[15] for they have
them not; nor sin they against the Gospell light, (which shines not amongst
them) as the men of Europe do:[16] And yet if they were greater sinners then
they are, or greater sinners then the Europeans, they are not the farther
from the great Ocean of mercy in that respect.[17]

Lastly, they are intelligent, many very ingenuous, plaine-hearted, in-
quisitive, and (as I said before) prepared with many convictions &c.[18]

Now secondly, for the Catholicks conversion, although I believe I may
safely hope that God hath his in Rome, in Spaine,[19] yet if Antichrist[20] be

13. Williams here is referring to Native Americans.

14. A partial quotation of several Bible verses, including Ps 113:3–4 and Isa 64:8.

15. A reference to the Corporal Works of Mercy (usually seven) within Catholic
teaching, usually drawn from Jesus's teaching in the New Testament. These include:
feeding the hungry, giving drink to the thirsty, sheltering the homeless, visiting the sick,
visiting prisoners, giving alms to the poor, and burying the dead. Williams is simply
observing that Natives were not hypocritical like some European Christians were in
that they did not profess a standard of practical holiness and then not live up to it.

16. "Gospell light" is a reference to the knowledge of salvation through Jesus that both
Catholics and Protestants believed but that Protestants made absolutely central to their
teaching. Williams is arguing that Europeans were aware of this salvation but did not live
by it, whereas Natives did not know about it, and therefore did not sin by not living by it.

17. Williams is verging on a sort of universalism here, in which Native "sins" (by
European definitions) might still be covered in God's mercy.

18. Williams's views of Native cultures were often contradictory; here he praises
Native culture and intelligence, although there are plenty of places in private correspondence where he refers to them in highly derogatory terms.

19. Williams, as a staunch Protestant, is trying to be a little bit nuanced here and
state that some Catholics are truly saved, in his view at least.

20. This is a specific reference to the Catholic pope, although the idea of the Antichrist has loomed large in Protestant theology, and was especially strong in early
modern England. In the Bible the Antichrist is described in partial ways in various
books, but is usually understood to gather forces against Jesus during the end times, as

their false head (as most true it is) the body, faith, baptisme, hope (opposite to the true, Ephes. 4.) are all false also; yea consequently their preachings, conversions, salvations (leaving secret things to God) must all be of the same false nature likewise.[21]

If the reports (yea some of their owne Historians) be true, what monstrous and most inhumane conversions have they made; baptizing thousands, yea ten thousands of the poore Natives, sometimes by wiles and subtle devices, sometimes by force compelling them to submit to that which they understood not, neither before nor after such their monstrous Christning of them.[22] Thirdly, for our New-england parts, I can speake it uprightly and confidently, I know it to have been easie for my selfe, long ere this, to have brought many thousands of these Natives, yea the whole country, to a far greater Antichristian conversion then ever was yet heard of in America. I have reported something in the Chapter of their Religion, how readily I could have brought the whole Country to have observed one day in seven; I adde to have received a Baptisme (or washing) though it were in Rivers (as the first Christians and the Lord [J]esus himselfe did) to have come to a stated Church meeting, maintained priests and formes of prayer, and a whole forme of Antichristian worship in life and death.[23] Let none wonder at this, for plausible perswations in the mouths of those whom naturall men esteem and love: for the power of prevailing forces and armies hath done this in all the Nations (as men speake) of Christendome. Yea what lamentable experience have we of the Turnings and Turnings of the body of this Land in point of Religion in few yeares?[24]

---

described in Dan 11 and Rev 13.

21. This is a strong but typical early modern Protestant indictment of Catholic teaching and practice. Williams refers to the pope as the Antichrist (which was exceedingly common among Protestants in this time period). Williams is saying that if the head of the Catholic church is the Antichrist and therefore false, then everything else in the church is also false, including the conversions of Natives.

22. Williams shows himself to be a wide reader of the literature of Spanish colonization. Large numbers of baptisms of Natives at the hands of Catholic priests were indeed reported in the sixteenth and early seventeenth centuries. This started with Franciscans in Mexico in the 1520s and continued on into New Mexico in the 1630s. Missionaries reported lining up hundreds of Indigenous people and sprinkling them with water in mass baptisms. For large numbers of baptized Natives, see, for example, *Memorial Que Fray Juan de Santander de la Orden de San Francisco* (1630). Fr Alonso de Benavides's "Memorial to King Philip IV of Spain of the Indian Missions of New Mexico," contained within this pamphlet, can be found in translated form at: http://nationalhumanitiescenter.org/pds/amerbegin/settlement/text5/BenavidesFranciscanReport.pdf. See also Don, *Bonfires of Culture*, 35.

23. Williams is massively exaggerating his own persuasive powers as well as the receptivity of New England Natives to Christianity, given his extreme vulnerability among the Narragansett and, before that, the Wampanoag.

24. As he goes on to explain, Williams seems to be referencing the way England's

When England was all Popish under Henry the seventh, how easie is conversion wrought to halfe Papish halfe-Protestant under Henry the eighth?[25]

From halfe-Protestanisme halfe-Popery under Henry the eight, to absolute Protestanisme under Edward the sixth: from absoluer Protestation under Edward the sixt to absalute popery under Quegne Mary, and from absolute Popery under Queene Mary, (just like the Weather-cocke, with the breath of every Prince) to absolute Protestanisme under Queene Elizabeth &c.[26]

For all this, yet some may aske, why hath there been such a price in my hand not improved? why have I not brought them to such a conversion as I speake of?[27] I answer, woe be to me, if I call light darknesse, or darknesse light; sweet bitter, or bitter sweet;[28] woe be to me if I call that conversion unto God, which is indeed subversion of the soules of Millions in Christen-dome, from one false worship to another,[29] and the prophanation of the holy name of God, his holy Son and blessed Ordinances America (as Europe and all nations) lyes dead in sin and trespasses:[30] It is not a suite of crimson Satten[31] will make a dead man live, take off and change his crimson into white. . .

Roger Williams, *The Bloody Tenent Yet More Bloody* (1652)[32]

Williams briefly addressed Native American evangelization in the midst of a lengthy pamphlet war between Williams and Boston minister John Cotton in the 1640s and 1650s regarding religious coercion. Cotton used Native

---

official religion followed the monarchs' preferences between the 1530s and the 1570s.

25. English King Henry VIII famously separated the Church of England from Catholicism, but theologically, he still favored Catholicism and resisted the Protestant movement under Martin Luther, John Calvin, Theodore Beza, and other reformers on the Continent.

26. Williams is rehearsing the complicated royal succession in England following Henry VIII. See the introduction to this book for a brief summary of these events.

27. Williams again shows he is feeling guilty about not having any conversions to show for his linguistic ability. This was especially true coming on the heels of his impressive *Key into the Language of America*.

28. These references come from Isa 5:20: "Woe unto them who call evil good, and good evil; that put darkness for light, and light for darkness; that put bitter for sweet, and sweet for bitter!" (KJV).

29. Williams in his writings repeatedly expresses concern that Natives were being incompletely converted to Christianity, which in his mind made that, too, another form of false worship (just as Native religion was in his mind also false worship).

30. By 1645, Williams had grown very doubtful that many people called Christians in Europe and America were actually Christians.

31. Satin.

32. Williams, *Bloody Tenent Yet More Bloody* in *Complete Writings of Roger Williams*, 4:3–547.

Americans as an example of how the Massachusetts Bay Colony (appropriately, in his mind) allowed Natives within its claimed boundaries to freely worship, but only privately. Cotton also referenced an important moment in 1644, when some Massachusett and Nipmuc sachems "submitted" as subjects to the English crown.[33] As part of their "submission," Cotton notes, they agreed to some principles that largely corresponded with the Ten Commandments. In response, Williams spends a few pages critiquing the evangelization methods of Roxbury minister and missionary John Eliot and others in Massachusetts Bay, and calls into question their proper apostolic commission and their linguistic ability.

More broadly, in The Bloody Tenent Yet More Bloody, Williams joined a longer debate regarding the extent of church and civil power over the inner lives of its residents (additional context and readings can be found in chapters 2, 3, and 7). In the excerpted section below, Williams discusses the conversion of Native Americans in the context of religious freedom as well as some complicated timing regarding authority to convert Natives to Christianity and convene true Christian churches.

Of propagating Religion by the Sword.

Peace. The close of this Chapter[34] seemes strange and wonder-full, for Mr Cotton acknowledged that Propagation of Religion ought not to be by the Sword, and yet instantly againe maintaines[35] "the use of the Sword when persons (which then must be judged by the Civill State) blaspheme the true God and the true Religion, and also seduce others to damnable Heresie and Idolatrie: But this (sayth he) is not the Propagation of Religion, but the preserving of it, and if it doe conduce to Propagation, it is onely Removendo prohibens."[36]

Truth. What is this Removendo prohibens, but as the weeding of a Field or Garden? And every Husbandman will say, that the end of such his work, is the propagation and increase of his graine and fruit, as well as the making of his fence, and planting and sowing of his Field or Garden: What therefore is this Confession, (though with this Distinction) but in truth an acknowledgement of what in Words and Tearmes, he yet denies (with Hilarie)[37] to wit, a propagating of Christian Religion and Truth by the Civill Sword?

33. We have included this document in chapter 4.

34. That is, chapter 66 of Cotton's book.

35. The original publication inserts an extra "he" here.

36. Williams here is quoting directly from *The Bloody Tenent Washed*, from the end of chapter 66. *Removendo prohibens* can be translated as "removing obstacles."

37. Likely Williams is referring here to Hilary of Poitiers, a fourth-century early Christian theologian whose work *De Trinitate* was often cited and quoted by early modern Christians, along with other early Christian leaders like Ambrose and Augustine, all early pillars of the church. Hilary of Poitiers was also held up, along with Tertullian

2. Besides it is the same hand and power that plucks up the weedes, and plants the Corne, and consequently, that same hand and Sword that destroyes the Heretick, may make the Christian, &c.

Exam: of Chap. 67. replying to Chap. 70.

Peace. Concerning Tertullians speech,[38] and especially that Branch, to wit, that [By the Law of naturall equitie, Men are not to be compelled to any Religion, but permitted to believe or not believe at all] Mr Cotton answers, that they doe permit the Indians, but it will not therefore be safe to tollerate the publicke Worship of Devills or Idolls. The Discusser replied, that they doe permit the Indians in the Paganish Worship, and therefore were partiall to their Countrymen and others: Mr Cotton answers; that it is not true, that they doe so permit the Indians, whatever they may doe privately: That the Indians submit to the ten Commandements, and that some of their Ministers have preached to them in English, which hath been interpreted: That one now preacheth in their owne Language:[39] Further, That they permit strangers in their Worship. And for their Countrymen, for the most part that they worship God with them: They which are distant have Libertie of publike prayer and preaching, by such as themselves choose without distur-bance.

Truth. Concerning the Indians, it is most true, that the Monahig-ganéucks, Mishawoméucks, Pawtuckséucks, and Cawsumséucks[40] (who professe to submit to the English) continue in their publike Paganish Worship of Devills, I say openly and constantly.

Peace. Yea but (saith Mr Cotton) they have submitted to the ten Commandements.

Truth. I answer; the ten Commandements contain a Renunciation of all false Gods and Worships, and a Worshipping of the true God, according to his owne Institutions and Appointments, which their practice is as farre from, as Mid-night is from Mid-day.

2. To put men upon observations of Gods Worship, as Prayer, &c. before the Foundations of Repentance from dead workes (their worshipping

---

and Lactantius, as a model of an early Christian leader who opposed religious coercion and who championed human liberty. Tyler, *Islam, the West, and Tolerance*, 69; Beckwith, *Hilary of Poitiers on the Trinity*, 210–11.

38. Tertullian (c. 155–c. 240) was an early Christian church father. The "speech" here is likely Tertullian's *Apologeticum* (Apology) from approximately 197 CE, which was a staunch defense of the religious freedom that should be accorded the "illegal" Christian church within the Roman Empire. See Keresztes, "Tertullian's Apologeticus," 131.

39. Cotton is likely referring here to John Eliot, the Roxbury minister who in the early 1640s learned Wôpanâak and by 1646 was feebly preaching to local Massachusett Natives west of Boston.

40. Williams refers to specific nations and bands of Natives here, seemingly the Mohegan, the Pawtuxet, and two other tribes that are not easily identifiable.

of Idolls, &c.) is as farre from the Order of Christ Jesus, and his Christian principles (whereof Repentance from dead workes is the first) as the building of an House or Palace, without the first Groundsell or Foundation laid.[41]

Peace. Mr Cotton therefore saith, they preach unto them.

Truth. I from my soule wish that all the Lords people in New England were Prophets, yea true Apostolicall Ministers or Preachers, truely furnished with Christs Abilities, and Christs Commission, to goe forth to convert and baptize the Nations, even these Wildest of the Nations of Adams Children: But Conversion of Nations Mr Cotton sayth (upon Revel. 15.) untill the seaven plagues of the seaven Angells be fulfilled, will not be great.

This Interpretation I acknowledge to be very probable, so far as concernes any great Conversion of the Nations before the downfall of Antichrist, and in the meane season I commend the pious Endeavours of any (professing Ministery or not) to doe good to the Soules of all Men as We have opportunitie. But that any of the Ministers spoken of are furnished with true Apostolicall Commission (Matth. 28.) I see not for these Reasons.[42]

First, The Minister or Ministers, whom Mr Cotton I conceive intends, professe an ordinarie Office in the Church of Christ, which is cleerely distinct, yea and another thing from the office of an Apostle, or one sent forth to preach and baptize, Ephes. 4. & I Cor. 12.[43]

Secondly, Such Churches as are invested with the power of Christ, and so authoriz'd to send forth, are seperate from the World, which many thousands of Gods people (dead and living) have seene just Reasons to deny those Churches so to be.

Thirdly, Were the Church true, and the Messenger or Apostle rightly sent forth with prayer and fasting, according to Act. 13. yet I believe that none of the Ministers of New England, nor any person in the whole Countrey is able to open the Mysteries of Christ Jesus in any proprietie of their speech or Language, without which proprietie it cannot be imagined that Christ Jesus sent forth his first Apostles or Messengers, and without which

41. Williams is taking issue with Massachusetts Bay colonists' evangelistic methods. Cotton boasted that the Natives observed the Ten Commandments (even if part of a political submission). Williams said their focus was wrong—that getting people to obey the Ten Commandments without first laying a proper foundation of awareness of sin and repentance is misguided.

42. Williams is setting forth a fairly radical view that no English ministers have the proper commission or authority from Jesus to evangelize Native Americans.

43. In terms of apostolic commission, Williams does not believe that regular ministers have been given the different and greater authorization as apostles, or ones who are sent out. That is why Williams doubted that any minister could legitimately evangelize Natives or any other non-Christian population.

no people in the World are long willing to heare of difficult and heavenly matters.[44] That none is so fitted;

First, The Natives themselves affirme, as I could instance in many particulars.[45]

Secondly, The Experience of the Discusser[46] and of many others testifie how hard it is for any man to attaine a little proprietie of their Language in common things (so as to escape Derision amongst them) in many yeares, without abundance of conversing with them, in Eating, travelling and lodging with them, &c. which none of their Ministers (other affaires not permitting) ever could doe.[47]

Peace. There being no helpes of Art and learning amongst them, I see not how without constant use or a Miracle, any man is able to attaine to any proprietie of speech amongst them, even in common things. And without proprietie (as before) who knowes not how hardly all men (especially Barbarians) are brought to heare matters of Heaven (so strange and contrary to Nature) yea, even matters of the Earth, except profit and other worldly ends compell them to spell out Mens minds and meaning?

Truth. 3. I may truely adde a third, an Instance in the booke of their Conversion,[48] written by Mr Tho: Shepheard,[49] there Mr Eliot (the ablest amongst them in the Indian Speech) promising an old Indian a suit of

44. Williams is leveling a critique of John Eliot and other Massachusetts Bay and Plimouth missionaries, namely, that they do not have a sufficient grasp of Native languages to truly and accurately communicate complex but essential Christian doctrine to Natives. And without this, there can be no true conversion in Williams's mind, even if there were an apostolic commission.

45. Natives themselves affirm the linguistic incapacity of English ministers and would-be missionaries, Williams claims.

46. That is, the imagined conversation partner in Cotton's text.

47. Here Williams is subtly bragging about his own linguistic abilities in comparison with those of the Massachusetts Bay missionaries, based, in part, on Williams's many days and weeks spent among both Wampanoag and Narragansett. After all, Williams had in 1643 published *Key Into the Language of America*, which demonstrated his long-term commitment to learning Native languages and his impressive facility with them. Over time, Eliot leaned on Native translators and linguists and eventually produced a full translation of the Bible in 1663.

48. This refers to the first book of the so-called "Eliot Tracts," which were a series of self-promotional pamphlets published by Thomas Shepard, John Eliot, and others describing the early successes of the Massachusetts Bay missionary efforts. The first of these was Thomas Shepard?, *The Day-Breaking, If Not the Sun-Rising of the Gospell with the Indians in New-England* (1647). For a modern edition of all of these pamphlets, see Clark, *The Eliot Tracts*.

49. Thomas Shepard was the Congregational minister in Cambridge, Massachusetts.

Cloths, the man (sayth the relation) not well understanding Mr Eliots speech, asked another Indian what Mr Eliot said.

Peace. Me thinks, the Native not understanding such a common and wellcome promise of cloths upon Gift, would farre more hardly understand Mr Eliots preaching of the garment of Righteousnesse Christ Jesus, unto which Men mutually turne the deafe Eare, &c.[50]

Truth. Neither you (sweet Peace) nor I Expresse thus much to dampe Mr Eliot or any from doing all the good they can, whiles opportunitie lasts in any truely Christian way, but to shew how great that mistake is, that pretends such a true preaching of Christ Jesus to them in their owne Language.

Peace. But to proceed, in the next Passage Mr Cotton affirmes their Impartialitie in permitting others as well as the Indians.

Truth. I answer; it is one thing to connive at a strange Papist in private devotions on shoare, or in the vessells at Anchor, &c. Another thing to permit Papists, Jewes, Turkes, &c. the free and constant Exercise of their Religion and Worship, in their respective Orders and Assemblies, were such Inhabitants amongst them.[51]

Peace. Doubtlesse the bloudie Tenent cannot permit this Libertie, neither to the Papists, Jewes, Turkes, &c. nor to the Indians, nor doth their practice toward their Countrymen hould forth a shew of such a freedome or permission.[52]

Truth. I wonder why Mr Cotton writes, that the most part of the English worship God with them, and the rest absent have Libertie to choose their Preachers! Since Mr Cotton knowes the Petition and Petitions that have been presented for Libertie of Conscience in New England, and he cannot but also know the Imprisoning and Fining of some of the Petitioners, &c. . .[53]

50. Williams continues casting doubt on Eliot's linguistic ability by stating that if Eliot is unable to communicate with Natives about clothing, how much less Eliot will be able to explain things regarding Christian teachings.

51. Williams is showing just how radical his commitment to full religious liberty is. He suggests that Catholics, Jews, and Muslims should be granted "the free and constant Exercise of their Religion and Worship."

52. William highlights that, no matter what Cotton claims for the religious tolerance of the Massachusetts Bay colonists, in reality they do not give freedom to Catholics, Jews, Muslims, Natives, or even to their own fellow colonists who differ in religious beliefs (as Williams himself had found out when he faced deportation for his views in 1635–1636).

53. Williams again highlights the shallowness of Cotton's claims to religious toleration and liberty when at the same time Massachusetts Bay officials were banishing, imprisoning, and fining (and would later execute) religious dissenters.

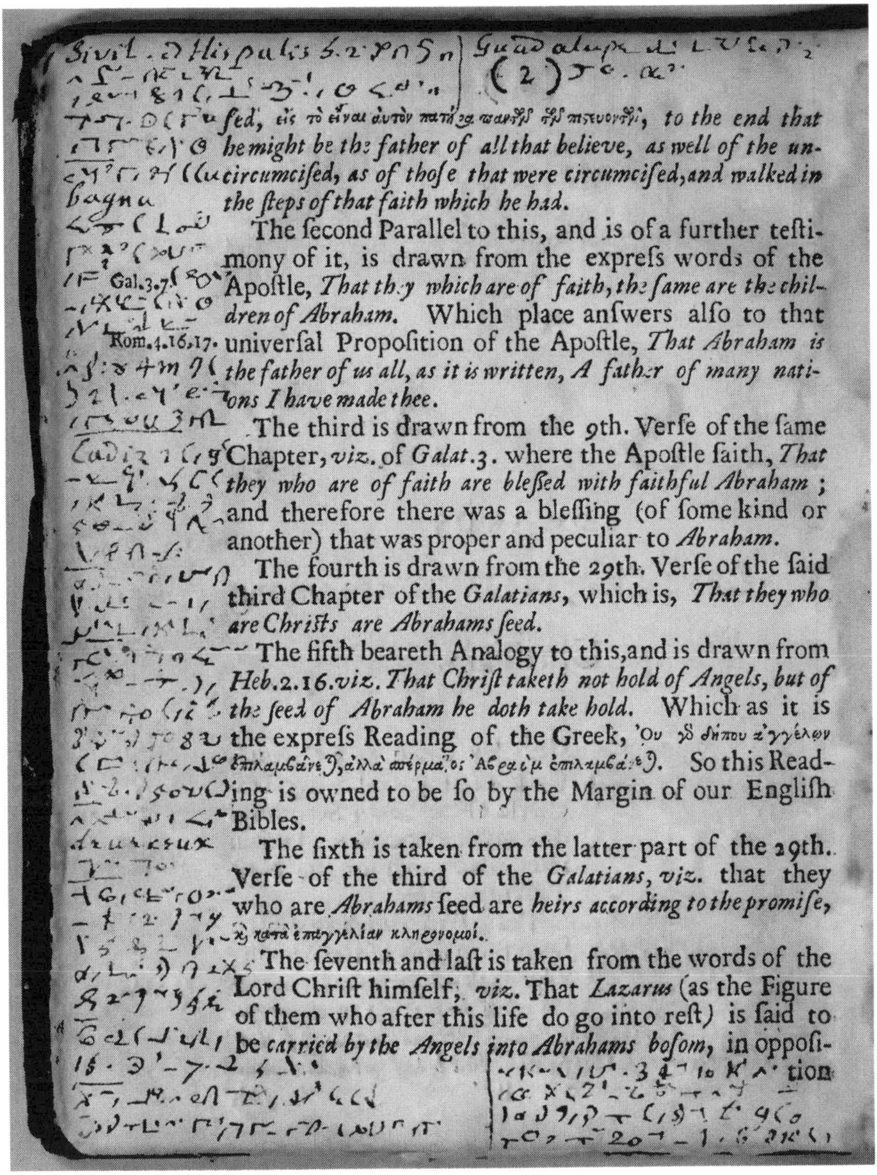

[handwritten marginalia in an unidentified shorthand/Native script along the left and bottom margins]

... D(*ufed*, εἰς τὸ εἶναι αὐτὸν πατέρα πάντων τῶν πιστευόντων, to the end that he might be the father of all that believe, as well of the un-circumcifed, as of thofe that were circumcifed, and walked in the fteps of that faith which he had.

The fecond Parallel to this, and is of a further tefti-mony of it, is drawn from the exprefs words of the *Gal.3.7* Apoftle, That th.y which are of faith, the fame are the chil-dren of Abraham. Which place anfwers alfo to that *Rom.4.16,17.* univerfal Propofition of the Apoftle, That Abraham is the father of us all, as it is written, A father of many nati-ons I have made thee.

The third is drawn from the 9th. Verfe of the fame Chapter, viz. of Galat.3. where the Apoftle faith, That they who are of faith are blefed with faithful Abraham ; and therefore there was a blefing (of fome kind or another) that was proper and peculiar to Abraham.

The fourth is drawn from the 29th. Verfe of the faid third Chapter of the Galatians, which is, That they who are Chrifts are Abrahams feed.

The fifth beareth Analogy to this, and is drawn from Heb.2.16.viz. That Chrift taketh not hold of Angels, but of the feed of Abraham he doth take hold. Which as it is the exprefs Reading of the Greek, Ου ϒδ δήπου ἀγγέλων ἐπιλαμβάνεϑ,ἀλλὰ σπέρμαᵗος Ἀϐραὰμ ἐπιλαμβάνεϑ). So this Read-ing is owned to be fo by the Margin of our Englifh Bibles.

The fixth is taken from the latter part of the 29th. Verfe of the third of the Galatians, viz. that they who are Abrahams feed are heirs according to the promife, ϰϳ ϰατὰ ἐπαγγελίαν ϰληϱονομοί.

The feventh and laft is taken from the words of the Lord Chrift himfelf, viz. That Lazarus (as the Figure of them who after this life do go into reft) is faid to be carried by the Angels into Abrahams bofom, in oppofi-tion

[handwritten marginalia in an unidentified shorthand/Native script along the bottom margin]

Page from "A Brief Reply," c. 1680, in the margins of *An Essay Towards the Reconciling of Differences Among Christians* ([London]: s.n., [1645]). Courtesy of John Carter Brown Library.

Roger Williams, "A Brief Reply to a Small Book Written by John Eliot," c. 1680[54]

The following text is an excerpt from a larger essay by Roger Williams that was only transcribed and published in 2014. The original essay exists in manuscript form, written in a difficult shorthand code in the margins of a book at the John Carter Brown Library in Providence, Rhode Island.[55] Scholars knew about this "mystery book" and its enigmatic marginal writings, but no one had been able to crack the shorthand code and decipher its meaning. In 2012, a team of undergraduate researchers at Brown University, supported by a few faculty members, began serious work on decoding the shorthand writing, which had been long suspected to be by Roger Williams. The team was able to determine that the shorthand system used was derived from John Willis, The Art of Stenographie (London, 1602). The team eventually discovered that there were actually three sections of marginal shorthand. The first section contained notes from a popular description of the world, Peter Heylyn's Cosmographie in Foure Bookes (1652). The third section contained notes from a well-known medical encyclopedia, Thomas Bartholin's Bartholinus Anatomy (1654). But it was the middle section of the marginal shorthand that proved to be the most exciting. It contained an essay written by Roger Williams that had remained completely unknown and unpublished.

As the team began to translate/transcribe this new essay, it became evident that it was a treatise defending believer's (or adult) baptism. Although such debates may seem mostly archaic today, in the seventeenth century one's views on the proper time for and mode of baptism was seen as a core Christian issue that could influence one's salvation. On the one side of the

---

54. Note: This transcription and annotation was previously published as Fisher and Mason-Brown, "'By Treachery and Seduction.'" The title is derived from the first line of the shorthand essay. See Williams, "Brief Reply," 146. For ease of reading, we have silently supplied punctuation where appropriate, even though the shorthand is almost entirely devoid of quotation marks, periods, and other punctuation. We have indicated with italics the portions of the original manuscript for which we have not been able to produce an exact word-for-word translation. In these instances, the italicized text represents an approximate translation, based on contextual clues and what shorthand we can decipher. Bracketed text is not derived from the original shorthand, but has been inserted to clarify the meaning of the translated text. Williams's system, like most shorthand systems, is strictly case-indifferent; it cannot distinguish between upper-case and lower-case letters. We have done our best to capitalize the translated text in a historically plausible manner, using Eliot's book and Williams's published essays as guides. For a more complete interpretation and contextualization, see Fisher et al., *Decoding Roger Williams*.

55. The book, which is missing the title page, is *An Essay Towards the Reconciling of Differences Among Christians* ([London]: s.n., [1645]), and is housed at the John Carter Brown Library in Providence, Rhode Island.

debate, Congregationalists, Anglicans, Lutherans, Presbyterians, Catholics, and most early modern Christians taught that infants should be baptized within a few days of birth. Even though Protestants did not believe baptism conveyed salvation, pro-infant baptism Protestants did believe there was a special covenant benefit of such baptism that aided a child until he or she could profess faith later in life. On the other side, a much smaller number of Protestants—mainly Anabaptists (like the Mennonites) and Baptists—believed that baptism should be reserved for believing and consenting adults and therefore not be administered to infants.

Williams, in defending believer's baptism, entered a wider debate that was taking place in the Anglophone Atlantic world. But he also entered a more specific debate that was taking place in print. In 1672, an English minister by the name of John Norcott published a treatise titled Baptism Discovered Plainly and Faithfully, According to the Word of God. *John Eliot, the missionary to Native Americans, responded to Norcott's book in 1679 with a treatise titled* A Brief Answer to a Small Book Written by John Norcot Against Infant-Baptisme. *Roger Williams, in turn, picked up Eliot's book late in his life and drafted a reply to Eliot, which he seemingly intended to publish. The title for Williams's essay comes from the first line in this section of the shorthand: "A Brief Reply to a Small Book Written by John Eliot." Although it is undated, it must have been written between 1679, when Eliot's book was published, and 1683, when Williams died. 1680 is the estimated date of writing by scholars working most closely with this project.*

The excerpt given here is just one small portion of the larger essay Williams wrote as a rebuttal to Eliot. In this section—which takes up only one page of the marginal shorthand—Williams critiques Eliot's missionary program to Native Americans in New England. Furthermore, Williams points out that some Native Americans have professed belief in Christianity without any benefit of infant baptism, which for Williams confirmed that infant baptism was not necessary. Williams was always skeptical of Natives (or English men and women, for that matter) having true and saving faith, but he uses this particular point to both criticize Eliot personally as well as to invalidate Eliot's point about the spiritual benefits of infant baptism.

The next thing that Eliot writes of is three to four pages [about] parental Covenant or a spiritual Patrimony,[56] which, sayeth Eliot, the Ana-

---

56. Eliot defines spiritual patrimony as "our Estate in Religion which our Parents conveigh unto us," a benefit that remained with baptized children throughout their lifetime, comforting them in difficult times and aiding them to make their own profession of faith. Eliot, *Brief Answer to a Small Book*, 11.

baptists[57] deny. [On] Page 12 Eliot sayeth that spiritual Patrimony is a great and sanctified means of conversion, though not the only means thereof; the Indians are converted without it. But, sayeth Eliot, in our churches all of the converts are converted by the improvement of their Patrimony or Covenant only, and this appears, sayeth Eliot, by their confessions when they come into full communion with the church.[58]

Answer: As for the conversion of the Indians by the Gospel (for those are [the] words written) it would be cause of great joy if they were feeling true.[59] But if the shepherd of their chiefs[60] [uses] treachery and seduction, [it] is much a sore to the wisdom of the gospel of Christ. As the first treatise[61] doth declare, there is first grounding to prepare one's soul before conversion. Eliot speaks out against the Indians.[62] They might speak [or] do something as they are taught[63] and this conversion [of the] Indians appears as the French and Spanish [conversions].[64] But if their leaders be prepared in error, how can their duties be considered true or according to the Gospel?

As for those whom Eliot calls true converts, [we must] wonder of the wisdom of their conversion. In contrast to the Indians whom Eliot says are

57. Eliot's use of the word "Anabaptists" for English Baptists like Norcott intentionally identified them with the infamous radicalism of the sixteenth-century Anabaptist movement—a rhetorical move clearly intending to mar Baptist credibility. Although Williams believed in adult baptism, he would not have identified as an Anabaptist, and he took umbrage regarding the negative associations Eliot made with the term.

58. For many Congregational churches in seventeenth-century New England, full membership (and therefore access to Communion, or the Lord's Supper) was reserved for individuals who could narrate their own conversion either to a minister or to the congregation. See Pope, *Half-Way Covenant*; Hall, *Reforming People*, 165.

59. That is, "if their feelings were genuine"; indicates sincerity.

60. The shorthand is a bit unclear here, but the most straightforward rendering is "shepherd of their chiefs," meaning John Eliot.

61. Here Williams is likely referring to Norcott's 1672 treatise *Baptism Discovered Plainly and Faithfully, According to the Word of God*, to which Eliot's essay was a response.

62. This phrase is not entirely clear. One possible interpretation is that Williams sees Natives and Baptists (as articulated by Norcott) to be in the same position of preparation apart from patrimony. By speaking out against Norcott, Williams argues, Eliot is inadvertently also speaking out against Natives, since they, too, come to Christ apart from spiritual patrimony.

63. Gloss: "They simply say and do what they have been taught" (i.e., the Indians are simply performing for the missionaries).

64. This is a pointed critique of Eliot's program of Indigenous evangelization, since Williams did not see Catholic conversions of Natives as authentic.

converted by the gospel, Christians are converted[65] only by the improvement of spiritual Patrimony and by the Covenant of the Spirit. Surely we be cautious of such conversions to Christ. The Apostle Paul [in] Romans 10.17 speaks clearly against this: "faith cometh by hearing and hearing by the word of God" to join the gospel out of feeling[66] not by patrimony.

65. Only a few isolated phrases here are decipherable, including "of the Indians" and "more for the Gospel."

66. The shorthand here is ambiguous, but the citation of Rom 10:17 is clearly intended to refute Eliot's claims about the role of spiritual patrimony in conversion.

Chapter 9

Pastoral Care to an Ailing Wife, 1652

HISTORIAN EDWIN GAUSTAD DESCRIBED *Williams's* Experiments of Spiritual Life & Health *as a "kind of love letter to his wife" written to encourage Mary Bernard Williams following a severe illness she suffered while he was in Indian country in 1650.*[1] *In the text Williams frequently compares his devotional book to a bouquet of flowers, sent to offer her comfort.*[2] *Williams spent many months of each year at his trading post, and twice traveled for extended periods in London. Williams refers to those absences in this text and admits how hard it is to be away from her: "My dear Love, since it pleaseth the Lord so to dispose of me, and of my affairs at present, that I cannot often see thee, I desire often to send to thee." There are glimpses of real affection between them in this text. Williams also acknowledges that marriage is hard: "it is not easie to keep in the first flame of Love, fresh and equall, although the fire of the truth and sinceritie of marriage love never die, or be extinguished." Readers may even detect a twinge of his guilt at frequently leaving Mary at home with six children in a busy household, where she was surely expected to host neighbors, visitors, and Indigenous leaders during his many absences. Throughout this text, Williams refers to writing the letter in the "wilderness," where the hospitality and kindness of his many Indigenous neighbors made his writing possible.*

1. Scholars have not always been this kind to *Experiments of Spiritual Life*. When Winthrop Hudson republished it in 1951, he suggested that readers would benefit from this "classic of devotional literature" and that ministers could mine it for a wealth of sermon material. But in reviewing the 1951 publication, Archibald Ward dismissed such marketing efforts as "nausea." Ward suggested that readers would have to dig out the "brighter and purer nuggets." It suggests Williams's power in American culture in the 1950s, however, that Hudson's republication of *Experiments* merited a book review in *Time* magazine.

2. Gaustad, *Roger Williams*, 108.

Originally written as a personal letter, Experiments *was published in 1652 in London during his second long stay. In its published form,* Experiments *is dedicated to Frances Wray Vane,[3] the wife of Henry Vane, the younger,[4] in gratitude for her kindness. Williams and Henry Vane were close friends and evidence suggests that Williams and Lady Vane corresponded regularly. During his two extended visits in England, Williams stayed with the Vanes both in London and in Lincolnshire, as the address line in many of his letters indicate. Whether he sent Lady Vane a transcribed copy of the text before it was printed, brought her one when he arrived, or waited to share it in its printed form is unclear. Williams wrote that he was convinced to publish it by "the earnest desire of some godly friends" and by his "own desire of sowing a little handful of spiritual seed while the short minute of my seedtime (the opportunity of life) lasteth."[5] How Mary may have felt about her husband dedicating to Lady Vane what was once a letter written solely for her—and publishing it with a florid dedication to Vane—is unfortunately impossible to know. Williams clearly missed Mary during his time away: for example, in 1653, he wrote a letter from England to the towns of Providence and Warwick describing how he implored Mary to join him in London, but unsettled wartime seas made travel dangerous and he left the decision "to the freedom of her spirit."[6]*

Although the original letter was a gift for his wife, the book was published with an English audience in mind. Devotional manuals like this one were a staple of reformed Protestant practice and a popular genre for booksellers. Williams published the guide to provide spiritual lessons to both men and women, lay and ecclesiastical, in both New and Old England. This genre was designed to offer consolation to the reader in times of affliction, especially by reminding them that struggles were opportunities for grace; therefore the reader's own lived experience was an important part of devotional practice.[7] Readers of Experiments *would have been familiar with the idea that*

---

3. Lady Frances Wray Vane was the daughter of Sir Christopher Wray of Lincolnshire. She and Henry married in 1640 and had ten children. *Correspondence of Roger Williams,* 1:301, 355, 360; Hudson, "Introduction," *Experiments of Spiritual Life* (1951), 19.

4. Henry Vane, the younger (1613–1662) emigrated to Massachusetts Bay in 1635 following an intense religious conversion. He was governor of Massachusetts Bay during the Antinomian Crisis, and left New England in 1637 after losing re-election, later serving in the House of Commons. After the Restoration of the Stuarts, Vane was executed in 1662 for treason for his service in Cromwell's Parliament. For more on Vane, see chapter 4.

5. Williams, *Experiments,* 52.

6. *Correspondence of Roger Williams,* 1:386.

7. Weimer, "From Human Suffering," 12.

afflictions needed to be "used" through prayer and meditation, and struggles were an expected part of a life dedicated to God.[8]

Women play a central role in this devotional manual. For example, when describing the foundations of the early Christian church, Williams mentions four women immediately after writing about the apostles: Jesus's mother, Mary, and Phoebe, Priscilla, and Persis. In Romans 16:1–2, Paul describes Phoebe as a "servant of the Church at Cenchrea," and Priscilla was a crucial supporter of Paul's, sometimes traveling with him. Paul refers to Persis as "beloved" who "labored much in the Lord" in Romans 16:12. In addition to drawing attention to these influential women of the early church, domestic imagery and marriage metaphors run throughout Experiments, with Williams sometimes comparing God to a father, sometimes to a husband. He describes believers as children of a loving, yet demanding, father. As he does in nearly every published piece, Williams defends the liberty of conscience by arguing that when prayer is forced by others, it is not true prayer.

Although he claims to follow "Heads of Discourse," the body of the work only loosely follows this structure and Williams himself digresses into so many tangents that it becomes difficult to follow his thinking. The work contains three key sections. In the first, Williams lists the trials of true believers, and how they are distinguished from false Christians, whom he calls "hypocrites." The second section details the work godly people do in the world, and how they should profess the faith. Finally, Williams ends his tract by giving Christians suggestions for recovering their faith and preventing "spiritual sickness." Williams's three sections are laid out in a conversational style. Like many devotional manuals, Experiments poses a question and an answer immediately follows.[9] This format is influenced by the catechetical style of early religious education that teaches doctrine in a question and answer format, and puritan sermons usually follow the same structure. The "objections" suggest that hypocrites can do all of the things true believers can do, which was an overwhelming worry of reformed Protestants: Is salvation truly mine? How can I really know if I am saved?

Roger Williams, *Experiments of Spiritual Life and Health* (1652)[10]

To the truly Honorable the Lady Vane, the Younger.
   Madam,

8. Weimer, "From Human Suffering," 12–13.

9. Weimer, "From Human Suffering," 23.

10. Williams, *Experiments of Spiritual Life* in *Complete Writings of Roger Williams*, 7:42–114. The word "experiments" is close to "experiences" or "evidences."

Your favourable, and Christian respects to me (both of former and latter date) your Godly and Christian Letters to me, so many thousand miles distant in America: And your many gracious Demonstrations of an humble and Christian Spirit breathing in you; are of a three fold Cord[11] which have drawn these lines into your presence.

While I have sometimes mused how to express a Christian gratitude, I am at last perswaded to crave your Ladyships acceptance of these poore Experiments of each true Christian personall union, and communion with the Father of Spirits.

It is true, I have been sometimes prest to engage in controversies, but I can really and uprightly say, my Witnes is on high, how harsh and doleful the touch of those strings are, especially, against such Worthies both in old and new-England, in whom I joyfully before the world acknowledge (in many heavenly respects) a lively character and Image of the Son of God. This broken piece, is a breath of a still and gentle voice, none but the God of this world, and the men of this world, can I lightly (at this turne) expect my opposites . . .

I confess (Madam) it was but a private and sudden discourse, sent in private to my poor Companion and Yoak-fellow,[12] occasioned by a sudden sickness threatening death, into which, and from which it pleased the Lord most graciously to cast and raise her.

The forme and stile I know will seem to this refined age, too rude and barbarous: And the truth is, the most of it was penned and writ (so as seldom or never such discourses were) in the thickest of the naked Indians of America, in their very wild houses, and by their barbarous fires;[13] when the Lord was pleased this last year (more than ordinarily) to dispose of my abode and travell amongst them. And yet, is the Language plaine? is it the

11. This refers to the "three-fold cord" in Eccl 4:12, which says that one person can be easily defeated by another, but two people together can "withstand" him. Even stronger is a threefold cord because it is not "easily broken." Williams adapts this metaphor to the three ways Lady Vane supported him: her respect to him, her "Godly" letters sent from England to Providence, and her own "demonstrations of an humble and Christian spirit."

12. His wife, Mary.

13. Again, Williams indulges in derogatory language, when in so many of his other published and personal writings, he praises his Indigenous neighbors and denigrates English practices in comparison. As we have written frequently in this collection, Williams's attitude toward Native Americans was complicated. But this example may hint at something else. Perhaps he resorted to this when addressing readers who far exceeded him in social status—like Lady Vane. It was a way for him to be obsequious and "apologize" for his own writing by reminding the reader of his life in the "wilderness" of Rhode Island. Clearly, apologies like this one are formulaic. If he really did not think his words were worth reading, then he would not have published them.

liker Christs: Is the composure rude? such was his outward Beauty: Are the tryals (seemingly) too close? such is the two edged Sword of his most holy Spirit, which pierceth between the very Soul and Spirit, and bringeth every thought into the obedience of Christ Jesus . . .

My humble cry (Madam) to the Lord shall never cease, those all those your many obligations of both temporall and eternal mercies, may (like chaines of Adamant) draw and bind your precious Soul more and more to resolve (by his grace assisting) to make his name great, who hath made your so and so to love his Name, his Son, his Spirit, his Truth, his Children, that others at the Torch of your exemplary meeknesse and fear of God, may light and kindle theirs; That your Souls-eye more and more brightly may see him who is invisible, and may so experimentally resent those invisible and internal Honors, pleasures, and profits that are in him that in comparison thereof the visible and worldly, may be accounted by you but dreams of shadows, &c. That your great desire may be a likenesse of so high and holy, and so dear a Savior, and (as in other excellencies so) in that especially of a desire of saving others, your Children, Kindred, Servants, Friends, yea, Enemies: that neither the pleasing calme of prosperity, nor the dreadfull storms of changes, may quench or dampe that holy fire of your souls love (in Life and Death) to Him whom your Ladyship hath so much infinite cause to love, but never yet saw, in whom, and for ever

I desire to be

Your Honours unfeignedly faithful.

R.W.

The Letter which the Author sent with this Discourse to his Wife M. W. upon her recovery from a dangerous sicknesse.

My Dearest Love and Companion in this Vale of Tears.

Thy late sudden and dangerous Sicknesse, and the Lords most gracious and speedy raising thee up from the gates and jawes of Death: as they were wonderfull in thine own, and others eyes, so I hope, and earnestly desire, they may be ever in our thoughts, as a warning from Heaven to make ready for a sudden call to be gone from hence: to live the rest of our short uncer-taine span, more as strangers, longing and breathing after another Home and Country. . . My dear Love, since it pleaseth the Lord so to dispose of me, and of my affairs at present, that I cannot often see thee, I desire often to send to thee. I now send thee that which I know will be sweeter to thee then the Honey and the Honey-combe, and stronger refreshment then the strongest wines or waters, and of more value then if every line and letter were thousands of gold and silver . . .

The holy and humble desires are strong, but I know thy writing is slow,[14] and that thou wilt gladly accept of this my poore helpe, which with humble thankfulnesse and praise to the Lord, I humbly tender to his holy service, and thine in him. I send thee (though in Winter) an handfull of flowers made up in a little Posey, for thy dear selfe, and our dear children, to look and smell on, when I as the grasse of the field shall be gone, and withered.

Wee know how it pleaseth the spirit of God, to distinguish between the outward and the inner man, 2 Cor. 4. It hath pleased the most high to cast downe thy outward man, and againe graciously to lift him up, and thereby to teach us both, to examine and try the health, and strength, and welfare of the inner . . . This Inner man, this new-man (which after God is created in holinesse and righteousnesse) I say, this Inner-man hath his temper and distempers, his health and sicknesse, as well as this outward-man this body of Clay . . . Now as this outward man desires not onely life, and being, but also health and cheerfulness in all the living motions and actions thereof: So, (and much more ten thousand fold) requires the inward and spirituall man, an heartfull and cheerful temper . . . Tis true, as it is between a loving couple, (and as it was in the Church as Ephesus) it is not easie to keep in the first flame of Love, fresh and equall, although the fire of the truth and sinceritie of marriage love never die, or be extinguished . . .

I am far therefore from passing the sentence of death upon the least of the little ones of Jesus (notwithstanding their spiritual weaknes, and sickness) in whom the least spark or breathing of the spirit of Life can be discerned. And I desire to see and lament the spirituall sicknesses, and diseases of mine own and others Spirits, which yet are not unto death (as Christ Jesus spake of Lazaraus) but for the glory of God, in the fall and rising of his servants.

Yea as Paul distinguished of Gods afflicting hand on his Saints of Corinth, so must I distinguish, between these three, death, sicknes and weakness: Every sicknes of Gods Children is not a death, for the inner man cannot die, no more then Christ himself. Rom: 6.

14. There is little evidence to judge whether Mary's letter-writing habits or penmanship skills were as slow as Roger suggests. Literacy rates in early New England were very high, especially if we see literacy as a bundle of different skills: reading printed text, reading handwriting, and producing handwriting. A busy household and the care of six children during Williams's many absences may better explain what he perceived as her "slow" writing. Scholars have explored women's education and women letter-writers in early modern England and New England: Daybell, *Women Letter-Writers*; Daybell and Gordon, *Cultures of Correspondence*; Dierks, *In My Power*; Monaghan, "Literacy Instruction and Gender"; Perlmann and Shirley, "When Did New England Women Acquire Literacy?"; Thornton, *Handwriting in America*.

Again, every weaknes is not a sicknes, for some are weak, little ones
in the knowledge and love of Christ, while others are grown to be strong
and aged in Christ Jesus; Yea, the strongest and oldest Souldiers of Christ
Jesus. . .have yet been troubled with some weaknes, and fits of spirituall
distempers: Weaknes in their Eyes is not discerning aright in the mind of
Christ Jesus, weaknes in their hands, and Feet, hindring their spirituall
chearfulnes, and activity in Christs wayes, which weaknesses yet have not
brought them to a down right halting in Christianity.

I propose therefore (with the assistance of Gods holy spirit) to examine these three particulars. First, what are the Arguments of that measure of
spirituall life in Christ, which may yet stand with great spirituall weaknesses
and diseases. 2ly. What is the measure of grace of Christ Jesus, which may
be called the health, and chearfull temper, and disposition of the inner man.
3dly. What are those spiritual preservatives, which may keep the Soul in
a healthful temper, free from spirituall sicknesses and distemper. In these
Examinations I professe two things: First not to oppresse thy thoughts and
memory, with any long discourse, intending only to send thee after thy
sicknes, a little posey fit and easie for thy meditation, and refreshing . . .

I begin therefore with such trialls and arguments as declare, the true
life of the inner man, notwithstanding spirituall weaknes, sicknes, and
distempers.

First then when the spirit of the Lord in 1 Joh[n]. 2. describeth the
severall Ages and grouths of this inward man. . .it pleaseth him to describe
the young or the little one by this difference, that [He knows the Father] to
wit, that he knows the Lord so, as to look upon him (in his measure) as to a
Father, that he fears him, loves him, obeys him, and calls upon him as on a
Father: according to that of Gal: 4. Because you are sons, he hath sent forth
the spirit of his Son crying in your Hearts Abba Father: Father pardon me,
Father help me, Father give me, &c.

Obj. But may not the Hypocrites call upon God (and sometime more
boldly then Gods little ones,) Lord Lord, Almighty and most mercifull Father, &c.

An. I answer, an Hypocrite hath many Lords, and many Fathers, besides, and joyned with their (pretended) heavenly Father. Whereas Gods
little ones cry out, (Isa. 63.) Doubtless thou art our Father, although Abraham be ignorant of us, as if they had said: Thou art our only Father, above
all Fathers, &c.

2ly. The Hypocrite saies Lord, Lord, but cares for no more of the will
of the Lord then may serve his owne turne: But a child of God declares
his child like submission, to an heavenly Fathers will in all things . . . The
difference lies not in the words, but in the Heart, in the upright submission

of a child of God, to all that he believes to be the will and pleasure of his heavenly Father.

For a second triall therefore: Where spirituall life is (notwithstanding weaknes or distempers) there is always a professed willingnesse to get more and more knowledge of this heavenly Father, of his name, of his works, of his word, of his Christ, of his Spirit, his Saints, and Ordinances.

Hence Beleevers in Jesus, both Men and Women, are called Disciples, or scholars of Christ Jesus, professing continually to learn more and more of this heavenly teacher. Hence his Disciples or Scholars petition to Christ Jesus, Lord teach us to pray: Lord increase our Faith, &c . . .

Obj.[15] But may not an Hypocrite desire to know more and more of God, of Christ, &c.

I answer, although an Hypocrite out of an itching desire, of knowledge, of novelty, and out of self love, to make use of so much of God, and of Christ, as may serve his own ends . . . The obedience of Hypocrites is but the task of a slave, or Hireling, when the obedience of a child of God, is that of a dutifull child to his Father, or an endeared Wife to her Husband, not caused by terrour or wages, but hearty Reverence and Affection . . .

While the Hypocrites find their natural delight in the word, as in musick, while yet they obey not: The child of God comes to the breast of the Church, as a child hangs upon the Mothers Breast, not only for the delight of sucking, but out of a vehement painfull longing, to have its soul satisfied, and its strength of spirituall life and grace increased in the ways of God: according to that in 1. Pet. 2[16] . . .

A 7th. Argument of the true life of grace (though in much weaknes or sicknes,) I observe to be a humble acknowledgement of, and a submitting unto the correcting and afflicting hand of God, in sicknesses, crosses, losses, &c . . . a true child of God desires, as to acknowledge his Fathers hand correcting his righteously, because he hath deserved it, so also graciously and faithfully, because he hopes God aims at his good, as a Father doth at a childs, in giving him fatherly correction, bitter Pills and Phisick.

And therefore (2ly:) as when the Lord strikes an Hypocrite, he either runs from him as a strange child striken by another man, or flies against him in a murmuring, or howls out for anguish as a Dog, (Hos: 7) They howl upon their Beds . . . The Hypocrite if he might have his own choice,

15. Objection.

16. In the verse Williams refers to here, Peter wrote that believers "crave pure spiritual milk." The "church as breast" metaphor would have been familiar to Williams's readers; New England children were taught using John Cotton's 1646 primer, *Milk for Babes. Drawn Out of the Breasts of Both Testaments*. Cotton's catechism was a best-seller and remained in print for almost 200 years.

had rather be rid of his pain than his sin, and therefore when his pain is over, he returns with the Dog to his Vomit: But a true child of God, truly (though weakly) desires to see, and abhor, and slay his dearest sins, because he knows they are but flattering traytors and guilded poysons . . .

A 9th discovery of true spirituall life, in weaknes, I find to be a painfull[17] and a restles mind, in temptations to sin, in yielding to sin, and lying in sin, the breach not being made up with the Lord in humble confession and suit for mercy, in the blood of a Saviour . . . Only a true Wife and Spouse of Christ Jesus can grieve and mourn for the displeased absence of Christ Jesus, and cries out in humble bitterness of soul, saw ye him whom my soul loveth? . . . [H]e might see and like righteousness in the end, and fruit of it, and yet not in the true nature and beauty of it . . . just as these Indians (amongst whom I write these lines) they see the excellency of the English industry, joined with plenty, and a better condition then their own, but endure not that life of labour and indeavour, wherein that plenty and better state is found . . . Grant this life is as the life of Christ, never again to be extinguished. Yet who rejoyceth not in health, who mourns not under the pains and weaknesses of a sick bed?

Next therefore to the discovery of spirituall life, all that are born of God must try their spirituall strength, and health, and chearfull temper: The particular instances whereof, being propounded as examples, copies, and samplars[18] for us to follow in the holy Scripture, I shall pick and gather, and bind up, for both our incouragement, and comfort . . . Thus the Lord Jesus frequently retired alone to private prayer, and sometimes spent the whole night in prayer to God with strong cries, tears and supplications: And therefore is it that all true Christians are the spiritual Israelites, that is, wrastlers and strivers with God in prayer . . .

Ob.[19] But may not Hypocrites be frequent and fervent in prayer to God? . . . And how easie is it by worldly engines to wheel about the Indians of America to become frequent prayers unto God, &c.

I answer: Many are the differences between the true prayers of Gods children, and the false of dissemblers and hypocrites: I will name a few for instance.

17. Pained or tormented.

18. "Samplar" is an older variation of "sampler," something that serves as a model or pattern to be copied. The earliest uses of the word usually referred to needlework, but seventeenth-century examples tend to use it in reference to God or Christ as "samplar." *OED*, 14:433–34.

19. Objection.

First then hypocrites pray but in a form and lip-labour,[20] as a task and work to be done for carnall respects, to merit at Gods hand, or to stop the mouth of conscience, which tels them they cannot be Gods children except they pray: But true prayer is the pouring out of the heart to God, the true breathing of the soul to God, arising as Incense and perfume unto God . . .

The second difference is, the Hypocrites prayers more respect the ears of men then God, as the Lord Jesus tells us: They pray that men may know so much, and esteem them Religious: Gods children, like true lovers, delight to be private, and fervent with their heavenly Father and Husband . . .

Obj. May not wicked men and Hypocrites acknowledge Gods afflicting hand, and humble themselves?

I answer, Hypocrites may see Gods hand, and humble themselves as the Egyptians, and the Philistins[21] did, but cannot possibly be thankfull for it: They acknowledge Gods hand as a Dog his Masters when he is beaten, but not as a child his Fathers. As a loving and dutifull wife, receiving Pills or Phisick from the hand of her loving Husband, a skilfull Physitian, who knows her sicknes, and out of love and care, prepares them for her, she cannot but be thankfull for those bitter medicins, and earnestly desire a kindly working . . .

Hence it is that in the heavenly Love Song, the love of Christians to Christ Jesus in his ordinances is most elegantly set forth by a similitude taken from the strong affection of married persons . . . True heavenly affection (like marriage love) at first kindles from some private sparks, to an open flame of publick profession, without shame before all men . . .

Object. Why then are many of Gods children so heavy in their sufferings and losses for Christ Jesus?

I answer, This hapneth sometimes out of distemper of body; sometimes out of distemper and weaknesse of mind, which they labour against, and chide themselves for as did David, Psal. 42. & 43. why art thou disquieted O my Soul, and why art thou so heavy within me? still trust in GOD, for I will praise him, who is the health of my countenance and my God.

It argues strength of Grace when we use this world, and all the comforts of it with a weaned eye and mind, as if we used it not: as English Travellers that lodge in an Indian house, use all the wild Indians comforts with a strange affection, willing and ready to be gone: or as Passengers in a Ship,

20. According to the *Oxford English Dictionary*, "lip-labour" is "empty talk" or "vain repetition of words in prayer." "Lip-labour" was replaced with "lip-service" in common usage by the mid-1800s. *OED*, 8:1006, 1009. "Lip-Labour" may also refer to Prov 14:23: "In all labor there is abundance: but the talk of the lips bringeth only want." (KJV)

21. The ancient Philistines were long-standing enemies of the Israelites.

willing and ready (when God will) to land, and goe ashoar in our own country, to our owne House, and comforts in the Heavens . . .

I Now come to . . . our conversation with men, in which First I argue,
that it is a strong argument of a strong constitution and spirituall health,
when we can make it our worke and trade, to aime at glorifying our Maker
in doing good to men . . .

Obj. Christ Jesus and his Apostles and messengers were endued with
power from on high, not only to preach the Word for conversion but also
with power of casting out Devils, and healing bodily diseases.

I answer, as an holy witnesse of Christ Jesus (a Woman) once answered
a Bishop, I am a member of Christ Jesus as wel as Peter himself. The least
Believer and Follower of Jesus pertakes of the nature and spirit of him their
holy head and husband, as well as the strongest and holiest that ever did or
suffered for his holy name.

Therefore it is that we read not only of the service of those great mas-
ter-builders and work-men of Christ Jesus, the Apostles, but also the service
and helpe of Christian women, for instance Phebe, Priscilla, Mary, Persis,
were eminently noted for helping forward the work of Christ Jesus, to wit,
the glorifying of God in the saving of the poor sons of men . . .

I Am now come (dear Love) to the third and last Head proposed,
which is some few means of recovering and preserving of Christian health
and cheerfulness, and the preventing of spirituall sickness and diseases: In
this I shall desire to be brief, lest by too long a discourse I discourage thy
reading, and hinder thy use and improvement of it . . .

First then, holy consideration of our estate, a deep and frequent examination of our spirituall condition is an excellent means of Christian health
and temper . . . This holy practice ought to be frequent, but then especially
when the hand, and Rods of the Lord are upon us: For then . . . God softeneth our Hearts, and we are most like then to be as the ground, mollified
upon a Thaw, fit to be broken up, or like the ground moistened with storms,
and showers from Heaven, then in some hopefull turn for the Lords most
gracious seed and heavenly planting.

Secondly, maintain an earnest longing, and endeavour to enjoy Christ
Jesus, who is our souls life in every holy Ordinance, which he hath appointed. If it be possible (with true satisfaction to our consciences, and doubts in
Gods presence) let us never rest from being planted into the holy society of
Gods children, gathered into the order of Christ Jesus, according to his most
holy will and Testament: Remembering that Christian health, growth, and
flourishing, are promised to the Trees planted in Jehovahs house . . .

Especially be much in holy prayer, and fasting before the Lord: this is
an Ordinance of which neither Pope nor Devill could ever deprive a child

of God: If it be possible to practice this duty with others, however before the Lord in secret: remembering how frequent the children of God in holy scripture were in this duty . . .

This holy Ordinance is of such admirable use among the Saints, that even in the first, and purest times of Christianity, we read of Christian yoak fellows, consenting to a separation from each other, for a time that they may give themselves to prayer, and fasting, 1. Cor: 7 . . . as it is in the restoring of the body to health, or in the preserving of it in an healthfull condition: it is often necessarie to use the help of sharp and bitter things, bitter pills, bitter potions, bitter medicines, sweatings, purgings, vomitings, blood-lettings, &c. So is it with our souls, and spirits, and preservation of the health and chearfulness of the spiritual and the inner man.[22]

The sharp and bitter things which it pleaseth God to make use of in these cases are of two sorts.

First, such as himself is pleased to use towards us in the way of his fatherly afflictions of all sorts: on our spirits, our bodies, our yoak-fellows, children, servants, cattel, goods, &c. out of which, yea also out of the injurious and slanderous, and persecuting dealing of others, yea and out of our own sins and failings his most holy and infinite wisdom, fetcheth all sorts of cleansing and purging, yea and sometimes a cordiall and healing physick.

The second sort of sharp and bitter means are such, as we voluntarily use and apply our selves unto our selves, for the slaying and the purging out of the filthy humours and corruptions of pride, securitie, uncleanness, self-love, covetousness, and what ever else remains behinde of the body of death in us . . .

The Kernell of truth is not the lesse sweet though wrapt up in the shels and husks; Beyond all question therefore Christ Jesus foretels most sure and inconceivable plagues to all that know not God: And by this Worme that never dyes, and this fire that never goes out,[23] declares a torment to be inflicted upon both men and devils which shall be extream like fire which shall be universal upon the whole sinfull creature, no part exempted, which shall be also eternall, never dying, never ending, yet we may adore Gods righteous judgements and (working out Salvation with fear and trembling) make sure of a Jesus a Saviour to deliver us from the wrath that is to come.

---

22. Perhaps Williams is offering another explanation for his many absences?

23. Williams is quoting Isa 66:24: "And they shall go forth, and look upon the carcasses of the men that have transgressed against me: for their worm shall not die, neither shall their fire be quenched, and they shall be an abhorring unto all flesh." (KJV) In the New Testament, Mark quotes Jesus saying, "Where their worm dieth not, and the fire never goeth out," in Mark 9:48. (KJV)

In the next place (my deare Love) let us downe together by the steps of holy meditation into the valley of the shadow of Death. It is of excellent use to walke often into Golgotha, and to view the rotten skuls of so many innumerable thousands of millions of millions of men and women, like our selves, gone, gone forever from this life and being (as if they never had life nor being) as the swift Ships, as the Weavers, shuttle, as an arrow, as the lightning through the aire, &c. It is not unprofitable to remember the faces of such whom we knew, with whom we had sweet acquaintance, sweet society, with whom we have familiarly eaten and lodged, but now growne loathsome, ugly, terrible, even to their dearest, since they fell into the jawes of death, the King of terrors . . .

Oh how weaned, how sober, how temperate, how mortified should our spirits, our affections, our desires be, when we remember that we are but strangers, converse with strange companies, dwel in strange houses, lodge in strange beds and know not whether this day, this night shall be our finall change of this strange place for one far stranger, darke and dolefull, except enlightened by the Death and Life of the Son of God.

How contented should we be with any Pittance, any Allowance of Bread, of Cloaths, of Friendship, of Respect, &c.? How thankfull unto God, unto man should we poor strangers be for the least crum, or drop, or rag, vouchsaf'd unto us, when we remember we are but strangers in an Inn,[24] but passengers in a Ship, and though we dreame of long Summer days, yet our very life and being is but a swift short passage from the bank of time to the other side or Banck of a dolefull eternity? . . .

How frequent, how constant (like Christ Jesus our Founder and Example) in doing good (especially to the Souls) of all men, especially to the Household of Faith, yea even to our enemies, when we remember that this is our seed time of which every minute is precious, and that our sowing is, must be our eternall Harvest: for so sayeth the Spirit by Paul to the Galathians: He that soweth to the flesh, shall of the flesh reap corruption or rottennesse, and he that sowth to the Spirit, shall of the Spirit reap life everlasting.[25] FINIS.

---

24. The commandment to offer food, clothing, and shelter to strangers occurs throughout the Old and New Testaments. For a few examples, see Lev 19:33–34, Heb 13:1–2, and Matt 25:31–40. Williams's reference to strangers echoes 1 Chr 29:15: "For we are strangers before thee, and sojourners, like all our fathers: our days are like ye shadow upon the earth, and there is none abiding." (KJV)

25. Gal 6:8–9: "For he that soweth to his flesh, shall of the flesh reap corruption, but he that soweth to the spirit, shall of the spirit reap life everlasting. Let us not therefore be weary of well doing, for in due season we shall reap, if we faint not." (KJV)

Chapter 10

"Civility" and the Quakers, 1672

ROGER WILLIAMS'S VIGOROUS DEBATE *with the Quakers in 1672 presents a Williams that modern readers may not expect. Since he was banished from Massachusetts Bay for religious heterodoxy, readers might reasonably assume that Williams would empathize with the Quakers, who were also banished from Massachusetts. Readers may anticipate that Williams's rigid separation between matters of religion and matters of government would lead him to support all forms of religious practice and may see his attitude towards the Quakers as an anomaly. But Williams's disagreements with the Quakers is another way to see how radical his ideas on religious toleration were: Williams believed in the governmental protection of religious freedom for all—even for those he despised, like the Quakers. But he was no modern pluralist, and he felt personally compelled to write and publicly argue against those with whom he disagreed. He believed that people should have full religious freedom and be free from governmental intervention or punishment, but at the same time, he accepted that individuals and churches would disagree with each other and even try to use the "sword of the spirit" (as he termed it in* The Bloudy Tenent) *to prove each other wrong. Williams did place limits on religious expression (even in terms of government intervention) when religious expression crossed the bounds of acceptable actions in a civil society, or broke the civil laws of the state. Williams, like his neighbors in the Massachusetts Bay and Plimouth colonies, saw the Quakers as challenging the very foundation of civil society.*

Anti-Quaker sentiment was widespread in Europe, and Protestants and Catholics alike opposed the new sect. Quakers posed a fundamental challenge to puritans in the New England colonies and Williams (like his puritan neighbors) found Quaker theology dangerous and wrong. Of all the English colonies in New England, only Williams's colony even allowed them to settle

*within its borders beginning in 1656.¹ While he disagreed with the extreme
measures taken by magistrates in Massachusetts Bay and did not prohibit
Quaker settlement in Rhode Island, he also worried about their proliferation.
So when Williams heard that the Quaker founder and leader George Fox was
planning to visit Newport in 1672, he immediately wrote to the Quakers in
Newport, challenging them to a public debate, with part of the debate to take
place in Newport, and the other part in Providence. In fact, so determined
was Williams to publicly disprove the Quakers that, according to Williams's
own account below, he hopped in a boat and rowed the twenty-five miles from
Providence to Newport—an arduous row on the Narragansett Bay that likely
took more than eighteen hours, which was pretty impressive for a seventy-
year-old man. But Williams was not alone in his strong feelings regarding the
Quakers; many Baptists in Rhode Island (some of whom were his fiercest critics) supported Williams during the 1672 debates.² This text—Williams's last
published work and the only one printed in the colonies—shows his eagerness
to debate Quakers, rather than banish, punish, or execute them, as his counterparts in Massachusetts Bay had done.*

*Quakers emerged out of the Church of England in the political and
spiritual chaos of the 1650s, when the puritans, Presbyterians, and Independents had more power after the beheading of King Charles I in 1649. Quakers
believed that the inner light of Christ was in every person, something their
puritan adversaries saw as far too close to believing in the divinity of mankind.
Massachusetts Bay authorities saw Quaker evangelism as aggressive, under-
mining, and even satanic—a fundamental threat to their "City on a Hill."
So in the Massachusetts Bay Colony, Quakers were "warned out," physically
abused, and between 1659 and 1661, William Robinson, Marmaduke Steven-
son, Mary Dyer, and William Leddra were hanged for "heresy." (In 1661, the
newly enthroned King Charles II ordered the colony to discontinue its harshest punishments.) The different treatment of Quakers in these two colonies is
stark. Williams believed they should be protected in their religious practice,
and chose to spend days debating Quakers and wrote more than 500 pages
detailing those debates in a book that was printed during King Philip's War,
of all times.*

*That said, this text shows Williams at his ornery, opaque worst. For
many readers, Williams's attack on the Quakers seems entirely unfair. Along
with disagreeing with their theology, Williams finds Quakers' daily behavior*

---

1. James, *Colonial Rhode Island*, 39–41.

2. Fisher et al., *Decoding Roger Williams*, 61. Despite ministerial and governmental
worries about the Quakers, the residents in Massachusetts Bay were often disturbed by
the colony's physical punishments and executions of them: Weimer, *Martyrs' Mirror*,
98–117.

unacceptable and dangerous. Several times during the debate, Williams alleges that Quaker women "appear in publick stark Naked," something he admits he never witnessed.[3] *What may surprise some readers is how essentially conservative Williams was or had become in his old age: he expected men to lift their hats and keep their hair short, children to address their parents as Mother and Father, and he found the idea that women might preach in public as "unnatural." Crowds gathered to watch the debates in Newport and Providence in August 1672 (even though George Fox had left Newport by the time Williams arrived), which dragged on for many days longer than expected. The Quakers consistently criticized Williams for being long-winded, even after they began limiting his time. The debates included dramatic moments and acrimony: An eclipse of the sun occurred during the first day of the debate, and on the second day, Williams's exhaustion led his opponents to describe him as drunk.*[4] *But, there are some remarkable scenes included in this text, and it highlights the complicated population of residents in Rhode Island as few other Williams texts can.*

George Fox described the invitation from Williams: "we had a long Dispute with one Roger Williams, that sent us a Challenge from Providence, with fourteen Propositions, as he called them, but they were Charges." Williams offered fourteen propositions for debate, but in the excerpts below we chose to focus primarily on three of them: Williams's first proposition, that Quakers are not true Christians and do not accept the essential dual nature of Christ; the fourth proposition, that Quakers do not read, understand, or follow the Bible; and the thirteenth, that Quaker writings are "poor and lame." Along with these three propositions, we have included many sections of Williams's comments on Quakers as residents in the colony, since their actions in the community often angered and worried him.[5] *[Note that Williams used the word "dumb" repeatedly in this text; he meant it as a synonym for "silent." Silence is an important part of Quaker devotional practice.]*

Williams completed the manuscript by March 1673, but struggled to find a publisher. It seems that the printer, John Foster, had set the type in 1673

---

3. This practice follows the example of Isaiah preaching naked "as a sign" [Isa 20:1–4]. Evidence of it happening in New England is scant: In 1662, Quaker Deborah Buffum Wilson walked through Salem and Lydia Wardell entered the Newbury meeting house naked. None of the Quaker missionaries visiting from England did this while in New England, so historian Carla Pestana suggests that these two women "must have adopted the practice after hearing about it from others." Pestana, *Quakers and Baptists*, 39–40; Winship, *Hot Protestants*, 149.

4. James, *Colonial Rhode Island*, 45–47.

5. One thing that Fox and Williams shared was a mutual dislike of Williams's nemesis Samuel Gorton. See J. L. Diman's introduction to *Fox Digg'd Out* in *Complete Writings of Roger Williams*, 5:xx.

before realizing that Williams could not pay for the printing.[6] *In a letter early in 1673, Williams wrote that "if it please God I cannot get it printed in New-England, I have great thoughts and purposes for old."*[7] *Eventually, Massachusetts Bay Governor John Leverett and Plimouth Colony Governor Thomas Prence, along with other puritan supporters, covered the costs of printing. The first preface is to King Charles II, and Williams asks for the "Majestyes continued Grace and Patience to this poor New-England," claiming that the book is "the Protestant Truth." Clearly keen to win the monarch's favor, Williams engaged in a pamphlet war with Quakers, who were equally eager to prove their loyalty.*[8] In 1678, Fox published a response to Williams's George Fox Digg'd Out, called A New-England-fire-brand quenched being something in answer unto a lying, slanderous book, entitled, George Fox digged out of his burrows, &c. printed at Boston in the year 1676, of one Roger Williams of Providence in New-England.

Roger Williams, *George Fox Digg'd Out of his Burrowes* (1676)[9]

To the People called Quakers.

Friends & Country-men:

1. The occasion of these Discourses you may see in the first Page: the 14 Proposals in the second Page, and the occasion of the Title in the 34.

2. The truth is (as Edmund Burroughs,[10] and others of you say of your selves) from Childhood (now above three-score years) the Father of Lights

6. LaFantasie suggests that lack of funds explains the almost four-year delay in printing. *Correspondence of Roger Williams* 2:689n6; Williams, *George Fox Digg'd Out* in *Complete Writings of Roger Williams,* 5:xlviii.

7. Williams to Samuel Hubbard, Winter 1673, in *Correspondence of Roger Williams,* 2:688.

8. Weimer, "Problem of Godly Loyalty," 295–98.

9. Williams, *George Fox Digg'd Out* in *Complete Writings of Roger Williams,* 5:1–503. Footnotes at the end of each section refer to the pages from which transcriptions were taken.

10. The title reference to "burrowes" is a pun on Burrough. Edward Burrough (1634–1663) was an early English Quaker prophet who published extensively in defense of Quakers, especially during the Restoration, when Quakers were eager to prove their loyalty to the monarchy. When Charles II became king and the Massachusetts Bay General Court wrote to him defending their punishments of Quakers, Burrough petitioned the king seeking toleration for Quakers in the New England colonies. That text—*A Declaration of the Sad and Great Persecution and Martyrdom of the People of God called Quakers, in New England, for the Worshipping of God*—was printed in 1662 and led Charles II to temporarily halt the harshest punishments in the colonies. Burrough was arrested in London for holding a Quaker meeting and died in Newgate prison in February 1663. For Burrough's quest to prove Quaker loyalty, often by comparison to New

and Mercies toucht my Soul with a love to himself, to his only begotten, the true Lord Jesus, to his Holy Scriptures, &c. his infinite Wisdome hath given me to see the City, Court and Country, the Schools and Universities of my Native Country, to converse with some Turks, Jews, Papists, and all sorts of Protestants, and by Books to know the Affairs and Religions of all Countries, &c.

3. My Conclusion is, that be of good chear thy sins are forgiven thee, Mat. 9. is one of the joyfullest sounds that ever came to poor sinful Ears: how to obtain this sound from the mouth of that Mediatour that spoke it, is the great dispute between the Protestants and the bloody Whore of Rome:[11] this is also the great point between the true Protestants and your selves . . .

4. Bear with me while I say, that as the Jesuits[12] pretend to deifie the Pope, but it is known, the end is to deifie themselves under the cloak of the Popes Name: so Satan pretends to exalt and deifie you, under the name of God, and Christ, and Spirit, &c. but his end as Peter tells us, to exalt himself, and fill his hellish Paunch with Souls.

5. I endeavoured, but could not procure a Short-hand writer, so that I am forced to recollect Transactions from my Memory, and I believe (in the holy presence of God) that I have not failed to present the true substance of passages without advantage to my self, or disadvantage to my Opposites.[13]

6. I have used some sharp Scripture Language, but not (as commonly you do) passionately and unjustly: I sometimes call you Foxians . . . because G. Fox hath appeared the greatest Writer, and the greatest Preacher amongst you, and the most deified that I can hear of, sure it is that here he subtly run for it: he ordered that my Letters to our Deputy Governour Captain Cranstone (in which my Proposals to G.F. were, should not be delivered to the Deputy, until G. F. was some hours under sayle, that he might say he never saw my Paper, though it is as clear as noon-day that he knew all matters by Copies, Letters and Relations, perfectly many dayes before his departure.

England Congregationalists, see Weimer, "Problem of Godly Loyalty," 287–93.

11. This refers to the Roman Catholic Church.

12. Jesuits are Roman Catholic priests from the Society of Jesus order founded in 1540 by Ignatius of Loyola.

13. Williams admitted here that he was recalling much of this from memory since he did not take notes during the debates, although he would have liked to have had a short-hand notetaker. The Quakers had a few notetakers and the 1873 editor of this text suggests that while they disagreed with Williams's condemnation of them, they did not dispute "the accuracy of the report." Williams prepared the manuscript in fall 1672 and winter 1672/1673—all of the prefaces are dated March 10, 1673—but it took three more years to find a publisher to print the book. Williams, *George Fox Digg'd Out* in *Complete Writings of Roger Williams*, 5:xlviii-xlix.

7. My disadvantage (in our Contests (especially at Newport) were great and many: for though J. Stubs[14] and J. Burnet were more civil and ingenious: yet W. Edmondson[15] was nothing but a bundle of Ignorance, and Boisterousness, he would speak first end all (though all three were constantly on me at once) no man might speak at all in favour of my Positions: any might freely speak against them: they sat in the midst of the Governour and Magistrates (of their Opinion) and the whole Assembly (of their way) W. Edmundson (though J. Stubs twice said in publick, that I had not inter- interrupted them) yet W. Edmundson would frequently and insolently interrupt me: so that I was not only forced to bear patiently (through Gods only help) but to suppress my thoughts, which here I have added in some places.

8. I know that a great weight of your Opinions and Actings lye upon your believing your selves guided by the immediate Spirit of God: but I believe that I have proved that it is no more the holy Spirit of God, that speaks and acts in you, then it was the true Samuel that spake such heavenly words in the appearance of Sam. Mantle amongst a cloud of other witnesses you shall never perswade Souls (not bewitched) that the holy spirit of God would perswade your Women and Maidens to appear in publick (streets & assemblies) stark naked, &c. of which I have spoke more particularly in our disputations.

9. It is hard to Perswade a Fox or a Wolf that his is so, &c. or that he doth Rob or Steal, or Murther; it is hard to perswade a man while he dreams that he is in a Dream: yea though he be a filthy Dreamer as Gods Spirit speaks: In our Dreams we believe lyes and impossibilities to be true as that we are many thousand miles of, that we talk with dead men, &c. that we are at Marriages or Burials and are Kings and Queens, &c.

10. All that I can hope for (without Gods wonderfull mercy) is to give my Testimony in my generation: for (as Solomon speaks of the Whore) few or none of you return. Yet I know Gods foundation is sure he knows

14. John Stubs (c. 1618–1675) converted to Quakerism while stationed with Cromwell's army in 1653 at Carlisle garrison, where George Fox was imprisoned. Unwilling to swear an oath to Cromwell, Stubs left the army shortly after his conversion. He served as an itinerant preacher throughout the British Isles, Holland, Germany, and Rome. Stubs accompanied Fox on his trip to the New England colonies, staying behind to debate Williams after Fox departed.

15. William Edmundson (1627–1712) also served in the army under Cromwell, fighting at the Battle of Worcester in 1651. He became a Quaker missionary after conversion in 1653, and is generally credited with the founding of the Quaker church in Ireland. Edmundson made three missionary trips to the British colonies: in 1671, he traveled to Barbados, Jamaica, South Carolina, and Virginia with George Fox; he returned to Virginia in 1675–1677; and he made a final trip to the southern colonies in 1683–1684.

who are his amongst you as amongst other perswasions. I have proved, and will prove (if God please) that spiritual Pride, that is Pride about spiritual matters, is the Root and Branch of your whole Religion, and that the King Eternal, who did cast out proud Angels out of his Palace, will hardly open his Gates to proud and scornful Dust and Ashes:

I am one of your best Friends,

R.W.

Providence, March 10 1672/3 (so called)

A Narration of a CONFERENCE OR DISPUTE,

This last August 1672 (so called) in the Colony of Rode-Island and Providence, Plantations in N. ENGLAND, between Roger Williams of Providence (who Challenged Fox by writing which followes) and all his Friends then met on Rode-Island, (and G. Fox withdrawing) John Stubs, John Burniat, and William Edmunston (three of their ablest Apostles) on the other, that is, (on the pretended Quakers) Party.

Having long heard of the great name of G. Fox, (a man cried up by the People called Quakers) and having read his book in Folio (some years since) against, as I think above six score Books and Papers (written by pious and able pens against them) and now this Summer hearing of his coming into these Parts of N England . . . I read over his Book afresh . . . and more clearly finding his Answers so weak and silly, so Anti-Christian and Blasphemous, and yet so Imperious and Scornfull, so Cursing and Censorious, Damning and Reprobating all that bow not down to their new Upstart Image, my Spirit rose up within me, and I believe the holy Spirit of God (in answer to my poor Petitions and Meditations) resolved and quickened my Spirit to the present Undertake and Service . . . For the vindicating of many of the precious Truths of the old Christian purity, and for the sake of so many precious Souls lying slain and bleeding before me, I made this Offer following to G. Fox, and any or all of his Followers or Associates, then together at New-port . . . Tis true G. Fox was at Providence some few dayes before, and spake publickly; and it was free for me publickly to have heard him, and opposed him; But going the last year to one of their general Assemblyes at New-Port, and having begun to present to them some Considerations about the True Christ and the false, the True Spirit and the False and being cut of in the midest, by sudden Prayer of one, and the Singing of another, and then by the Prayer of another and the sudden dissolving of the Assembly, I resolved to try another way, and to offer a fair and full Dispute . . .

To G. Fox or any other of my Countrey-men at New-Port who say they are the Apostles and Messengers of Christ Jesus, In humble Confidence of the help of the Most High, I offer to maintain in Publick, against all Comers, these 14 Propositions following, to wit, the first seven at New-Port, and the other seven at Providence . . .

Only I desire

1 To have three dayes Notice, before the day you fix on.

2 That without Interruption (or many speaking at once) the Conference may continue from Nine in the morning till about four in the afternoon. and

3 That if either of the seven Propositions be not finished on one day, the Conference may continue and goe on some few hours the next day.

4 That either of us Disputing shall have free uninterrupted liberty to speak (in Answers and Replyes) as much and as long as wee please, and then give the Opposite the same Liberty.

That the whole may be managed with Ingenuity and Humanity . . . the Propositions are these that follow.

First That the People called Quakers are not true Quakers according to the holy Scriptures.

2 That the Christ they profess is not the True Lord Jesus Christ.

3 That the Spirit by which they are acted is not the Spirit of God.

4 That they doe not own the holy Scriptures.

5 Their Principles and Professions, are full of Contradictions and Hypocrisies.

6 That their Religion is not only an Heresy in the matters of Worship, but also in the Doctrines of Repentance Faith. &c

7 Their Religion is not but a confused mixture of Popery, Armineanisme, Socineanisme,[16] Judaisme&c.

8 The People called Quakers (in effect) hold no God, no Christ, no Spirit, no Angel, no Devil, no Resurrection, no Judgment, no Heaven no Hell, but what is in man.

9. All that their Religion requires (externall and internall) to make Converts and Proselites, amounts to no more than what a Reprobate may easily attain unto, and perform.

10 That the Popes of Rome doe not swell with and exercise a greater Pride, then the Quakers Spirit hath expresst, and doth aspire unto, although

16. Popery was a common derogatory term for Catholicism. Based on the teachings of the early seventeenth-century Dutch Protestant reformer Jacobus Arminius, Arminianism denied predestination and suggested that people could choose or reject salvation. (It was considered heretical by puritans.) Socinianism was based on works of sixteenth-century Italian theologian Faustus Socinus, and denied the doctrine of the trinity.

many truly humble Soules may be captivated amongst them, as may be in other Religions.

11 The Quakers Religion is more obstructive, and destructive to the Conversion and Salvation of the Souls of People, then most of the Religions this day extant in the world.

12 The Sufferings of the Quakers are no true evidence of the Truth of their Religion.

13 That their many Books and writings are extremely Poor, Lame, Naked, and sweld up only with high Titles and words of Boasting and Vapour.

14. That the Spirit of their Religion tends mainly, to reduce Persons from Civility to Barbarisme, to an Arbetratry[17] Goverment, and the Dictates and Decrees of that sudden Spirit that acts them, to a sudden cutting off of People, yea of Kings and Princes opposing them, to as fiery Persecutions for matters of Religion and Conscience, as hath been or can be practised by any Hunters or Persecutors in the world.[18]

At this point in the text, Williams includes transcribed letters that he exchanged with John Throckmorton (J.T. in the text) in the last two weeks of July 1672.[19] He describes that letter exchange below as "the Skirmishings of my Forlorn-Hope." Williams considered Throckmorton a friend, as Throckmorton and Williams had traveled to New England together, and Throckmorton was one of the original proprietors of Rhode Island. He was a successful merchant and coastal trader who converted to Quakerism—a conversion Williams clearly struggled with. Williams now turns his attention to narrating the logistics of planning the 1672 debates in Newport, his long journey by rowboat from Providence to Newport, and the first "conferences."

Hitherto (gentle Reader) have been the Skirmishings of my Forlorn-Hope; I hasten now to the relation of the main Battle, for after this my third Letter and Answer, I heard no more of that foul and slanderous Spirit: I should rejoice to be instrumentall to his casting out of my ancient friend J.T. however he pluckt in his horns as G Fox himself did, and I have yet hear no further.

Within some few dayes after that our Deputy Governour had delivered my Paper to them, the strange Quakers (as was agreed with G. Fox) came to Providence. John Stubs, John Burnet, and others, and came to my house six

17. Arbitrary.

18. Williams, *George Fox Digg'd Out* in *Complete Writings of Roger Williams*, 5:1–5.

19. The Throckmorton letters are included in *Correspondence of Roger Williams*, 2:654–77.

or seven together: their Salutations were (like the meetings of their dumb Spirit) in silence. I bid them welcome &.c. John Stubs began and said, they had received a Paper from me, and they came to me to tell me, that they accepted my Offer, and that they had appointed (according to the liberty given them by my self in my Paper) the 9th. of the present August to be the day at Newport. I told them they were welcome, and the more welcome because they brought me tidings of their Resolution: for I longed for the Opportunityes of such Exercises, to which I thought the most High invited us by our precious Libertyes &.c. I added that my Paper was in the first place directed to G. Fox: but . . . John Burnet told me that G. Fox was departed before my Letters were opened, and that G. Fox never saw my Paper (and probably as afterward in the dispute he spake honestlie not knowing the Mistery) John Stubs added that my Paper gave liberty to G. Fox or his friends. I said therefore I would not fail (if God pleased) to meet them at the place, and by nine in the morning, on the day they had appointed.

They departed (after drink offered and accepted by some) but the next morning being the first of the Week I sent them word in writing, that diverse of our Neighbours were grieved that the Conference should be carried away from Providence to Newport wholly, (as some of them had also spoken) I told them that the accepting of my proffer necessarily included the Conference about the latter seven at Providence: I told them their Consciences and Credits lay on it . . . This Paper was delivered to one of their Company in the room where they were together, but whither on purpose or (as tis possible) by mistake, they say the Paper was lost: so receiving no Answer from them, I late in the evening sent them another writing, signifiing, that I could not hold my self ingaged to meet them at Newport about the first seven, without their promise of discussing the latter seven at Providence. Then they wrote to me that I had seemed willing, and they had given notice, and the Countrey would come in, therefore they challenged me to appear and prove my malicious and bitter charges against them . . . Upon receipt of this, I sent them a third writing signifiing that I rested in their Promise, and therefore (if God pleased) I would not fail to be with them at the time and place appointed. And God graciously assisted me in rowing all day with my old bones so that I got to Newport toward the Midnight before the morning appointed . . .

When I came into the place aforesaid I found three able and noted preachers amongst them, viz John Stubs, John Burnet, William Edmunson sitting together on a high Bench with some of the Magistrates of their Judgment with them: I had heard that John Stubs was learned in the Hebrew and the Greek (and I found him so) as for John Burnet I found him to be of a moderate Spirit, and a very able Speaker. The third W. Edmundson was newly come (as was said) from Virginia, and he proved the Chief Speaker, a man not so able nor so moderate as the other two: For the two first would speak Argument, and discuss and produce Scripture: but William Edmundson was very ignorant in the Scripture or any other Learning: He had been a souldier in the late warres,[20] a stout portly man of a great voice, and sit to make a Bragadocia (as he did) and a constant exercise meerly of my Patience: he would often Vapour and preach long, and when I had patiently waited till the Gust was over, and began to speak, then would he stop my mouth with a very unhandsome Clout of a grievous Interruption . . . It pleased God to help me with such Patience to weather them . . .

I took my Seat at the other end of the house opposite to them, and began telling them that the most High was my witness, that not out of any prejudice against, or disrespect to the persons of the Quakers (many of whome I knew and did love and honour) nor any foolish Passion of pride or boldness (for I desired to be sensible of my many decayes of my house of Clay, and other wayes) nor any earthly or worldly ends I had occasioned this trouble to my self and them.[21]

Williams begins outlining and elaborating on his fourteen proofs.

I began with the first Position, which I think W. Edmunson also read out of the paper. viz. That the people called the Quakers are not true Quakers according to the Scriptures. I said I knew they did not owne that name Quakers, as imposed on them by God, or taken up by themselves, but given them in scorn and derision . . . And yet I had cause to judg that the name was given by Justice Bennet and others to them from that strange and uncouth possessing of their bodyes. with quaking and shaking of their Bodyes even in publick Assemblyes and Congregations, which extraordinary motions I judged to come upon them, not from the holy Spirit and Power of God, but from the spirit and power of Sathan for diverse Reasons.[22]

Some of these Particulars I could not then express, but I think fit here to remember the former dayes, for Information of such as doe desire it. These

20. Williams is referring to Edmundson's service in Cromwell's army in Scotland, and his participation in the Battle of Worcester (1651), which was a decisive victory for the New Model Army against the Royalist forces of the new king, Charles II.

21. Williams, *George Fox Digg'd Out* in *Complete Writings of Roger Williams*, 5:35–39.

22. During meetings, Quakers could tremble and quake from what they said was the working of Christ within them. Williams, like many other puritans, dismissed this physical movement as false witness at best or demonic possession at worst. As Williams notes here, they were called "Quakers" by their enemies, and it was not a name they chose. Winship, *Hot Protestants*, 149. Williams, *George Fox Digg'd Out* in *Complete Writings of Roger Williams*, 5:41.

People come from Lancashire and other northern parts to the Southward of England and to London. I spake with some of their Chief then in London, I knew it was the old proud spirit which had appeared in so many foul lyes in their former deceived and deceiving Leaders, and I was more confirmed in my thoughts when I saw their foul spirit to transport them, not only in lying Doctrines, but lying Quakings and Tremblings, lying preaching through the Streets Repent, Repent . . . To my face and to the world in print they maintaind, there were no sins in them: Saying That the Saints could not sin, and God did all and was all, and they were as pure as Adam and God himself. . . .

Again I said unto my Antagonists that the manner of these quakings and shakings were not as of those quakings and tremblings of David, Moses, and the Corinths receiving Titus with Trembling, or the working out Salvation with Fear and Trembling . . . Beside, as it is naturall for the Body to tremble when the mind doth, as we see in many Persons in the beginning of a Battle, or going over a deep Water, or going to suffer Death, or looking over a high Clift into the sea &c. . . .

But the quaking and shaking motions of the Quakers (as I shall prove) they proceeded not from the holie Affections proper to Gods Children, so also they were horrid and monstrous casting their bodies into horrid and monstrous motions and Gestures which mine eyes have seen . . . which cannot be imagined to proceed from the holy Spirit of God, but from Sathan to delude and cheat poor sinners with. To this purpose I told them at the first coming of this spirit to London and Westminster, some Parliament men told me that themselves went to one of the Quakers Meetings about Charing Cross, but were so affrighted with the shakings of their own bodies, and of their Chairs and Stooles under them, that they could never again be got into their Assemblyes. I added, that such Shakings, Motions, Extasies, &c. were known to be the frequent workings of Sathan upon his Servants in all ages . . . John Burnet and William Edmunson rose up and said that I had laid many deep and heavy Charges upon the people of the Lord, which I should never be able to prove: I had denied them to be Christians, and so had wronged the good Spirit of God in them, and their Profession of worshiping God in the Spirit: Yea I had taken away their being (as men) out of the World, as a dangerous People to Nations and Kingdoms & Commonweales, yea to Kings & Princes, and so not fit to live amongst men in the World . . . I waited patiently till these Gusts of their angry Spirit was over, and then I told them I had not wronged them in a tittle: But by the help of the most High I would . . . leave it to every mans and womens Soul to judge at their own Perill.

About this time John Stubs alleadged that of Paul, Phil 2. Work out salvation with fear and Trembling. I replyed I in no way opposed the awfull

and most serious impressions of Gods Majesty in all his appearances & ordinances upon the Soules and Spirits, yea the Bodyes of Gods Children. But
I denied that those places to the Corinthians and Philippians concerned
any such bodily shakings and quakings as we now debated . . . But the plain
truth is, the Devill will be Gods Ape in most things: He subornes and sub-
stitutes a bastard Quaking and Trembling of the body in Imitation of David,
Moses, &c. on purpose to thrust out the true Fear and Trembling which
ought to be constantly in us . . .[23]

*Williams often compares the Quakers to Catholics, knowing the power
that this derogatory comparison had in the reformed Protestant world. There
is little he could say that would better illustrate how deeply he disagrees with
the Quakers, especially given what he sees as both groups' utter disregard for
the Bible. He also seems bothered by what he sees as unacceptable behavior by
Quakers, including, as the excerpt below shows, their unkempt hair.*

I told them God was little beholding to the Pope and the Quakers for
their humble Reverence and great Affection to his holy Letters, Declara-
tions and Proclamations. The Pope had his Infallibility as well as they, his
immediate Inspirations as well as they: They both owned, and yet did not
owne the holy Scriptures, the Pope and they only must interpret Scriptures,
they only give the Sense, they only judge all Controversies: yet they dispence
with the Scriptures . . . one Thurston[24] an Apostle of theirs who came to
Providence with extraordinary long hair hanging over his shoulders . . . [a
woman] demanded of him why he ware it so long since nature it self did
teach it to be a shame for a man to wear long Hair, as the holy Scripture
affirmed? . . . This mans hair was so offensive and odious . . .[25]

23. Williams, *George Fox Digg'd Out* in *Complete Writings of Roger Williams,* 5:43–46.

24. Thomas Thurston (1622–1693) traveled to New England in 1656, was imprisoned as a Quaker in Boston as soon as he arrived, and was deported to England a few
months later. He returned to the colonies in November 1657, landing in Virginia, where
he was immediately imprisoned. Repeatedly Thurston was imprisoned, banished, and
exiled in Virginia, Maryland, and New Netherland, eventually returning to England in
1659. He came back to the colonies and settled with his family in Maryland in 1663;
by this time, he was considered radical even by fellow Quakers, including George Fox.
Fox tried to reason with Thurston during Fox's 1673 visit to Maryland, which led to
Thurston's penitent confession in 1675. His moderation did not last though, and in
1683 the Maryland Quakers described him as an "evil instrument." Carroll, "Thomas
Thurston: Renegade Maryland Quaker," 170–93.

25. Williams, *George Fox Digg'd Out* in *Complete Writings of Roger Williams,* 5:49–51.

Throughout the text, Williams describes the alleged nakedness of Quakers, especially Quaker women. As the introduction to this text explains, Williams was particularly bothered by this practice (perhaps in part because he thought it was an unacceptable violation of civil society), but scholars of early America suggest that it rarely, if ever, happened. Williams admits that he never witnessed it himself.

I told them . . . that they were so far from being Christians . . . being fallen beneath the common temper and nature of the Humanity of men, and women, yea of the Savage and Barbarous in the world, viz. their stripping stark naked their Men and Women and Maidens and passing along in publick places and Streets unto the Assemblyes of Men and Youths and so were beheld and gazed upon by them! and this under a pretence of being stirred up by God as a Service or Worship unto God, as an act of Christian Religion proceeding from the immediate moving of the most holy Spirit of God . . .

John Burnet said that the people called Quakers, were a People known to abhor all Impurity and Uncleanness and the Appearance of it, and if any of their women should so practice, they should condemn it in them, yet nevertheless if it should please the Lord God to stir up any of his Daughters so to appear as a Sign and Testimony against the Nakedness of others, that they durst not condemn it. . . . John Stubs read the 20th of Isa. where Isaiah was commanded to goe naked for a Sign to the Egyptians and Ethyopians, to prophesie and denounce that they also should go naked with their buttocks uncovered as the words are: and this is (said they) a proof that the People of the Lord might be stirred up by God to such actions for Signs unto others.

I Answered, that this was in the dayes of Figures and Signs, Shadows and Ceremonyes . . . The difference of Nakedness of Mankind and Womankind is very great in all Nations. The Sex of Women is more fitted and framed by God for a Covering, for Retiredness and keeping at home and for Modesty and Bashfulness; nor do we ever read that ever God commanded such a thing to Women, or that ever it came into his heart, or that ever any Godly Woman did so practice: there is no shadow or colour of Proof from the holy Scripture, nor from any Civill and sober People, no nor from the naked Barbarians themselves, who though they suffer their Male Children to go naked till about seven year old, yet they cover their Females from their birth . . .

They still answered they would not Countenance any such Practice but if the Lord God so commanded his Sons and Daughters it must be obeyed. I demanded of them how it should be known that it was the voice and command of God, the God of Holiness, and not the command of the unclean Spirit? . . . Edmundson fel into a great heat against me and said I spoke Blasphemy . . . he added, that I had kept them long and had proved nothing.[26]

Williams woke up on August 10, the second day of the debate, feeling unwell. He admits, sarcastically, that he would "rather have kept my Bed then have gone forth to a whole days fresh Dispute with such (reputed) able and noted Champions." The Quakers seemed equally exhausted by the debate. They had spent an entire day and had only engaged the first of Williams's fourteen propositions, despite their mutual agreement that they would cover the first seven propositions on that first day. Williams's voice was hoarse from "continued loud Speech all the day before," and his head was pounding. He opted to sit closer to his "Antagonists" so as to reserve his voice. Despite this precaution, Williams heard that many in the audience believed he was drunk because his voice was weakened. Horrified by this "foul Slander," Williams reassures the reader: "[others who] lodged with me can testifie that I complained of Illness . . . my daughter kindly offered me a Dram for my Illness, but I refused it knowing it might curdle the milk I had taken, and so increase my cold and Obstruction."[27] Throughout the days of debate, Williams often commented on the uncivil behavior of the Quakers. According to Williams, he was rarely allowed to speak without interruption.

Still my Opposites were catch in their own Craftiness they seemed well pleased that G. Fox should be heard in his Answere to his Adversaries, and I restrain'd and stopt from making out my Proofs from the Sense, and Scope and Meaning: . . . I intended to make use of this present Advantage (which I from the first intended, when I saw I should be stopt, and they would not afford me the liberty I gave to them without the least Interruption) as John Stubs confessed.[28]

The Quakers raised an uncomfortable comparison for Williams. They reminded him that he accused them of denying a visible church, while Williams himself abstained from attending church services. Williams admits that he cannot "finde rest" for his soul with any gathered church.

I told them that G. Fox his Book and all their Books and Professions denied any visible Church of Christ at all: and though they maintained and kept up Congregations (of pretended Christian) Worship and Worshippers

26. Williams, *George Fox Digg'd Out* in *Complete Writings of Roger Williams,* 5:59–63.

27. Williams, *George Fox Digg'd Out* in *Complete Writings of Roger Williams,* 5:65–67.

28. Williams, *George Fox Digg'd Out* in *Complete Writings of Roger Williams,* 5:91.

(in a direct contradiction unto their own Tenants, yet) they maintained the Church was in God and so not visible: the Officers of the Church were invisible and immediately made by the immediate and invisible Spirit . . . The Lords Supper appointed by the Lord Jesus to be a Spiritual Feast remembring him until his coming was with them nothing else but Spiritial Joy, which they have one in and with another . . . Upon this (as I remember) there fell out some words between my Opposites, and some of the people called Baptists: But some of them (especially John Stubs) demanded of me, why I thus charged them and was my self so guilty, not living in Church Ordinances myself.

I answered . . . After all my search and examinations and consideration I said, I do profess to believe, that some come nearer to the first primitive Churches . . . then others, as in many respects so in that gallant and heavenly and fundamental Principle of the true matter of a Christian Congregation, Flock or Society, viz. Actual Believers, true Disciples & Converts Living Stones, such as can give some account how the Grace of God hath appeared unto them, and wrought that Heavenly Change in them; I proferred that if my Soul could finde rest in joyning unto any of the Churches professing Christ Jesus now extant, I would readily and gladly do it, yea unto themselves whom I now opposed.[29]

Williams turns to one of the most upsetting errors he accuses the Quakers of committing; he argues that they do not "own the Holy Scriptures." In Williams's fourth proposition, he passionately defends the Bible as the revealed word of God. Below, he describes the scriptures as "Love Letters of Christ Jesus to his Church." While many aspects of Quaker society and doctrine trouble him, this error might be the worst for Williams.

After some few interchanges and altercations, we descended to the fourth Position, which they read out of the Paper (as they did all the rest) which was this, viz. That the people called Quakers did not own the Holy Scriptures. I said there was a twofold owning the Holy Scriptures or the Writings of God . . . The one is verbal and literal, viz. that such a writing or Declaration, or Treatise is extant, and that it proceeds from the Kings Authority and Command. The second is real and actual, when the Authority of it is in all humble obedience submitted to and obeyed . . .

I said the Jews owned verbally and wonderfully that Writings of the Old Testament and the Papists owned both old and new but it is known that in many particulars they do in effect deny and damn them. 1. They both set

---

29. Williams, *George Fox Digg'd Out* in *Complete Writings of Roger Williams*, 5:102–3.

up their rotten Traditions, their unwritten Verityes (as they speak) of equal authority with, if not (in cases) above the holy Scripture. 2. They set up the Papists by the authority of the Council of Trent, a most defective Translation notoriously false . . . 3. The Papists set up the Pope as the only infallible Judg & Interpreter in all Questions about the Scriptures and the Jews make their Rabbies[30] as so many Popes also. 4. Their Interpretations are so forraign and strange and many of them so absurd & monstrous from the genuine & proper Sense of the Scriptures, and adulterated with Wresting and allegorizings &c. that is truly said of them that they bring not their Doctrines, Disciplines and Conversations to the Scriptures but force the holy Scriptures of God to attend and wait upon their Abomination as a Negro Slave and Lacquey.

I said the Jews and Papists did not more disowne the holy Scriptures upon the account of their Popes and Traditions and Interpretations than the Quakers did upon account of their Light and Spirit and Interpretations also. Who knows not that in the beginning of their Profession, they generally fell from the reading of them by themselves or in their Families, or in their Publick Assemblyes, only crying up the Light within, the Spirit within, the Scriptures within, their Teacher within. They stil say The Scripture was not the Word of God, the Scripture is but a dead Letter, they have no need of Paper-Teachers having the spirit that gave it forth? . . . what should hinder but that the Scripture is but a dead Letter, and (compared with their spirit) a weak and needless Paper unto them that hath such a light and Spirit within to guide them?[31]

Upon this occasion I told them that the Scriptures were the Love Letters of Christ Jesus to his Church . . . they are dear, not as common Paper and Ink, but as the Good-Will, the dearest Love and heart of the King and Emperour himself: and thus are holy Scriptures highly prized and embraced, and laid up in the heart and bosome of the true Children of God, believed listned to, and followed as the voice of Christ Jesus to his true sheep and Spouse.[32]

Williams returns frequently throughout the text to condemn the ways that Quakers conduct their meetings. In the section below, Williams offers a substantial list of their flawed practice, as he sees it. That list includes having female ministers, silent meetings, shaking hands, children addressing their

30. That is, rabbis, or Jewish teachers of the law.

31. Williams, *George Fox Digg'd Out* in *Complete Writings of Roger Williams*, 5:137–39.

32. Williams, *George Fox Digg'd Out* in *Complete Writings of Roger Williams*, 5:143.

parents by their first names, and bad singing. This list concludes his days in debate at Newport.

1. I named some of the Quakers Traditions and Inventions in our publick Conference, (unto which I shall now name some more) I told them, and now do, of the Un-Christian and unnatural Invention of Women Ministers, Women Apostles, Women Embassadors to all Nations: a business that all the Apostolical first Christian practice, and all Sober and modest Humanity abhor to think of.

2. Their dumb and silent meetings (their dumb and deaf Spirit[33]) without Colour of Common Humanity or precept or practice, or promise of Christ to such a worship.

3. Their bruitish Salutations of strangers, yea, and of acquaintance, Foes or Friends: It is true that some of them will admit of those two words, How do you, and Farewel, as if there were some holiness in these two, and in none other, and they might practice this holiness toward the worlds, &c.

4. Their New Way of feeling and grabling the hand in an uncouth, strange and Immodest way,[34] and this instead of kissing, called the holy Kiss amongst Christians, and a token of Love and Reverence to men also in sober and Civilizd Nations.

5. Their bruitish Irreverence to all their Superiours either in Age, or in any other way of Preheminence, a most proud and monstrous Bestiality against so many Commands and Examples of holy Scripture, and against the very Light of Barbarous Nature it self, for the Indians use both Reverent words and Gestures towards their Sachims, Wiyouhs and Rulers. Contrary to which, some of us have heard the Children of the Quakers brought up by and taught to say to their Fathers George thou lyest: Mary thou lyest to their Parents, a Language which deserved little less then Death by the Law, which God delivered to the Jewish Nation, and surely deserveth severe Punishment at this day.

6. Their crying down of Musicians and musick,[35] (so Excellent a gift of God[36]) as a foolish and Devilish practice, though confirmed by so many

33. Again, Williams uses "dumb" as a synonym for "silent."

34. Williams's preference for kissing over shaking hands as a form of greeting may surprise some modern readers.

35. Early Quakers saw music and singing as a distraction from prayer.

36. For puritans, singing psalms was a form of prayer: "by singing, the devout glorified and praised God . . . through singing, the worshipper was also brought closer to the divine." Focusing on singing as a form of piety, early New Englanders sang text in unison based on the psalms translated into meter in the *Bay Psalm Book* (1640), which was the first book printed in the colonies. Goodman, "Tears I Shed," 692, 701; Russo,

Reasons from, and before Christs time in Scripture, and in all sober Nature and Civility, though it is abused, as all the gifts of God are.

7. Their own un-Christian, Fantastical, absurd, and unprofitable way of Toning and singing.[37]

8. Their Condemning of the Commendable and Ingenious Arts of Carving, Embroydering, and Painting, so approved of, and Commended by God himself in Scripture, &c.

9. Their Crying out against Ornaments of Garments, and otherwise, against that Order God hath set in his works, and that Variety of his gifts for necessity, for Conveniency, for delight, even to Astonishment and Admiration in all his glorious works.

All these particulars (and more) I had not time, now have I to reckon up and amplifie, I remember no Material Exception, or Objections I had from my Antagonists. Only John Burnet spake against my great charging of them, and William Edmundson he thundred out continually how deep my Charges were, and how weak my proofs, and that I had proved nothing.[38]

Williams departed Newport, and the debate was set to resume in Providence. Before he set off, Williams was pleased with an "Unexpected yet Seasonable and true Testimony from Elizabeth Williams," his sister-in-law in front of the gathered crowd.

Just here it pleased God so to Order it, that from the Boat (ready to set Saile for Providence) I and others were called upon to depart: So I was stepping down, the Lord opened the mouth of Elizabeth Williams my Brothers wife, one of the Society of the Baptists in Newport, who hearing their Clamours, their only Refuge, he hath proved nothing and said loud: The man hath discharged his Conscience: He hath fully proved what he undertook to prove against you, and the words that he hath spoken shall Judge you at the last day. And thus the Father of Lights, the first and last, the Alpha and Omega graciously carried me through all alone these three days Contests, as in a shadow of Death with these Deceived, and Deceiving Souls: through my Labours of making out my proofs the burthen whereof lay wholly upon

"Sonic Piety," 610–22; Rath, *How Early America Sounded*, 97–119.

37. Many early New Englanders disliked Quaker singing, which they labeled "ranting." But many Quakers also sought to distance themselves from "ranters," who disrupted Quaker meetings with "wild" singing and dancing; these songs often lacked words, and seemed closer to humming. Rath, *How Early America Sounded*, 127–44; Carroll, "Singing in the Spirit," 1–13.

38. Williams, *George Fox Digg'd Out* in *Complete Writings of Roger Williams*, 5:210–12.

me though they had been silent, (through their Censures Reproaches, Fall-ing on me so many at once, Interruptions, and other Disadvantages and Provocations, his holy Name be ever praised and magnified.[39]

The debates continued in Providence on August 17, where Williams explored the remaining seven points. John Stubs and William Edmundson, on behalf of the Quakers, wrote to Williams expressing their willingness to continue, but insisted on brevity. So throughout the remainder of the text, Wil-liams inserts arguments he did not have time to make verbally. In many of the positions he took at Providence, Williams worries that Quaker beliefs would lead to chaos because there is not enough distinction among levels of family or society. In the brief example below, he uses George and Margaret Fox's own marriage as an example.

And thus though GF and MF be one in marriage, and one in a Spirit of notorious railing, yet she her self will not say but she is the Woman and he is the Man, she the wife and he the husband, and this Distinction God in Nature the Law of our Countrey and all Nations will force them . . . to acknowledge: otherwise (like the man possessed in the Gospel) I fear no Chains of Humility nor Modesty would hold them from throwing off all Chains of Conscience, and from flinging all upon heaps of confusion with-out all due respective respects and distinctions.[40]

Williams frequently attacks Fox as a thinker and, more importantly, as a writer. Time constraints limited his in-person challenges (a sand hourglass was apparently used to keep time) but he alludes to Fox's poor writing skills and grammar flaws in his thirteenth proposal. At one point Williams suggests that God "delights" in Fox's poor grammar because it undermines his writings.

We now descended to the thirteenth Proposal (the sixth to be discus'd at Providence) which was read by them, and is this, viz. These many Books and Writings are extreamly Poor, Lame, and Naked, swelld up only with High Titles and Words of Boasting and Vapour. . . .

Let a man read the Works of the Papists, Lutherans, Arminians, and amongst our selves, the Episcopal and Presbyterian Writings: a man shall have wherein to exercise his Judgement, Memory, &c. he shall have Scrip-ture proposed, Arguments alleadged, yea he shall read Answers and Replies, whereby to satisfie a rational Soul and Understanding. But in the Quakers

39. Williams, *George Fox Digg'd Out* in *Complete Writings of Roger Williams,* 5:213–14.

40. Williams, *George Fox Digg'd Out* in *Complete Writings of Roger Williams,* 5:230.

Books & Writings, Peter & Jude tells us (what I have found) clouds high of an imaginary Christ and Spirit: high swelling words . . .

I said, let who will that understands true English, and are able to read and write true English, (though he know no more) take G. Fox his Folio Book in hand, and tell me whether (through his whole Book) he writes like an English-man: And though he upbraids all his Opposites scornfully and ridiculously (as poor Children that know not the Bible nor their Accidence in saying you to a singular, &c.) whether in many scores of places in his Book he confounds not the singular and the Plural: I confess when I urged this in publick, my Opposites desired of me no proof of this out of Foxes Book and therefore (remembering my quarter hour Glasse) I spared Quotations, but now (through Gods patience and my Readers) my Tedder being longer, I shall give one or two brief Proofs and Instances.

In page 282. in G. Fox his second Answer his saith, You where you are sees him not where it should be the Plural see him not, if this Proud Bruit had known either his Accidence or the Bible.

In Page 300. he saith The Scriptures is able to make wise unto Salvation which should be are able, &c.

. . . And abundance more of this Boyes English all his Book over, which I cannot impute to his Northern Dialect (having been so long in the South, and London, and read and answered (as he dreams) so many English Books: nor to the Printer (the faults of that kinde being so numerous) but to the finger of the most High, and most Holy, whose property it is, and therefore delights to run thwart and cross the shins of proud and insulting Souls and Spirits.[41]

Williams worried that he had not sufficiently countered the "Lame writings of our G.F" so he took "the liberty (if God please) of presenting the Reader with a further Appendix or Addition of some few further Instances out of G. Fox his Writings." Following that promise to the reader, he concludes the text with his fourteenth proposition. As a final attack, he compares Quakers to Native Americans, and generally finds the Quakers wanting; he also offers a sly dig at Fox for writing about Indigenous peoples in North America before he had even traveled there. The Quakers push Williams to prove that Quaker women go naked, and they imply that Williams obsesses on this alleged nakedness for his own prurient purposes.

41. Williams, *George Fox Digg'd Out* in *Complete Writings of Roger Williams*, 5:276–81.

I hasten to the 14 Proposition, the last of the seven at Providence. They read it publickly, viz. the spirit of the Quakers tends mainly to reducing of Persons from Civility to Barbarisme, to an Arbitrary Goverment, and the Dictates and Decrees of that sudden Spirit that acts them . . .

I told them that in our Native Countrey, and in all civilized Countreys, that civility, Courteous Speech, Courteous Salutation, and respective Behavior was generally practised, opposite to the cariage of Barbarous & Unciviliz'd People . . . We English were our selves as first wild and savage Britains: Gods mercy had civilized us, and we were now come into a wild and savage Countrey, without Manners, without Courtesie, so that generally except you begin with a What Chear or some other Salutation, you had as good meet a Horse or a Cow, &c. And hath not the Quaker Spirit been such a Spirit amongst us? have we not known persons formerly loving, courteous &c. and as soon as this Spirit hath come upon them have not our eyes seen them pass by their Familiars, their Kindred, their Elders and Superiours, and though kindly spoken to, not give a Word or a Look toward them? as if they were not worthy of a word or a look from such High Saints? . . .

G. Fox in his book affirms that the Conversation of these very Barbarians, in many things were better then his Opposites &c. I mused in my self (being much acquainted with the Natives) what G. Fox should mean, he not having been in N. England when he wrote that passage; but since I have heard that Quakers have commended the spirit of the Indians, for they have seen them come into English Houses and sit down by the fire, not speaking a word to any body: But this cariage of the Indians proceeds from a bruitish spirit, for generally they have boldly come in without Knocking or asking of leave, and sit down without any respect or word or gesture to the Governour or chief of the Family whoever (just the Quakers general fashion and Spirit)

Further I told them, that in some respect the spirit and cariage of the Quakers was worse then that of the Indians, for if they were saluted by the English in the high-way or coming into an House, they are very ready to receive your Salutation kindly, and return you another: But commonly we know that it is not so with the Quakers bruitish spirit. 2. The Indians morning and evening, and upon all meetings, they give a respective and proper Salutation to their own Superiours, and sometimes in gesture as well as speech. 3. Although the Indians are bruits in their Nakedness both men and women, yet they never appear (no not in private houses) stark naked as the Quaker men and women doe: yea they so abhor such a bruitishness, (except it be in their mad Drunkenness, for then they will be stark naked) that as to their Female kind, they will carefully from their birth keep on some modest covering before them.

W.E. rose up and said they did abhor Uncleaness as well as our selves or any, their women were sober, holy and Modest, and would not endure (some of them) to have a Toe to be seen naked: but he said if the Lord God did stir up any of his Daughters to be a Sign of the nakedness of others he believed it to be a great Cross to a Modest womans Spirit, but the Lord must be obeyed . . . John Stubs said he had been a Quaker 19 years and had never seen a woman Naked, and some of their Quakers said to me aloud, when didst thou see any of our women Naked? and another of them said, We did not think that thou wouldest have been such a wicked man. These two (though of the Quakers spirit) yet of long time had been Loving and respective to me, but now they were enraged . . .[42]

42 Williams, *George Fox Digg'd Out* in *Complete Writings of Roger Williams,* 5:307–11.

Chapter 11

Unraveling, 1675–1677

FROM WILLIAMS'S PERSPECTIVE IN 1674, *he surely thought he had accomplished most of his goals. Rhode Island was firmly established; freedom of religion was protected; church and state were separated; and Rhode Island maintained relatively peaceful relationships with the Narragansett. However, an Indigenous perspective might have described things very differently. Rhode Island from the beginning proved to be invasive and expansionist— just another English colonial presence to manage and deal with. Underneath the surface—even in Rhode Island—decades of discontentment boiled to the surface and eventually ruptured all of New England during King Philip's War in 1675–1676. This violent and bloody war—provoked by ongoing English colonial invasion and settlement—broke out between the English colonists and their Mohegan, Pequot, and other Native allies on the one side, and the Pokanoket chief, Pumetacom (or "King Philip" as he was named by the English) and his many Native allies on the other side.*

The letters below illustrate Williams's tortured thought processes through these difficult times, from grappling with the burning of his beloved Providence in 1676 to the selling of Native captives into slavery and servitude. It is here that we see Williams the least differentiated from wider colonial sentiment, and perhaps the beginning of the end of a multicultural Rhode Island that Williams envisioned, no matter how Anglo-centric that vision had always been. The loss in English communities was astounding—some 1,000 English men, women, and children dead, twenty-five English towns severely damaged and sixteen entirely destroyed, and thousands of cows, sheep, and pigs slaughtered. Grimmer still were the losses in Native communities that reduced the entire region's Indigenous population by half. Those events and losses haunt New England Native communities to this day.

King Philip's War, 1675–1676

In the mid-1670s, most of the Indigenous peoples of New England revolted against an increasingly onerous English settler colonial presence. Despite the 1621 peace treaty between Plimouth and Ousamequin (the Wampanoag sachem), over the next half century a new generation of Native leaders grew up experiencing the never-ending land-grabbing sprawl of English colonialism. Before long, rumors of war swirled. In mid-June 1675, Rhode Island Deputy Governor John Easton met with Pumetacom, or "Philip," the son of Ousamequin and now a Wampanoag sachem of the Pokanoket. Surrounded by forty of his men, Pumetacom succinctly leveled a series of charges that described the nature of his grievances. The list was comprehensive and summarized fifty-five years of aggressive English colonial presence: land loss and theft; political humiliation; disregard for Wampanoag jurisdiction; being disarmed (turning over guns); English missionary intrusions; lack of justice in English courts; English livestock constantly damaging and feeding upon Indian cornfields; and that the English encouraged Indian drunkenness by readily selling liquor to any and all Natives (thereby creating debt dependence as well as more favorable negotiating and sale conditions).[1] All of this added up to a tangible challenge to Native political, cultural, and religious autonomy. Pumetacom and his people had had enough.

On June 24, 1675, one week after that conversation, Native warriors loyal to Pumetacom attacked the southeastern Massachusetts Bay town of Swansea. Warriors quickly advanced through the town, killing twelve colonists, burning houses, and destroying property. Colonists retaliated, and what became known as King Philip's War soon spread across the region. Native successes surged through 1675, as Pumetacom and his allies attacked and burned town after town in southern and central Massachusetts. Williams desperately tried to keep the Narragansett and Rhode Island out of the war, although that all fell apart when Rhode Island permitted the United Colonies (Massachusetts Bay, Plimouth, and Connecticut) to invade Narragansett homelands on December 19, 1676, with a combined force of 1,000 soldiers, including 150 Mohegan and Pequot allies. The devastating raid on a Narragansett fortress in southern Rhode Island led to the slaughter of between 350 and 600 Natives, plus an additional 350 Narragansett taken as captives. This attack pushed the Narragansett into the war against the English, and Rhode Island paid dearly for enabling the attack. Native forces burned Providence to the ground on March 29, 1676, as they did most other towns on the west side of the Narragansett Bay.

---

1. Easton, "Relacion of the Indyan Warre," 7–17.

The war ground to a slow end as English forces, their Native allies, and starvation stalked Pumetacom, his allies, and their communities. On August 12, 1676, English and Indian-allied forces hunted down and killed Pumetacom, although the fighting continued in what is now New Hampshire and Maine into 1678. The results were devastating for the region's Indigenous populations, with thousands killed and another 2,000 enslaved, approximately 1,000 of whom were shipped out of New England to be sold as slaves. In the letters that follow, we see an elderly Williams trying to comprehend the blood and carnage visited on his colony and the Narragansett. And yet, in the end, Williams fully sided with the English colonial project, even heading a militia and overseeing the sale of Native captives into slavery.

Roger Williams to [Robert Williams?], April 1, 1676[2]

This letter describes a chaotic scene during King Philip's War and the seeming destruction of Williams's dream with Narragansett and other Natives burning Providence on March 29, 1676. Though some puritan leaders (including Williams, it seems) cast the war as punishment from an angry Christian God, conversations such as the one captured here give voice to Narragansett explanations. With the air thick from the smoke of smoldering English homes and farms, Williams and Native men from various tribes confronted each other, both looking for reasons and explanations for the others' actions. What unfolds is a rare look into the differing perspectives on the war and its meaning at a particularly raw moment. The Native men pointed to specific betrayals, including the taking of Native land and joining with Plimouth and Massachusetts Bay against the Narragansett (which Williams falsely denies). Interestingly, both sides claim God was on their side and pointed to evidence for that in recent victories. Williams, clearly exasperated, speaks rather menacingly to the assembled Native soldiers, stating that "God would help us to Consume them" and that "King Charles would spend Ten Thousands before He would loose this Countrie." Williams ends the letter to his brother by instructing colonists in Newport to build forts and hunker down or else they would meet the same fate as Providence.

These conversations also reveal other deep trade and personal connections between specific English and Native men. See for example the Narragansett request to speak with Valentine Whitman ("Vall")—an Englishman

---

2. This letter is most likely a flawed or altered copy of an original letter. For a full consideration of the letter's complicated provenance and the caveats it raises for the reader, see LaFantasie's editorial note preceding this letter in *Correspondence of Roger Williams*, 2:717–20.

with plenty of interpreting experience—or the reference to "friend" Arthur
Fenner. Equally, Williams recognized quite a few Native men from the crowd
and called them by name. Such familiarity on the part of both parties reminds
readers that King Philip's War was not fought between strangers, but between
neighbors who knew each other.

[Providence]

Dear Brother,

By my Wife I wrote to You some particulars of the Goings of God at Rehoboth.[3] I thought fitt to acquaint your dear Self, and my Dear Wife, and Children, and Friends, with the goings of the Most Hight at Providence, with whome he hath not dealt according to our transgressions, nor as he hath dealt with many other Towns of our Countrimen in New England.[4] All that were in Forts Men, Women, and Children, were Saved. H. Wright would trust God in his own Hous. There they Killed Him with his own Hammer.[5] Elizabeth Sucklin was preparing to goe from Her own Hous to A Fort but delaying they Killed Her. Lord Sanctifie this Example of not useing means but tempting God presumptuously, and of Neglect, and delay, in the applying of our selves to them. . . . This Morning wee hear their Camp is between Notaquonckanit, and Patuxet[6] and at this present Wee see smoaks rise from Pawtuxet and from my Daughter Mercies House in the Woods, . . . In the afternoon of this burning Day of Gods Anger, an Indian that Knew Vall[7] Called from the other Side of the Mill Hill that they two might speak together peaceably Without their Guns. Vall went gently towards the poynt of Land . . . Word was brought me. I hasted out and came up to Vall, and Heard them ask for me. Vall said He is here. They then desired that we Would come to the point Without Arms as they would Doe. The Town Cried out to us not to Venture. My Sonns came Crying after me. Vall Went

3. Native bands attacked the town of Rehoboth on March 28, 1676. *Correspondence of John Cotton Jr.*, 151n3.

4. Williams sent his wife, Mary, to Aquidneck Island for safety. This letter suggests that some of their children also evacuated Providence, along with many of the town's residents.

5. Wright refused to move to a garrison, choosing to remain at home. Other contemporary accounts indicate that he was killed with a hammer. *Correspondence of Roger Williams*, 2:725n3.

6. Neutaconkanut hill and the Pawtuxet River were the western and southern boundaries mentioned in the original deed of Providence to Williams, meaning that Indigenous troops were literally on Providence's doorstep.

7. Valentine Whitman, a servant who had moved up in the world and had settled in Providence.

back. My Heart to God and the Countrie forced me to go on to Throg-mortens poynt.[8] They mett Without Arms.

I asked who they were. They said Nahigonsets, and Cowwesets, and Wompano[torn] and Neepmucks, and Qunticoogs.[9] I asked (for We heard so) Whither Phillip[10] [torn] amongst them. They said no. I asked Whither He was not in these parts. They said no; I asked where he was; They Said on this side Qunitiult. I asked if the Nahigonsit Sachims were amongst them: they said they were at their Houses at Nahigonsit. I asked who Commanded Here: they Said many Captains and Inferior Sachims, and Counsellors. I asked the Names [of] these present: they Said Wesauamoge (Commonly called Wesamog) and [illegible and torn] Spake aloud and Said I am Wesauamog, What Cheere,[11] this is my Ground Which You have gott from me. Then said Pawatuck (the old Queens Counseller)[12] I am Pawatuk and Suckamog, Capt Fenner's[13] Great Friend. I asked if they were the Company that burned Re-hoboth and Swansie. Since they owned it and that their Number was about 1500: I asked them Whither they were bound. They Said to all the Towns about Plimoth. They would Stay about two dayes more with us (which they Did not but [went?] away yesterday afternoon the day after their coming). I asked them Why they assaulted us With burning and Killing who ever were kind Neighbours to them (and looking back) said I this House of mine now burning before mine Eyes hath Lodged kindly Some Thousands of You these Ten Years.[14] They answered that we were their Enemies Joyned with Mas-sachusetts, and Plimouths, Entertaining, Assisting, and Guideing of them, and I said we had Entertained all Indians being A Throughfare Town, but nither Wee nor this Colloney had acted Hostilitie against them. I told them they were all this While Killing and burning themselves Who had Forgot they were Mankind, and ran about the Countrie like Wolves tearing, and

8. "Throckmorton's Point" does not appear on any town records. Glenn LaFantasie suggests it is likely a "slight bulge in the east bank of the Moshassuck River near John Throckmorton's house lot at the northern end of the settlement." *Correspondence of Roger Williams*, 2:726n17.

9. Referring to Narragansett, Cowesett, Wampanoag, and Nipmuc. The "Qunti-coog" were likely a smaller community in the Connecticut River Valley.

10. That is, King Philip, or Pumetacom, the leader of the Pokanokets.

11. The greeting "What Cheer?" or "What Cheer Nétop?" was a phrase some Native men and women used to greet Englishmen. *Nétop* was an Algonquian word for friend.

12. The Old Queen was a female sachem, known as a sunksquaw, in this case spe-cifically Quaiapen. She was the sister of Ninigret, the Niantic sachem.

13. Captain Arthur Fenner of Providence. The language of friendship even in the middle of the war is striking.

14. A reminder that Roger Williams's own house was burned to the ground in the attack on Providence.

Devouring the Innocent, and peaceable. I told them they had noe regard for their Wives, Relations [*torn*] ones, nor to God Whome they confessd made them and all things. They Confessed they were in A Strange Way. 2ly we had forced them to it. 3ly that God was with them and Had forsaken us for they had so prospered in Killing and Burning us far beyond What we did against them. I answered it was false for They began with us and God had prospered us so that wee had driven the Wampanoogs with Phillip out of his Countrie and the Nahigonsiks out of their Countre, and had destroyed Multitudes of them in Fighting and Flying, In Hunger and Cold etc.: and that God would help us to Consume them Except they Hearkned to Counsel. I told them they knew many times I had Quenched fires between the Bay and them, and Plimoth, and Quniticut, and them.[15]

And now I did not doubt (God assisting me) to Quench this and help to restore Quietness to the Land againe. They Heard and Understood me quietly. They desired me to come over the River to them and Debate matters at large. I told [them] it was not Fair without Hostage to desire it.[16] Sucka-mog A. Fennors Friend asked where he was. I said at his Garrison, Shall I fetch him, and Vall. They said Yea and promised Cessation. I went. All ours Diswaded me affirming itt was A plot to shoot us three. Yett I went till some came running, and affirmed that J. Laphams House in the Way was full of Indians: I then retreated Yet held my Self bound to goe or send word of the reason of my not comming with A. Fennor, yet none would goe or suffr me to goe. At Last I got to the poynt againe, and told them the truth and how since we parted Divers Houses were fired as J. Mattisons on that Side and Ep. Olnys on this. They Said they Had sent to all to be quiet but Some Would not stop. They prayed me to come over. I desired one of them to come over Saying they Had bin Burning all the Day on this side and were they affraid of an old unarmed Man in the same place. They Desired me to open my Cloak that they might See I had noe Gun. I did so. Then Came one Nawham, Mr R. Smith's John Wall Maker (an Ingenious Fellow and peaseable), then Matta-log (A Neepmuck Sachim), then Cuttaqune (A Qunniticutt Sachim, A Stout lustie brave Fellow, and I think the Chief in Command amongst them). We had much repetition of the former particulars Which were debated at the

15. Williams is here pointing to his long role as a navigator of Native politics in the region, although he is surely seeing it through his own perspective at this moment. The Natives present see things differently, as they clearly indicate. For another perspective on this meeting and on the attack on Rehoboth, see Noah Newman to John Cotton Jr., April 19, 1676, *Correspondence of John Cotton Jr.*, 148–51.

16. In moments of tense negotiation, it was common for each side to retain a hos-tage as a way of ensuring the safety of individuals from both sides who were meeting together.

Poynt. Nawwhun Said that we broke Articles and not they (as I alleadged). He said they Heartilie Endeavoured the Surrender of the Prisoners. They were abroad in Hunting, at Home. They were Divided and could not Effect it. He said You have driven us out of our own Countrie and then pursued us to our Great Miserie, and Your own, and we are Forced to live upon you.[17] I told them there were Wayes of peace. They asked how. I told them if their Sachims would propound something and Cause A Cessation I would presently Write if (it were to morrow) by two of theirs to Boston. I told them planting time was a coming for them and Us. Cuttaqueen Said they cared not for Planting these Ten Years. They Would live upon us, and Dear. He said God was with them for at Quawbaug and Quoneticut (Excepting old Men and Women) we had Killed noe Fighting Men but Wounded some (Shewing me his Wound upon his Arm) but they had Killed of us Scores, and Hundreds and bid me goe look upon three Score and five now unburied at Blackstones.[18] I told them they Confessed they were all most 2,000: and might Well over run half an Hundred, but How many Killed they at Warwick when 22 of ours fought With all Your Burners.

I said they were A Cowardly People and got nothing of ours but by Commuotin[19] our Houses our Cattle and Selves by Ambushes, and Swamps, and Great advantages, and told them they durst not come Near our Forts. We entered theirs, and if Providence Men Would yield to Me we would Viset them with an Hundred out of [illegible] by Mid-night. Cuttaqueen Said we will meet you an Hundred, to an Hundred, to Morrow upon A Plain. I said it was not an Hundred, to an Hundred, Except we Had an Armie nigh acquivalent etc.: but I told them they Should find many Thousands would be on them, and King Charles would spend Ten Thousands before He would loose this Countrie. . . . We parted and they were so Civill that they called after me and bid me not goe near the Burned Houses for their might be Indians that might mischief me, but goe by the Water Side.[20] My Dear Brother and Friends, The Most High offers to Humble us more and make

17. This is an excellent representation of an Indigenous view of the war: it was the English who had breached their obligations, not Native peoples.

18. "Blackstones" is a reference to a battle near the Blackstone River, in present-day Central Falls, Rhode Island, led by Scituate captain Michael Pierce against a much-larger force led by Nananautunu (Canonchet). It was a disaster for the English; Noah Newman wrote that 52 English and 11 Indigenous allies from Cape Cod were killed. Noah Newman to John Cotton Jr., March 27, 1676, *Correspondence of John Cotton Jr.*, 141–42.

19. Meaning to acquire something by cheating or stealth.

20. This is a fascinating end to this rather raw and tense standoff: even as they threaten each other, the Native men warn Williams of a potential ambush and point him towards a safer route.

us more Heavenly Seing our burnt Walls etc. Shure you must prepare Forts for Women and Children at Newport and on the Island or it will be shortly worse With You then us. Your Unworthy

R.W.

The Father of Mercies Direct Protect and Save You here and for Ever.

Roger Williams to John Leverett, January 14, 1675/1676[21]

In this letter to the Massachusetts Governor John Leverett, Williams discusses one of the most important events in King Philip's War, the attack on a Narragansett fort on December 19, 1675, in what English writers named the "Great Swamp Fight" but is often called the "Great Swamp Massacre" (described above). In particular, Williams shared the information he and other English learned from the examination of Joshua Teft,[22] an Englishman who had been living with the Narragansett at the time of the battle. Normally, the English authorities would have considered an inside account of this nature to be a godsend, but instead they accused Teft of treason. Based on a couple of sources, they accused him of firing on and killing English troops during the fighting in the Great Swamp. Four days after Williams wrote this letter, English authorities found Teft guilty of treason for which they hanged and quartered him.

For readers new to King Philip's War, Williams's account may be disorientating. References in this letter remind readers that English and Indigenous ties extended in many different directions. In this battle, as was the case with the larger war itself, there was no simple line that divided Englishmen and Indigenous people. In this account, Pequot and Mohegan warriors helped English troops attack the Narragansett while an Englishmen stood next to Narragansett men to fend off the attackers.

Providence

Sir, This night I was requested by Cap: Fenner[23] & other officers of our Towne to take ye Examination & Confession of an English man who hath bene with ye Indians before & since ye fight: his name is Joshua Tift & he was taken by Capt: Fenner this day at an Indian howse halfe a mile from where Capt: Fenner house (now burnd) did stand.[24] Capt Fenner &

21. *Correspondence of Roger Williams*, 2:711–17.

22. Also spelled Tift, or Tefft.

23. Arthur Fenner was named co-captain of the Providence militia, along with Williams, during King Philip's War.

24. The "Fenner Castle" was located in what is now southern Cranston, almost thirty miles northeast of the Narragansett Fort, which suggested Teft was moving with

others of us proposed severall questions to him which he answered & I was requested to write, which I did, & thought fit—having this bearer (Mr Scot) brought by Gods gracious hand of Providence to mine, to present you with an Extract of ye pith & Substance of all he answered to us:

He was askt by Capt: Fenner, how Long he had bene with the Nahigonsiks: He answered about 27 days more or lesse:

He was demaunded how he came amongst them He said yt he was at his farme a mile & halfe from Puttuckquomscut[25] where he hired an Indian to keepe his Cattell himselfe purposing to goe to Rode Iland, but yt day which he purposed & prepared to depart there came to his House Nananawtenu[26] (ye young Sachim) his Elder brother (Panpauquivnout) with their Captaine Quaquackis & a partie of men & told him he must die: He said yt he begd for his Life & promised he would be servant to ye Sachim while he lived. He Saith ye Sachim then caried him along with him having given him his Life as his slave: He said yt he brought him to their Fort where was about 800 fighting men & about 200 howses. He said ye Indians brought 5 of his Cattell & killd them before his face: So he was forced to be Silent but praid the Sachim to Spare ye rest: who answered him what will Cattell now doe you good, & ye next day they sent for ye rest & killd them all, whereof 8 were his owne.[27]

Being askt whether he was in ye Fort in ye fight,[28] he Saith yes & waited on his master ye Sachim there untill he was wounded (of which wound he lay 9 days & died) He Saith yt all ye Sachims were in ye Fort & staid 2 vollies of shot & then they fled with his master & passed through a plaine & rested by ye side of a Spruce Swampe, but he saith Himselfe had no Arms at all.

He Saith that if the Monhiggins and Pequts had bene true they might have destroyed most of the Nahiggonsiks, but, the Nahigonsiks parlied with them in the beginning of the Fight so that they promised to shoote high which they did and kild not one Nahigonsik man except against their Wills.[29]

Narragansett troops that had been burning English houses and towns.

25. Pettaquamscutt is a region within present-day Kingston, in southern Rhode Island.

26. Nananautunu, who was also known as Canonchet, was an important Narragansett sachem and a son of Miantonomo, an influential early seventeenth-century Narragansett sachem.

27. The destruction of cattle by Native troops was common throughout the war, largely because domesticated cattle were signs of an intrusive English colonial presence, and often roamed onto Native lands and destroyed their fields and gardens.

28. That is, the Great Swamp Fight, in southern Rhode Island, on December 19, 1675.

29. Teft is suggesting what some English soldiers and magistrates feared, namely, that the Pequot and Mohegan soldiers were not fully fighting against the Narragansett and other Native nations the English declared to be enemies.

He saith that when it was duskish, Word was brought to the Sachims that the English were retreated. Upon this they Sent to the Fort to see what their Loss was, where they found 97 slaine and 48 wounded beside what slaughter was made in the houses and by the burning of the Houses, all of which he saith were burnt except 5 or 6 thereabouts. He Saith the Indians never came at the Fort more that he knows of. He saith they found 5 or 6 English bodies and from one of them a bag about I li [pound] ½ of Powder was brought to the Sachims. And he Saith that abundance of Corne and provisions and goods were burnt allso. He Saith Some powder belonging to the Young Sachim which was in a box was blown up but how much he can not tell.

He Saith the Nahigonsiks powder is (generally) gone and spent but Phillip[30] hath sent them word that he will furnish them enough from the French. He saith they have caried New England money to the French for Ammunition, but the money he will not take but Beaver or Wampam. He Saith that the French have sent Philip a present viz a Brass gun and Badaliers Sutable.[31]

He said allso that the Nahigonsiks have sent 2 baskets of Wampam to the Mowhauks (Mauquawogs) where the French are for their favour and Assistance.[32]

He saith that the Sachims and people were about 10 mile Northwest from Mr Smiths[33] whether the Cowwesets and Pumhom[34] and his men brought to the Sachims all the Powder they Could, but Caunounicus[35] said it was nothing for they had 400 guns (beside Bows) and there was but enough for Every Gun a charge. The young Sachim Said that had he known that they were no better furnished he would have been Elsewhere this Winter.

He saith that while they were in Consultation an Indian Squaw came in with a Letter from the Generall.[36] Some advised to send to Phillip for one of his Councellours to read it: but at last they agreed to Send a

30. Pumetacom, or "King Philip," was the sachem of the Pokanoket band of Wampanoag who was seen as the leader of the Indian uprising, or King Philip's War.

31. One of the English strategies was to cut off supplies of gunpowder and ammunition for Native troops, which explains the interest in Native munition supplies.

32. Reports that Pumetacom and his men were potentially finding support from the French and the Mohawk was surely alarming.

33. Richard Smith had a large house at Cocumscussoc, the former site of Roger Williams's Indian trading post near Wickford, Rhode Island.

34. Pomham was a Shawomet Indian sachem who often operated independently (and slightly at odds with) regional Native groups as well as colonial officials. See chapter 6 for more on Pomham.

35. Canonicus was a Narragansett Indian sachem, or tribal leader.

36. This is likely General Josiah Winslow, governor of Plimouth Colony and head of the joint colonial army that attacked the Narragansett fort.

Councellour to the Gen. who brought word that the Gen. Said that there had bene a Small Fight between them and asked him how many Indians were slain and how the Sachims liked it: that he desired the Sachims would shew themselves men and come and parley[37] with him: that if they feared they might bring what Guard they pleased who might keepe at a distance from ours who should not offer them any Afront, while the Sachims were at the House with the Gen. from whom they should depart in Peace if they came to no Agreement.

Their Councellours said that the English did this only in policie to intrap the Sachims, as they had done Philip many times who when he was in their hand made him Yield to what they pleased.

Nananawtenu the young Sachim said he would not goe but thought it best to use policy and to send word to the Gen. that they would Come to him 3 dayes after. But Cawnounicus Said that he was old and would not lie to the English now, and said If you will fight, fight for tis a folly for me to fight any longer. The young prince Said he might goe to Mr Smiths then but there should never an Indian goe with him. Their Chief Captaine allso said that He would not yield to the English so long as an Indian would stand with him. He Said he had fought with English and French and Dutch and Mowhauks and feared none of them, and said that if they yielded to the English they should be dead Men or slaves and so worck for the English.[38] He Saith that this Quaquackis bears chief sway and is a midling thick Set man of a very stout fierce Countenance.

Being asked whether he was present at this Consultation he Saith no, but that Quaquackis acquainted the People what the Sum of the Consultation was.

. . .

[*missing portion*] asked what was the English child which was brought [*missing*] to the Gen: he Said that Pumhoms men had taken it at Warwick. Allso he said that there is an English youth amongst them (his name he forgot:) one that Speaks good Indian and was wounded and taken in the fight, whom they spake of killing with torture, but he was yet with Quawnepum.

Sir you may Suppose it to be now Past midnight and I am to write forth the Copie of this to goe tomorrow to the Gen. and therefore I dare not add my foolish Comment but humbly beg to the Father of mercies for his mercy

---

37. That is, negotiate or meet. As the next sentence shows, however, Pumetacom and his councilors were (rightfully) afraid that the calls for negotiations were a trap.

38. The "Chief Captaine" here repeats a common fear of Natives during the war, namely, that to surrender would mean being enslaved by the English—fears that were largely well-founded. See Fisher, "'Why Shall Wee Have Peace to Bee Made Slaves."

Sake to guide You by his Councell (Psal. 73) and afterward receave you unto Glory. Yours most unworthy

R.W.

My humble respects presented to such honrd friends to whom Your wisedome may thinck fit to Communicate etc.

Sir, Josh. Tift added that this Company intended to stay with Philip till the Snow melt and then to divide into Companies.

Allso that many of Ninicrafts[39] men fought the English in the Fort, and 14 of the Monhiggins are now marcht away with the Nahigonsiks.

Sir since I am oft occasioned to write upon the Publike busines I shall be thanckfull for a litle paper upon the publike account being now neere destitute.

Sir I pray present my humble respects to the Govr Winthrop[40] and my thancks for his loving Letters, to which I cannot now make any returne.

Providence Committee Authorizes Sale of Indian Slaves, August 16, 1676[41]

During and after King Philip's War, roving English militias (including one nominally headed by an aging Roger Williams) gathered up Natives for sale into slavery. Individuals, families, and even whole groups of Indigenous people from various nations surrendered to officials in different colonies, including Rhode Island. Magistrates were not exactly sure what to do with these surrendering Natives. The colony of Rhode Island had passed a law in March 1676—during the war—that stated that "noe Indian in this Collny be a slave," a statute often quoted by historians. But there was a loophole in this law: "but only to pay their debts or for their bringinge up, or custody they have received." This clause allowed Rhode Island magistrates to sell off Indian captives and surrenderers to colonists for a set amount of time. Providence had a complicated set of guidelines and Newport had another. But in both places, Natives were supposed to be free by approximately twenty-five to thirty years of age. While this sounded better than lifetime enslavement in theory, there are plenty of examples of this limited-term enslavement being extended beyond the allotted time. After all, who, really, was going to enforce such a nebulous contract after twenty years? Enslaved Natives—even when enslaved for the

39. That is, Ninigret, a sachem of the Niantic and Narragansett.

40. John Winthrop Jr., governor of Connecticut Colony.

41. *The Early Records of the Town of Providence*, 15:156. Note that this is only the reverse side of the document; the front side contains additional descriptions of the capture and sale of Natives under the guidance of this same committee.

short term—could be sold within and out of the colony. Once sold elsewhere,
the original contract could be lost. And what about the children of Natives who
labored unwillingly under a limited term slavery contract? Records suggest
that they, too, were forced into slavery, sometimes for multiple generations.

This document shows that Rhode Island, too, dealt with Indian captives
in much the same fashion as other colonies: by selling them into slavery. Nota-
bly, nothing is said about servitude or contracts of specific years. The terminol-
ogy is simply one of being sold, which most commonly brings to mind lifelong
slavery. The date of the document is also striking. English and allied Indian
forces killed Pumetacom on August 12. Just four days later, this subcommittee
was authorized to transport and sell Natives into slavery. The capture and sale
of these Natives in Providence was not directly related to Pumetacom's death
necessarily, but it does remind us that the war dragged on in various ways even
after his death. This was especially true in New Hampshire and what is now
Maine well into 1678.

It is not clear if these enslaved Narragansett and other Natives were sold
out of the country as lifelong slaves or sold locally. This committee of sixteen
leading men in Providence, Rhode Island, having been empowered to sell In-
digenous captives and surrenderers into slavery, turned around and authorized
Arthur Fenner, William Hopkins, and John Whipple Jr. to conduct the sale
and transportation of the Indian captives. Any associated costs related to the
transportation and sale of the Natives, along with payment for themselves, was
to be taken out of the money generated by the sale of Natives. The rest should
be returned to the committee. Notably, Roger Williams is the first name listed.

We whose names are here unto Subscribed having Right to the sayd Indians, as by an Act of a Comitty doth Appeere;[42] Doe betrust impower, and
fully Authorise Capt: Author Fenner, William Hopkins, and John Whipple
Junr: to hire, and procure a Boate to transport the sayd Indians where they
may be sold,[43] and to make sale and Delivery thereof as fully, and as firmly,
as if we were all personally present, And to doe all such things as shall any
ways belong to the transporting making sale, or Disposion of all and Every
of the sayd Indians as above sayd, and to see all such Charges as doth arise
by the sayd Indians, after to them Comitted Defrayd out of the product of
the same, and them selves reasonably sattisfied for theire paines, and then

42. It is not entirely clear which committee passed an act empowering this committee, but likely a council of war or one within the Providence city government or the
colony's General Assembly.

43. Providence sits at the head of the Narragansett Bay, so transportation by boat
would have allowed shipment to almost any other area in Rhode Island, adjacent colonies, or, as was also common, out into the wider Atlantic.

to make returne of the remainder of the product of the sayd Indians to the sayd Company.[44]

This being our Reall act and Deed as Wittness our hands this: 16th: day of August: 1676:

Roger Williams   John pray

Daniell Abbott

john mawry

Henry Eusten[45]

Nathaniell Waterman

Ephraim pray

Joseph Woodward

Abraham. Man

Eliazur whipple

John Angell:

James olney:

James Angell

Vallintine whittman,

Edward Bennett:

Thomas Field

Roger Williams to John Leverett or Josiah Winslow, October 16, 1676[46]

This short but layered letter from Williams to the governor of Massachusetts Bay contains all of the rawness of a post-battlefield report. Two Indigenous children from the Native village of Mettabiscut (in central Rhode Island; perhaps part of the Narragansett confederacy) survived a raid by the English-allied Pequot and Mohegan forces as they were peaceably digging for clams on the shores of the Narragansett Bay. The young Native boy and girl—brother and sister—seemingly survived largely on their own for ten weeks until an older Native youth named Mittonan told them to go seek bread (and likely shelter) from Thomas Clemence of Providence, whose house had been burned in the war. Clemence, in turn, took the children to Williams, who promptly plied them for information about nearby Indigenous survivors. Williams refers to the Native children being brought to him as a "providence," perhaps

44. Fenner, Hopkins, and Whipple Jr. were allowed to keep some of the profit of the sales for themselves, in addition to being reimbursed for costs incurred along the way. The rest was to be returned to the larger committee.

45. Probably Henry Esten.

46. *Correspondence of Roger Williams*, 2:728–29.

inadvertently invoking where he lived. English Protestants understood many events to be evidence of God's presence in their lives—everything from a healthy harvest to a comet to a devastating war. But by 1676, Williams's "providence" shifted from describing where he found refuge when he was exiled from Massachusetts Bay to the arrival of two children who might provide post-war intelligence to land-hungry English.

Williams quickly moves on from the children to a more pressing matter, in his mind: land. King Philip's War not only caused a massive rupture in Native families and livelihood, but it also led to large-scale English-driven dispossession and land-grabbing. Williams understood this and wanted to make sure that Rhode Island's claims to this land were fairly considered. He understood that the land that belonged to this particular band of Natives (who seemed to lay claim to an area within the boundaries of the land claimed by Warwick) might have claims from Plimouth and Massachusetts Bay. He therefore suggested that a militia be sent out to round up the remaining Natives who were residing in two different locations so that the land could be properly "improved" by the English. And to make sure that this land (and likely other land) was divided up equally among the English (without attracting too much attention from the king in London), Williams suggested a committee with representatives from Rhode Island, Connecticut, Massachusetts Bay, and Plimouth. This interrelated land clearing of Natives through warfare and enslavement and land grabbing was an essential part of the immediate and long-term aftermath of the war, and dramatically reduced Native land holdings.

Providence 16. 8. 76 (ut vulgo)

Sir

With my humble and lo. [loving] respects to your selfe and other honrd friends etc. I thought fit to tell you what the providence of the most high hath brought to my hand the evening before yesterday: 2 Indian children were brought to me by one Tho. Clements who had his howse burnt on the other side of the River.[47] He was in his Orchard and 2 Indian Children came boldly to him, the boy being about 7 or 8: and the guirle (his sister) 3 or 4 years old. The Boy tells me that a youth one Mittonan brought them to the sight of Tho. Clemments and bid them goe to that man and he would give them bread. He saith his Father and Mother were taken by the Pequts and Monhiggins above 10 weeks agoe as they were clamming (with many more Indians) at Cowwesit:[48] that their dwelling was and is at a place calld

47. Thomas Clemence was a Providence resident whose house was on the west side of the Providence River (instead of on the east, where the Providence lots were generally laid out, as can be seen in chapter 4).

48. Cowesett was on the Narragansett Bay, on the southern side of the present-day

Mittaubscut: that it is upon a branch of Pawtuxet River,[49] to Cowwesit (their neerest salt Water) about 7 or 8 mile: that there is about 20 houses. I can not learne of him that there is above 20 men beside Women and children: that they live on Ground nuts etc. and deare: that Aawaysewaukit is their Sachim: and 12 days agoe he sent his Son Wunnawemenseeskat[50] to Onkus with a present of a basket or 2 of Wompam. I know this Sachim is much related to Plymmouth to whom he is said to subject, but he said (as all of them doe) [he] deposited [i.e., laid aside] his land. I know what bargains he made with the Browns and Willets and Rode Island and Providence men and the Controverses [Controversies] between the Nahigonsiks and them about those lands.[51] I know the talke abroad [i.e. around] of the right of the 3 united Colonies (by Conquest) to this Land: and the plea of Rode Iland by the Charter, and Commrs [Commissioners]. I humbly desire that this party may be brought in: the Countrey improved (if God in mercy so please) the English not differ about it and Complaints run to the King, (to unknowne trouble [,] charge and hazard etc.) and therefore I humbly beg of God that a Committee from the 4 Colonies may (by way of prudent and godly wisedome) prevent many inconveniences and mischiefs. I write the Summ of this to the Govrs of Conecticut and Rode Island, and humbly beg of the Father of mercies to guide You in mercy. For his mercy sake

    Sir Your unworthy

                                             R.W.

    Excuse my Want of Paper

    This boy saith there is anoter [another] Towne to the northeast of them with more howses then 20: who as tis like correspond to the Eastward.

---

town of Warwick.

    49. The Pawtuxet River formed the northern boundary of Warwick.

    50. Williams wrote Wunnawmeneeskat in the margin.

    51. Williams perhaps hoped to avoid a situation Rhode Island had dealt with thirty years prior, when colonists used local Native bands as a point of leverage with Massachusetts Bay in the Shawomet purchase.

Sale of Indian Captives, August 16, 1676.
Courtesy of the Rhode Island Historical Society.

Receipt from the Committee regarding Indian Slave Sales, January 1, 1676/1677[52]

On August 16, 1676, a committee comprised of Authur Fenner, William Hopkins, and John Whipple Jr. was authorized to sell Indian captives as slaves. This document is simply a certificate verifying these sales, as well as the amount (or "share") that each of the committee members received: sixteen shillings and four pence (a pound was and is twenty pence). The men who received money from the sale of Natives included—near the bottom of the list—Roger Williams. There is no information given regarding where these enslaved Natives were sold, to whom, and whether for life or for a shorter term.

1 January 1676/7 [Providence]

We whose names are here unto Subscribed having implyed [employed] Arthor Fenner, William Hopkins, and John Whipple junr:: to make Sale of a Company of Indians to us belonging as by Act of the Comittey doth Appeare,[53] they having made Sale of the Same,[54] and received a part of the pay for the Same, and having proportioned Each man his shaire of what they have received the which amounteth to Sixteene shillings and fower pence halfe penney per shaire the which sayd sum wee say wee have received, And Doe hereby fully Acquitt and disschareg the abovenamed persons of the same as witness our hands this first day of January one thousand, Six hundred, Seaventy and Six or 77[55]

The marke of
Richard pray
Joseph Woodward
John pray
Thomas Arnold
Samuel Winsor
Ephraim pray
John Whipple: 4
Abraham man : 7:
John Whipple : in

52. Bartlett, *Records of the Colony of Rhode Island and Providence Plantations*, 15:161.

53. This nebulous language is interesting and raises many questions. Who authorized this committee to be formed? Who gave it the authority to sell Natives?

54. There are very few records about where these enslaved Natives were sold. Many of them were likely sold locally, to Rhode Island colonists. Some of them perhaps ended up in Newport, maybe to be transferred to a larger ship and sold out of the colony.

55. That is, 1677, by the modern calendar.

behalfe of Jame olney, : 4 :
Samuel Wipell 2
William Haukens junr: 4
James Angell
Edward Smith: 2
Eliazvr Whipple: 2
Vallintine Whittman : 4:
John Angell: 4
Thomas Field: 4
John Smith: 2
Nathaniel Waterman : 8
Roger Williams
Dan: Abbott
Tho: Wallinge:

Epilogue

ON MAY 6, 1682, writing from his rebuilt Providence house, an elderly and infirm Roger Williams scrawled out one of his last surviving letters that encapsulates his energy and commitments, as well as the limitations of his life.[1] Huddled up to his fireplace and dealing with illness and lameness in both of his feet, Williams's mind had finally outpaced the physical limitations of his body. Ever the connector, he was once again trying to exert influence over the spheres of his world, but without fully recognizing how much the world had changed around him, and how much he had been part of those changes. Likely feeling isolated and alone, he wrote to Massachusetts Bay governor Simon Bradstreet, hoping to continue connections with those in the Boston area, even as he admitted that, in some cases, "Death hath stript me of all of my Acquaintance." Ever the controversialist, he told Bradstreet he was trying to publish another diatribe against the Quakers, although his friends advised him to stop creating additional discord among Protestants, since such quarrels played into the anti-Protestant designs of the Catholic church.

His most tone-deaf request was an attempt to reach out to the Narragansett nation, despite his role in fighting, enslaving, and displacing them only five years prior—as we saw in the receipt for Indian captive sales in the last chapter. Williams reported to Bradstreet that he had written up thirty pages of musings on twenty-two theological and biblical topics, including "of Atheisme," "Mistakes about Christianitie," thoughts on the latest "blazing starr" (comet), and "Meditations on Harvest, especially our Indian Harvest." Williams was desperate to get this little tract published and distributed to the Narragansett, and so had written to potential donors in Connecticut, Plimouth, Rhode Island, and Massachusetts Bay in an attempt to raise money to do so. One can only imagine how the Narragansett leaders would have received such a tract had it ever been published and delivered. After

---

1. Roger Williams to Governor Simon Bradstreet, May 6, 1682, *Correspondence of Roger Williams*, 2:777–80.

King Philip's War, Connecticut and Rhode Island veterans, speculators, and colonists forced the remaining Narragansett communities to the southwest corner of Rhode Island. As they watched their English neighbors gobble up their ancestral homelands, surely the Narragansett were in no mood for preaching by someone who had so fundamentally betrayed them.

What are we to make of Roger Williams? How can we evaluate the life and contributions of such a central and yet conflicted soul? For generations, Williams has been cited and used selectively to demonstrate early examples of key developments in core values that would later characterize the United States. This includes freedom of religion and the separation of church and state. Williams has also been used to demonstrate that some colonists, at least, had inherent interest in Native cultures, and went out of their way to protect Native land rights and interact with them in culturally non-coercive ways.

The Williams you have encountered in this volume, however, looks a little different, and we recognize that this Williams may not be the one you were expecting. What we have tried to present is the Williams that emerges from the sources—a person full of contradictions who wrote and acted in ways that seem self-serving. Slowly but surely a more complete Roger Williams emerges into view, a less flattering figure than appeared before, but also far more interesting and all too human. Williams can and did go from spending time with Natives in their wetus and learning their language to enabling a genocidal war against a different nation only a few years later. He could establish a colony based on full religious freedom and yet bitterly complain and campaign against residents with whom he disagreed, such as Samuel Gorton or the Quakers.

This, then, has been the rationale for this volume. Our compilation was not driven by the discovery of new letters from Roger Williams or a recently unearthed publication, but rather, a desire to reintegrate Williams back into the complexity of his life and times by bringing various kinds of writings together, side-by-side, no matter how incongruous they might be. While reconstructing Williams in his entirety is impossible, maybe thinking of Williams in only one way now is also impossible. Williams's writings continue to offer an unrivaled look into a particular time and place. They do not provide a perfect look, nor an unproblematic one, for they are decidedly both imperfect and troubling at times. But his writings are unparalleled in their ability to delve into intellectual, cultural, and religious conversations that animated the day. Our understanding of seventeenth-century religious and political culture and the Narragansett would be vastly different without him. Troubling as he is, he was an on-the-ground observer of people around him, intertwined with almost every aspect of colonial activity in Rhode Island, Massachusetts, and England.

How should we understand Roger Williams's legacies over time? In the realm of ideas, while he was one of the earliest colonists to articulate values that became central to the founding of the United States, it is less clear that he had a direct influence on James Madison and other framers of the Bill of Rights. This includes the supposed separation of church and state and the protection of religious liberty, both of which are enshrined in the First Amendment of the United States Constitution. And, as history has shown, public support for equal and full religious liberty for all faiths or clear church-state separation has ebbed and flowed over time, rarely living up to the radical freedom and separation that Williams established in Rhode Island that included atheists, Muslims, and Jews.[2] Then again, such values were challenging to ensure even in Rhode Island, where within seventy years of Williams's death, Jews were prevented from obtaining the rights of citizenship.[3]

In the realm of Indian affairs, Williams's actions portended the future of the English colonies and, after 1776, the new United States. For Williams, protecting English colonies and land was what really mattered the most in the end, even if such protection came with incalculable costs in life and land for Indigenous peoples. Like the Narragansett, Native nations all across the North American continent experienced the never-ending demands of American leaders and missionaries who, having been welcomed as guests to Native homelands, proceeded to dispossess, remove, and wage war against Indigenous nations. Such collective greed would not cease until every Native nation was cornered onto reserved lands and, even now, continues in the form of ongoing treaty violations and neglect of Native peoples by state and federal governments. In Rhode Island, the processes that Williams initiated led to two centuries of injustice and attempted erasure of the Narragansett within the borders of their own ancestral land. Even so, the Narragansett Indian nation remains today in Rhode Island, on the lands of their ancestors, which is an incredible testimony to the deep and abiding strength of Indigenous nations everywhere who celebrate their heritage and culture, even as they continue to reclaim language, land, and rights. The historical trauma caused by these events is palpable for modern Narragansett tribal members. As Chrystal Mars Baker reflected after reading this collection, "It has been 300+ years since conquest but feels like now. Though I sit in

2. Sehat, *Myth of American Religious Freedom.*
3. Snyder, "Rules, Rights, and Redemption."

modernity, the spirit of my ancestors are present with me as I read this text as I experience the loss that they could not forsee would exist now."[4]

What, then, is left of Williams that can be of service to modern readers? Perhaps Williams represents an unfulfilled potential and a warning: a call to more robustly engage in the radical religious freedom and church-state separation he envisioned, and also to commit to a more just present and future regarding the Indigenous nations who are still here, and on whose land we now reside.

4. Chrystal Mars Baker, correspondence with the authors, January 24, 2023.

Bibliography

Published Works by Roger Williams (in order of publication date)

A Key into the Language of America, or, An help to the language of the natives in that part of America called New-England together with briefe observations of the customes, manners and worships, &c, of the aforesaid natives, in peace and warre, in life and death: on which are added spiritual observations, generall and particular, by the author. London: Gregory Dexter, 1643.

Mr. Cottons letter lately printed, examined and answered: by Roger Williams of Providence in New England. London: [s.n.], 1644.

Queries of Highest Consideration, proposed to the five Holland ministers and the Scotch Commissioners (so called) upon occasion of their late printed apologies for themselves and their Churches. In all humble reverence presented to the view of the Right Honourable the Houses of the High Court of Parliament. London: [s.n.], 1644.

The Bloudy Tenent of Persecution, for cause of Conscience, discussed, in a A Conference betweene TRUTH and PEACE. Who In all tender Affection, present to the High Court of Parliament, (as the Refute of their Discourse)there, (among other Passages) of highest consideration. London: [s.n.], 1644.

Christenings Make not Christians, or A briefe discourse concerning that name heathen, commonly given to the Indians. As also concerning that great point of their conversion. Published according to order. London: Iane Coe, 1645.

Fourth Paper, presented by Major Butler, To the Honourable Committee of Parliament, for the Propagating the Gospel of Christ Jesus. London: [s.n.], 1652.

The hireling ministry none of Christs, or, A discourse touching the propagating the Gospel of Christ Jesus humbly presented to such pious and honourable hands whom the present debate thereof concerns by Roger Williams. London: [s.n.], 1652.

Experiments of Spiritual Life & Health, and their Preservatives In which the weakest Child of God may get Assurance of his Spirituall Life and Blessednesse, And the Strongest may finde proportional Discoveries of his Christian Growth, and the means of it. London: [s.n.], 1652.

The Bloody Tenent yet more bloody: by Mr Cottons endevour to wash it white in the blood of the lambe; of whose precious blood, spilt in the blood of his servants; and of the blood of millions spilt in former and later wars for conscience sake, that most bloody tenent of persecution for cause of conscience, upon a second tryal, is found now more apparently and more notoriously guilty. In this rejoynder to Mr Cotton, are

247

principally I. The nature of persecution, II. The power of the civill sword in spirituals examined; III. The Parliaments permission of dissenting consciences justified. Also (as a testimony to Mr Clarks narrative) is added a letter to Mr Endicot governor of the Massachusetts in N.E. By R. Williams of Providence in New-England. London: Giles Calvert, 1652.

The Examiner Defended In a Fair and Sober Answer to the Two and twenty Questions which lately examined the Author of Zeal Examined, in this Answer are (not unseasonably) touched. London: James Cottrel, 1652.

George Fox digg'd out of his burrowes, or, An offer of disputation on fourteen proposals made this last summer 1672 (so cal'd) unto G. Fox, then present on Rhode-Island in New England by R.W. : as also how (G. Fox slily departing) the disputation went on being managed three dayes at Newport on Rhode Island, and one day at Providence between John Stubs, John Burnet, and William Edmondson on the one part, and R.W. on the other : in which many quotations out of G. Fox and Edward Burrowes book . . . are alleadged: with an appendix of some scores of G.F. his simple lame answers to his opposites in that book quoted and replyed to. Boston: Printed by John Foster, 1676.

The Complete Writings of Roger Williams. 7 vols. New York: Russell and Russell, 1963. Volumes 1–6 are reprinted facsimiles from the Narragansett edition, 1866–1874. Volume 7 includes material not included in the Narragansett edition.

LaFantasie, Glenn, ed. *The Correspondence of Roger Williams.* 2 vols. Providence: Rhode Island Historical Society, 1988.

Other Edited/Excerpted Collections of Williams Texts

Davis, James Calvin, ed. *On Religious Liberty: Selections from the Works of Roger Williams.* Cambridge: Harvard University Press, 2008.

Fisher, Linford D., et al., eds. *Decoding Roger Williams: The Lost Essay of Rhode Island's Founding Father.* Waco, TX: Baylor University Press, 2014.

Green, Theodore P., ed. *Roger Williams and the Massachusetts Magistrates.* Boston: DC Heath, 1964.

Groves, Richard, ed. *The Bloudy Tenent of Persecution, for Cause of Conscience, discussed in a conference between Truth and Peace.* Macon, GA: Mercer University Press, 2001.

Miller, Perry, ed. *Roger Williams: His Contribution to the American Tradition.* New York: Bobbs-Merrill, 1953.

Polishook, Irwin H., ed. *Roger Williams, John Cotton, and Religious Freedom: A Controversy in New and Old England.* Englewood Cliffs, NJ: Prentice-Hall, 1967.

Spears, Lorén, et. al., eds. *A Key into the Language of America: The Tomaquag Museum Edition.* Yardley, PA: Westholme, 2019.

Teunessen, John J., and Evelyn J. Hinz, eds. *A Key into the Language of America.* Detroit: Wayne State University Press, 1973.

Primary Sources (other than those written by Williams)

The Modell of Church and Civil Power, composed by Mr. Cotton and the Ministers of New England, And sent to the Church at Salem, as a further Confirmation of the bloody Doctrine of Persecution for cause of Conscience. Examined and Answered in Roger Williams, *The Bloudy Tenent*, Samuel Caldwell, ed. *Complete Writings of Roger Williams* 3:221–425. Providence: Narragansett Club Publications, 1867; New York: Russell & Russell, 1963.

Bartlett, John Russell. *Records of the Colony of Rhode Island and Providence Plantations, in New England.* Providence: A. C. Greene, 1856.

Bradford, William. *Of Plimouth Plantation.* Kenneth Minkema et al., eds. Boston: Colonial Society of Massachusetts, 2020.

Chapin, Howard M. *The Trading Post of Roger Williams, with those of John Wilcox and Richard Smith.* Providence: Freeman, 1933.

"Charter of Rhode Island and Providence Plantations, 15 July 1663." https://avalon.law. yale.edu/17th_century/ri04.asp#1.

Clark, Michael, ed. *The Eliot Tracts: With Letters from John Eliot to Thomas Thorowgood and Richard Baxter.* Westport, CT: Praeger, 2003.

Bush, Sargeant, Jr., ed. *The Correspondence of John Cotton.* Chapel Hill: University of North Carolina Press, 2001.

Easton, John. "A Relacion of the Indyan Warre, by John Easton, 1675." In *Narratives of the Indian Wars, 1675–1699*, edited by Charles H. Lincoln, 2–17. New York: Scribner, 1913.

Flinn, J. William, ed. *Complete Works of Rev. Thomas Smyth, D.D.* Columbia, SC: Bryan, 1908.

McIntyre, Sheila, and Len Travers, eds. *The Correspondence of John Cotton Junior.* Boston: Colonial Society of Massachusetts, 2009.

New Englands First Fruits. London: Printed by R.O. and G.D. for Henry Overton, 1643.

"Parliamentary Patent for Providence Plantations, 1643." https://avalon.law.yale. edu/17th_century/ri03.asp.

Rogers, Horatio, et al., eds. *The Early Records of the Town of Providence.* Providence: Snow & Farnham, 1892.

Shurtleff, Nathaniel B., ed. *Records of the Governor and Company of the Massachusetts Bay in New England.* Boston: White, 1853–1854.

"Submission of the Chief Sachem of the Narragansett to Charles I, April 19, 1644." Native Northeast Portal Transcription. https://nativenortheastportal.com/anno tated-transcription/digcoll3983.

Tanner, J. R., ed. *Constitutional Documents of the Reign of James I, A.D. 1603–1625.* Cambridge: Cambridge University Press, 1964.

Winthrop, John. *The History of New England from 1630–1649.* Edited by James Savage. Boston: 1835.

———. *The Journal of John Winthrop, 1630–1649.* Edited by Richard Dunn et al. Cambridge: Belknap Press of Harvard University Press, 1996.

Wood, William. *New-England's Prospect.* London: Cotes, 1634.

Secondary Works

Barry, John M. *Roger Williams and the Creation of the American Soul.* New York: Penguin, 2012.

Beckwith, Carl. *Hilary of Poitiers on the Trinity: From De Fide to De Trinitate.* Oxford: Oxford University Press, 2008.

Bejan, Teresa M. *Mere Civility: Disagreement and the Limits of Toleration.* Cambridge: Harvard University Press, 2017.

———. "'When the Word of the Lord Runs Freely': Roger Williams and Evangelical Toleration." In *The Lively Experiment: Religious Toleration in America from Roger Williams to the Present,* edited by Christopher Beneke and Christopher S. Grenda, 65–81. New York: Rowman & Littlefield, 2015.

Beneke, Christopher, and Christopher S. Grenda, eds. *The First Prejudice: Religious Tolerance and Intolerance in Early America.* Philadelphia: University of Pennsylvania Press, 2011.

———. *The Lively Experiment: Religious Toleration in America from Roger Williams to the Present.* New York: Rowman & Littlefield, 2015.

Bozeman, Theodore Dwight. "Religious Liberty and the Problem of Order in Early Rhode Island." *New England Quarterly* 45 (1972) 44–64.

Bremer, Francis J. *John Winthrop: America's Forgotten Founding Father.* Oxford: Oxford University Press, 2003.

Brockunier, Samuel Hugh. *The Irrepressible Democrat: Roger Williams.* New York: Ronald, 1940.

Brooks, Lisa. *Our Beloved Kin: A New History of King Philip's War.* New Haven: Yale University Press, 2019.

Brown, David C. "The Keys of the Kingdom: Excommunication in Colonial Massachusetts." *New England Quarterly* 67 (1994) 531–66.

Burnham, Michelle. *Folded Selves: Colonial New England Writing in the World System.* Lebanon, NH: University Press of New England, 2007.

Byrd, James P. *The Challenges of Roger Williams: Religious Liberty, Violent Persecution, and the Bible.* Macon, GA: Mercer University Press, 2002.

Cambers, Andrew. *Godly Reading: Print, Manuscripts, and Puritanism in England, 1580–1720.* New York: Cambridge University Press, 2011.

Cameron, Euan. *Waldenses: Rejections of Holy Church in Medieval Europe.* Oxford: Blackwell, 2000.

Camp, L. Raymond. *Roger Williams, God's Apostle of Advocacy: Biography and Rhetoric.* Lewiston, NY: Mellen, 1989.

Carlino, Anthony. "Roger Williams and his Place in History: The Background and the Last Quarter Century." *Rhode Island History* 58 (2000) 34–71.

Carrington-Farmer, Charlotte. "More than Roger's Wife: Mary Williams and the Founding of Providence." *New England Quarterly,* forthcoming 2024.

Carroll, Kenneth L. "Singing in the Spirit in Early Quakerism." *Quaker History* 73 (1984) 1–13.

———. "Thomas Thurston: Renegade Maryland Quaker." *Maryland Historical Magazine* 62 (1967) 170–192.

Cave, Alfred. *The Pequot War.* Amherst, MA: University of Massachusetts Press, 1996.

Cesarini, J. Patrick. "The Ambivalent Uses of Roger Williams's *A Key into the Language of America.*" *Early American Literature* 38 (2003) 469–94.

Chu, Jonathan M. *Neighbors, Friends, or Madmen: The Puritan Adjustment to Quakers in Seventeenth-century Massachusetts Bay.* Westport, CT: Praeger, 1985.

Cogley, Richard W. "The Ancestry of the American Indians: Thomas Thorowgood's 'Iewes in America' (1650) and 'Jews in America' (1660)." *English Literary Renaissance* 35 (2005) 304–30.

Coker, Joe. "John Murton's Argument for Religious Tolerance: A General Baptist's Use of Non-Biblical Sources and Its Significance." *Baptist History and Heritage* 54 (2019).

Cohen, Charles. "Post-Puritan Paradigm of Early American Religious History." *William and Mary Quarterly* 54 (1997) 695–722.

Collinson, Patrick. *The Elizabethan Puritan Movement.* Berkeley: University of California Press, 1967.

Covey, Cyclone. *The Gentle Radical: A Biography of Roger Williams.* New York: Macmillan, 1966.

Davis, Jack L. "Roger Williams among the Narragansett Indians." *New England Quarterly* 43 (1970) 593–604.

Daybell, James. *Women Letter-Writers in Tudor England.* London: Oxford University Press, 2006.

Daybell, James, and Andrew Gordon, eds. *Cultures of Correspondence in Early Modern Britain.* Philadelphia: University of Pennsylvania Press, 2016.

Dierks, Konstantin. *In My Power: Letter Writing and Communications in Early America.* Philadelphia: University of Pennsylvania Press, 2011.

Don, Patricia Lopes. *Bonfires of Culture: Franciscans, Indigenous Leaders, and the Inquisition in Early Mexico, 1524–1540.* Norman: University of Oklahoma Press, 2012.

Ernst, James. *Roger Williams: New England Firebrand.* New York: Macmillan, 1932.

Felker, Christopher. "Roger Williams' Use of Legal Discourse: Testing Authority in Early New England." *New England Quarterly* 63 (1990) 624–48.

Field, Jonathan Beecher. *Errands into the Metropolis: New England Dissidents in Revolutionary London.* Hanover, NH: University Press of New England, 2009.

———. "A Key for the Gate: Roger Williams, Parliament and Providence." *New England Quarterly* 80 (2007) 353–82.

Fisher, Julie A. "Roger Williams and the Indian Business." *New England Quarterly* 94 (2021) 352–93.

Fisher, Julie A., and David A. Silverman. *Ninigret, Sachem of the Niantics and Narragansetts: Diplomacy, War, and the Balance of Power in Seventeenth-Century New England and Indian Country.* Ithaca, NY: Cornell University Press, 2014.

Fisher, Linford D. "'Why shall wee have peace to bee made slaves': Indian Surrenderers during and after King Philip's War." *Ethnohistory* 64 (2017) 91–114.

Fisher, Linford D., and Lucas Mason-Brown. "'By Treachery and Seduction': Indian Baptism and Conversion in the Roger Williams Code." *William and Mary Quarterly* 71 (2014) 175–202.

Gallay, Alan, ed. *Indian Slavery in Colonial America.* Lincoln: University of Nebraska Press, 2010.

Garrett, John. *Roger Williams: Witness beyond Christendom.* New York: Macmillan, 1970.

Garrison, Becky. *Roger Williams's Little Book of Virtues.* Eugene, OR: Resource, 2020.

Gaustad, Edwin S. *Liberty of Conscience: Roger Williams in America.* Grand Rapids: Eerdmans, 1991.

———. *Roger Williams.* New York: Oxford University Press, 2005.

———. *Roger Williams: Prophet of Liberty.* New York: Oxford University Press, 2001.

Gilpin, W. Clark. *The Millenarian Piety of Roger Williams.* Chicago: University of Chicago Press, 1979.

Goodman, Glenda. "'The Tears I Shed at the Songs of Thy Church': Seventeenth-Century Musical Piety in the Puritan Atlantic World." *Journal of the American Musicological Society* 65 (2012) 691–725.

Goodman, Nan. *Banished: Common Law and the Rhetoric of Social Exclusion in early New England.* Philadelphia: University of Pennsylvania Press, 2012.

———. "Banishment, Jurisdiction, and Identity in Seventeenth-Century New England: The Case of Roger Williams." *Early American Studies* 7 (2009) 109–39.

Gordis, Lisa. *Opening Scripture: Bible Reading and Interpretive Authority in Puritan New England.* Chicago: University of Chicago Press, 2003.

Grandjean, Katherine. *American Passage: The Communications Frontier in Early New England.* Cambridge: Harvard University Press, 2015.

Grenda, Christopher S. "Faith, Reason, and Enlightenment: The Cultural Sources of Toleration in Early America." In *The First Prejudice: Religious Tolerance and Intolerance in Early America*, edited by Christopher Beneke and Christopher S. Grenda, 23–52. Philadelphia: University of Pennsylvania Press, 2011.

Gura, Philip. *A Glimpse of Sion's Glory: Puritan Radicalism in New England, 1620–1660.* Middletown, CT: Weslyan University Press, 1984.

Haefeli, Evan. *Accidental Pluralism: America and the Politics of English Expansion, 1497–1662.* Chicago: University of Chicago Press, 2021.

———. "How Special Was Rhode Island: The Global Context of the 1663 Charter." In *The Lively Experiment: Religious Toleration in America from Roger Williams to the Present*, edited by Christopher Beneke and Christopher S. Grenda, 21–36. New York: Rowman & Littlefield, 2015.

Hall, David D. *The Antinomian Controversy, 1636–1638: A Documentary History.* Durham: Duke University Press, 1990.

———. "Not in Print yet Published: The Practice of Scribal Publication." In *Ways of Writing: Practice and Politics of Text-making in Seventeenth-century New England*, 29–80. Philadelphia: University of Pennsylvania Press, 2008.

———. *The Puritans: A Transatlantic History.* Princeton: Princeton University Press, 2019.

———. *A Reforming People: Puritanism and the Transformation of Public Life in New England.* Durham: University of North Carolina Press, 2012.

Hall, Timothy L. *Separating Church and State: Roger Williams and Religious Liberty.* Urbana, IL: University of Illinois Press, 1998.

Hambrick-Stowe, Charles E. *The Practice of Piety: Puritan Devotional Disciplines in Seventeenth-Century New England.* Chapel Hill: University of North Carolina Press, 1982.

Hodge, Frederick Webb, ed. *Handbook of American Indians North of Mexico.* Washington, DC: Government Printing Office, 1910.

Isham, Norman. "The House of Roger Williams." *Rhode Island Historical Society Collections* 18 (1925) 33–39.

Keary, Anne. "Retelling the History of the Settlement of Providence: Speech, Writing, and Cultural Interaction on Narragansett Bay." *New England Quarterly* 69 (1996) 250–86.

Keresztes, Paul. "Tertullian's Apologeticus: A Historical and Literary Study." *Latomus* 25 (1966) 124–133.

LaFantasie, Glenn W. "A Day in the Life of Roger Williams." *Rhode Island History* 46 (1987) 95–111.

———. "Roger Williams and John Winthrop: The Rise and Fall of an Extraordinary Friendship." *Rhode Island History* 47 (1989) 85–95.

Lemons, J. Stanley. "John Clarke: The Neglected Founder." *Baptist History and Heritage* 55 (2020).

———. "Roger Williams not a Seeker, but a 'Witness in Sackcloth.'" *New England Quarterly* 88 (2015) 693–714.

Lepore, Jill. *The Name of War: King Philip's War and the Origins of American Identity.* New York: Vintage, 1999.

Lovejoy, David S. "Roger Williams and George Fox: The Arrogance of Self-Righteousness." *New England Quarterly* 66 (1993) 199–225.

Lowenherz, Robert J. "Roger Williams and the Great Quaker Debate." *American Quarterly* 11 (1959) 157–165.

Mackie, John M. "Life of Samuel Gorton." In *Library of American Biography*, edited by Jared Sparks, Second Series, 5:317–411. Boston: Little & Brown, 1834–1848.

Penrose, Elizabeth Cartwright. *A History of England from the First Invasion of the Romans down to the Present Time.* London: Murray, 1891.

Monaghan, E. Jennifer. "Literacy Instruction and Gender in Colonial New England." In *Reading in America: Literature and Social History*, edited by Cathy N. Davidson, 53–80. Baltimore: Johns Hopkins University Press, 1989.

Miller, Nicholas P. *The Religious Roots of the First Amendment: Dissenting Protestants and the Separation of Church and State.* New York: Oxford University Press, 2012.

Moore, J. K. *Primary Materials Relating to Copy and Print in English Books of the Sixteenth and Seventeenth Centuries.* Oxford: Oxford Bibliographical Society, 1992.

Moore, Leroy. "Religious Liberty: Roger Williams and the Revolutionary Era." *Church History* 34 (1965) 57–76.

———. "Roger Williams and the Historians." *Church History* 32 (1963) 432–51.

Morgan, Edmund. *Roger Williams: The Church and State.* New York: Norton, 1967.

Murphy, Andrew R. *Conscience and Community: Revisiting Toleration and Religious Dissent in Early Modern England and America.* University Park: Pennsylvania State University Press, 2003.

———. "'Livelie Experiment' and 'Holy Experiment': Two Trajectories of Religious Liberty." In *The Lively Experiment: Religious Toleration in America from Roger Williams to the Present*, edited by Christopher Beneke and Christopher S. Grenda, 37–51. New York: Rowman & Littlefield, 2015.

Myles, Anne G. "Arguments in Milk, Arguments in Blood: Roger Williams, Persecution, and the Discourse of Witness." *Modern Philology* 91 (1993) 133–60.

———. "Dissent and the Frontier of Translation: Roger Williams's *A Key into the Language of America*." In *Possible Pasts: Becoming Colonial in Early America*, edited by Robert Blair St George, 88–108. Ithaca: Cornell University Press, 2000.

Najar, Monica. *Evangelizing the South: Social History of Church and State in early America.* New York: Oxford University Press, 2008.

Naumec, David, et al. "Battle of Pequot (Munnacommock) Swamp, July 13–14, 1637." Department of the Interior, National Park Service American Battlefield Protection

Program. September 13, 2017. https://www.fairfieldhistory.org/wp-content/uploads/Battle-of-Pequot-Swamp-Archeological-Report-2017.pdf.

Newell, Margaret Ellen. *Brethren by Nature: New England Indians, Colonists, and the Origins of American Slavery*. Ithaca: Cornell University Press, 2015.

Nussbaum, Martha. *Liberty of Conscience: In Defense of America's Tradition of Religious Equality*. New York: Basic, 2008.

Oberg, Michael Leroy. *Uncas: First of the Mohegans*. Ithaca: Cornell University Press, 2006.

Perlmann, Joel, and Dennis Shirley. "When Did New England Women Acquire Literacy?" *William and Mary Quarterly* 48 (1991) 50–67.

Pestana, Carla Gardina. "The City Upon a Hill Under Siege: The Puritan Perception of the Quaker Threat to Massachusetts Bay, 1656–1661." *New England Quarterly* 56 (1983) 323–53.

———. *Quakers and Baptists in Colonial Massachusetts*. Cambridge: Cambridge University Press, 1991.

———. "The Quaker Executions as Myth and History." *Journal of American History* 80 (1993) 441–69.

Pope, Robert G. *The Half-Way Covenant: Church Membership in Puritan New England*. Princeton: Princeton University Press, 1969.

Roger Williams Family Association. https://www.rogerwilliams.org.

Rosenmeier, Jesper. "The Teacher and the Witness: John Cotton and Roger Williams." *William and Mary Quarterly* 25 (1968) 408–31.

Rubertone, Patricia E. *Grave Undertakings: An Archaeology of Roger Williams and the Narragansett Indians*. Washington, DC: Smithsonian Institution, 2001.

———. *Native Providence: Memory, Community, and Survivance in the Northeast*. Lincoln: University of Nebraska Press, 2020.

Russo, Francis. "Sonic Piety in Early New England." *New England Quarterly* 95 (2022) 610–44.

Sehat, David. *The Myth of American Religious Freedom*. New York: Oxford University Press, 2011.

Scott, Mack H. "From a 'Great Tree' to a New Dawn: Race, Ethnogenesis, and Indigeneity in Southern New England." PhD diss., Kansas State University, 2019.

Settle, Mary Lee. *I, Roger Williams: A Fragment of Autobiography*. New York: Norton, 2001.

Simpson, Alan. "How Democratic Was Roger Williams?" *William and Mary Quarterly* 13 (1956) 53–67.

Simpson, Percy. *Proof-Reading in the Sixteenth, Seventeenth, and Eighteenth Centuries*. London: Oxford University Press, 1935.

Skaggs, Donald. *Roger Williams' Dream for America*. New York: Lang, 1993.

Snyder, Holly. "Rules, Rights and Redemption: The Negotiation of Jewish Status in British Atlantic Port Towns, 1740–1831." *Jewish History* 20 (2006) 147–70.

Sowerby, Scott. "Toleration and Tolerance in Early Modern England." In *The Lively Experiment: Religious Toleration in America from Roger Williams to the Present*, edited by Christopher Beneke and Christopher S. Grenda, 53–63. New York: Rowman & Littlefield, 2015.

Spurgin, Hugh. *Roger Williams and Puritan Radicalism in the English Separatist Tradition*. Lewiston, NY: Mellen, 1989.

Staloff, Darren. "John Cotton, Roger Williams, and the Problem of Charisma." In *The Making of an American Thinking Class: Intellectuals and Intelligensia in Puritan Massachusetts*, 26–39. New York: Oxford University Press, 1998.

Stern, Jessica. "*A Key* into the *Bloudy Tenent of Persecution*: Roger Williams, the Pequot War, and the Origins of Toleration in America." *Early American Studies* 9 (2001) 576–616.

Thornton, Tamara Plakins. *Handwriting in America: A Cultural History*. New Haven: Yale University Press, 1996.

Tyler, Aaron A. *Islam, the West, and Tolerance: Conceiving Coexistence*. New York: Palgrave Macmillan, 2008.

Walsham, Alexandra. *Charitable Hatred: Tolerance and Intolerance in England, 1500–1700*. Manchester: Manchester University Press, 2008.

———. "Sermons in the Sky: Apparitions in Early Modern Europe." In *Superstition and Magic in Early Modern Europe: A Reader*, edited by Helen Parish, 163–68. London: Bloomsbury, 2015.

Warren, James. *God, War, and Providence: The Epic Struggle of Roger Williams and the Narragansett Indians against the Puritans of New England*. New York: Simon & Schuster, 2018.

Wenger, Tisa. *Religious Freedom: The Contested History of an American Ideal*. Chapel Hill: University of North Carolina, 2017.

Weimer, Adrian Chastain. "From Human Suffering to Divine Friendship: 'Meat out of the Eater' and Devotional Reading in Early New England." *Early American Literature* 51 (2016) 3–39.

———. *Martyrs' Mirror: Persecution and Holiness in Early New England*. Oxford: Oxford University Press, 2011.

———. "Quakers, Puritans, and the Problem of Godly Loyalty in the Early Restoration." In *The Worlds of William Penn*, edited by Andrew R. Murphy and John Smolenski, 283–302. New Brunswick, NJ: Rutgers University Press, 2019.

Widmer, Ted. "A Nearer Neighbor to the Indians." In *A New Literary History of America*, edited by Greil Marcus and Werner Sollors, 30–34. Cambridge: Belknap Press of Harvard University Press, 2012.

Winship, Michael P. *Hot Protestants: A History of Puritans in England and America*. New Haven: Yale University Press, 2018.

Winslow, Ola E. *Master Roger Williams*. New York: Macmillan, 1957.

Zimmermann, Zoe. "This Little One with the Red About His Neck": A Microhistory of Roger Williams' Indigenous Servant." Unpublished paper, 2022.

Index